MW01054865

Richard Wagner and the Anti-Semitic Imagination

RICHARD

AND THE ANTI-SEMITIC IMAGINATION

WAGNER

MARC A. WEINER

University of Nebraska

Press

Lincoln and London

1995

Library of Congress
Cataloging-in-Publication-Data
Weiner, Marc A.
Richard Wagner and the anti-
Semitic imagination /
Marc A. Weiner. p. cm. – (Texts
and contexts ; v.12)
Includes bibliographical referen-
ces and index.
ISBN 0-8032-4775-3 (cloth : alka-
line paper)
1. Wagner, Richard, 1813–1883 –
Symbolism.
2. Antisemitism. 3. Body, Human,
in literature. I. Title.
II. Series. ML410.W19W23 1995
782.1'092–dc20 94-12187 CIP
MN
Set in Linotype Janson Text by
Keystone Typesetting, Inc.
Book design by Richard Eckersley
Publication of this book
was assisted by a grant from The
Andrew W. Mellon Foundation.

TO BOBBIE WEST WEINER,
whose love for Wagner has
been a most precious affinity

CONTENTS

To write a book on Wagner is to draw upon the expertise and patience of specialists in many fields, disciplines, and walks of life. In my case, the discussions and exchanges that contributed to my work unfolded within a host of contexts, and always with close friends. I should like first and foremost to thank Dr. John Deathridge of King's College at the University of Cambridge, Great Britain, and Klaus Schultz, Generalintendant of the State Theaters in Mannheim, Germany, for some of the most rewarding and intellectually satisfying conversations of my life on a complex subject fraught with ambiguity. A suggestion of Sander Gilman's led me to undertake this project, and I owe him a personal and intellectual debt of gratitude for his encouragement and, as the reader shall see, his investigations into the ideology of race in nineteenth- and twentieth-century German culture, from which my own work has benefited. Thanks, too, to Professor Dr. Dieter Borchmeyer, who sponsored my application to the Alexander von Humboldt Foundation for research fellowships that took me to Cambridge and to Heidelberg in 1992–93, during which I wrote a large part of the manuscript. I am very grateful to the foundation for its support of a controversial project, and to Indiana University's Research and University Graduate School for a research leave supplement grant during my year abroad, and to it and the Indiana University Department of Germanic Studies for grants covering the production of the music examples used in this book, which were produced with enthusiasm and impressive expertise by Lynn Gumert, a composer and specialist in computer-generated musical calligraphy. Sincerest thanks, too, to Elizabeth Starr for her aid in completing the index.

Many other friends and colleagues read drafts of the following chapters and offered helpful insights: Eva Knodt and William Rasch urged me to question some of my methodological premises, and Hinrich Seeba, with the warmth and friendly precision I've come to expect of him, contributed a host of historical references and encouraging observations. Sue Olsen helped me to merge computer systems of different national provenance at a time when I would have gone crazy if she hadn't.

I developed many of the ideas for this book while co-teaching, with Professor Paul Eisenberg, a course on 'Nietzsche and Wagner' offered in the departments of Philosophy and Germanic Studies at Indiana University in the spring of 1990. Working with Paul and with the exceptionally gifted students in that course was an immensely rewarding experience, and Paul, my thanks to you for rejuvenating my faith in the redemptive-stimulative powers of team pedagogy.

Unless otherwise noted, all translations are my own, but I should like to thank Antje Petersen for her suggestions concerning renderings into English of Wagner's thornier German passages. I should also like to thank her, with love, for putting up with years of Wagner quotations and quizzes at the least appropriate times, many of them at the dinner table.

Portions of chapters 2 and 3 have appeared in the following publications: 'Wagner and the Vocal Iconography of Race and Nation,' in *Re-reading Wagner*, edited by Reinhold Grimm and Jost Hermand (Madison: University of Wisconsin Press, 1993), 78–102; 'Wagner's Nose and the Ideology of Perception,' *Monatshefte* 81.1 (Spring 1989): 62–78. I have revised these essays extensively but wish to acknowledge gratefully the editors' permission to draw upon them in this book.

DS   Richard Wagner. *Dichtungen und Schriften*. Ed. Dieter Borchmeyer. 10 vols. Frankfurt am Main: Insel, 1983.

GS   ———. *Gesammelte Schriften*. Ed. Julius Kapp. 14 vols. Leipzig: Hesse & Becker, 1911.

L   ———. *Lohengrin: Texte, Materialien, Kommentare*. Ed. Attila Csampai and Dietmar Holland. Reinbek bei Hamburg: Rowohlt, 1989.

MN   ———. *Die Meistersinger von Nürnberg: Texte, Materialien, Kommentare*. Ed. Attila Csampai and Dietmar Holland. Reinbek bei Hamburg: Rowohlt, 1981.

P   ———. *Parsifal: Texte, Materialien, Kommentare*. Ed. Attila Csampai and Dietmar Holland. Reinbek bei Hamburg: Rowohlt, 1984.

RN   ———. *The Ring of the Nibelung*. Trans. Andrew Porter. New York: Norton, 1976. (Porter's edition contains the German text found in Wagner's scores, which differs on occasion from that in the *Dichtungen und Schriften* edition. References to the *Ring* dramas are to the German in Porter's edition, not to his English translation.)

T   ———. *Tannhäuser: Texte, Materialien, Kommentare*. Ed. Attila Csampai and Dietmar Holland. Reinbek bei Hamburg: Rowohlt, 1986.

TR   ———. *Tristan und Isolde: Texte, Materialien, Kommentare*. Ed. Attila Csampai and Dietmar Holland. Reinbek bei Hamburg: Rowohlt, 1983.

We feel certain that in Wagner all that is visible in the world wants to become more profound and more intense by becoming more audible, that it seeks here its lost soul; and that all that is audible in the world likewise wants to emerge into the light and also become a phenomenon for the eye; that it wants as it were to acquire corporality. . . . [Wagner] . . . is continually compelled . . . to see the most deeply concealed inner activity as visible phenomenon and to clothe it with the appearance of a body. — Friedrich Nietzsche, *Richard Wagner in Bayreuth*

The evidence of the senses is also an operation of the mind in which conviction creates the evidence. — Marcel Proust, *The Captive*

There is no anti-Semite who does not basically want to imitate his mental image of a Jew, which is composed of mimetic cyphers. — Horkheimer and Adorno, *Dialectic of Enlightenment*

Gleaming or dripping eyes, a resonant or screeching voice, the bodily aromas of youthful love or the stench of sulfur and flatulence, the steady tread of a muscle-bound warrior or the lopsided, hobbling gait of a diminutive, hairy, goatlike creature whose skin is ashen or deathly pale — these are images of the body through which Richard Wagner metaphorically expressed his theories concerning the failings of nineteenth-century Europe and his vision of a superior and future Germany. For Wagner the body is the site in which the ideological becomes visible; it is both metaphor and physical reality, a vehicle for communicating abstract aesthetic and social concepts and, at the same time, a physiological manifestation of the purported veracity of the issues with which it is associated. But while the ideas with which Wagner identified the body in his essays and music dramas were often novel, iconoclastic, and even weird, the corporeal images through which he expressed them were not his invention but part of a widespread motivic vocabulary laden with specific connotations in his culture. The body in Wagner's works thus takes on two dimensions: it both expresses — virtually incorporates — his revolutionary theories concerning social-aesthetic issues and reveals him to be, like his contemporary audience, a member of his culture steeped in beliefs and values characteristic of his age.

This book, accordingly, examines two interrelated subjects: the function of corporeal images within Wagner's theoretical reflections and music dramas, and the iconographic traditions in his culture from which he drew these images. I approach Wagner from two complementary vantage points: as an idiosyncratic, iconoclastic individual who created some of the most innovative works of the nineteenth century, and as a man steeped in — and hence representative of — a host of beliefs and ideological forces that defined his age. The configurations of his personal makeup, though often unusual, shed light on the assumptions and pressures shared by his contemporaries, and their values also often illuminate beliefs and associations involved in the creation of Wagner's works. Beliefs concerning the body provide a nexus linking the composer's personal agenda and the response granted his works by his nineteenth-century audience, for by using bodily imagery, Wagner was able to evoke specific associations linked to the body in his culture and to grant his ideas a degree of persuasive credibility to a nineteenth-century audience that can only be imaginatively reconstructed today. I hope to show that Wagner's music dramas did not only come to be associated with ideas ranging from anti-Semitism to the longing for an imagined German community through the composer's many pronouncements on these subjects and through his later association with Nazism (though many of his apologists make precisely this argument) but through a host of culturally pervasive bodily images that in his world were already understood as signs of racial, sexual, and national identity.

Since the nineteenth century, and especially since the end of World War II, such ideological implications in Wagner's writings and music dramas have been increasingly denied or repressed as the cultural vocabulary of the world in which he is read and performed has changed, thereby making what I believe in his time was an obvious dimension of the Wagnerian artwork an issue of open debate in the post-Wagnerian age. But in Wagner's world, the body was the site in which identity could be read (and for Wagner, that meant above all racial identity), and its signs are everywhere apparent, both as metaphor and as physiological phenomenon, in his works. Inscribed upon the body, Wagner read the signs of everything he despised in the modern world and discerned in it the possibility of a different social order as well.

Any discussion of the body in Wagner's thought must begin with the psychological significance of racial identity for the composer, because in his time the appearance of the body was deemed an obvious and reliable indication of race, and throughout his life Wagner strove to distance himself from the 'race' of Jews with whom he feared comparison. For those critics receptive to the arguments of depth psychology, there is no question but that Wagner's documented hatred of Jews was intimately connected to the composer's uncertainty regarding his paternal heritage. It is possible, they argue, that Wagner feared his father was Jewish. It has become a staple of Wagnerian scholarship that Wagner never knew whether his father was Carl Friedrich Wilhelm Wagner, who died six months after the composer's birth, or the actor, poet, and portrait painter Ludwig Heinrich Christian Geyer, whom Wagner's mother married nine months after the death of her first husband and whom Wagner may have suspected of being a Jew.[1] (Some scholars have also maintained that Wagner was even worried about his mother's potentially Jewish pedigree.)[2] Shortly after Wagner's death, in 1888, Nietzsche played upon this fear in *Der Fall Wagner* (The case of Wagner) in his pun concerning the name of Ludwig Geyer. After having come to know the composer's hopes, frustrations, and fears through years of nearly familial intimacy, it was Nietzsche who suggested to Wagner that he create a family crest containing not an eagle (*Adler*) but a vulture (*Geier*), and Wagner indeed used such a crest as the frontispiece in the private first edition of his autobiography *Mein Leben* (My life) of 1870 (figure 1). Playing upon the two names — *Adler* and *Geier* — replete with racial associations, Nietzsche lampooned in 1888 the racist composer's pretensions to Germanic 'purity,' implying instead that Wagner may well have been (and presumably feared being) precisely that creature most removed from the German in his own thinking — a Jew: 'Was Wagner even a German? . . . His father was an actor named Geyer. A Geyer is almost an eagle. . . . I admit my distrust of every point that is only attested to by Wagner himself. . . . He remained . . . true to himself even

1. Wagner's family crest for the first edition of
Mein Leben, 1870, showing the *Wagen* and *Geier*
(Nationalarchiv der Richard Wagner–Stiftung/
Richard Wagner Gedenkstätte, Bayreuth)

in the biographical, — he remained an actor.'³ In nineteenth-century European culture Nietzsche's point was clear: Wagner's father could have been a Jewish artist. Nietzsche exaggerates the point by erasing the ambiguity of the father's identity — an ambiguity that Wagner acknowledged when he accepted Nietzsche's suggestion for the two images in the family crest — but he preserves it when he implies that the vulture 'is almost an eagle [*Adler*].' Nietzsche's attack was of a posthumously personal nature, for it was based upon insight into the mind of the composer available to few.

Yet we must not ground our argument on remarks Wagner may or may not have made to his philosopher friend, for even if he did not discuss the matter with Nietzsche, Wagner's preoccupation with the uncertainty of his father's identity, laden with racial implications, is still discernible in virtually all his most celebrated music dramas. The postrevolutionary, technically most iconoclastic of his works for the stage focus time and again on figures who either have never known their fathers (Siegfried, Tristan, and Parsifal), did not know their true identity (Siegmund and Siegfried do not even know their fathers' names), or lived with them only for a short time before they disappeared (Siegmund) or died during the hero's youth (Walther von Stolzing), dramatic testimony to the importance of the motif in the composer's thinking.⁴ (I feel that the degree of such repetition saves the critic from the accusation of the intentional fallacy, for it suggests, if nothing else, the composer's heightened fascination or preoccupation with a motif, without reducing his works to mere embodiments of his personality.) But what if that long-lost father were in fact not the shining image of a knight or hero but its opposite in Wagner's system of thought and culture — a Jew? Perhaps the most celebrated instance of Wagner's horror at the all-too-autobiographical potential of the hated Jew was the moment when he may have recognized his own image in his first description of the Nibelung dwarf Mime, contained in the verse draft of *Der junge Siegfried* (Young Siegfried) of 1851 (which Wagner later revised and retitled *Siegfried*, the third of the *Ring* dramas [1876]). Theodor W. Adorno pointedly argues that Wagner expunged the following, initial description of Mime of 1851 from the final text of the music drama precisely because the dwarf appears here so similar to Wagner himself (figure 2):

Mime, the Nibelung, alone. He is small and bent, somewhat deformed and hobbling. His head is abnormally large, his face is a dark ashen colour and wrinkled, his eyes small and piercing, with red rims, his grey beard long and scrubby, his head bald and covered with a red cap. He wears a dark grey smock with a broad belt around his loins: feet bare, with thick coarse soles underneath. There must be *nothing approaching caricature in all this*: his aspect, when he is quiet, must be simply eerie: it is only in moments of extreme excitement that he becomes *exteriorily* ludicrous, but never too uncouth. His voice is husky and harsh; but this again ought of itself never to provoke the listener to laughter.[5]

The figure of Mime is a vehicle for the representation of a number of anti-Semitic stereotypes from Wagner's time (as I will discuss in detail in chapters 1 to 4), and, given Wagner's small stature, large head, and excited demeanor made note of by so many of his acquaintances, his decision to suppress this passage from the final text of the *Ring* may be a clue to the psychological investment underlying his exploitation of anti-Semitic stereotypes in the creation of a number of figures in his music dramas.[6] Wagner's vehement hatred of Jews may have been based on a model of projection which itself suggests a deep-seated fear of precisely those features within the Self (diminutive stature, nervous demeanor, and avarice, as well as a lascivious nature) that are projected upon and then recognized and stigmatized in the hated Other. If Adorno is correct, the incident illustrates both Wagner's secret potential affinity with his image of the Jew — his surreptitious fear concerning his own paternity and the nature of his genetic and even artistic identity — and his violent desire to disavow such an affinity. In the final version of *Siegfried*, bereft of its initial description of Mime, Wagner's answer to that most tenacious and pernicious of questions — am I a Jew? or could others perceive me as

Mime (Breuer).

2. Hans Breuer as Mime at Bayreuth, ca. 1899
(Nationalarchiv der Richard Wagner–Stiftung/
Richard Wagner Gedenkstätte, Bayreuth)

one? — would find its most violent dramatic expression. (Many of Wagner's contemporary detractors exploited this possibility, presenting the composer as a caricature of that being he most despised; figures 3 and 4.)

Wagner inherited his belief in the physical difference of the Jew from a host of traditions within German culture. In his world, the Jew's difference was discerned in his purportedly idiosyncratic corporeal signs (such as stature, voice, smell, hair, gait, gestures, sexuality, and physiognomy) that I will discuss in detail in the following chapters. Belief in such signs thus links Wagner's personal psychological needs — and the corporeal images of his essays and music dramas — with the larger cultural vocabulary of his time. His own psychological dynamic concerning Jews — documented through his letters, essays, and autobiographical writings (as well as in Cosima Wagner's diaries) and, I will argue, discernible in his music dramas — would be of only anecdotal interest were it not for the shared beliefs it betrays, for though Wagner often stylized himself as a Promethean, romantic genius creating original works out of a void, his theoretical writings and the music dramas based upon them demonstrably incorporate those images of the body that were part of the culture in which he lived — and to which he wished to communicate. A key to the ideological function of such signs in that culture is that they are never recognized as the products of collective fears; instead, they are simply deemed credible indications of physiological reality. Both Wagner and his contemporaries believed that things are as they appear, but that belief itself was fueled by psychological needs and social tensions, especially when it was applied to groups that were identified as different and rejected by a society seeking to establish its own identity. His statement that 'there must be *nothing approaching caricature*' in Mime's appearance (the emphasis is Wagner's) betrays the psychological function of the aesthetic representation of the Jew for the composer and for his fellow nineteenth-century Germans, because in formulating such a wish, Wagner sought to

3. Left: Caricature of Wagner by
K. Klic, from *Humoristische Blätter*,
Vienna, 1873 (From Eduard Fuchs
and Ernest Kreowski, *Richard Wagner
in der Karikatur* [Berlin: B. Behr's
Verlag, 1907])

4. Below: 'Richard Wagner and Judaism,' caricature, from *Floh*, Vienna, 1879
(From Eduard Fuchs and Ernest Kreowski, *Richard Wagner in der Karikatur*
[Berlin: B. Behr's Verlag, 1907])

efface the image of the Jew as a cultural construct, insisting instead that it was true to life and 'real.'[7]

At least since Foucault there has been no shortage of investigations into the status of the body within Western culture as the site upon which values are inscribed.[8] Far from constituting a value-free, neutral, and objective entity, the body has emerged as an iconographic map upon which are found the signs of commonality and of difference imagined there by Western minds to ensure the sanctity and the identification of borders of community. It was precisely to the establishment of such borders that Wagner devoted his life's work. Many studies have been done in recent years on the various corporeal iconographies of racial and sexual difference that developed within nineteenth-century European culture and that came to form a standard repertoire through which those deemed foreign, such as blacks, Orientals, Gypsies, and Jews, were viewed, as well as those deemed sexually deviant or disenfranchised, such as homosexuals, masturbators, and women. It is within the context of these standard, stereotypical bodily images that Wagner's musical-dramatic creations should be understood as cultural constructs of, for his time, enormously evocative power, because the libretti, stage descriptions and directions, and the dramatic music Wagner wrote, often intended to portray fundamentally different kinds of human beings, employ precisely those value-laden images of the body with which he and his contemporaries were familiar.[9]

Given the voluminous nature of Wagner's extant letters, diaries, and autobiographical writings, as well as Cosima Wagner's lengthy diary entries, we have a remarkable wealth of information that provides insight into the composer's concern with the physical appearance of others as a clue to their identity, as well as with his own body, health, and appearance. Wagner's pronouncements on these subjects are couched in terms suggesting neurotic compulsions and compensations; his preoccupation with diet (especially his penchant for a strict vegetarianism), ill health (ranging from his remarks on gastrointestinal maladies to diseases of the skin [erysipelas] and cardiovascular deterioration), and various cures (he was especially interested in the nineteenth-century literature on the regenerative powers of water) emerges as the psychological flip side of his aggressive portrayal of himself as larger than life and loftier than his mundane contemporaries. As the Self suffers physical deterioration within a world that stigmatizes and categorizes physical difference, it threatens to revert in the eyes of the would-be superior being (and of the would-be superior community) to the status of the hated and feared object of derision — to resemble the image that the Self has so vociferously rejected. No wonder the Volsungs, Walther von Stolzing, and Parsifal — who represent the German community in the *Ring*, *Die Meistersinger von Nürnberg*, and Wagner's final music drama — are so exaggeratedly bursting with health, youthful exuberance, and blond-haired, blue-eyed beauty; they are the longed-for image of the Self designed as a counter to that all-too-familiar part of Wagner's own physical (and psychological) identity he so adamantly refused to recognize as his own — a physical identity that in the nineteenth-century anti-Semitic imagination came dangerously close to that of the Jew.[10]

Owing to the associations that attended physical appearance in nineteenth-century Western culture, the moment Wagner employed the body as a metaphor for his often highly idiosyncratic theories concerning the arts and society, his unusual ideas took on connotations that were already grounded in the repertoire of racist, xenophobic, misogynist, and homophobic imagery central to his age. That is, many of Wagner's ideas concerning social-aesthetic revolution may have been iconoclastic or new in his time, but when he couched them in diverse metaphors of the body, he connected in the minds of his contemporary audience these novel ideas with all the ideological baggage associated with corporeal iconographies in his culture. One could argue, of course, that the opposite is true, that it was their exclusionary connotations that led Wagner to employ such value-laden images in his essays and music dramas in the first place; but it is less important to determine which came first — the cultural context or the poetic intent—than to appreciate how the metaphors in Wagner's theories and their dramatic representations lent his works powerful and reprehensible connotations in the nineteenth century that have been lost or repressed since his time. By using corporeal signs, Wagner was able to express his ideas in an evocative, metaphorical, symbolic, and nonexplicit manner that resonated against a repertoire of physiological images linked in his culture to contemporary prejudices and fears.

For example, as I will discuss in chapter 1, Wagner believed modern, hypercivilized culture (which he associated with Jews) to be distressingly superficial, and tradition-laden and communally defined German culture (as he characterized it) to be wonderfully authentic, worthy of veneration, and 'deep.' But, as I will show in chapter 2, Wagner invested this polarized spatial metaphor of superficial (as inferior) and deep (as superior) with polarized, fundamentally antithetical images of the Jewish and German bodies that were taken from his culture. Wagner's image of the Jewish voice was that of an instrument virtually higher than, and hence physiologically altogether different from, the Teutonic voice; as Sander Gilman has shown, such an image is to be found in European culture both in the early nineteenth century (as reflected in the works of Rossini) and in the period immediately following Wagner's death (as discernible in the music of Richard Strauss).[11] Thus, the polarization of high versus low voices in Wagner's music dramas has a metaphorical dimension ('high' culture being inferior to the 'deep' essence of German culture) that was singularly Wagnerian but that found aesthetic manifestation in an image of the body that was part of the composer's culture, in which such images were not seen as ideological constructs but as manifestations of real, universally verifiable, and collectively perceived difference. This image in Wagner's vocal music suggests a connection between the physiological dimension of musical material and its function as an ideological metaphor that resonated within the context of the cultural vocabulary of Wagner's time but that, since the early twentieth century (since Strauss), is no longer automatically evoked in performance today. The issue is not simply that Wagner *intended* to convey his notion of Jewish culture as different through the metaphor of his elevated vocal music (though I believe he did) but rather that the image of the Jewish body in which he expressed his idea made sense both to him and to his audience as members of an interpretive community that no longer exists; Wagner and his audience viewed the Jewish body as physiologically different from that of the non-Jew, and both heard the Jew's voice as a manifestation (and, in Wagner's anti-Semitic caricatures in *Die Meistersinger*, the *Ring*, and *Parsifal*, as a representation) of that difference. Couched within a corporeal sign that was widely accepted as real, Wagner's notion of a Jewish threat to the development of German culture may have — literally — sounded familiar in its metaphorical-physiological setting to his nineteenth-century audience.

Thus I will argue that both Wagner and his contemporaries perceived his works through associations — linking a given set of values and beliefs to specific bodily imagery — that may no longer be automatically evoked in performance today; it will be my task to reconstruct hypothetically these associations within which Wagner's essays and music dramas could have, and indeed may have, resonated for the composer and his nineteenth-century audience. As the cultural context in which the works are performed and the essays are read undergoes transformation, so too do the associations that an opera-going and reading public brings to a work. Ironically, however, such a shift in the horizon of expectations — which Wagner, like any artist living within a given cultural context, no doubt took for granted when writing his works — has led to a widespread *disavowal* of precisely the racist and exclusionary dimension of his essays and music dramas that would have been so obvious to a nineteenth-century audience. Wagner never included the word *Jude* in his works for the stage because he didn't need to; the corporeal features deemed obvious signs of the Jew in his culture would have made the anti-Semitic nature of his representations of purportedly Jewish characteristics self-evident in his time, but it is precisely the lack of such irrefutable connections between anti-Semitic intent and musical dramatic representation that has led, since the end of World War II, to a widespread rejection of the notion that Wagner's works ever contained a racist dimension.[12]

The music dramas of no other composer have been the object of such a pervasive desire among scholars, stage directors, and the general public alike to rid them of the ideological and specifically racist component with which—as I hope to demonstrate—they were conceived and initially performed and received. Such widespread disavowal has involved at least four distinguishable yet intimately related strategies: scholars have (1) minimized the extent of anti-Semitism in Wagner's life; (2) disavowed any connection between the artist's 'private, personal' antipathies and his works; (3) sought to separate Wagner's theoretical and essayistic pronouncements from a discussion of his music dramas; and (4) above all, and with only a few noteworthy exceptions, refused to acknowledge any 'evidence' of racism 'in' Wagner's music, restricting instead, when hard pressed, analysis of the relationship between Wagner's documented Judeophobia and the makeup of his works to an examination of his libretti, and this often in only a most superficial fashion.[13]

With the exception of Adorno's iconoclastic and pioneering *Versuch über Wagner* (In search of Wagner) of 1952, it has only been within the last twenty-five years, since the publication of Robert W. Gutman's often-maligned but perceptively critical *Richard Wagner: The Man, His Mind, and His Music* of 1968, that a public discussion has unfolded concerning the relevance of Wagner's anti-Semitism to an appraisal of his music dramas.[14] This omission is due in part to a historical factor. When, in 1933, Thomas Mann made light of Wagner's theoretical writings, dismissing them in his celebrated essay 'Leiden und Größe Richard Wagners' (The sorrows and grandeur of Richard Wagner) as an aberration not worthy of serious attention, he laid the foundation for a host of future scholars who would write numerous examinations of Wagner's life and dramas that would eschew discussion of the composer's writings concerning the reformation of society and what Wagner believed to be the role of Jews in the corruption of the modern world. 'What I [objected] to,' Mann wrote, 'right from the beginning—or rather, what left me totally indifferent—was Wagner's theory. In fact, I have hardly ever been able to convince myself that anyone could ever have taken it seriously.'[15] While Mann may not have intended to draw attention away from Wagner's anti-Semitism (he had in mind above all the arguments in *Oper und Drama* [Opera and drama] of 1851 concerning the interrelationship of the arts), his remarks, given his stature in the world of letters in general and in German studies in particular, nevertheless paved the way for postwar defenders of Wagner who would dismiss the composer's essayistic writings as a personal matter or an aberration, as mere marginalia, and hence as unnecessary to an appreciation of the works for the stage. In this way such explicitly anti-Semitic Wagnerian texts as 'Das Judentum in der Musik' (Jewishness in Music), 'Modern' (Modern), 'Erkenne dich selbst' (Know thyself), and 'Was ist deutsch?' (What is German?) (as well as a number of other equally but less explicitly racist tracts) were shelved in the post-Holocaust era as scholars focused on more palatable features of the Wagnerian music dramas.

It was not until Dieter Borchmeyer's *Das Theater Richard Wagners: Idee, Dichtung, Wirkung* of 1983 (1991: *Richard Wagner: Theory and Theater*) that a scholar seriously addressed the relationship between Wagner's essays and his musical-dramatic production.[16] But though he rigorously and extensively discusses many of the theoretical, sociocritical writings as a key to an understanding of the dramas, Borchmeyer stopped short of taking the anti-Semitic tracts seriously and consequently omitted them from his ten-volume collection of Wagner's works published in Germany by the Insel Press on the centennial anniversary of Wagner's death. Borchmeyer maintained that those who 'object to a beautification [*Beschönigung*] of Wagner's image' could read these texts elsewhere, and even stated that their omission, 'for reasons of the intellectual level' of the edition, was 'rather to be welcomed [*eher erfreulich*]' (*DS* 10: 185). Thus, while for the first time a scholar recognized the fundamental link between Wagner's pronouncements on social and aesthetic reform and his music dramas, such a link was incomplete, for it silenced the essential component of Wagner's racism both within his model of utopian revolution and in the motivic makeup of his 'Artworks of the Future.'[17]

Such an omission, with only few exceptions, has been typical of a pervasive post-Holocaust approach to Wagner. To an extent this is understandable, given Wagner's association with the National Socialists, which is embarrassing to his apologists and seen by them as an unfortunate exploitation and falsification of Wagner's works rather than as a consistent legacy of his thought — which is not to say that Wagner was a Nazi *avant la lettre*, but only that the National Socialists saw in Wagner's writings and works for the stage formulations of many of their ideas. Examples of scholarship's penchant for ignoring or refusing to take seriously the anti-Semitic dimension of Wagner's works can be seen in the popular studies by Martin van Amerongen, Carl Dahlhaus, Martin Gregor-Dellin, Burnett James, Brian Magee, L. J. Rather, Geoffrey Skelton, Ronald Taylor, Peter Wapnewski, Derek Watson, and Curt von Westernhagen, to mention only some of the most prominent Wagnerian specialists of the last quarter century, as well as in many others writing in a similar vein.[18] Until most recently, a lone voice in the landscape of scholarship on Wagner was that of Hartmut Zelinsky, who has continually attempted to draw public attention to the need for consideration of Wagner's anti-Semitism in a discussion of the composer's theoretical and dramatic works, but he has been largely ignored (or vituperatively ridiculed) by the majority of the scholarly community.[19]

That this is not simply an academic matter is borne out by the Wagner renaissance that has pervaded both the academic landscape and popular culture with ever-increasing fervor for the last twenty-five years, as reflected not only in a glut of publications and conferences on the figure and his works but especially in the films and televised broadcasts of Wagnerian performances that have reached a wide, diversified, and often enthusiastic audience. A case could be made, for example, that the current spectrum of Wagnerian stage productions is defined by (or, some would say, fraught with) the same ideological issues that inform (or are either ignored or suppressed from) current Wagnerian scholarship. In the last twelve years two complete, and in terms of their ideological implications, antithetical productions of *Der Ring des Nibelungen* have been broadcast on American television that demonstrate manifest parallels between Wagnerian scholarship and dramaturgy, the ideological underpinnings of which have yet to be examined in a comprehensive fashion. Each production constituted a rejection of the kind of approach found in the other. The first, broadcast in 1983, was directed by Patrice Chéreau in 1976 for the centennial celebration of the tetralogy's premiere in Bayreuth and caused international controversy due to its iconoclastic and, many felt, irreverent and willful staging of the dramas.[20] The neo-Marxist and, given its ideological agenda, surprisingly postmodern thrust of Chereau's direction emphasized the political implications of the cycle, including its anti-Semitic content.[21] Presenting the work as a product of the nineteenth century, complete with attire from the period and numerous references to the initial growth of industrialization, Chereau emphasized the anti-Semitic implications of the Nibelung dwarves. The other production was designed by Günther Schneider-Siemssen and directed by Otto Schenk for the Metropolitan Opera over a period of several years in the late 1980s and broadcast complete in the early 1990s; it used modern stage technology in an attempt to fulfill what the designer and director interpreted as Wagner's original scenic intentions, while at the same time *effacing* Wagner's use of nineteenth-century anti-Semitic stereotypes.[22] The result was a series of neo-Romantic tableaux that glossed over the political and racial tensions in the cycle, emphasizing instead its motifs of nature and fairy tale imagery.

One parallel between these productions and recent Wagnerian scholarship lies precisely in the tension between those who directly address the issue of Wagner's anti-Semitism and those who either make light of it or simply ignore it altogether (or who admit that it is important, but lambaste anyone who discerns evidence of it in Wagner's work). Another is the popularity that both the conservative production and the apologetic publications have enjoyed, which is quite different from the resistance, skepticism, and general distaste with which the academic and general public alike have greeted the less adulatory staging and more overtly critical studies of Wagner and his works. Because, as I will argue, Wagner's music dramas were intended and initially understood as programmatic documents of a racist utopian agenda, the tendency of numerous scholars, stage directors, and apparently a large and grateful public as well to make light of this dimension of his theoretical reflections and music dramas emerges as troubling indeed.

It was only recently that two writers, Paul Lawrence Rose and Barry Millington, have seriously considered Wagner's anti-Semitism as pertinent to a discussion of both the libretti and the music of his dramas, but, ironically, their work demonstrates a problem for which Wagner's champions are grateful, namely, the problem of analyzing Wagner's music in connection to his anti-Semitism. Instead, they primarily establish connections between the composer's private pronouncements concerning Jews, reflected in his letters and Cosima Wagner's diaries, his essays, and the texts of his stage works, while nevertheless maintaining that his racism also found expression in the musical material. This is even the case in Rose's controversial and highly informative *Wagner: Race and Revolution* (1992), in which the author devotes only four pages, for example, to the caricatures of Jews in the *Ring*.[23] While Millington's article, 'Nuremberg Trial: Is There Antisemitism in *Die Meistersinger*?' does attempt to reveal elements of racism in the specific musical material of that drama, it is, given its spatial restrictions, necessarily cursory.[24]

Thus, whether for methodological reasons (as in Gutman, Zelinsky, and Rose) or due to a desire to separate and save the work of art from the tribulations of nasty sociopolitical reality, a common feature of the writings of both Wagner's severest critics and his most ardent apologists has been the paucity of discussions linking Wagner's ideological program and his musical material. Derek Watson, for example, notes that both Nietzsche and Gutman attack the man even as they admit their admiration for his works; but Watson makes this claim in *defense* of Wagner and of the beauty of his artistic creations and implicitly seeks solace therefore in the notion of musical art as inviolate: 'Wagner was a *musical* dramatist and the greatest part of his work can only be fully understood through the music. Most of the prejudice against his art ignores the music completely.'[25] On the other side of the debate, such a penchant for distinguishing between the greatness of the music and the meanness of the man can be found in Leon Stein's *The Racial Thinking of Richard Wagner*, and here, too, such a division serves to save Wagner's art from the undeniable shortcomings of his personal animus, as seen in such statements as the following: 'If, in truth, Wagner's music were felt to distil the same evil as his ideas there would be every reason for condemning it. . . . But, even accepting those moments when his music and his racial thinking may seem to spring from the same emotional morass, the *greatest* part of his art may be understood and appreciated as music rather than an expression of his racial and political thinking.'[26] A similar claim is even made by Jacob Katz in his book-length examination of Wagner's anti-Semitism when he writes: 'In fact, without forced speculation, very little in the artistic work of Wagner can be related to his attitude toward Jews and Judaism.'[27] The discussion by Katz is the kind deemed sound and judicious by Wagner's supporters, for while he cannot help but make mention of the composer's more heinous pronouncements and writings on Jews, he does so with the understanding that such matters have no bearing on an evaluation of the music. Time and again, Wagner's champions separate the man and the music even as they censure anyone who cannot prove that the anti-Semitism of his life and writings has a demonstrable connection to his aesthetic production. Such is the case with the response of those defenders who have criticized Zelinsky most vociferously for his analyses of Wagner's anti-Semitism, for they have repeatedly drawn attention to the fact that he — perhaps Wagner's most outspoken critic of the 1970s and 1980s — has *little* to say about Wagner's music.[28] This is the very argument raised in one of the most vituperative attacks thus far from a scholar who prefers a more palatable and respectable Wagner, a Wagner worthy of veneration: Hans Rudolf Vaget's review of Rose's *Wagner: Race and Revolution* from 1993: 'One of the striking features of Mr. Rose's book is its distribution of weight: approximately 90% of the text is devoted to Wagner's political and metapolitical utterances, only some 10% to the operas. . . . one would expect a detailed engagement with the poetic and musical texts of the operas . . . *the only manifestations of* [Wagner's] *creativity that really matter*' (my emphasis).[29] These remarks are actually based on — and mask — a fear of acknowledging the more repugnant features of Wagner's works, and I suspect this fear propels much of the writing on the figure that would divorce Wagner's personal antipathies and his Judeophobic essays from his aesthetic production. Tellingly, Vaget's criticism manifests his desire ultimately to shield and to protect the works from the kind of ideological issues with which Rose is concerned, as another passage from his review makes apparent:

If *Der Ring des Nibelungen*, *Tristan und Isolde*, *Die Meistersinger*, and *Parsifal* were indeed vehicles for the propagation of anti-Semitism, as Mr. Rose believes, they would have no place in any cultural practice that we consider acceptable, and we could not, in good conscience, go on listening to the music of Wagner as though it were music like any other. What is ultimately at stake, then, is the survival and acceptance of Wagner's musico-dramatic oeuvre as an indispensable element of Western culture.[30]

This is the key issue, the ideological agenda and impasse behind the remarkably (and otherwise inexplicably) vehement criticism against anyone who entertains the possibility that Wagner's anti-Semitism may be related somehow to his music, for it is precisely in order to preserve that music as above reproach that so many of Wagner's critics disavow any relationship between it and the composer's writings on social issues, especially those that openly manifest his racism. Even as the defenders of the 'Master of Bayreuth' criticize his detractors for *not* demonstrating that their attacks on Wagner's thought are pertinent to a discussion of his aesthetic material, they take solace in the purportedly inviolate nature of those works, because they feel (naively, I believe) that if the music dramas are understood to represent morally nefarious ideas, then they as listeners will be morally obligated to reject the works as a whole. For this reason they argue (either explicitly, as in Vaget, or implicitly, as in the writings of many of the other critics cited thus far) that the anti-Semitism is of interest *only* if it can be demonstrated to be pertinent to an analysis of the music, assuming, of course, that it cannot. At the same time, those who *do* address Wagner's anti-Semitism unfortunately have yet to provide the kind of extensive demonstration their opponents demand.

It is precisely this gap that I address in this book. Wagner's music is not the focus of my study, but I do wish to persuade my reader that discussion of nineteenth-century anti-Semitism, including Wagner's personal hatred of Jews, is indeed relevant to an analysis of his works for the stage — and that includes his music — because his music and dramatic texts, as I will show, were intended and initially perceived to evoke a host of corporeal iconographies associated with Jews and with other groups deemed different and therefore foreign in Wagner's time. It is only with the cultural context of that age in mind that the anti-Semitic implications of the music can be demonstrated — indeed, only through consideration of such a context can such a discussion make sense at all.

If one examines the racist iconographies of the body in Wagner's works that were pervasive in nineteenth-century German culture, the ideological component of his essays and music dramas becomes manifestly apparent. These iconographies are found in virtually all aesthetic dimensions of Wagner's works — in the verse his figures sing, in the written descriptions of their physical appearance and attire, in the stage directions indicating how they move, and even in the music Wagner composed for them. Yes, even Wagner's music should be understood within the context of nineteenth-century images of the body as signs of commonality or difference, for it is precisely as somehow 'physical' in nature that it was conceived and initially received — as a music that reflected the physical states of the beings it accompanied and portrayed. Already within Wagner's lifetime, and not only later in the nineteenth century and the fin de siècle, his music took on connotations, both in his own writings and within the popular imagination, of an explicitly corporeal nature, because it was intended and interpreted as an acoustical equivalent to the visual impressions made on stage. The notion that it conveyed physical and often specifically corporeal states provides the basis for many of Wagner's theoretical reflections on the 'Artwork of the Future,' which he hoped would appeal not to the intellect (as the all-too-cerebral, Judaized artwork would) but to the 'feeling' of the audience through the 'sensual impressions' that the musical material and the corporeality of the singing actor would make.[31] Wagner's remarks on the role of the *Gebärde*, or 'gesture,' in the future art work concern precisely this connection between acoustics and corporeality, between musical and visual motion.[32] The following, characteristically convoluted passages from the theoretical reflections in *Oper und Drama* concerning the development and interdependence of the various arts after the breakup of a lost, unified *Gesamtkunstwerk* underscore Wagner's own understanding of his music as an acoustical manifestation of physical states that could be perceived through diverse senses:

Gesture — let us understand it as the complete exterior manifestation of the human appearance to the eye . . . gesture *and* orchestral melody form . . . a totality, something comprehensible per se. . . . Dance-gesture and orchestra . . . [are] mutually interdependent. . . . Just as the

gesture . . . manifests to the eye only what *it* can express, so the orchestra communicates to the ear that which corresponds exactly to this
manifestation. . . . The farther the gesture distances itself from its most
specific, yet also most limited basis in the dance . . . the more manifold
and finer it now shapes the sonic figures [*Tonfiguren*] of instrumental
language which, in order to convincingly communicate the inexpress-
ible element of gesture, gains the most idiosyncratic kind of melodic
expression. (*DS* 7: 317, 312–313)

Central to Wagner's aesthetics is the notion that the 'orchestral language' and the physical appearance of the singing actor
(whose movement on stage constitutes the visual component
of an aesthetic accomplishment also expressed through corresponding sounds) are two interdependent, aesthetically symbiotic manifestations of the poetic idea. The semantic pretensions
of Wagner's revolutionary music, then, in terms of his intentions
and theoretical formulations, are grounded in the physicality of
the body: With bodily movement comes sound, and the sounds
of the orchestra are the acoustical correlations to the movement of the dancer and the singing actor. Visual and acoustical
phenomena are simply two manifestations of the same being,
and thus a physiological icon connoting commonality or difference in Wagner's works will find its expression not only in the
visual appearance of the body—in the information granted to
the eye—but in its sonic expression as well. As I shall discuss in
chapter 1, the eye in Wagner's theories and dramas—so central
in this passage—is the organ that discerns the body's physiological features in order to identify the perceived being as a member,
or as an enemy, of the community: The eye perceives the body of
the other, whose identity as similar or different, friend or foe, is
encoded in its appearance. But music is the symbiotic acoustical
corollary to visual impressions in Wagner's thought; hearing
serves the same function as seeing. Music is an art that appeals to
a different sense but that does so in order to convey the same
physiological states that the eye discerns through visual impressions. Wagner's music, then, is a sonic expression of the body.

This notion is not solely to be found in Wagner's own interpretations of his works; it is not only a product of his personal imagination, for his contemporaries perceived his music as a corollary to corporeality as well. In *Der Fall Wagner* (The case of Wagner) Nietzsche expressed the close proximity of the image of the physical body and the new, revolutionary music thus: 'With Wagner at the beginning there is hallucination: not of sounds, but of gestures. It is for these that he then seeks the sound-semiotics.'[33] By the time Nietzsche penned this observation in 1888, the association of sound and the body within Wagner's works had become central to the understanding of his music dramas in nineteenth-century culture. *Tristan und Isolde*, for example, came to be viewed by Wagner's contemporary audience as an explicitly erotic work, shocking to bourgeois sensibilities of the time, not simply because of the drama's text but because of the notion that its music itself evoked physiological—and, in this case, overtly sexual—states. Wagner intended his revolutionary music dramas to be perceived in these terms, and his own interpretation of his works appears to have seemed credible to his contemporary audience. The 'immorality' of *Tristan* was attributable in no small part to what were understood in the nineteenth century to be the gestural connotations of the music, as seen (or heard) for example in the incessantly increasing rhythmic pulse of the love duet of act 2, which was understood in Wagner's lifetime to be so obvious and so pronounced an example of the evocation of corporeal reality through music that its performance was often deemed inappropriate for women.[34] (Isolde Vetter points out that Duchess Sophie of Bavaria was not allowed to attend the 1865 premiere of *Tristan* in Munich 'out of moral considerations'!)[35] Thus the notion that the music of *Tristan* was explicitly sexual and that it included acoustical representations of bodily (sexual) sensations was in part attributable to the idea that the music itself reflected the physiology of its protagonists. This notion was essential to the role of Wagnerian music in German literature of the late nineteenth century, as seen in the works of Thomas Mann and Ferdinand von Saar, for example (which even posited a connection, derived from Nietzsche, between such physiologically mimetic sounds and their effect on the body of the listener), and it was put forth in the twentieth century by Christian von Ehrenfels, George Bernard Shaw, and a host of other enthusiastic Wagnerites.[36] In his 1931 'Wagner und seine neuen Apostaten' (Wagner and his new apostates) Ehrenfels would argue that the acoustical material of the music drama evoked the rhythms of sexual intercourse, even claiming that one could 'point to the bars' in act 2 of *Tristan* 'in which the orgiastic ejaculations of that night twice burst forth and detumesce.'[37] If such a response seems all too literal to listeners today, it may serve to underscore the distance between Wagner's world and our own; in Wagner's time, his music—like his texts and stage directions—was both intended and perceived to convey physiological states, and this perception tied in with the pervasive role of corporeal imagery in his works. It is upon this general, widely accepted association of music and physiology that the more specific musical references to the idiosyncratic corporeal imagery of the German and the Jew in Wagner's music dramas are based, which I will address in detail in chapters 2 through 5.

A discussion of the context in which musical mimesis unfolds must take into account the different dimensions of music as a code, all of which are subject to the ephemeral, constantly shifting nature of the expectations of a cultural community. As the cultural context in which Wagner's music dramas were composed and heard changed, so did the connotations initially linked to the iconographies they employed; the associations connected to Wagner's music in his lifetime are not necessarily those of today. One dimension of this music—not having to do with physiology but concerning the association of given ideas with acoustical art in a given cultural context—serves to illustrate the distance between the horizon of expectations in his world and in the culture of the post-Wagnerian age and provides an example of a musical code not based on mimesis: Today, few listeners bring to the perception of a given tonal key the associations that were a staple of musical culture in the eighteenth century and that still held forth in Wagner's time. As several musicologists have pointed out, the fact that specific keys in the *Ring* cycle are associated with specific dramatic configurations demonstrates the continuing influence in the 1850s of the eighteenth-century *Affektenlehre*, which linked diverse moods and meanings to specific keys. Wagner may have chosen the key of B♭ minor, for example, for his portrayal of the Nibelung dwarves because for the musically acculturated in Wagner's time the key carried connotations of 'evil' and 'darkness' due to its function in the musical traditions of Europe. The key of B♭ minor was described in just these terms by Johann Friedrich Daniel Schubart in his *Ideen zu einer Ästhetik der Tonkunst* (Ideas for an aesthetic of the art of tone), first published in 1806 but written in the 1780s: 'A strange creature, clad quite often in nocturnal garments. It is somewhat surly and assumes a pleasant countenance only on the rarest of occasions. Contempt for God and the world; dislike of oneself and everything else; preparation for suicide, all resound in this key.'[38] This is often the key heard in conjunction with the appearance of the 'evil,' surly, ugly, strange, and decidedly nocturnal creatures Alberich and Mime; with the exception of suicidal tendencies, Schubart's text could read as a description of the Nibelung brothers, and such connotations would have made the choice of this key appropriate in the mid-nineteenth century, when they were still linked in the minds of the composer and his audience to this tonal material.[39] Such a link between sound and meaning is not mimetic, but it is nevertheless associative and temporally (and culturally) defined, linked to Wagner's age, but not to our own, and thus provides an example of one kind of associative pattern involved in the initial reception of Wagner's art.

If such associations attended the conceptualization and the reception (that is, the composition and the performance) of music in Wagner's lifetime, the meaning of the music then would have been somewhat different from what it is today. The issue of the associations evoked by the use of specific keys is but one example of the culturally circumscribed status of Wagner's music as an associative code system.[40] Music can also function in a more mimetic capacity, as the perception of rhythms of sexual intercourse in *Tristan* suggests; the temporally and culturally transitory nature of this perception is less pronounced than that of, say, the link between B♭ minor and attributes of evil and threatening darkness, but it is still based on the expectations of an audience that assigns meaning to music.

Most important to my investigation, however, is a third level of musical associations, a kind of music that is perceived to refer mimetically to something (an image of a body, for example) that is understood to be real (and that is widely accepted as such) but that is a cultural construct, a stereotype. The bodies of the German and the racial and sexual Other are the examples with which I deal here. With this kind of musical reference, one representation (the 'gestural' music, for example) refers to another (the iconography of the body), which is culturally defined. When the interpretive community changes in which such a code (the iconography of the body) functions, so too do the associations members of that community—both composers and listeners—bring to the work of art. As we move away from Wagner's age, the associations of a specifically racist nature linked to the purportedly reliable signs of the body change, because the perception of the body changes. While our age today still has its stereotypes and still locates them in bodily imagery, our spontaneous associations are no longer those of Wagner's culture. In the latter half of the twentieth century, however, most scholars would prefer to ignore or disavow altogether the fact that such a dimension *ever* existed in Wagner's works and view them instead, in terms of their ideological portent, in a cultural and historical vacuum.

Thus, by analyzing a host of corporeal iconographies of difference—racial, sexual, and otherwise—that were central to the Wagnerian artwork and to the culture in which the composer lived, I wish to demonstrate that those strands in the literature on Wagner and those stagings of his works that would disavow (either categorically or implicitly) the role of anti-Semitism in his theories, his libretti, and the music he composed for his works for the stage are either indefensibly wrong or, at best, incomplete. I also wish to expand upon those recent, more ideologically insightful investigations that have not gone far enough in their attempts to show how perhaps virtually all the aesthetic components of Wagner's writings and music dramas (even the music) may have resonated in his time against a cultural matrix of corporeal imagery that lent his concerns a persuasive and obvious credibility that so many of his apologists would repress today. I want to make clear, however, that in discussing the ideological import of the body in Wagner's works, I am engaging in a kind of cultural archaeology which seeks both to reconstruct and to posit a horizon of expectations in a culture in which these works were first received but which no longer exists. That is, my argument will move between the desire to persuade my reader that the associations of which I am writing did actually occur in the minds of some listeners — as seen, for example, in Gustav Mahler's remark that Mime's music was an obvious parody of traits deemed Jewish (discussed in chapter 2) — and that such associations were *plausible*, given what we know from diverse expressions of the time. I am not insisting that all members of Wagner's culture *necessarily* responded consciously to his representations of the body in like fashion according to the ideological connotations of the iconographies I analyze here, for what interests me is the cultural context in which a series of related motifs — in a society and in a work of art — may potentially take on ideological meanings, consciously or unconsciously, at a given time. Enough evidence is available today to allow for the hypothetical reconstruction of the ideological parameters within which Wagner and his audience may have perceived the imagery of his works as obvious signs of racial, sexual, and national identity, and such reconstruction, I feel, is particularly necessary in an age that prefers a Wagner cleansed of, as one Wagnerian apologist has put it, 'the darker side of genius.'[41]

I also wish to state emphatically that, unlike Wagner's apologists, I do not feel that one is morally obligated to reject his works or to feel embarrassed about enjoying them as soon as one acknowledges their reprehensible connotations, for such an approach is based on an extremely limited and unimaginative appreciation of the complexity and multilayered ambiguity of the work of art and views it in a cultural vacuum, omitting any consideration of the volatility of the cultural imagination. The concomitant appreciation of Wagner's aesthetic constructs and discernment of their nefarious intended meaning for which I argue is a far cry from the aesthetically, historically, and ideologically simplistic approach of his apologists. It is precisely because they ignore cultural permutations that Wagner's defenders have been forced to make light of the racist and exclusionary dimensions of his works altogether. Personally, I refuse to receive Wagner's works as he would have had them received, and the fact that our culture is not Wagner's may constitute our redemption (to use one of his favorite terms) from the Wagnerian agenda and may allow us to experience his breathtakingly beautiful and stirring musical-dramatic accomplishments as works that can be enjoyed *despite* their initial, intended message of racial exclusion. That, however, is altogether different from insisting that such a message never existed at all.

This book, then, examines the interplay between the role of corporeal images as metaphors within Wagner's revolutionary theories and their status as culturally encoded signs. Chapter 1 situates the function of the bodily iconography of those deemed similar or foreign within Wagner's social and aesthetic theories, in which demarcations of race, provided by the body, appear as key concepts that underscore the socially redemptive status for Wagner of his Artworks of the Future intended as models of a world rid of Jewish influence. The chapters that follow investigate specific iconographies of the body dividing Germans and foreigners in Wagner's writings and in his music dramas and situate these images within various German cultural traditions: the iconography of the voice as a sign of race and sexual identity (chapter 2); of smell (as well as Orientalism, associated with both aroma and skin color) (chapter 3); of the clubfoot (so closely associated with the demonic in European culture) (chapter 4); and of the iconography of degeneration, especially of that attributed to masturbation, one of the most heinous of sexual crimes for the nineteenth-century imagination believed at the time to have physiological repercussions discernible in the exterior of the body, and hence that offered yet another sign of difference and, not surprisingly, that shared much in Wagner's time with the corporeal images associated with Jews (chapter 5).

I will close this introduction, however, with a question that runs counter to the temporally based argument I have been making thus far and that will hover in the background of the book that follows: I have been suggesting that those who refuse to acknowledge evidence of anti-Semitism in Wagner's works fail to see them in the cultural context in which they were composed and first performed. But what if the opposite were true? What if the meaning behind those corporeal icons has not completely vanished over time? That is, do today's scholars and audiences *continue* to respond to the nineteenth-century ideology associated with these images, even as they refuse to acknowledge their implications? Phrased somewhat differently, my cynical question reads as follows: Despite the attempts of many scholars and stage directors to ignore or make light of the more obvious manifestations of anti-Semitism in Wagner's works against the background of the cultural vocabulary of nineteenth-century Europe, could the 'continuing appeal' that Wagner's music dramas hold for audiences today be based, in part, on their continuing capacity to evoke within Western society, in which Wagner is still primarily performed, those very images of race, sex, and nation that continue to underscore and perpetuate the notions of difference so fundamental to Western culture?[42] Do these works occupy such a prominent position within the Western canon precisely because they dramatize so forcefully the process of exclusion? The answer to the former question is, in terms of the ideological forces of our own world, one of the most important gauges of our distance from Wagner and his age, while the answer to the latter may reveal what our world continues to share with his.

A NOTE ON THE ILLUSTRATIONS

Perhaps a few remarks concerning the prominence in this book of Arthur Rackham's 1910–1911 illustrations to *The Ring of the Niblung* are in order. It may seem unusual to include in a study concerning the iconography of the body within nineteenth-century German culture several illustrations by an English artist from the early twentieth century. But it is important to bear in mind that both Rackham — himself an avid Germanophile and Wagnerite who traveled widely in the German-speaking countries, attended performances at the Bayreuth festivals in 1897 and 1899, and was intimately familiar with German culture of the time — and his contemporaries understood his work on the *Ring* to be more 'German' than English.[43] The English perception of Rackham's Wagner illustrations as essentially German in nature conflates with a controversy in which the artist was involved concerning his championing of caricature, because both Rackham himself and many of his contemporaries deemed the genre of caricature un-English, believing that it typified Continental culture. Rackham's biographer James Hamilton writes that the English paper *The Morning Leader* 'accused German and French caricature as being "simply a degradation, brutalisation, 'uglification' of life,"' while others said that it exuded a 'rancour and bitterness that infuse the French and German papers.'[44] This notion of caricature as more German than English is important to an understanding of both Rackham's and his contemporaries' perception of his *Ring* illustrations as felicitous expressions of the spirit of the work, for they are replete with exaggerated, even parodistic and stereotypical iconographic representations of a number of figures and, therefore, from the perspective of Rackham's culture, they appeared commensurate with German cultural proclivities. Moreover, many of the images in Rackham's illustrations (those of the Nibelungs), I would

5. Arthur Rackham, 'Alberich drives a band of Nibelungs laden with gold and silver treasure,' 1910 (From *The Ring of the Niblung*, trans. Margaret Armour, vol. 1 [New York: Abaris Books, 1976])

argue, are of an overtly anti-Semitic nature (figure 5). (This is not to say that Rackham himself need have been an anti-Semite, only that his work on the *Ring* contains iconographic features of anti-Semitic stereotypes.) Indeed, this would account in part for Rackham's remarks on the work's 'grimness' and his fear that he would 'make as many enemies with it as friends.'[45]

These illustrations, then, constitute a cultural documentation of sorts, because they represent Rackham's interpretations of those aspects he deemed characteristic of the *Ring* less than a generation after the work's premiere. The aspects imbued with caricature that Rackham chose to emphasize or exaggerate underscore both what the artist believed would be self-evident to a German audience of the time (especially, I would argue, the cycle's employment of anti-Semitic stereotypes) and his attempt to faithfully reflect what he perceived to be the essence of the work. His contemporaries viewed his renditions precisely in these terms. C. S. Lewis, an ardent admirer of his compatriot Rackham and of the *Ring*, described these illustrations as 'the very music made visible.'[46] It is precisely the fidelity of the latter to the former that is at issue here. Through their exaggerations of the body of the Nibelungs, endowed with a virtual catalog of anti-Semitic imagery, these illustrations provide visual parallels to Wagner's music from the perspective of a culture still close to Wagner's age. Accordingly, they have an important place in a book devoted to examining the corporeal iconography of Wagner's works.

By including images from the nineteenth century (only illustration 15 is closer to our age than to Wagner's), I hope to show that the iconographies I am discussing, so central to Wagner's aesthetics and music dramas, were symptomatic of his time. These diverse photographs and drawings provide insight into the visual dimension of the nineteenth-century anti-Semitic imagination, upon which Wagner's theories and referential, "gestural" music were often based.

If things are dressed up in heroic guise, they cease to be immoral, as we have learnt from Wagner's analytical textbook. — Georg Groddeck, 'The *Ring*'

In Wagner's theoretical writings on the Artwork of the Future and on the social issues associated for him with the revolutionary music drama, the most prevalent and indeed the most portentous image of the human body is the eye. For Wagner, the eye is many things: It is the organ that makes possible the most significant of sensual impressions for the theoretician of the theater (vision being primary in Wagner's hierarchy of the senses, with hearing, touch, and smell all subservient though related to it); and, for the champion of a reprehensible, revolutionary worldview that longs for a homogeneous society rid of disparate racial elements, it is the organ that guarantees the recognition of corporeal signs denoting similarity or difference. The eye is thus the site of the body in which Wagner's aesthetic and social concerns merge, providing a focal point for his various and yet remarkably consistent pronouncements on what he perceived to be the aesthetic and social malaise in modern Europe.

Wagner often employed the motifs of the eye and of vision in the essays devoted to aesthetic and social reform that he wrote in exile following the failed 1848 revolution: especially 'Die Kunst und die Revolution' (Art and revolution) of 1849, 'Das Kunstwerk der Zukunft' (The artwork of the future) and 'Das Judentum in der Musik' (Jewishness in music) of 1850, and his most extensive theoretical tract, *Oper und Drama* of 1851.[1] The motif of the eye first appears in 'Die Kunst und die Revolution' in a discussion of social and aesthetic matters, but though it is initially used in this essay in a discussion of an idealized communal-aesthetic experience in ancient Greece, it always functions as a vehicle that makes possible the recognition of physical signs that serve to define the borders of a community, and that means for Wagner the community of Germany: The eye always has racist implications in Wagner's thought and provides a link between the essays apparently bereft of overt anti-Semitism and the more obviously anti-Semitic tracts. It also provides, as we shall see, a direct link between Wagner's theoretical reflections and the texts of his music dramas.

The key to Wagner's vision of the theatrical experience in ancient Greece was its role as a metaphorical 'mirror' for the community, which saw itself 'reflected' in the drama. Like so many of the images and ideas in Wagner's works, this metaphor of recognition was not his invention: he borrowed it from Hegel's *Phänomenologie des Geistes* (The phenomenology of mind) of 1807, in which the philosopher discusses the development of 'self-consciousness through mutual *recognition*,' a concept later taken up by Ludwig Feuerbach as well, to whom much of the ideational content of Wagner's *Ring* is indebted and, as Sandra Corse has shown, one central to much of the imagery and plot of the musical-dramatic cycle.[2] For Wagner, when the Greek spectators observed the unfolding of a tragic drama, they saw therein a mirror which reflected back to their gaze the 'essence' of themselves and — even more important for him — *of their community*. The experience thus served in Wagner's interpretation of the classical theatrical event to reinforce the Greek's identity by confirming his place within the communal group (and, though his utopian agenda implies that these thoughts pertain equally to men and women, Wagner writes of the Greek as a man). In Wagner's idealized image of the reception of Greek tragedy described in 'Die Kunst und die Revolution' the viewer recognized himself, 'for in the tragedy he found himself again, and moreover the noblest part of his being, united with the noblest parts of the total being of the entire nation' (*DS* 5: 277). The optical metaphor of the theatrical experience is thus based upon the notion that the sense of vision serves to reinforce one's place within the social whole. In his longer and more aesthetically detailed revolutionary tract *Oper und Drama*, Wagner repeats this notion so central to his theory of the utopian role of art and emphasizes again that the Greek viewer not only saw himself 'reflected' in the drama but, more important, saw therein his ties to the rest of the community. For Wagner, the function of the myths presented on stage in the Greek drama was to reflect, and thereby to reinforce, the unification and the bonds of the people: 'Art . . . is nothing other than the fulfillment of a longing to recognize oneself [*sich selbst zu erkennen*] in a represented, admired, or beloved object, to find oneself again in the phenomena of the outer world through their representation. . . . Myth is the condensed aesthetic experience of a *common* view of life [*das Gedicht einer gemeinsamen Lebensanschauung*]' (DS 7: 153–155, my emphasis). According to Wagner's social-aesthetic theory, by gazing upon the work of art one recognizes oneself in the reflection provided by the aesthetic accomplishment, and in so doing one establishes and reinforces one's place within a group: These two notions constitute the fulcrum of his nostalgic and utopian thoughts, couched in the social and aesthetic metaphor of vision, as his discussion in 'Die Kunst und die Revolution' of Aeschylus's image of Apollo makes clear:

Apollo, who had vanquished the chaotic dragon Python, had destroyed the vain sons of the braggart Niobe with his lethal arrows, who through his priestess at Delphi proclaimed to those who asked the primeval law of the Greek spirit and being, and thus held up to the man caught up in the most passionate actions an unsullied mirror of the innermost, unchanging Greek nature, — Apollo was the executor of Zeus's will on Greek soil, he was the Greek people. . . .

Thus the Athenian saw him, when all the drives of his beautiful body, of his restless spirit propelled him to the rebirth of his own being through the ideal expression of art. (DS 5: 274–275)

According to the concepts expressed in Wagner's metaphors, myth and tragedy provided concentrated representations of fundamental components of Greek culture, and thus Aeschylus recognizes himself in Apollo even as the Greek populace sees itself reflected in the Athenian's dramas. For Wagner, this vision-as-recognition is a decidedly social, collective experience. He describes this process as a corollary to the merging of social spheres in the theatrical performance, to which the Greek people flocked 'from the government and judicial buildings, from the country, from ships, from military barracks and from the furthest regions' in order to be united in the collective, theatrical event. In the theater, the Greek populace cast its gaze into the socially regenerative mirror of the drama 'in order . . . to understand itself . . . to dissolve its being, its community . . . into innermost unity and thus in the noblest, deepest peace to be that once again which a few hours before it had also been in restless excitement and isolated individuality' (DS 5: 276). As a dramatic representation, Apollo 'is the people,' and the drama serves to underscore not individuality but community and to highlight the common ties of the Greeks. Thus, the tragedy acts both as a reflection of the unified nation and as a narcissistic vehicle for reinforcing that unity.

For Wagner, this act of social cohesion is the very raison d'être of the superior work of art, and it is based on the metaphor of reflection. In his theoretical tracts, Wagner time and again draws attention to the function of the theater in classical Greece as a vehicle for the visual confirmation, that is, for the recognition, of a *previously known* communal truth reflected in its representation through aesthetic signs. The etymological affinity of the German verbs *kennen* and *erkennen*, which Wagner so often exploits in his essays, underscores the idea that to 'know' something in this system of thought is to 'recognize' it through one's innate, *predisposed* familiarity with it. The Self knows itself by recognizing itself and by seeing itself reflected in the theatrical embodiment of a community to which it belongs and hence that also appears familiar.

The concept of recognition in Wagner thus also harbors an exclusionary dimension, because the knowledge of that which is familiar and communal is (here implicitly and elsewhere explicitly) determined by the boundaries segregating and excluding that which is foreign. And just as Wagner did not invent but borrowed the cognitive model of recognition from Germany's intellectual traditions (as seen in its appearance in Hegel's writings of the early nineteenth century), so too the notion of exclusion that accompanies it is already found in the works of other writers from the German past whom he greatly admired, especially E. T. A. Hoffmann, Eichendorff, and Novalis. The notion of privileged recognition was central to Romantic hermeneutics and manifest in Hoffmann's famous dictum that 'only the artist knows the artist' [*nur der Dichter kennt den Dichter*],' a statement that summarized the Romantic artist's belief in a privileged access to a superior community of like-minded souls.[3] In 'Die Kunst und die Revolution' and the other post-revolutionary essays, it is clear that the act of recognizing oneself is based on one's status as a member of an established and sharply circumscribed group, which for Hoffmann was the community of artists and for Wagner a larger community sharing common ties. For Wagner, when the Greek recognizes himself in the representation of his essence in the work of art, that recognition is vouchsafed no other.

The notion of recognition-as-privilege is coupled with another conceptual model in these Romantic writers as well that is also based on vision and that is also found in Wagner, a model of thought expressed in the metaphor of a superior *depth* hidden beneath a mundane surface appearance. Hoffmann claimed that the artist's privileged capacity to recognize his fellow artist was linked to his ability to discern the essence of art, or 'Truth,' *beneath* the insignificant and multifarious phenomena of everyday life. Using a spatial metaphor, Hoffmann juxtaposed an impoverished and often irrelevant system of superficial signs with the superior, hidden knowledge available only to those exalted few who could perceive and uncover it. But in Hoffmann, too, the hermeneutic event is characterized by the perception of hidden knowledge as an act of *recognition*, of sensing something with which the privileged individual has had a predisposed, innate affinity. Hoffmann's metaphor of superior depth, accessible only to a few, opposed to inferior surface reappears repeatedly in Wagner's writings and in his works for the stage. Sensing the truth behind the signs, whether it provides the key to one's identity as an artist for Hoffmann or as a member of a community for Wagner, the Romantic disregards the mundane appearance of external phenomena and delves into the wondrous, exalted 'depths,' 'recognizing' there, and thereby 'knowing,' the essence that he had previously anticipated. (Before writing his most celebrated essays during the years immediately following the failed revolution, Wagner had already exploited this metaphor of artistic insight earlier in his career — albeit coupled with the motif of social *isolation* — in *Tannhäuser*, which owes much of its imagery to Hoffmann's short story 'Die Bergwerke zu Falun' [The mines of Falun]).[4]

Novalis's famous description from his novel *Heinrich von Ofterdingen* of the aesthetics of poetry (*Dichtkunst*) as superior to the other arts is based on precisely the spatial model, also found in Hoffmann, that polarizes a privileged access to the hidden depths and the unenlightened perception of mere surface phenomena: 'All is internal [*innerlich*], and just as those artists [painters and musicians] fill the external senses with pleasant sensations, so the poet fills the interior sanctuary of the soul [*Gemüt*] with new, wondrous, and pleasurable thoughts. . . . As if out of deep caverns past and future times, immeasurable numbers of people, *wondrous* places, and the strangest occurrences ascend within us.'[5] That this juxtaposition of superior depth and inferior surface conflates with that of privileged poetic sensibility versus mundane and pervasive insensitivity also emerges in a poem from another passage of the Romantic novel:

Der ist der Herr der Erde
Wer ihre Tiefen mißt,
Und jeglicher Beschwerde
In ihrem Schoß vergißt.

Wer ihrer Felsenglieder
Geheimen Bau versteht,
Und unverdrossen nieder
Zu ihrer Werkstatt geht.[6]

[He is the Lord of the earth who measures its depths and forgets all troubles in her womb. Who understands the secret formation of its adamantine limbs, and unperturbed journeys down into its smithy.]

Such depth-defying poetic forays are vouchsafed only those with the inborn sensitivity and predilection to discern what lies hidden beneath the vagaries of surface appearance, as Eichendorff, in one of his most celebrated verses that functions as a hallmark of German Romanticism, implies:

Schläft ein Lied in allen Dingen,
Die da träumen fort und fort,
Und die Welt hebt an zu singen,
Triffst du nur das Zauberwort.[7]

[Sleeps a song in all the things that are dreaming on and on, and the world begins to sing, if you find the magic word.]

It is only the Romantic who can perceive that hidden world and find its magic formula. This topos juxtaposing impoverished surface appearance and superior and above all *privileged* depths functions as the fulcrum of Wagner's aesthetics, providing a motif upon which many of the metaphors of his theoretical writings and music dramas are based. The polarity of superior depth and inferior surface with which *Das Rheingold* (The Rhinegold) closes is based on this very idea and contains within it the rejection of all that is not sensed as already known. It constitutes a legacy of an intellectual tradition whose final representative, as the late-Romantic artist par excellence, Wagner would become:

Rheingold!
Reines Gold!
O leuchtete noch
in der Tiefe dein lautrer Tand!
Traulich und treu
ist's nur in der Tiefe:
falsch und feig
ist, was dort oben sich freut! (*RN*, 72)

[Rhinegold! Pure gold! O if only your simple bauble still shone in the

depths! Trusted and true it is only in the depths: false and cowardly is
what rejoices above!]

A central aspect of Wagner's metaphors of recognition, depth,
and surface is the notion that the work of art somehow provides a
parallel or a representative corollary to the audience that views
it. Wagner's metaphorical description, in part 1 of *Oper und
Drama*, of music in the superior Artwork of the Future employs
the very images of depth, surface, and visual reflection found in
his discussion of the theater in ancient Greece precisely because
that work is understood as an aesthetic reflection of the human
audience.[8] According to Wagner, in classical antiquity the arts
were not divided into separate genres as we know them today but
were merged into one, organically whole, single aesthetic unity,
and that unity mirrored the bonds holding together the community that beheld it. With the disintegration of Greek society,
however, went hand in hand the disintegration of that ideal,
unified aesthetic work, and the various arts became segregated
into the distinct genres of dance, painting, sculpture, architecture, music, and poetry.[9] It would be the despairing agenda
of the revolutionary Artwork of the Future to bring together
these disparate elements for a future society, for a community
whose reunified makeup would be mirrored in the reunification
of the formerly distinct aesthetic elements of the future of art. In
that world, like in ancient Greece, the viewer shall recognize
himself and the cohesion of his social sphere in the representation on stage. For this reason, Wagner can use the same images
for both artwork and audience, and the image he chooses most
often is a corporeal one, the eye. The artwork, couched in
the metaphors of the bodies of those who perceive it, contains
within its 'depths' the essence of those who innately know by
viewing, and thus itself contains its focal point in the metaphor
of ocular perception. Wagner's description of the future artwork
runs thus:

Just as the interior is probably the basis and the condition for the
exterior, but only from the exterior does the interior clearly and de-

cisively emerge, so *harmony* and *rhythm* are probably the formative organs, but only melody is the true shape of music itself. Harmony and rhythm are blood, flesh, nerves, and bones with all the inner organs, which like the former remain closed to the beholding eye in the contemplation of the completed, living human being; melody on the other hand is this completed human being itself, just as it presents itself to our eyes. When we look at this human being we behold only the slender shape as it expresses itself to us in the form-giving delineation of the exterior coat of skin. We immerse ourselves into the contemplation of the most expressive realization of this shape in its facial features and finally stop at the eye, the most lively and communicative realization of the entire human being, which, through this organ that derives its capacity for communication in turn only out of the most universal talent to receive the expressions of the surrounding world, at the same time communicates to us its interior in the most convincing fashion. In this way melody is the most perfected expression of the interior being of music, and every true melody determined by this innermost being also speaks to us through that eye which most expressively communicates to us this interior. (*DS* 7: 106–107)

To the discerning gaze the Artwork of the Future reveals its depths through its physiognomy — it is a being that mirrors the audience that beholds it, and the symbiosis of vision between artwork and community forms a link between the aesthetic construct as metaphorical body and the community as the body politic made up of real, human bodies with genuine physiognomies. No wonder the eye is the most important image here; as a metaphorical correlate to the social body, the Artwork of the Future will itself be based on the act of vision as a metaphor, making possible through its aesthetic makeup the recognition and 'knowledge' for the future community that unfolded within the idealized classical Greek past. Thus the terms that Wagner chose for that future work and that ideal forerunner of the future German community are also similar; *Gesamtkunstwerk* describes the reformatory artwork, recalling his description of the 'total being' (*Gesamtwesen*) of the Greek spectator in the process of becoming united with the entire community in the theatrical experience (*DS* 5: 277), the very goal of the newly conceived, unified German artwork of tomorrow. As metaphor, the work itself will enact — and thus provide a model for and a mirror of — the very utopian agenda of unification for which, in the idealized social context of a future Germany, it is intended. The social body and the artwork-as-body are two interdependent manifestations of the same phenomenon in Wagner's imagination, and its central metaphors — the eye and the body — are keys to his conceptualization of the ideal society and of its representative work of art.

But the superior work of art — be it the Greek tragedy or the Artwork of the Future — is not for each and every body. While the conceptual metaphors of depth and vision in Hoffmann, Novalis, and Eichendorff had *implicitly* harbored the elitism of privilege, Wagner uses his metaphors to explicitly separate the elect from the lowly. Wagner argues that the act of recognition vouchsafed by the superior work of art is privileged precisely because it is based on the *exclusion* of those deemed different, and the recognition of difference is determined, as we shall see, by the body and by the ability to recognize its signs. In 'Die Kunst und die Revolution' it becomes clear that only the Greek — and no other — can know and recognize himself and his fellow Greeks. In the middle of his discussion of the Greek's self-recognition in the theater, Wagner writes the following, ideologically key passage:

having contempt for that soft trust that accumulates in indolent and egotistical rest beneath the flattering shadow of a foreign care, always on the lookout, tirelessly defending against external influence, giving no tradition, no matter how time-honored, power over his free contemporary life, activity, and thought, — the Greek fell silent before the call of the chorus, gladly subordinated himself to the sensual agreement in the scenic directions, willingly obeyed the great need proclaimed to him by the tragedian through the mouth of his gods and heroes on the stage. (DS 5: 277)

Only those who share the 'common view of life' can 'know' (and that means, for Wagner, can recognize [*erkennen*]) themselves in the unified artwork designed to appeal to a unified people, to a

people, therefore, that is by implication *homogeneous*. The flip
side of the communal bonds reinforced through the recognition
and knowledge of one's ties to one's fellow citizens is thus *the
perception of one's difference* from those who do not belong to
the idealized community, those whose characteristics are defined through their opposition to the privileged order: They are
'external' and 'foreign' and harbor an 'egotistical' nature associated with individualism, the antithesis of the community. These
characteristics have no place in the essence of the Greek spirit
and serve to establish, through their rejection, the borders of the
superior idealized Greek communal group. Wagner's entire social theory, and his concept of the role of art in society, is based
on the rejection of that which is recognized as foreign and different. In Wagner, recognition never serves to segregate the
individual from his *own* kind but only to reinforce social bonds:
He who recognizes his difference from others also recognizes
his ties to those who are *not* different, who are like him. In 'Das
Kunstwerk der Zukunft' Wagner states explicitly: 'That which
should be distinguished must necessarily have *that* from which it
is to distinguish itself. He who wants to be completely himself
must first recognize what he is; this he recognizes however first
in the difference from that which he is not: if he wanted to
separate from himself that which is different from himself, he
would not be anything different, and thus no longer something
recognizable' (*DS* 6: 39). Recognition, then, serves not simply to
establish one's own identity but to do so through a process of
exclusion. The Self 'knows' itself by sensing its ties with its
community and by discerning its difference from those who are
foreign. With ever-growing clarity, Wagner forms a consistent
image of community as based on *homogeneity*, as comprised of
individuals who are *similar*.

In all his essayistic productions and in many of his dramatic
conceptualizations, Wagner's arguments unfold through the use
of oppositional, polar models based on exclusion; the polarity of
like and foreign, of friend and foe is fundamental to his thought.
In 'Die Kunst und die Revolution' the development of his ideas

progresses through the juxtaposition of images of diametrically opposed elements: classical Greece versus Rome; Greece versus Christianity; and the role of art in the lost, ancient, idealized classical paradise versus its role in the modern world, where it is little more than fodder for the culture industry. Behind all these antithetical images lies the juxtaposition of irreconcilable kinds of societies — one homogeneous and containing only like-minded and similar, communally unified people who can recognize the commonality they already know, and another that is *heterogeneous*, mixed, filled with dissimilar and disparate foreign elements and hence, in Wagner's thinking, inferior. Friend and foe, kind and un-kind constitute the uncompromising poles of Wagner's social reflections based on the recognition of the familiar, and the chasm between them remained irreconcilable for him throughout his life. (One of the last of his essays — 'Erkenne dich selbst' [Know thyself] of 1881, whose title itself repeats his ubiquitous preoccupation with the concept of recognizing that which is already known — again employs the metaphor guaranteeing the preservation of communal boundaries through the rejection of that which is different: 'What is not recognized,' Wagner continues to maintain toward the end of his life, 'will be beaten [*Was nicht erkannt wird, darauf wird losgeschlagen*]' [GS 14: 182].)

The demise of ancient Greece is directly linked for Wagner to the individualism and heterogeneous particularism he locates in the later societies of Rome, of Christianity, and of the modern world, a particularism that attacked the communal familiarity and homogeneity of Greek society and that he associates with foreigners of diverse national origins (as well as with their preoccupation with money, as we shall see). It is clear that ancient Greece and Rome function here as screens for Wagner's reflections on the role of the arts in nineteenth-century Germany and the non-German countries, for Wagner explicitly links the decay of the post-Hellenic age, associated with the 'egotistical individuation' of the nationally diverse foreigners, to the heterogeneity of a decaying modern Europe:

The Romans had a god *Mercury*, whom they compared with the Greek god Hermes. But for them his winged endeavors took on a practical meaning: for them these were a matter of the moving industry of the wheeling and dealing merchants [*bewegliche Betriebsamkeit jener scha-chernden und wuchernden Kaufleute*] who came together from all corners of the earth to the center of the Roman world in order to gain access, for their own profit, for the rich gentlemen of their world to all the sensual pleasures which nearby nature was not able to offer them. To the Roman . . . the god of the merchants thus also became the god of swindlers and vandals. . . .

If you crown his head with a halo of Christian hypocrisy and adorn his breast with the spiritless medal of deceased feudal orders of knights, you'll have him, the god of the modern world, the holy highly noble god of 5 percent, the benefactor and director of today's — art. Incorporate you see him before you in a bigoted English banker . . . when you see him allowing the foremost singers of the Italian opera . . . to sing to him. That is *Mercury* and his gifted servant, *modern art*. (DS 5: 284–285)

The movement in Wagner's argument from the world of ancient Greece to modern Europe is based on the link he perceives between foreigners and commerce (between disparate and untrustworthy foreign cultural elements and the commodification of art); the move from the 'sensual pleasures' acquired through the wandering merchants of ancient Rome to the modern conflation of national identities in the performance of Italian opera for the English banker makes the epithets associated with Rome readily applicable to Wagner's view of non-German civilization (especially that of Italy, France, and England). Conversely, the superiority of the idealized Greek community provides a model for Wagner's utopian vision of a future fatherland. The irreconcilable poles of Greek and non-Greek take on increasingly specific contours ever more pertinent to Wagner's critique of the modern age as his essay unfolds; multifolkish plurality, commerce, egotism, and individuation come to characterize the non-Greek (and non-German) world, while similarity, homogeneity, and communal spirit constitute the hallmarks of Greek society and of its theater, which reflected its unified and similar essence, the very attributes within Wagner's thinking of Germany and of a German theater as well, especially in his image of a future Germany cleansed of the characteristics of the non-German world imposing on his beloved and privileged fatherland. As I will show, these antithetical images of society are also related to Wagner's metaphors of the eye and of visual recognition.

'Die Kunst und die Revolution,' so illustrative of Wagner's ideological program, concerns the concept of egotism as antithetical to community (and, therefore, as represented in the aesthetic sphere by the particularism of the distinct, isolated, individual artistic genres symptomatic of the post-Hellenic artwork and the 'egotistical' world ruled by commerce). As the title of the essay suggests, Wagner's thoughts concern a revolutionary agenda for a different kind of art, a different kind of theatrical experience, and a different society redeemed from such self-serving egotistical individuation. In the ancient world, according to Wagner, art was not a commodity, and thus it emerges in his description of the Roman and the modern world as antithetical to the idealized public sphere and to the function of art in the idealized communal theatrical experience of ancient Greece. In the Wagnerian imagination, commerce is a concept belonging to a world bereft of communal unification, lacking the affinity of those who belong to a group of similar and like-minded people. It is a post-Hellenic, a modern phenomenon with solely negative connotations, the modus vivendi of *foreigners*, of 'swindlers and vandals,' and of 'bigoted English bankers':

[The Greek's] spirit lived only in the public sphere [*in der Öffentlichkeit*], in the people's community [*in der Volksgenossenschaft*]: his worries were occupied by the needs of this public sphere. . . . To the enjoyment of the public sphere the Greek walked out of a simple, unadorned domesticity: shameful and base it would have seemed to him to indulge in a refined abundance and sensuality behind the splendid walls of a private palace, which today constitute the sole content of the life of a hero of the stock exchange; for herein the Greek distinguished himself from the egotistical Orientalized barbarian [*dem egoistischen orientali-sierten Barbaren*]. (*DS* 5: 293)

Wagner argues that while once all men were free to celebrate their communal equality through art, now, in the particularized interests of multicultural nineteenth-century European society, the majority are 'slaves who today are taught by bankers and the owners of factories to seek the reason for existence in artisanry and manual labor [*Handwerksarbeit*] for their daily bread' (*DS* 5: 294). This state of affairs characterizes precisely the life of the modern artist, Wagner maintains, who is merely paid for producing works composed of isolated, segregated, disparate arts intended for the culture industry and destined to be received in an institution — the (Parisian) Grand Opéra — that furthers social particularization, stratification, and alienation. The bankers and factory owners of the modern world, and the merchants, swindlers, and vandals of Rome, all united under the 'god of 5 percent' and found within the most diverse national locations, have vanquished the long-lost unity of the homogeneous single national community in which a unified art, unalienated from the common man and part of the public sphere, reflected a unified nation.

Wagner maintains that within the idealized Greek past, the work of art could be 'conservative' because it reflected and itself reinforced a genuine public sphere, but in the modern world the authentic work of art (as opposed to the hackwork created for the culture industry) would have to be 'revolutionary,' opposed to the public sphere, in order to bring about a transformation of the social context in which it can authentically exist. Thus, according to Wagner's utopian agenda, the revolutionary (Wagnerian) Artwork of the Future will serve both as a model and *as an anticipatory mirror* of a future, superior world. While the unified artwork in ancient Greece reflected the community of a unified and homogeneous people, the revolutionary work, which does not yet have a social context commensurate with its unified makeup, can only anticipate, in an exemplary fashion, its future audience: it can only posit the world for whose realization it was created, but that does not yet exist. Recalling its long-lost Greek model, the Artwork of the Future will itself contribute, through its metaphorical capacity to reflect an ideal, to the reestablishment of communal identity and hence to the creation of that superior, future world. Thus, fundamentally irreconcilable kinds of art works — one a conglomeration of disparate, isolated, egotistical elements and the other a unified, 'organic' whole — represent antithetical social orders characterized by the diametrically opposed spheres of commerce or community.

Even the different physical configurations of the theaters of ancient Greece and the modern world, by which Wagner means Epidaurus and the modern (Parisian) Grand Opéra house, reflect for him the diverse functions of theater within each society, one intended for inclusion based on equality, the other representative of alienation and social segregation fostered by the power of capitalism and egotism. In ancient Greece, the stage extended into the audience, which surrounded it on three sides, and this spatial configuration manifests for Wagner a populist, inclusive kind of theatrical experience altogether different for him from that of a modern opera-going audience separated from the spectacle on stage by a proscenium and an orchestra pit. It was with these antithetical representations of diverse societies in mind, each with a different relationship to art, that Wagner conceived of the festival theater in Bayreuth — the modern, German-Greek theater that would have no boxes and would be intentionally egalitarian (figure 6).

How do Wagner's metaphors of vision tie into his polar models of societies in the ancient world and in the modern age, and to their representative theaters? These images of society are based on the notion that the unified community comprised of similar members defines itself by rejecting what is different, while the other, multifarious group comprises an assemblage of disparate elements apparently bereft of such a visual mechanism guaran-

6. Interior of the
Bayreuth Festival
Theater (without
seats). Drawing by
Louis Sauter, 1875
(Nationalarchiv der
Richard Wagner–
Stiftung/Richard
Wagner Gedenk-
stätte, Bayreuth)

teeing identity. But what are the signs delineating difference?
How does the Greek or the German recognize the 'wheeling
and dealing merchants' from foreign lands, the 'egotistical Orientalized barbarian'? He does so in the modern world *through
the corporeal, visual signs of race*. It is at this juncture that Wagner's
thoughts on the recognition of like kind, egotism, commerce,
and the makeup of the modern heterogeneous world and its
representative, disjunctive artwork merge, for all these concepts
are intimately related in Wagner's theories to Jews, and the Jews
are distinguishable in Wagner's culture — and throughout his
own works — by the idiosyncratic physiognomy of their racial
makeup.

The single most corrupting factor in the dissolution of the
modern world for Wagner was the development of the power
interests of industry and state, and he closely associated these, in
typically nineteenth-century anti-Semitic fashion, with Jewish
financial influence.[10] It was Wagner's argument that the Jews,
through their prominence in banking institutions and the grow-

ing publishing industry, were non-Germans who exerted an unprecedented influence on the modern world in general and on the theatrical and musical institutions of Europe in particular. He regarded them as endowed with a host of the very 'non-German' traits he had associated with post-Hellenic culture in 'Die Kunst und die Revolution': avarice, egotism, lovelessness, immorality, a carnal nature, and an ability to mimic (though imperfectly) the society in and from which they lived.[11] As early as 1841, long before his concentrated production of essays in the immediate postrevolutionary period spent in exile, Wagner directed anti-Semitic remarks at the composer Giacomo Meyerbeer, whose 'Jewish' aptitude for mercantile advance had brought him, according to Wagner, wealth and success in Paris and who influenced the makeup and reception of music in the international culture scene, as he baldly stated in his essay 'Pariser Fatalitäten für Deutsche' (Parisian fatalities for the German), written for a German readership under the pseudonym V. Freudenfeuer:

[If the German musician] attains to higher levels of achievement, for instance if he becomes a law-giving composer (a composer who sets precedents) [*gesetzgebender Komponist*] at the Grand Opéra, like Meyerbeer, he will have achieved this only as a banker; for a banker can do everything in Paris, even compose operas and have them produced. . . .

Yet the *German bankers*, of whom there are a good many here, no longer count as Germans; they are above all nationality, and therefore above all national prejudices; they belong to the Universe and the Paris stock exchange. . . . In the eyes of the French, Rothschild is more a universal Jew than a German. (*DS* 5: 62)

As a wealthy Jew influential in the music world (as a member of the 'stock exchange'), Meyerbeer is not a German but a member of a multicultural, pluralistic society; he belongs to the sphere of 'the egotistical Orientalized barbarians' that in ancient Rome had been comprised of mixed and disparate 'wheeling and dealing merchants' and that now, in modern Europe, is populated by the 'bigoted' bankers for whom modern art is a 'gifted servant.' (Forty years later, in 'Erkenne dich selbst,' Wagner would still decry the state of contemporary civilization as 'a barbaric-Judaistic mishmash [*ein barbarisch-judaistisches Gemisch*]' [GS 14: 186].) For Wagner, Meyerbeer loses his national identity and implicitly endangers German art through his commodification of culture in the modern world.[12] Because art and its reception are always hallmarks of the society in which they function for Wagner, the Jewish presence in the arts constitutes and represents a threat and a hindrance to the establishment of a unified, homogeneous society, to the rebirth of the Greek spirit in a future Germany rid of the foreign element of the Jew.

Wagner's anti-Semitism is already discernible in his essays from the early 1840s penned during his stay in Paris, but the conflation of Judeophobia and his sociocritical concerns is most clearly developed in the disparate and at first glance primarily aesthetic and sociocritical reflections of the early years spent in exile, 1848 to 1851 (figure 7). This is particularly the case in 'Das Judentum in der Musik,' which so many apologetic critics seek to decontextualize and treat as an aberration but which, both chronologically and in terms of its significance for Wagner's utopian agenda, lies squarely in the middle of his other revolutionary writings.[13] In this essay (the racism of which is only more overt but not more vehement or essentially different from that upon which the other essays are based), Wagner states emphatically that the Jews' financial control of European cultural institutions had come to corrupt public taste and hence the public reception of music: 'That the impossibility to further create natural, necessary, and true beauty without completely changing the basis of the level to which the development of art has now advanced has brought the public taste in art under the mercantile fingers of the Jews, for that we have now to examine the causes' (GS 13: 10). (In a letter to Ferdinand Heine of 14 September 1850 — the year in which he published 'Das Judentum in der Musik' — Wagner expressed his 'terrible disgust over the banker-music whoring [*furchtbaren ekel für die banquier-musikhurerei*],' another formulation conflating his hatred of both the Jews' prominence in finance and their success and in-

7. Wagner in Paris, 1850, the year of 'Das Judentum in der Musik.' Photo by Ernest Benedikt Kietz (National-archiv der Richard Wagner–Stiftung/ Richard Wagner Gedenkstätte, Bay-reuth)

fluence in the music industry.)[14] This is the very idea that emerges less explicitly, though with equal vehemence, in the book-length essay *Deutsche Kunst und deutsche Politik* (German art and German politics) of 1867, in which Wagner coined the often-cited maxim: ' "German" [means] doing the thing one does for its own sake and for the joy of it; whereas utilitarianism, i.e., the principle whereby a thing is done because of an external personal objective, shows itself to be un-German' (DS 8: 320). If one thinks of financial gain as an 'external personal objective,' the un-German is clearly the Jew in Wagner's view of the world as controlled by Judaized bourgeois capitalism. In 1865, in an effort to answer the titular question of his essay 'Was ist deutsch?' (What is German?) (first published in 1878) through negative examples, Wagner again wrote of the mercantile nature of the Jews and of their pernicious influence in the modern world, which he described as

this invasion of German essence by an utterly alien element. . . . It everywhere appears to be the duty of the Jew to show the nations of Europe where haply there may be a profit they have overlooked. . . . None of the European nations had recognized the boundless advantages for the nation's general economy of an ordering of the relations of labor and capital in accordance with the modern spirit of bourgeois enterprise. The Jews laid hand on these advantages, and upon the hindered and dwindling prosperity of the nation the Jewish banker feeds his enormous wealth. (DS 10: 91–92)[15]

'What is German' is defined by what it is not; the commercial 'nature' of the Jew constitutes a foreign element, the negation of which defines the borders of the homogeneous German community. This constellation of related ideas (the corrupt modern state, impersonal interaction based on finance, the Jew's parasitic power, and above all the foreign nature of the Jew) appears repeatedly in Wagner's thinking. The superior German artist, isolated within a culturally and racially heterogeneous world characterized by the avaricious particularism of the Jews, themselves the modern descendants of the roving Oriental barbaric tribes who contributed to the downfall of the ideal, cohesive, and unified Greek community and of its art, longs for a world rid of such multifarious, individual competition so bereft of folkish spirit. His superior, future Total Works of Art will reject the modern commercial theatrical institutions and will hold up a mirror to a different society yet to come, one characterized by the familiarity and community of — literally — *anti*-Semitic, like kind.

Those who have examined Wagner's anti-Semitism, especially Leon Stein, Robert Gutman, Hartmut Zelinsky, and Paul Lawrence Rose, have written extensively of the racist thrust behind many of the composer's essays concerning what Wagner viewed as the corrupting, mercantile influence of the Jews on the development of art in general and of music in particular in the Western world. None, however, has discussed the importance of the motif of vision as a link between Wagner's anti-Semitic writings and his essays on social and aesthetic reform. Vision functions as a metaphor that ties together these various concerns and that provides a key to the ideologically consistent, racist program underlying Wagner's disparate pronouncements on aesthetic issues, cultural history, and the modern world, because in Wagner's thinking it is the metaphorical vehicle through which a society defines itself, and in the nineteenth-century imagination, the Jew — and all the vile characteristics with which he is associated for Wagner and for many of his contemporaries — can be recognized and rejected due to his purportedly idiosyncratic and characteristic visual appearance. As I shall show, the metaphor of reflection also connects Wagner's prose works to his music dramas.

When discussing the mirror metaphor in conjunction with Wagner's anti-Semitism, it is important to realize that for the discussion of the Jew, the *physiological dimension* of that metaphor is of paramount importance: Wagner's model of recognition guarantees for the German the demarcation, and hence the preservation, of racial and national boundaries precisely because in his culture the Jew was understood to be endowed with a corporeal iconography that distinguished him from the non-Jew. It is at this juncture that Wagner's notion of sensing the 'essence' of the Self and of the community emerges not simply as an abstract conceptualization — as a metaphor — but as a notion purportedly *grounded in physical reality* for those who experience it. The German, like the hypostasized Greek, may discern some ill-defined 'essence' in his artwork in general, but he does so, we should recall, by recognizing that which is different from himself, and to the nineteenth-century German imagination, that different Other par excellence was the Jew, defined and revealed by a body that was viewed as essentially, fundamentally different from that of the German. When Wagner's model of recognition in Greece is transferred to the modern world, the physical presence of those who are deemed antithetical to the German people emerges as the constitutive marker indicating the borders of the modern community: here, metaphor and physical image, laden with racist implications in Wagner's culture, merge.

Wagner uses his metaphor in an idiosyncratic fashion, but the corporeal signs with which he associated it were not his own, for his image of the Jew was drawn from a host of German cultural traditions with widespread currency in his time. 'Das Judentum in der Musik' documents the belief, pervasive in Wagner's age, that the Jew reveals his difference through a host of iconoclastically and yet stereotypically foreign corporeal signs: through his appearance and through the sounds he makes (that he also stinks and limps are still other components of the repertoire of anti-Semitic stereotypes in Wagner's time that are discernible in his music dramas, as I shall discuss in chapters 3 and 4). One of the most notorious of Wagner's statements from this essay is the following: 'In everyday life the Jew strikes us first of all by his external appearance, which, no matter what European nationality we belong to, has something unpleasantly foreign to this nationality: we desire instinctively to have nothing to do with/ nothing in common with a person who looks like that [*wir wünschen unwillkürlich mit einem so aussehenden Menschen nichts gemein zu haben*]' (GS 13: 11). Precisely, 'with a person who *looks* like that': Community has its signs, and those signs are available to those who belong to it; they are distinguishable, and indeed fundamentally different, from the signs of others. The metaphors of vision, recognition, and differentiation are based on the physiology of the perceived object, who is deemed different pre-

cisely because his body evinces features that fall outside the catalog of the national physiognomy. Those foreign, non-German
signs, moreover, will always constitute corporeal indications of
the psychological traits also deemed non-German: avarice, egotism, and a lack of familial and communal piety. It is by his
appearance that the Jew reveals his 'foreign' characterological
essence to the German, and, because of this appearance, the
German wishes to have nothing to do with him. In his extensive
clarification on this tract, 'Aufklärungen über "Das Judentum in
der Musik"' (Elucidations on 'Jewishness in Music') published
when he reprinted the earlier text in 1869, Wagner made the
connection between the corrosive influence of the Jews on German art and their physiological nature explicit: 'of *one thing* I am
certain: just as the influence that the Jews have gained on our
spiritual life, and as it manifests itself in the distraction and
falsification of our highest artistic tendencies, is not a simple,
perhaps even a purely physiological coincidence, so it must also
be acknowledged as undeniable and decisive' (*GS* 13: 50). The
body of the Jew is intimately linked to his nefarious essence, and
it provides the marker that distinguishes the foreign element so
threatening to the future of German culture. Even when Wagner employs his metaphor of vision in a more abstract, theoretical context, the physiology of the foreigner will always be
implied, accompanying and providing a negative corporeal substratum, as it were, to the lofty conceptual reflections on the
good of the superior community.

Wagner's metaphorical discussion in *Oper und Drama* of music in the Artwork of the Future as somehow corporeal in nature
thus takes on a larger dimension when compared with these
more explicitly anti-Semitic statements, for it implies that such
a work as a bodily metaphor of its audience is intended to reflect
a community *that looks different* from those it rejects. It is the
task of that work to provide a model for a different, uniquely
German world, and its characterization as a body has connotations for the physicality of those it is supposed to represent. The
eye is foremost in the metaphorical description of that work

precisely because the eye guarantees the demarcation of communal borders on the basis of physical appearance, and the Jew is deemed physiologically different from, indeed antithetical to, the German. In section 2 of 'Das Kunstwerk der Zukunft' (The artwork of the future) entitled 'Der Mensch als sein eigener künstlerischer Gegenstand und Stoff' (The human being as his own aesthetic object and material), Wagner discusses the superior work of art as *primarily concerned with the corporeality of its protagonists*, and in this context he mentions the eye as a vehicle allowing for the process of distinction: 'The eye takes in *the corporeal form of the human being*, compares it with its surroundings, and distinguishes it from them. Corporeal man and the direct expressions of his impressions of sensual pain and sensual pleasure received through exterior touch are immediately accessible to the eye' (*DS* 6: 32). Because the function of the Total Work of Art for Wagner is the establishment of the borders of community and these are determined by corporeal markers, the work itself is conceived in terms of those markers, of that physiology. The artwork does not simply reflect the image of the community, then, but also does so by physiological distinction, and this it achieves through the assessment of physical appearance. Thus, when the future German audience beholds its image in the aesthetic representations of the Total Work of Art, that work will metaphorically constitute a body reflecting the bodily presence of those who view it, but the physicality of that metaphorical idea will be essential, for the difference between their bodies and those of the world it rejects will be perceived as real, as grounded in verifiable physiology. The work as metaphor will itself be based on vision as the guarantor of social demarcation vouchsafed by the distinctive iconography of the body.

It is only consistent, then, that Wagner was so concerned with the senses as the basis of his new aesthetic-social theories. The audience of the future and superior artwork, he maintained, would perceive the unified work through the empathy of its 'feelings' and not through the intellect (deemed cold and characteristic of the Jew) and thus would be sensually united with the work as the communally rejuvenative theatrical experience unfolded. As a reflection of the utopian community, 'art,' Wagner writes in 'Die Kunst und die Revolution,' will be 'the highest activity of the . . . sensually beautifully developed human being [*des . . . sinnlich schön entwickelten Menschen*] at one with himself and with nature' (*DS* 5: 281). The first plan for the revolutionary music drama that Wagner developed in conjunction with his post-1848 essayistic production — *Siegfrieds Tod* (Siegfried's death), which would later be expanded into *Der Ring des Nibelungen* (Wagner's paradigm of the evils of the modern world and of the need for the rejuvenation and de-Jewification of Germany, and a work whose most basic tension is that between Nature and money) — focused on the *corporeal impression* that its hero would make on its audience. Siegfried, and especially his body, was to provide an aesthetic model for the world of the future rid of the Jew's body and of Jewish particularism. Wagner's initial conceptualization of the figure, whom he described in a letter of 25 January 1854 to his friend August Röckel as 'my ideal for the perfect human being' and as a 'man of the future [*Mensch der Zukunft*],' [16] was based on the physical impression of the hero, on Siegfried's body, as he made clear in 'Eine Mitteilung an meine Freunde' (A communication to my friends) of 1851: 'What I recognized here was no longer the historical conventional figure, whose attire must interest us more than his true appearance, but rather the genuine naked human being, in which I could recognize every surge of blood, every twitch of the powerful muscles in unfettered, freest movement: the *true human being* per se' (*DS* 6: 290). The physical, corporeal dimension of Siegfried took the fore in Wagner's imagination, for it was the appearance of the hero, as that aspect immediately discernible to the eye, that provided the basis for his identity and for the drama that would present him to the empathetic and sensually discerning gaze of the future audience. The body of the Volsung hero and the metaphor of the work-as-body both constitute vehicles for the reflection of the German audience, whose physiology,

too, is central to its identity. Physiological appearance and metaphor are never far apart in Wagner's aesthetic theory of social
redemption. In 'Eine Mitteilung an meine Freunde' he went on
to say that he even conceived of the kind of verse commensurate
with his young hero as a linguistic corollary to Siegfried's body,
which was superior to the physiologically inferior body of the
intellectual, rational drama:

> Just as this human being moved, so his spoken expression necessarily
> had to be; here the merely *rationally conceived* [*gedachte*] modern verse
> with its fleeting, bodyless shape [*mit seiner verschwebenden, körperlosen
> Gestalt*] no longer sufficed; the fantastical deception of the end-rhymes
> no longer was able as apparent flesh to disguise the absence of all living
> bone structure, which this verse-body contains within itself as an ar-
> bitrarily expandable, disintegrating compilation of cartilage [*Schleim-
> knorpelwerk*]. . . . At the primeval mythical spring, where I found the
> youthfully beautiful human being Siegfried, I also found automatically
> the sensually perfected linguistic expression in which alone this human
> being could express himself. It was the . . . *alliterative verse* [*der . . .
> stabgereimte Vers*] in which the *Volk* itself once created poetry, when it
> was still poet and creator of myths. (*DS* 6: 308–309)

When Siegfried appears on stage before the gaze of the German
audience, his image and his sounds provide a hierarchy of metaphors based on his superior physiology: As the locus in which
rhythm and movement converge (as mentioned in the introduction in the discussion of Wagner's theory of 'gesture'), he represents the reunification of aesthetic elements that were once indistinguishable within the ideal of the Greek Total Work of Art
and that were thereafter isolated in the age of particularization;
the relatedness and similarity of the component parts of his
alliterative discourse constitute a metaphor for the social relationships based on the similarity of those for whom the superior
artwork is created, while the exaggerated and intentional physicality of his verse and of his music and visual presence underscores his purported proximity to nature; his is a verse that
constitutes the deep interior 'essence' of German art, discernible to the German audience as the opposite of an inferior and

modern kind of verse which had been little more than a superficial system of semantic surface phenomena that might satisfy the gaze of those who cannot truly see but that would be insufficient to the powerful vision of the German community endowed with the ability to penetrate beneath the surface into the depths suggested by Wagner's 'sensually perfected linguistic expression.' And finally, all these meanings, grounded in the physiological impression of Siegfried's body, constitute the rejection of that other, inferior kind of body which would have no place in the future audience: the body of Siegfried's opposite, the 'merely rational' being without 'living bone structure,' a 'disintegrating compilation of cartilage' which the German eye would immediately recognize and 'know' as foreign. (Wagner's age was sensitive to the racist implications of his hero; twenty years after the composer's death, Otto Weininger, in his sensationally popular *Geschlecht und Charakter* [Sex and character], stated that the figure of Siegfried was 'the most un-Jewish thing imaginable [*das Unjüdischeste . . . was erdacht werden konnte*].')[17]

It is no coincidence that the body is likened to language here, because throughout Wagner's theoretical writings, language is viewed as a *folkish* accomplishment linked to the community of like kind. In 'Was ist deutsch?' for example, Wagner made the connection between language and circumscribed community explicit when he answered his eponymous question with the (incorrect) explanation that the word *deutsch* is etymologically related to *deuten*, 'to explicate' or 'to make "clear" [*deutlich*],' implying that that which is 'clear' is immediately and innately 'known' and recognizable to the German community, to those with shared, common ties, and that such clarity is discernible in the language of a community:

'*deutsch*' is accordingly that with which we are familiar, what we are used to, what we have inherited from our fathers, what has sprouted from the earth. . . . It denotes therefore those peoples [*Völker*] who remained in their place of origin, continuing to speak their primeval mother tongue [*Urmuttersprache*], while those [previously German] lines [*Stämme*] ruling in the former Romanic countries gave up their mother tongue. The concept '*deutsch*' is therefore attached to language and to the primeval homeland [*Urheimat*]. (*DS* 10: 85–86)

Wanderers from foreign lands signified degeneration in Wagner's image of the downfall of ancient Greece and the emergence of Rome, that forerunner of the modern world, and the diasporatic, migratory 'Oriental barbarians' associated with a different blood and soil, as well as with a different language and appearance, constitute the elements that blurred the homogeneous 'clarity' of ancient Greece and that form the antithesis to all that is familiar or clear in nineteenth-century Germany — to that which is *deutsch*. Little wonder, then, that Wagner perceives the Jew as a foreigner incapable of assimilating, of participating in, this linguistically defined communal idiom. As a folkish accomplishment, language can only be imperfectly and superficially mimicked by those outside that community, as Wagner's remarks in 'Das Judentum in der Musik' on the Jew's speech patterns suggest:

A completely unidiomatic use of our national language and an arbitrary distortion of words and phrase constructions give the Jew's locutions the unmistakable character of an intolerably confused babble of sounds. (*GS* 13: 13)

[The Jew's speech is the] merely senseless repetition of a painfully accurate and deceptively similar nature, just as parrots imitate human words and phrases, but without any expression or real emotion as these stupid birds are wont to do. (*GS* 13: 17)

Language functions here as the body does in Wagner's essays: Just as the metaphor of vision reveals to the ancient Greek and to the modern Romantic German initiate the deep interior beneath the outwardly similar superficial physiognomy, so speech also provides a sign of identity. Wagner's description of Siegfried's verse as a superior body is thus both consistent and ideologically significant; his linguistic corpus is the kind of body no Jew in Wagner's imagination could ever convincingly adopt, let alone possess.

Because the authentic artwork reflects the physiological and linguistic (the visual and acoustical) likeness of like-kind to those with the affinity of a homogeneous community, the antithesis of superior German art—the Jewish music of Meyerbeer and Mendelssohn—cannot provide a reflected image but only a blurred distortion of the German appearance, language, and essence. Their art cannot be 'clear,' or *deutsch*. It is precisely because the Jew, who does not innately 'know' the German as only the German can, cannot sense the hidden depths of the German identity beneath the exterior, superficial appearance of German art that he is condemned to mimic, and thus to provide only an inauthentic, superficial distortion of the German community. Whether semantic, corporeal, or dramatic (as in Meyerbeer's case), the mirror is not available to the foreigner, because his eyes, both those of the nomadic merchants of classical antiquity and those with which the modern banker views the world, are focused on less lofty ideals than the German's, as Wagner states in 'Das Judentum in der Musik': 'The Jews' sensual ability to behold [*Anschauungsgabe*] was never able to bring forth visual artists from their midst: their eye was always occupied with far more practical matters than beauty and the spiritual content of the formal world of appearances' (GS 13: 15). Because the Jew sees solely the superficial matters of commerce, he can only mimic the exterior but not the deeper truths of German art:

His entire position among us does not seduce the Jew . . . into penetrating our being completely: either intentionally . . . or by chance . . . he therefore only listens to our artistry and its life-giving inner organism in a very superficial manner. . . . Therefore the accidental exterior form of appearances in the area of our musical life and art must necessarily appear to him as its very being, therefore his reception of it, when he reflects it back to us as an artist, must appear to us foreign, cold, strange, indifferent, unnatural, and distorted. (GS 13: 20–21)

In 'Was ist deutsch?' Wagner adopts this metaphor to emphasize the purported *threat* of the Jewish artwork, which can only act as a fun-house mirror, reflecting back to the German not a 'clear' image of German culture but only a parody of its superior essence: 'and thus we see an odious travesty of the German spirit upheld today before the German *Volk* as its imputed likeness. It is to be feared that before long the nation may really take this false image for its mirrored image; then one of the finest natural dispositions in all the human race would be done to death, perchance for ever. We have to inquire how to save it from such a shameful doom' (*DS* 10: 92). This distortion—a false, Judaized artwork that can only convey an untrue image of those who observe it—threatens to undermine the purity and the integrity of the communal audience, should that German community fail to recognize the parrotlike foreign mimicry of the barbaric Oriental artwork as a travesty of its own true linguistic-corporeal nature and therefore as inimical to German culture.

Thus the metaphor of vision by itself reveals that Wagner's anti-Semitism is not some minor, passing aberration limited to his personal antipathies but a fundamental component in the ideological program of his social theories and his tracts on the aesthetic makeup of a future and different, socially redemptive work of art. Moreover, that ideological, racist program is not solely discernible in Wagner's prose texts, not merely to be dismissed as an interesting, albeit largely abstract component of his multivolume theoretical writings, but constitutes the very raison d'être of his works for the stage. Indeed, his mature, post-revolutionary music dramas, written and composed in conjunction with diverse social-aesthetic anti-Semitic tracts, constitute dramatic representations of the ideas found in his writings. Many Wagner scholars have been at great pains to dissociate his theories from the dramatic works for which he is largely remembered today, and especially to disavow any connection between his racism and his most celebrated Total Works of Art, but comparison of these works with the motifs and arguments in Wagner's prose writings demonstrates that the former are dramatic enactments of Wagner's theories concerning the preservation of the German community threatened by the Jew in the modern world.

The notion that the development of German art is threatened by foreign influence is central, for example, to the ideological program of *Die Meistersinger von Nürnberg*, the third act of which Wagner was composing when he wrote 'Was ist deutsch?,' and the work may be read both in terms of Wagner's personal theories concerning Jews and as a dramatic construct based on a repertoire of nineteenth-century anti-Semitic images. Act 3 of the drama presents on stage the very idea of the foreigner's distortion of — and threat to — German art that Wagner discussed in the contemporaneous essay. In this respect the music drama constitutes a tale with a moral for Germany's future. When Wagner had his hapless town notary, Sixtus Beckmesser, reproduce an 'authentic German' art work in a garbled, 'foreign, cold, strange, indifferent, unnatural, and distorted' fashion, the ideas of 'Das Judentum in der Musik' and 'Was ist deutsch?' found dramatic representation. (I will discuss Beckmesser's anti-Semitic corporeal iconography — his voice, smell, and gait — in chapters 2 through 4.) In the final act of *Die Meistersinger*, Beckmesser happens upon a copy of the poetic dream-text that Walther von Stolzing has just composed out of spontaneous creative fantasy and dictated to Hans Sachs; having failed to woo Eva with his nocturnal serenade in the previous act, Beckmesser is in need of a new song for the impending Meistersinger contest and thus is delighted when Sachs presents this text to him. But the querulous and pedantic notary — despised, significantly, by the town's folk, repellent to the German maiden Eva, and associated with intellectualism rather than manual labor (he alone among the Meistersinger does not belong to a craft guild) — fails to take heed of Sachs's warnings concerning the difficulty of the song-text (*MN*, 118), a creation which, given its ultimate status as a work to which the *Volk* immediately feels drawn when it is sung at the conclusion to the drama, must prove illusory to the parasitic and lascivious representative of everything that is foreign to the German spirit. Beckmesser will never be able to penetrate into the 'depths' of the 'life-giving inner organism' of Walther's prize song and will instead reflect back to the audience — the communal *Volk* — only a distortion of the superficial 'exterior form of appearances' contained in its — Walther's — artistry. In his parrotlike mimicry, and through his foreign eyes, the 'organism' of German art will metaphorically die. The first stanza of Walther's text had run thus:

Morgenlich leuchtend in rosigem Schein,
voll Blüt' und Duft
geschwellt die Luft,
voll aller Wonnen
nie ersonnen,
ein Garten lud mich ein
Gast ihm zu sein. (*MN,* 110)

[Beaming with morning's rosy splendor, and filled with blooms and scents, with all the joys as yet unknown, a garden beckoned me to be its guest within.]

From this pantheistic panoply Beckmesser, by virtually taking surreptitious peeks at the manuscript (*MN,* 133) and thus only imperfectly perceiving bits and pieces of its calligraphy, is not able to grasp the image and the essence of which Walther sings and in its place unwittingly produces a travesty:

Morgen ich leuchte in rosigem Schein,
voll Blut und Duft
geht schnell die Luft; —
wohl bald geronnen,
wie zerronnen, —
im Garten lud ich ein —
garstig und fein. (*MN,* 133)

[Tomorrow I shine in rosy shimmer, full of blood and aroma the air goes quickly; — surely soon curdled, as if evaporated, — in the garden I invited — ugly and fine.]

Beckmesser's parody is effected through the subtlest and most inconspicuous of textual shifts; from 'Blüt' to 'Blut,' 'blooms' become 'blood'; from 'Gast ihm zu sein' to 'garstig und fein,' 'to be its guest within' is transformed into 'ugly and fine.' In German, Wagner is able to present nearly antithetical oppositions with only the slightest of textual modifications, thereby making it clear that what appears so self-evident to his audience and to the audience on stage with whom that real public is supposed to identify remains hidden behind the plethora of potentially interchangeable superficial signs beyond which the caricature of the Jew cannot see. Language forms the boundaries of the unified and homogeneous *Volk*, excluding and marking the difference of the foreigner. This was the very idea spelled out in 'Das Judentum in der Musik' when Wagner described 'Jewish' speech as 'an arbitrary distortion' [or transposition: *Verdrehung*] of words and phrase constructions,' for precisely such distortion-qua-transposition characterizes Beckmesser's verbal failure. Walther's organic, life-affirming text progresses further:

Wonnig entragend dem seligen Raum
bot goldner Frucht
heilsaft'ge Wucht
mit holdem Prangen
dem Verlangen
an duft'ger Zweige Saum
herrlich ein Baum. (*MN,* 110)

[Radiantly rising out of the blessed space, a tree thus offered with grace and beauty to quell my desire with balsamic force of golden fruit lightly hanging from airy branches.]

Beckmesser's convoluted and insensitive version of that vision runs thus:

Wohn' ich erträglich im selbigen Raum, —
hol' Gold und Frucht —
Bleisaft und Wucht: —
mich holt am Pranger —
der Verlanger, —

auf luft'ger Steige kaum —
häng' ich am Baum. (MN, 133)

[I live passably in the same room, — fetch gold and fruit — lead and
weight: — the demanding man takes me to the pillory — scarcely on the
airy steps — I hang on the tree.]

It becomes ever clearer that, as Beckmesser's distorted re-pre-
sentation of Walther's folkish art progresses, it serves not only
to express his inability to grasp its essence and to fashion an
appropriate vehicle in which the *Volk* might recognize itself; his
song also serves to surreptitiously express the fantasy of retribution Wagner will visit upon his object of anti-Semitic ridicule,
for as Beckmesser's hapless and imperfect parody unfolds (complete with the stereotypical Jewish attribute of financial gain —
'gold'), he comes to verbally stage his own murder, first through
his references to torture ('pillory,' 'lead and weight') and then to
his own public execution by hanging.[18] Following this stanza
the *Volk* exclaims:

Schöner Werber! Der find't seinen Lohn:
bald hängt er am Galgen; man sieht ihn schon. (MN, 133)

[Nice wooer! He'll find his reward: soon he'll hang on the gallows; we
see him there already.]

This vision of the scapegoat's demise is made even clearer in the
final stanza, which drives the point home that the Jew's appropriation of German art can only distort an essence that is foreign to his nature and that therefore, according to the justice
of Wagner's imagination, demands his death. Walther's next
stanza runs thus:

Sei euch vertraut
welch hehres Wunder mir geschehn:
an meiner Seite stand ein Weib,
so schön und hold ich nie gesehn;
gleich einer Braut
umfaßte sie sanft meinen Leib;
mit Augen winkend,

die Hand wies blinkend,
was ich verlangend begehrt,
die Frucht so hold und wert
vom Lebensbaum. (*MN*, 111)

[May it be revealed to you what wondrous miracle I experienced: at my
side a woman stood, so beautiful and gracious I had never seen; like a
bride she gently embraced my body; beckoning with her eyes, her hand
shiningly pointed to what I had so longingly desired, the fruit so gracious and precious of that tree of life.]

Beckmesser kills that tree — the central image of the 'life-giving
inner organism' of German art — and describes his own murder
as well:

Heimlich mir graut —
weil hier es munter will hergehn: —
an meiner Leiter stand ein Weib, —
sie schämt' und wollt' mich nicht besehn.
Bleich wie ein Kraut —
umfasert mir Hanf meinen Leib;
Die Augen zwinkend —
der Hund blies winkend —
was ich vor langem, verzehrt, —
wie Frucht, so Holz und Pferd —
vom Leberbaum. (*MN*, 133–134)

[Secretly, I am terrified — because things are going to get lively here: —
at my ladder stood a woman, — she was ashamed and didn't want to
look at me. Pale like a weed — hemp winds about my body; his eyes
blinking — the dog blew waving — what I ate a long time ago, — like
fruit, so too wood and horse — of the liver tree.]

The phantasmagoric paranoiac fantasy at the conclusion of the
diminutive, second-prize song is just about the only feature that
grants it a retributive dimension, for it suggests at least at some
level of Wagner's imagination a semblance of sympathy with his
victim. As for the rest, it is a linguistic tour de force dramatizing
both the Jew's inability to understand and to appropriate Ger-

man art and therefore to adequately and truthfully 'reflect' the German's essence in an aesthetic creation — a metaphorical mirror of the German community. Wagner's drama is the scenic representation of the ideas he had expressed in 'Das Judentum in der Musik,' 'Was ist deutsch?' and elsewhere concerning the Jew's fundamental exclusion from the German *Volk* and from its aesthetic representation. Though Beckmesser does not die in the course of his drama, he is beaten and expelled, and his public execution is sublimated into the horrific fantasy of ritual exclusion contained within this, Beckmesser's final song.

The *Volk*, however, participates sympathetically in the aesthetic experience of Walther's prize song, because his art is the reflective conduit of its own essence. As his second stanza reaches its conclusion, the German community exclaims:

So hold und traut, wie fern es schwebt;
doch ist es grad', als ob man selber alles miterlebt! (*MN*, 136)

[So gracious and familiar, how distant it sways; yet it is as if one experienced it all oneself!]

As Walther nears the final lines of his artistic creation, the chorus spontaneously sing the lines with him, lines that they have never heard but that reflect their own being and therefore simultaneously emerge from both their bodies and from the voice of their reflective representative, their German Meistersinger. They innately 'know' the work which allows them to 'recognize' themselves and the borders of their community.

This polarization of Walther's and Beckmesser's diverse relationships to the *Volk*, with their commensurate antithetical aesthetic works (one organic and whole, one disjointed and inferior), recalls in detail Wagner's remarks concerning the juxtaposition of the *Dichter* and the *Denker* in 'Das Judentum in der Musik.' The terms, of course, refer to the phrase describing Germany as the 'Land der Dichter und Denker,' the 'country of poets and thinkers [or philosophers],' but instead of viewing both poetry and philosophy as diverse yet related forms of creative activity, Wagner radically distinguishes between them in his polarization of the upwardly mobile, would-be assimilationist, educated Jew and the superior German:

> Foreign and impassive, the educated Jew stands in the middle of a society that he does not understand. . . . In this position we have seen *Denker* emerge from among the Jews: the *Denker* is the backward-looking *Dichter*; the true *Dichter*, however, is the prophet who tells of future things. Only the deepest, most soulful sympathy with a great community of common goals, whose unconscious expression the *Dichter* interprets according to its content, enables one to exercise such a prophet's office. (*GS* 13: 16)

Walther's 'deepest, most soulful sympathy' with the *Volk* is underscored through the foil of the all-too-cerebral and elitist, egotistical Beckmesser, whose only 'office' is that of the local notary and who looks back to a tradition of artistic rules but never forward to an artwork reflecting more than his own egotism and profit. The *Volk* senses its innate affinity with Walther's emotional and revolutionary, forward-looking art and rejects the cerebral constructions of the local intellectual.

Yet a connection between the ideological program of Wagner's essays and that of his music dramas is not only manifest in *Die Meistersinger* of the 1860s. The metaphors and attendant concerns found throughout Wagner's essayistic production of the 1840s and early 1850s also bear directly on the texts of his other postrevolutionary music dramas, as seen most clearly perhaps in the musical-dramatic tetralogy of *Der Ring des Nibelungen* with which he was involved — and which he had in mind — while writing his reflections on aesthetic-social reform from 1849 to 1851. Its horrendous notions of race and, to the modern ear, often embarrassingly pompous diction and clumsy punning notwithstanding, the *Ring* constitutes an impressive and subtly consistent musical-dramatic emplotment of diverse motifs concerning Wagner's model of recognition as the guarantor of the homogeneous community. The eye as the vehicle of such recognition is the key image linking the social-aesthetic agenda of the essays to the dramatic configurations of the cycle; it acts as a focal point in which the metaphor of reflection as the bulwark of communal and folkish boundaries finds dramatic representation.

It is in the interaction of the Volsungs Siegmund and Sieglinde that Wagner introduces the metaphor of the eye — and with it, all of its attendant ideological implications — into the *Ring*. Indeed, their recognition is the moment when the drama truly begins, the machinations of *Das Rheingold* having provided only the necessary background to *Die Walküre* (The Valkyrie) (hence Wagner's characterization of the cycle as a 'trilogy with a prelude'), which opens with the reunion of the Volsung twins. The fact that they are twins serves to underscore their physical likeness, which itself functions as the realistic component of the Volsungs-as-metaphor. They constitute a metaphorical-dramatic parallel to Wagner's pronouncements, scattered throughout his revolutionary tracts, concerning the German *Volk*. Beleaguered yet resilient, primitive (in the sense of uncivilized) and yet superior, self-sufficient and suspicious of the foreign, and desperately in 'need' of redemption out of the alienating, unnatural, and treacherous strictures of the modern world (Wagner repeatedly defined the *Volk* as those 'who sense a common need' [*DS* 6: 15]), the Volsungs, like Wagner's German people, seek freedom from the pressures of foreign authority and find themselves — *recognize* themselves — in their hour of 'highest need.' In the dramatic text 'Jesus von Nazareth' (Jesus of Nazareth) of 1849, whose temporal proximity to the reformative writings and the early stages of the *Ring* project was no coincidence, Wagner employed the metaphor of the family as the *Volk* when he described 'the egoism of the family [as that of] the egoism of the fatherland,'[19] thereby clearly linking the motif of the family with that of the nation, and in 'Das Kunstwerk der Zukunft' from the same year, he used the family as a key component in his definition of the *Volk*: 'The *Volk* has always been the essence [*der Inbegriff*] *of all the individuals* who constituted a *commonality* [*ein Gemeinsames*]. In the beginning it was the family and the races [*Geschlechter*]; then the races united through linguistic equality as a nation' (*DS* 6:14).

Commonality, language, family, race, and nation form closely related, at times even interchangeable, components of a single concept in Wagner's thought. If we recall that it is language that defines and binds together the *Volk* in Wagner's other writings from this period, it becomes clear that family, race, and *Volk* are diverse expressions for a group of like-minded, similarly speaking, and physiologically related (and similar) beings, beings defined by their physiological difference from others. This motif, like those found in other nineteenth-century thinkers — Hegel, Feuerbach, Hoffmann, Novalis, and Eichendorff — was not Wagner's invention, but part of the repertoire of ideas and images that comprised the cultural vocabulary of his world. Friedrich Ludwig Jahn had already described the family as the biological foundation of the Volk in his *Deutsches Volk* (German Volk) of 1810, and it was a notion with wide currency by the time Wagner employed it as a metaphor in his tetralogy concerned with the downfall of the homogeneous German community.[20] In the *Ring* cycle, this equation of family and *Volk* characterizes the metaphorical function of the Volsung race and of the antithesis between it and its foes, who are foreign to it, such as the Neidings in *Die Walküre*, and the race of the Nibelungs in *Siegfried* and *Götterdämmerung* (Twilight of the gods). When, in the opening scene of *Die Walküre*, Siegmund and Sieglinde gaze into each other's eyes and recognize therein both the reflection of their own identity and that of their familially familiar, long-lost partner, they provide a metaphor for like kind recognizing its own hidden essence in the external signs of its similarity.

After Sieglinde has given the exhausted man a drink of water, he looks upon her and makes a statement that, initially, must seem cryptic but that will emerge as the first manifestation of a metaphorical motif central to the ideational program of the entire cycle:

Kühlende Labung
gab mir der Quell,
des Müden Last
machte er leicht;
erfrischt ist der Mut,
das Aug' erfreut
des Sehens selige Lust. (RN, 77)

[Cooling refreshment the drink gave me, it lightened the burden of the weary man; my courage is refreshed, my eye enjoys the blessed delight of sight.]

Armed with the courage of the elect whose seeing is superior and hence sets him off from lesser men, Siegmund fears that his own glance-filled presence may bring danger and misfortune to the woman he beholds before him and thus exclaims:

Dir Frau, doch, bleibe sie fern!
Fort wend ich Fuß und Blick. (RN, 79)

[Yet from you, woman, may they stay far away! Farther I shall turn foot and gaze.]

After she has persuaded him to remain, there follows a series of stage directions in which the motif is visually enacted: '*he searches her expression; embarrassed and sad she lowers her eyes. Long silence. . . . his gaze fastens on Sieglinde with calm and resolute sympathy: she again slowly raises her eye to him. Both gaze upon each other in a long silence, deeply moved*' (RN, 79). The paradigm has been established, verbally and visually, and will provide an ideationally central motif for the rest of the music drama and will always convey in metaphorical dramatic enactment the ideas associated with the gaze in Wagner's writings.

Following their visual exchange, Hunding enters his hut, and when he sees Siegmund for the first time, he immediately notices the Volsung's likeness to Sieglinde, which he discerns in the similarity of their enigmatic and iconoclastic gaze:

Wie gleicht er dem Weibe!

Der gleißende Wurm
glänzt auch ihm aus dem Auge. (RN, 80)

[How he resembles the woman! The gleaming dragon also shines from his eye.]

It is illuminating to reflect for a moment on the philological origins of this passage in Wagner's drama. Wagner borrowed this line nearly verbatim from the *Völundarkvitha* (The lay of Völund) of *The Poetic Edda*, where it reads thus:

Seine Augen gleichen   dem gleißenden Wurm;
die Zähne fletscht er,   zeigt man ihm sein Schwert,
erblickt er den Ring   an Bödwilds Arm.

[The glow of his eyes is like gleaming snakes, / His teeth he gnashes if now is shown / The sword, or Bothvild's ring he sees.][21]

In the *Edda*, the 'gleaming dragon' of the eye is found in a figure altogether different from the heroic Volsungs, for in the sources to the *Ring* it is Völund, or Wieland (one of the models for Wagner's Nibelung Alberich) who is described thus. But, as I will discuss shortly, Alberich and the Volsungs are at opposite ends of the racial spectrum of the tetralogy, and thus Wagner removed the motif of the distinctive and heroically threatening eye from the body of the Nibelung and vouchsafed it instead to his physically superior Germanic twins. (Wagner's modification of his sources often sheds light on the ideological plan underlying his dramatic conceptions, and I will draw attention on further occasions to such changes.) This motif of familial resemblance was even more obvious in Wagner's initial conception of the drama, in which Wotan (called Wodan) is present as a witness to the incestuous union of his children, and Hunding notices the eerie resemblance between all three heroic-godly figures: 'Wodan, who offers Balmung [later Nothung] as a gift, resembles Wälse; this is apparent not only to Sieg. (who is more occupied with Siegl), but also to Hunding, which makes him afraid.'[22] The importance of like kind resembling one another is everywhere apparent in this initial plan for the drama and is underscored even in the original version of its final line, in which Wotan, surrounding the Valkyrie rock with fire and casting a spell to protect Brünnhilde from inferior suitors, says not simply 'May he who fears the point of my spear never pass through the fire!' (the line Wagner ultimately set to music) but 'Durch das feuer, das ich durchschreite, wage sich keiner der mir nicht gleich! [Through the fire, through which I pass, may no one dare who is not like me!].'[23] The verb *gleichen*, meaning 'to resemble,' underscores the physical appearance of the subject.

That this resemblance is due to the siblings' status as relatives and as physically superior, potentially immortal half-gods, children of Wotan, is made clear when Sieglinde relates to her brother the events of her wedding night, when 'an old man in grey attire' (whom the orchestra reveals, through the Valhalla motive, to be Wotan) entered Hunding's hut bearing a magic sword. Sieglinde emphasizes the terrifying effect the gleam of the old man's gaze had for the others while it offered solace to her:

ein Fremder trat da herein:
ein Greis in grauem Gewand;
tief hing ihm der Hut,
der deckt' ihm der Augen eines;
doch des andren Strahl,
Angst schuf er allen,
traf die Männer
sein mächt'ges Dräu'n:
Mir allein
weckte das Auge
süß sehnenden Harm,
Tränen und Trost zugleich.
Auf mich blickt' er
und blitzte auf jene. (*RN*, 88)

[A stranger entered: an old man in a grey cloak; his hat hung low, it covered one of his eyes, but the gleam of the other created fear in everyone, when its powerful, threatening gaze struck the men: For me alone the eye awakened sweet yearning pain, tears and solace at once. On me he gazed and like lightning glared at the others.]

The Wanderer's gaze is the sign of his familial relationship to his children, and thereby it offers Sieglinde comfort, allowing her to recognize her father, an act vouchsafed only the privileged members of a circumscribed group and one that thereby provides protection to Sieglinde against those who are so different from her — from those who see differently. Only the German's superior eye can recognize familial, communal likeness, and it is only this eye, too, that not only receives but that can also *communicate*, as Wotan does here through his eye to his daughter. In both the passage cited above from *Oper und Drama* and in section 2 of 'Das Kunstwerk der Zukunft' Wagner emphasizes the function of the eye — for the superior being, and for the superior artwork commensurate with that being — as a vehicle for both recognition and communication: 'namely . . . through the expression of the eye itself, which meets directly the observing eye, he [corporeal man — the subject of the Artwork of the Future] manages to communicate [to the eye] not only the sentiments of the heart but also even the characteristic activities of the brain' (*DS* 6: 32). The scene in act 1 of *Die Walküre* can thus also be read as a dramatic description of the metaphorical process of communication between the superior artwork and the authentic public sphere, an exchange vouchsafed only those of like kind. Such a process characterizes precisely the privileged, mutual exchange between godly father and daughter described in Sieglinde's monologue.

When Siegmund and Sieglinde are reunited, they fall in love because they sense their affinity as physically similar, related beings. Their love duet concerns nothing less than the process of verifying and establishing that affinity *as familial*, which in the associative patterns of Wagner's social-aesthetic theories means as members of a homogeneous and clearly defined group — the *Volk*. They do so by interpreting their physical appearance; they come to 'know' each other by 'recognizing' each other. The eye provides an ideal image for Wagner's ideas here, because it both acts as an organ receiving visual impressions of another subject and itself provides a watery, mirrorlike surface reflecting the image of the subject who views. It both receives the physical signs of the Other and allows for the reflection, and hence the recognition, of one's own features in the physiologically similar comrade and those that distinguish the Self from the foe. This narcissistic imagery is exploited explicitly throughout the recognition scene of *Die Walküre* and later in *Siegfried* as well, because it serves to reinforce the theme of recognizing one's self in others as a guarantee of solace and community.[24] As Sieglinde gazes into Siegmund's eyes she exclaims:

Fremdes nur sah ich von je,
freundlos war mir das Nahe;
als hätt' ich nie es gekannt,
war, was immer mir kam.
Doch dich kannt' ich
deutlich und klar:
als mein Auge dich sah,
warst du mein Eigen;
was im Busen ich barg,
was ich bin,
hell wie der Tag
taucht' es mir auf, . . .
als in frostig öder Fremde
zuerst ich den Freund ersah. . . .
O laß in Nähe
zu dir mich neigen,
daß hell ich schaue
den hehren Schein,
der dir aus Aug'
und Antlitz bricht
und so süß die Sinne mir zwingt. . . .
Im Bach erblickt' ich
mein eigen Bild —
und jetzt gewahr ich es wieder:
wie einst dem Teich es enttaucht,
bietest mein Bild mir nun du! (*RN*, 91–92)

[Only strange things had I ever seen, that which was near was friend-less, as if I had never known it, was everything that came my way. But I knew you clear and true: when my eye saw you, you were my own: what I harbored in my breast, what I am, rose shining within me like the day, . . . when in the frosty barren foreign place I recognized my friend for the first time. . . . O let me bend down close to you, so that I may brightly behold the wondrous glow that breaks forth from your eye and visage and so sweetly forces my senses. . . . In the brook I recognized my own image, and now I perceive it again as once it rose from the water, now you offer my image to me.]

Other than Siegmund, everyone Sieglinde has seen was 'for-eign,' because she had never 'known' them, but she 'knows' Siegmund 'clearly' (*deutlich* — they are *Deutsche*, after all), for he is the very image of that which rises within her as the recogni-tion of her own being. The image of her own face reflected to her by the natural mirror of the brook is precisely the image she beholds in the mirror of her like kind. To Sieglinde's narcissistic image Siegmund replies succinctly, consistently, and passion-ately, 'You are the image that I harbor within me!' Their narcis-sism is reciprocal, for they are truly kindred spirits: These Vol-sungs experience and enact the metaphor of the community recognizing itself in the reflection of its bonds which are based on the physiology of similar appearances. As part of Wagner's Total Work of Art, they both provide for the *Volk*, and meta-phorically enact, that recognizant reflection.

But the metaphorical implications of a privileged reunion-as-reflection vouchsafed by the physical signs of familial familiarity are not expressed solely in this act 1 exchange, nor are they lim-ited to the Volsungs alone, for the metaphor of family has many representatives who, like Siegmund and Sieglinde, also reveal their familial-folkish metaphorical affinities through the image of their similar eyes. When Brünnhilde nears Siegmund in the *Todesverkündigungsszene* (the Annunciation of Death scene) of act 2 of *Die Walküre*, seeing him, presumably, for the first time (he has never seen her), these motifs again come to the fore. They must, because Siegmund is Brünnhilde's half-brother, and

Wagner's motivic vocabulary tying together the racial system of
the *Ring* must reinforce their blood ties, though, in a modification of the motif dictated by the intricacies of the plot, Siegmund
never learns that they share the same father — that Wälse was
Wotan in disguise. But Brünnhilde knows this and recognizes
her brother's nature as she *sees* him. Wagner's text emphasizes
this visual event as she relates her meeting with Siegmund to her
reproachful father in act 3:

Tod kündend
trat ich vor ihn,
gewahrte sein Auge,
hörte sein Wort; . . .
tönend erklang mir
des Tapfersten Klage: . . .
Meinem Ohr erscholl,
mein Aug' erschaute (RN, 146)

[Announcing death I approached him, I noticed his eye, heard his
word; . . . ringing out the bravest man's cry resounded to me: . . . My ear
reverberated, my eye saw.]

The subtleties and motivically rich texture of this passage have
led to some remarkable interpretations concerning the role of
the senses involved in this scene. Is the Angel of Death, as a
family member, perceived primarily through the eye's gaze or
through the ear's sonic impressions? Carolyn Abbate, one of the
most innovative of Wagnerian critics today, maintains that the
motif of vision is of only secondary importance here: 'Seeing is
neutral (sehen, gewahren, erschauen). But hearing is charged,
as "heard" words "ring, resound" with sound that thunders into
her ear (hören, tönen, erklingen, erschallen). . . . Arriving at the
full texture of truth, as [Brünnhilde] has explained, entails not
seeing (reading a face, or a text) but, rather, hearing (voices).'[25]
While this reading makes sense within the larger development
of an argument concerning Brünnhilde's capacity as an adept
listener, it misses the recurring motif of the glance within the
cycle as a whole that serves to underscore familial relationships

as emblems of like kind. The irony of the scene is that, as a half-god and superior being with an eagle's gaze, Siegmund 'appropriately' belongs in Valhalla, the home of the gods and of the great, and his refusal of immortality is incredible to one who, literally, shares his views and lives there as a member of the godly family (though Brünnhilde seems little troubled, I must admit, by Sieglinde's summary exclusion). Seeing is the guarantor of such interconnections, of blood ties such as theirs. Brünnhilde's first command, her first statement to Siegmund, had been 'sieh auf mich [look upon me]' (RN, 117), to which he had replied with a question:

Wer bist du, sag,
die so schön und ernst mir erscheint?

[Who are you, say, who appear so beautiful and serious before me?]
(See example 10)

The Annunciation of Death scene opens with an exchange of glances, and the visual dimension of the Volsung's and the Valkyrie's interaction continues through a series of verbs that elaborate upon this central motif when Brünnhilde explains:

Nur Todgeweihten
taugt mein Anblick;
wer mich erschaut,
der scheidet vom Lebenslicht.
Auf der Walstatt allein
erschein ich Edlen:
wer mich gewahrt,
zur Walhall kor ich ihn mir! (RN, 117)

[Only those destined to die are worthy *of my sight*: he who *sees* me parts from the light of life. On the field of death I *appear only to the noble*; whoever *sees* me, to Valhalla I have chosen him!] (My emphasis)

Sight is central here, and it is supposed to reinforce the bonds of those who are superior. Only when he becomes dismayed at

Brünnhilde's refusal to allow Sieglinde a place beside him in Valhalla, that is, to preserve the elect family, does Siegmund's visual impression of the Valkyrie become clouded:

So jung und schön
erschimmerst du mir:
doch wie kalt und hart
erkennt dich mein Herz. (RN, 120–121)

[How young and beautiful you shimmer before (literally, 'to') me, yet how cold and hard my heart knows (recognizes) you.]

Wagner's use of metaphor is remarkably consistent. The goal of recognition is the preservation of communal ties, represented here by the metaphor of the family, but if those bonds that have already been reinforced (that is, that have been recognized in act 1 by Siegmund and Sieglinde) are threatened, the act of recognition will falter. Siegmund now recognizes Brünnhilde as *different* from him and his sister; she grows increasingly 'cold' as she threatens the familial bonds of those defined by their similarity and by their negation of that which is foreign. As I will argue in the next two chapters, icons of sound (the voice) and aroma (the sensuous, flowerlike smells that Wagner associates with incest) serve in act 1 of *Die Walküre* to reinforce the paradigm of visual recognition, but for that paradigm, sight is of central, primary importance. (All three motifs — image, voice, and smell — function in the successful, consummated unions characterized by the mutual recognition of Siegmund and Sieglinde and of Siegfried and Brünnhilde.) Here, in the frustrated exchange, only the first two — sight and sound — apply, and they only do so imperfectly, but of the two, vision is the key. *Die Walküre* thus contains a dramatic presentation of ideas found in Wagner's postrevolutionary essays concerning the definition and the preservation of the boundaries of the *Volk*; in both the music drama and its essayistic forerunners, the motifs of vision and recognition serve to ensure the integrity of the community, represented here by the small communal unit that precedes the communities of nation and race in Wagner's writings, the family.

Such imagery is not restricted to the first of the *Ring* dramas portraying superior human beings but reappears whenever the relationships of the Volsung race are at issue. Wagner uses repeatedly the motifs of vision, reflection, and recognition in order to establish and to reinforce the status of Siegfried as the child of these heroic, eye-catching siblings and, consequently, as a superior being descended from the gods. Siegfried constituted the focal point of the initial plan for the *Ring*, because for Wagner the young hero is the representative of the essence of the German race. The composer therefore imbued him with characteristics Wagner deemed typical of the German: He is straightforward and honest, fearless, and he possesses the physiological features of a male image Wagner would have loved to call his own. (Little wonder that the composer characterized the goal of his aesthetic-social revolution as 'the beautiful and strong human being' [*DS* 5: 300]; the artwork is the representation of its social order, and Siegfried, the 'youthfully beautiful human being' endowed with 'powerful muscles,' would be the model and the reflection of that future world.)

Siegfried is the antithesis of his dramatic and racial foil, the Nibelung dwarf Mime, brother of the arch-Nibelung, Alberich, and it is in the interaction between Siegfried and Mime that the tension between the race of the Volsungs and that of the dwarves comes to the fore. Their relationship makes *Siegfried* the most blatantly anti-Semitic drama in the *Ring*, comparable in this respect to the equally racist *Die Meistersinger von Nürnberg*.[26] Just as identity is established in Wagner's essays through the recognition of difference, so Siegfried comes to 'know' himself through the perception of Mime's physiology as different from his own. Wagner's German recognizes himself not only in the similar and related appearance of kith and kin, kind and kindred, but in the recognition of that which is deemed unlike, unkind, and decidedly foreign. This polarity is at the heart of the imagery of the *Ring* dramas, the motifs of which assume urgency precisely through the extreme polarization of its figures into similar, superior, and sympathetic beings versus those perceived as foreign, inferior, and threatening. Mime's relationship to Siegfried is that of a foster father, but such a constellation only serves to reinforce their difference, especially within the *Ring*'s paradigms, which equate family with like kind and, ultimately, with communal nation. Mime (an operatic Jewish mother if there ever was one) is as unlike his foster child as he could be (figure 8). He is sly and adept at the craft of dissembling, attempts to use the boy as a means of furthering his own gain, is cowardly and even paranoiac, and is imbued with physical features that, within the spectrum of stereotypical corporeal iconographies of race in the nineteenth century, characterize him as diametrically opposed to the young superman. That the Volsung-as-German-hero is the opposite of the Nibelung-as-Jew is suggested in 'Das Judentum in der Musik' when Wagner writes that 'we cannot imagine an antique or modern character, be it a hero or a lover, represented by a Jew on stage, without in the process sensing the inappropriateness — to the point of comedy — of such an idea' (*GS* 13: 11–12). In terms of racial stereotypes, Mime, Wagner's ridiculous antithesis of a 'hero,' is Siegfried's Other.

Siegfried himself repeatedly draws attention to the difference between his physiology and that of his foster parent and in so doing underscores Wagner's belief in the indelible appearance, in the corporeal encoding, of racial difference. When the dwarf attempts to convince Siegfried that he is 'both father and mother' to the boy (*RN*, 163), the young Teuton recalls an epiphanic, visionary moment that has defined for him his own identity as fundamentally different from Mime (figure 9):

Das lügst du, garstiger Gauch!
Wie die Jungen den Alten gleichen,
das hab ich mir glücklich erseh'n.
Nun kam ich zum klaren Bach:
da erspäht' ich die Bäum'
und Tier' im Spiegel;

8. Arthur Rackham, 'Mime and the infant Siegfried,' 1911 (From *The Ring of the Niblung*, trans. Margaret Armour, vol. 2 [New York: Abaris Books, 1976])

9. Arthur Rackham, 'Siegfried sees himself in the stream,' 1911 (From *The Ring of the Niblung*, trans. Margaret Armour, vol. 2 [New York: Abaris Books, 1976])

Sonn' und Wolken,
wie sie nur sind,
im Glitzer erschienen sie gleich.
Da sah ich denn auch
mein eigen Bild;
ganz anders als du
dünkt' ich mir da:
so glich wohl der Kröte
ein glänzender Fisch;
doch kroch nie ein Fisch aus der Kröte! (RN, 163)

[You're lying, ugly fool! How the young resemble the old I happily saw for myself. I came upon a clear brook: there I saw the trees and creatures in the mirror; sun and clouds, just as they are, in the glitter they appeared the same. Then I also saw there my own image; completely different from you I seemed to be there: thus would a shining fish resemble a toad; but never a fish crawled out of a toad!][27]

Siegfried's instinctive revulsion toward Mime is based on their physiological difference, for he hated and distrusted the dwarf long before finding his disgust explained and justified through his narcissistic glance into the reflective waters of the spring. In 'knowing himself,' he recognizes what is not like himself, and in doing so he establishes for Wagner's audience his innate affinity with his Volsung parents, who themselves recognized their own identity in a similar fashion, viewing their reflections either in a brook or in the watery image of their sibling's eyes. Siegfried's 'natural' aversion to Mime is a healthy one, for the dwarf constitutes a being that is bereft of familial (communal) ties and that threatens the very life of the hero. (The juxtaposition of the Volsungs' familial love and the Nibelungs' sibling rivalry, portrayed in the Nibelheim scene of *Das Rheingold* and act 2 of *Siegfried*, goes hand in hand with the function of the family as a metaphor for the German *Volk*, fundamentally different from the purportedly cold, egotistical, avaricious, and loveless Jews.) In discussing Wagner's conception of Siegfried's foster father, Ernest Newman went to some lengths to emphasize this fact: 'Mime is a powerful thing of evil, one who would do all that

Alberich has done were he fortunate enough to possess the Ring: he is dangerous in spite of his appearance and build: and the actor who does not make us conscious of all this, but so handles the character that the audience feels that Mime is pitiable rather than dangerous and loathsome, and Siegfried, consequently, a monster of boyish ingratitude, completely misrepresents the part.'[28] Wagner's intention, Newman surmises, was to convey a situation that would create sympathy between the audience and the hero and that would make Siegfried's derision and ultimate murder of the dwarf seem not only credible but *justified* and, in the truest sense of the word, (app)laudable. Mime poses a threat to the embodiment of all that is German, and his malevolent difference is readily apparent in his foreign and inferior corporeal makeup.

The *Ring* functions as a metaphorical work on a number of levels, and these figures simultaneously represent a number of issues. Siegfried's and Mime's physical polarity is also the dramatic manifestation of ideas found in *Deutsche Kunst und deutsche Politik* (which, moreover, can be read as an ideological corollary to, or a commentary on, the ideas represented on stage in *Die Meistersinger von Nürnberg*),[29] in which Wagner describes the differences between the kind of artwork he associates with France (whose theater, for him, had fallen under the sway of the Jews) and his own superior Artwork of the Future intended solely for Germans. Wagner explicitly likens the difference between the 'imitating' (*nachahmenden*) and the 'reproducing' (*nachbildenden*) artist — the former involved in a process of mere copying, and hence a term of invective, while the latter implies the creative activity with which Wagner wished to be associated — to the difference between the 'ape' (*Affen*) and the human being (*DS* 8: 290–292). The *nachahmender* artist is Francophilic, non-German, and hence either philo-Semitic or outright Jewish and so shares much with the backward-looking, aesthetically impoverished *Denker* upon whom the figure of Beckmesser is based. The *nachbildende* artist, on the other hand, is like the *Dichter*; he is the German prophet of future artworks intended

for a future society. *Denker* and *Dichter* find their *corporeal* counterparts here in the forms of the ape and the human. And, significantly, Wagner explicitly describes the imitative artist as a
Mime.[30] The mime is like an ape and is associated with an inferior kind of art found in the French theater that merely mimics,
in a parrotlike manner, the superficial world around him (recalling the association of the Jew and the parrot in 'Das Judentum in
der Musik'), while the superior artist, the 'idealist,' is concerned
with a superior essence that he seeks to recreate (*DS* 8: 291–293)
(I will have more to say about Mime's apelike features in chapter
3). The *nachbildende* artist's artistic reproduction is clearly based
on his ability to discern beneath the myriad phenomena of the
superficial exterior of things a superior essence harbored in the
depths, as indicated in Wagner's term for reproduction, 'nach-
bild-en,' or literally, 're-*image*-ing,' a term that evokes the empathetic imagination (*Einbildung*, or literally, ' "into"-imaging')
dramatically portrayed in Sieglinde's sympathetic fascination
with the similarity between her own *Bild*, seen in the stream, and
the image before her in the face of her brother.

The Mime of *Siegfried*, then, is an apelike Francophilic copy-
cat: Metaphorically, he is that which his name reveals him to be,
a mime, while Siegfried, among other things, is a metaphor for
the superior artist, the idealist, privy to the essence of relationships discernible for him behind appearance. Wagner, of
course, maintained that the creator of the Artwork of the Future
would be a conduit for the expression of the *Volk*, whose metaphorical embodiment in the *Ring* is the race of the Volsungs:
Siegfried represents both the *Volk* and the superior artist as the
voice (and the body) of the people. Dieter Borchmeyer has
pointed out that the metaphorical nature of Siegfried's forging of the sword is revealed through comparison with Wagner's study for the *Ring*, the dramatic prose sketch 'Wieland der
Schmied,' an overtly obvious parable of artistic creation.[31] No
wonder, then, that Mime is unable to refashion the sword, itself
a metaphor for the Total Work of Art, a work that once, in the
idealized Greek past, was unified but that has fallen into dispa-

rate pieces (the distinct genres of music, dance, poetry, painting, sculpture, and architecture) and has been harbored by an inferior race (the Jews who control the theatrical institutions of modern Europe), only to be reunified by the superior being, the embodiment of all that is German. Mime is a master smith — portrayed as the greatest among the 'race' of smiths in the *Ring*, but his artistry is inferior to that of the naive hero. The juxtaposition of Mime's inadequate attempts at forging at the opening of act 1 of the drama and Siegfried's triumphant blending of the (aesthetic) pieces of the sword at its conclusion underscores their metaphorical function as the embodiments of two kinds of artist, one apelike and the other the quintessential image for Wagner of everything German. Little wonder, too, that the sword's name is 'Nothung,' or 'Need-ung'; just as his Volsung father as a representative of the *Volk* had been driven to the sword in his hour of 'highest need' (as both he himself and Wotan repeatedly remind us [RN, 86, 94, 102]), so Siegfried-as-*Volk* will claim 'Nothung' in the hour in which he liberates himself from his foreign dwarf-father, a representative of the *Volk*'s enemy, the Jew, and in so doing metaphorically raises aloft the Artwork of the Future, an instrument for the destruction of non-German art and of the foreign presence in the realm of the future *Volk*.

Animal imagery within the music drama itself reinforces the motifs of familial affinity and natural antipathies separating Wagner's hero and the Nibelung. The animal motifs in the *Ring* are consistent metaphorical representations of the physiological signs that Wagner, in his essays, interprets as highlighting differences between races. In the tetralogy, heroes are associated with beautiful, lithe, and powerful animals, while those figures evincing traits associated with Jews, such as avarice, egotism, and lovelessness, are likened to lowly, disgusting, and clumsy creatures. As the superhuman, superior being, Siegfried is close to Nature, to the creatures of the forest (birds, foxes, wolves, bears, and deer), and even to the fish of the streams with which he compares himself. As such, it is fitting that he comes to understand the Forest Bird in act 2 of the drama after having partaken of the dragon's superior, magical blood. As has often been noted, the music of the Forest Bird is remarkably (and intentionally) similar to that of the nature-spirits of the first *Ring* drama, the Rhinemaidens; Siegfried's affinity with both bird and fish is thereby subtly reinforced through musical echoes.[32] This affinity is significant and motivically consistent, for it is part of a larger web of animal motifs used to convey the fundamental incompatibility of different races. The juxtaposition of fish and toad, from the opening scene of *Das Rheingold* to the demise of Mime in act 2 of *Siegfried*, is a prominent example of animal motifs representing the antithetical natures of the German and the Jew; bird, fish, and toad act as dramatic equivalents to what Wagner and his culture believed were the distinctive and distinguishing corporeal signs of race.[33] Siegfried, so close to Nature that he converses with birds, likens himself to a fish and in so doing distances himself from the Nibelung, whom he describes in terms suggestive of a fundamentally different kind of creature — lowly, slimy, and amphibian.

The motivic opposition of fish and toad, with its implied polarity of natural beauty versus foreign and unnatural ugliness, harks back to the first scene of *Das Rheingold*, in which Mime's brother Alberich curses two of the slippery Rhinemaidens for their fishlike nature; to Woglinde he exclaims:

Wie fang ich im Sprung
den spröden Fisch? (RN, 7–8)

[How can I catch the springing, coy fish?]

and then to Wellgunde:

Falsches Kind!
Kalter, grätiger Fisch! (RN, 9)

[False child! Cold, bony fish!]

The Rhinemaiden, he says, should 'whore with eels' if she doesn't like his hunchback:

Hei! So buhle mit Aalen,
ist dir eklig mein Balg! (RN, 9)

But within the motivically consistent bestiary of the *Ring*, it is to a creature most like an eel, and quite unlike the gleaming, superior, and seductively elegant fish, that the final Rhinemaiden, Flosshilde, likens Alberich — to a toad: she speaks explicitly of his 'Krötengestalt' (RN, 11), or 'toad shape.' Thus it is simply appropriate that when Alberich transforms himself into other animal shapes in the presence of Loge and Wotan in the Nibelheim scene, he chooses those creatures who are closest to his own nature: first the eellike dragon and then the toad. The formulation of his toad-invoking spell echoes the description of his physical appearance by Flosshilde:

Krumm und grau
krieche, Kröte! (RN, 50)

[Twisted and grey, creep, toad!]

The juxtaposition of fish and toad, then, discernible within *Siegfried*, is part of a larger constellation of animal imagery used consistently throughout the *Ring* to underscore fundamentally antithetical physiological essences. Because Alberich and Mime are both members of the same family, which in Wagner always means the same *Geschlecht* (race), they are viewed independently by various figures in the cycle (the Rhinemaidens, Wotan, Loge, and Siegfried) as possessing the features of the same lowly and slimy animal. Siegfried, on the other hand, automatically senses his affinity with a creature already associated in the audience's mind with unsullied, pure Nautre, with the fish. Indeed, it is the entrance of the foreign, toadlike Alberich into the golden and virginal waters of the fish-filled Rhine that brings about the demise of the purely natural state, and when Siegfried senses Mime's difference, there is an implication of natural antitheses as well. The fish is an exemplar of the shining, sunny side of Nature, while the toad is a ground-dweller, a creature of the dark. No wonder Siegfried exclaims to the Nibelung:

Seh ich dir erst
mit den Augen zu,
zu übel erkenn ich,
was alles du tust: . . .
Alle Tiere sind
mir teurer als du:
Baum und Vogel,
die Fische im Bach,
lieber mag ich sie
leiden als dich. (RN, 161)

[When I watch you with my eyes, I recognize with disgust everything you do: . . . All creatures are dearer to me than you: Tree and bird, the fish in the brook, I like them more than you.]

His eyes allow him to recognize his own reflection in the stream, the very place where he also discerns his affinity with a superior animal. When he runs off into the forest, after having learned that Mime is indeed not his father, Siegfried likens himself explicitly to the fish and the bird — to the two forms of metaphorically higher animal life reserved in the *Ring* for superior beings:

Wie der Fisch froh
in der Flut schwimmt,
wie der Fink frei
sich davonschwingt:
flieg ich von hier,
flute davon . . .
dich, Mime, nie wieder zu sehn! (RN, 167–168)

[As the fish gladly swims in the flood, as the finch freely flies off: I'll fly from here, flood away . . . you, Mime, never to see again!]

Wagner is famous for having radically adapted and amalgamated a number of sources for his *Ring* — primarily *The Poetic Edda, The Prose Edda, The Saga of the Volsungs*, and *The Song of the Nibelungs*[34] — but what has received less attention is the consistency with which he transformed this source material in order to fashion a coherent web of motifs designed to convey his ideological program. Just as he transferred the 'dragon's glance' from one of the models for Alberich in the *Völundarkvitha* to his Volsung twins, so he modified the motif of the fish as found in his sources to similar ends. Wagner emphasizes the antithetical nature of the Nibelungs' and the Volsungs' physiologies by juxtaposing fish and toad, but such a motivic polarity is nowhere to be found in the sagas; indeed, it even contradicts the motivic vocabulary of the sources. In the fourteenth tale of *The Saga of the Volsungs*, 'The Otter's Ransom,' for example, it is none other than the dwarf Andvari, another model for Alberich, who is likened to, and even transforms himself into, a *fish*, as Regin (the son of Hreidmar in the saga and a model for Wagner's Mime) relates to Sigurd (Wagner's Siegfried) when he recounts the story of his brother's murder:

'There was a dwarf named Andvari,' said Regin. 'He was always in the waterfall named Andvari's Fall. He was in the shape of a pike and caught food there for himself, for there were many fish in the falls. My brother Otr used to go into the waterfall and bring up fish in his mouth, laying them one by one on the bank. Odin, Loki, and Hoenir were traveling and came to Andvari's Fall. Otr had caught a salmon and was eating it, half dozing on the riverbank. Loki took a stone and struck the otter to death. The Æsir considered themselves fortunate in their catch and skinned the otter.

'That evening they came to Hreidmar's and showed him the catch. Then we seized them, imposing as their fine and ransom that they must fill the skin with gold and cover the outside with red gold. They sent Loki to obtain the gold. He went to Ran and got her net. Next he went to Andvari's Fall and cast the net out for the pike, and it leapt into the net. . . .

'Loki saw Andvari's gold. And when Andvari had handed over the gold he kept one ring back. But Loki took it from him. The dwarf went into the rock and said that the gold would be the death of whoever owned it.'[35]

Wagner modified the motif of the fish, distributed in the sagas among dwarves and greater beings alike, by assigning it to his Volsung alone. At the same time, he transformed Andvari-as-fish (pike) into Alberich-as-toad in the scene in which Loge (Loki in the saga) captures the dwarf, his gold, and his ring. Many of the elements of the plot of *Das Rheingold* are discernible here, but Wagner adapted them to a consistent motivic pattern that emphasizes physiological, racial difference.[36] The form of the fish is reserved for those natural and superhuman beings close to Nature in the cycle — for the Rhinemaidens and the man to whom those fishlike creatures will speak in earnest in *Götterdämmerung*, Siegfried.

Because appearance is the key to identity in Wagner's social-aesthetic theories and in their dramatic representations in the *Ring*, the first question Siegfried asks himself regarding his parents in the Forest Murmurs scene of act 2 concerns not the idiosyncracies of their lives, their fate, or their feelings but only their appearance.[37] He wonders what they *looked* like, not what they *were* like, for the former is the signature of the latter in Wagner's imagination, and in his culture. Siegfried begins his ruminations on each of his parents with the same question:

Wie sah mein Vater wohl aus? . . .
Aber — wie sah
meine Mutter wohl aus? (*RN*, 202)

[What did my father look like? . . . But — what did my mother look like?]

Yet Siegfried knows the answer, at least to the first of these questions, for essence is expressed in the signs of the body, and essences are circumscribed by the identity of family-as-race. In wondering what his father must have looked like, he recognizes what in Wagner's cosmology is obvious:

Ha, gewiß, wie ich selbst!
Denn wär' wo von Mime ein Sohn,
müßt' er nicht ganz
Mime gleichen? (*RN*, 202)

[Ha, surely, like myself! For wherever there were a son of Mime, would he not have to resemble Mime completely?]

It is against the appearance of the Nibelung dwarf that Siegfried reconstructs the shape of his father, and what follows is a host of images by now familiar, associated with the toad and taken from a catalog of nineteenth-century anti-Semitic stereotypes:

Grade so garstig,
griesig und grau,
klein und krumm,
höckrig und hinkend,
mit hängenden Ohren,
triefigen Augen. (RN, 202)

[Just as ugly, disgusting and gray, small and crooked, hunchbacked and limping, with hanging ears, dripping eyes.]

Siegfried imaginatively recognizes his father's appearance through the same process through which he had defined his own identity and through which in Wagner's essays the German always defines himself—through the perception of another's appearance as different and foreign from one's own. Listening to the kindred spirit of the birds in the heart of German Nature, the superman imagines (or, as a metaphor of the idealist artist, re-imagines, *nach-bild-et*) the appearance of his similar family member through the counterfactory rejection of a physiology he deems naturally antithetical to his own. In this context, the reference to Mime's eyes here is significant. While the eyes of the Volsungs are superior organs able to recognize the affinity of like kind, those of the Nibelungs betray their inferiority and isolation, and they are described in the vilest of terms. Mime's eyes—dripping, repulsive, and, in the initial description of the dwarf that Wagner later omitted from the drama, 'small and piercing, with red rims'[38] (like those of his brother Albe-rich, whose glance is derided by Flosshilde as *stechend*, or 'stab-bing' [RN, 101])—are contrasted to the doelike ('der Rehhinden gleich'), 'hellschimmernden Augen [brightly shining eyes]' (RN, 202) of Siegfried's mother. Here, the eye itself provides a sign of physiological identity; as in act 1 of *Die Walküre*, it is both a metaphor of vision and itself a corporeal icon providing a sign of race. (Mime's red and dripping eyes also make his appearance caninelike, recalling the nature of another enemy of the Volsung family, Sieglinde's husband, Hunding, or, literally, 'hounding.') Siegfried's eyes are his vehicle for recognizing Mime's foreign nature, and thus, following his description of the dwarf's 'hanging ears' and 'dripping eyes,' his most immediate desire is to be rid of the Nibelung's *image*, as he exclaims:

Fort mit dem Alp!
Ich mag ihn nicht mehr sehn. (RN, 202)

[Away with the elf! I don't want to see him anymore.]

By viewing the racially distinctive signs of Mime's appearance, Siegfried recognizes their natural difference and in so doing recalls for the audience the superior and beautiful eyes of his Volsung parents, who themselves had read their own familial identity in the glance of another being.

That Siegfried imagines his mother's eyes to be like those of a doe is no coincidence either but is part of a motivic constellation that reinforces his closeness to Mother Nature. In observing the couplings of the forest animals, he learns of love (which the loveless and egotistical Mime could teach no one) and finds in them natural images of himself and his family:

So ruhten im Busch
auch Rehe gepaart,
selbst wilde Füchse und Wölfe:
Nahrung brachte
zum Nest das Männchen,
das Weibchen säugte die Welpen.
Da lernt' ich wohl
was Liebe sei:
der Mutter entwand ich
die Welpen nie. (RN, 162)

[Thus rested at times also pairs of deer, even wild foxes and wolves: To the nest the male brought food, the female breastfed the cubs. There I learned what love is: I never stole the cubs from the mother.]

When Mime calls Siegfried a 'wolf's son,' he underscores the boy's natural qualities and, for the audience familiar with *Die Walküre*, the child's affinity with both his father, Siegmund, who called himself 'Wölfing,' and his grandfather Wotan, who, disguised as the berserker 'Wolfe,' roamed the forest in the shape of a wolf with the Volsung warrior, a wolf's cub. Thus, it is motivically appropriate for Siegfried to learn from the wolves and the deer what his parents would have taught him, and it is consistent for him to dwell not simply upon the certain beauty of his mother's appearance but, above all, upon her doelike eyes, those eyes that viewed her own image in her natural twin, her brother and the father of Siegfried.

Siegfried voices his natural antipathy under the linden tree, the home of his natural soulmate, the Forest Bird, and therefore it is fitting that, after having murdered Mime, he speaks to the bird of its brothers and sisters, whom he sees in the branches above him, and longs for a similar family (RN, 217). Having been raised in the company of the unfamilial/r, he longs for his own kind, and it is precisely to a close relation that the bird will guide him, first to his grandfather Wotan, and then to his parents' half-sister, Brünnhilde. No wonder he believes when he first sees her that she is his mother: As he quests for his own identity, what else could a true Wagnerian superhero expect to find but a relative?

Wagner repeats the eye motif in Siegfried's encounter with the one-eyed Wanderer in act 3, who, in conversing with his grandson, remarks:

Mit dem Auge,
das als andres mir fehlt,
erblickst du selber das eine,
das mir zum Sehen verblieb. (RN, 228)

[With the other eye that I am missing, you yourself behold the one that is left to me for seeing.]

But Wotan caused his father's death, and thus, in a motivically consistent continuation of the impoverished vision that attends the Annunciation of Death scene when Brünnhilde threatens the Volsung family, Siegfried fails to recognize the figure before him as his godly grandfather. Indeed, he will never learn the figure's full identity, only that he is his 'Vaters Feind' (his 'father's foe') (RN, 231), and thus takes revenge upon the old man before he ventures on in quest of the being who, unbeknownst to him, attempted to save his parents and whom he therefore can know and recognize.

Once united, Siegfried and Brünnhilde recognize themselves and each other much as their related Volsungs had. Siegfried exclaims to her: 'Oh . . . that I behold the eye that now shines upon me, blessed man!' (RN, 235), to which she consistently replies: 'Only your gaze was allowed to see me!' (RN, 236). Their courtship, as brief as that of Siegmund and Sieglinde, is comprised of an exchange of glances. As she grows afraid of losing her virginity, Brünnhilde covers her eyes, and in an effort to win her, Siegfried implores her to look at him, removing her hands from her face. She then employs the very image Sieglinde had used in comparing her own face to that of her brother but transforms it in her passing fear of sexual awakening, saying that Siegfried will lose the joy of narcissistic recognition if he disturbs the reflection she offers:

Sahst du dein Bild
im klaren Bach?
Hat es dich Frohen erfreut?
Rührtest zur Woge
das Wasser du auf;
zerflösse die klare
Fläche des Bachs:
dein Bild sähst du nicht mehr,
nur der Welle schwankend Gewog'.
So berühre mich nicht,
trübe mich nicht! (RN, 240)

[Have you seen your image in the clear brook? Did it please you, happy man? If you brushed the water into waves, the clear surface of the brook would vanish: You would see your image no longer, only the tottering rocking of the waves. Thus do not touch me, do not darken me.]

His counter is really a reaffirmation of the motif as it appeared in the first act of *Die Walküre*, for by stating that he longs only to be 'Aug' in Auge' with her (RN, 242), Siegfried reestablishes the narcissistic desire of his parents, and it is this desire, shared by his aunt Brünnhilde, who is related to him through their superior, godly blood, that wins over her resistance. In the end, as they are tempestuously united, the 'rays of their glances devour one another [*wie der Blicke strahlen sich verzehren*]' (RN, 243) and the affirmation of their kindred identity is confirmed in the optical imagery of their consummated passion. The orchestral accompaniment to this passage contains the leitmotif of the serpent, a quotation that has caused some consternation in Wagner's listeners, but one that makes sense through its connection to the theme of familial similarity in the *Ring*, for by employing the motif of the 'Wurm,' Wagner subtly recalls Hunding's observation in act 1 of *Die Walküre* that 'der gleißende Wurm' shines both from his wife's and from the strange intruder's — Siegmund's — eyes and reminds the audience that Siegfried was described by Mime in act 1 as 'the little dragon [*den kleinen Wurm*]' (RN, 160) (as well, of course, as implying that Siegfried has already 'conquered' one dragon and is about to make another conquest).[39] The music, too, underlines then the theme of the gaze so central to all the scenes involving the meeting and mating of kindred and superior beings. Toward the end of his life, after his anti-Semitism had found a purportedly scientific confirmation in the writings of Count Joseph Arthur Gobineau, Wagner would recall this very scene explicitly in racial terms and when doing so would underscore the central function of the motif of the gaze as a guarantor of racial identity, as Cosima Wagner noted in her diary on 17 October 1881: ' "That is Gobineau music," R. says as he comes in, "that is race. Where else will you find two beings who burst into rejoicing when merely looking at each other?" '[40]

That the *Ring* is so motivically consistent is testimony to the subtlety of its construction and to the importance of the meanings its diverse motifs convey. The *Ring* is not simply a mythic parable of good versus evil or of greed versus love but a dramatic representation of these themes against the background of racial difference. Without recognizing the component of anti-Semitism so central to its design, the drama's numerous and repeated images of human and animal physicality, and especially of physiological difference, would seem little more than fairy tale embellishments to a work dealing with nature and magic. But Wagner's music dramas constitute visual, textual, and sonic representations of the ideas he spelled out in detail in diverse essays following the 1848 revolution regarding the corrupting role of Jews in the modern world and the need for the redemption of the German community from Jewish influence; that he employed the motif of the recognizing gaze in his tetralogy as a dramatic counterpart to the motif of recognition in his social revolutionary tracts is suggested both by the temporal conflation of these diverse projects and by the extraordinarily consistent implications accompanying the motif's numerous appearances in the music dramas.

Yet the gaze is no mere metaphor but the basis of a conceptual model that is very much rooted in the perception of physiology as a sign of innate, real difference in nineteenth-century culture. Inscribed upon the body of the nation, the signs of the individual's body reveal for Wagner and for his contemporary audience racial and national identity. In dramatizing the metaphors of the eye, reflection, recognition, and self-definition through the rejection of all that is foreign, Wagner drew upon a repertoire of anti-Semitic stereotypes deeply entrenched within his culture in order to lend persuasive credibility to his portrayals of social issues. Though his ideas were often highly idiosyncratic, personal transformations of conceptual models taken from other early nineteenth-century German thinkers (from Hegel, Feuerbach, Hoffmann, Novalis, Jahn, Eichendorff, and others), he infused them in their dramatic representations with a wealth of connotations attending specific iconographies of the body that had widespread currency in his world. In so doing, he established his Artworks of the Future as documents of segregation that conveyed their agenda of hatred through a host of images that implied for his culture fundamental physical differences separating peoples, communities, and races. It is to the investigation of the specific features of such bodily imagery in Wagner's essays and dramatic works that we must now turn.

Wagner himself seeks to interpret the promotion of music by the Germans by supposing among other things that, denied the seductive stimulus of a naturally melodious voice, they were compelled to take the art of music with something of the same degree of seriousness as their religious reformers took Christianity. —Friedrich Nietzsche, *Richard Wagner in Bayreuth*

The human voice is the practical foundation of all music. —Wagner, 'Bericht an Seine Majestät den König Ludwig II. von Bayern über eine in München zu errichtende deutsche Musikschule'

The eye is a key metaphor in Wagner's social-aesthetic theories and in his music dramas, but it is not the only one, nor does it function alone. In Wagner's thought other images of the body are metaphorically likened to the eye and also serve in his writings and works for the stage, like the eye, either to recognize similarity or to distinguish the German from the foreigner. Self and Self, or Self and Other—the two models of identity underlying the act of vision for Wagner— also emerge for him in the act of receiving other sensory impressions. When considering the works of a composer of music dramas, it should come as no surprise that the sense closest in importance to vision for him is that of acoustical perception, of sound, and, given the central model of recognition of like kind or of the foreign in Wagner's social-aesthetic theories, it is consistent that the composer metaphorically likens hearing to seeing, for the two sensory acts provide information to the same ideological ends. As previously noted, Wagner uses the eye as a metaphor in his description of the extravisual components of the Artwork of the Future in *Oper und Drama*, where it functions as a metaphor for melody: 'Every true melody,' Wagner claims, 'speaks to us through that eye which most expressively communicates to us [the] interior [of the entire human being]' (*DS* 7: 107). Vision can be related here to sonic perception, because in Wagner's theories all 'sensual impressions' serve to define the position of the Self, either as a member of a community based on shared experience and similarity or as different from the being it perceives as foreign. In *Oper und Drama*, the discussion of the future artwork's appeal to the senses, to the emotions of the German *Volk*, conflates and makes comparable vision and hearing: 'We see . . . that where the ear is to be stimulated to a greater sensual participation [*Teilnahme*], he who wishes to communicate must in the process also turn to the eye: Ear and eye must mutually assure themselves of a superior communication [*müssen sich einer höher gestimmten Mitteilung gegenseitig versichern*] in order to convincingly lead to the feeling' (*DS* 7: 310). The path to the heart of the folkish community leads through the senses, and sight and sound are mutually and equally involved in this sensuous-folkish endeavor that is based on the exclusion of nonfolkish elements (associated with intellectualism and bereft of feeling) and that has as its ultimate goal the establishment of a community based on kindred identity. Thus sounds, too, participate in Wagner's metaphors of this social-aesthetic process so central to his theories.

But because it is the body that acts as a guarantor of identity in Wagner, it is above all the sounds of the body that reveal the individual as familial or foreign, and the most important corporeal sound for him is that of the human voice. The sound of one's voice provides a physiological signature guaranteeing the verification of identity, of friend or foe, and it appears in this capacity both in Wagner's reformative tracts and throughout his works for the stage following the failed 1848 revolution. In 'Das Kunstwerk der Zukunft,' for example, the following passage is typical:

It is to the ear that the inner human being communicates directly, precisely through the *sound of his voice*. The sound is the immediate expression of feeling, as it has its physical origin in the heart, the point of departure and return of the blood's circulation. Through the sense of hearing the sound moves directly out of the heart's feeling back to the heart's feeling: The pain and joy of the feeling human being once again communicate directly through the varied expression of the sound of the voice to the feeling human being. (*DS* 6: 32)

And 'feeling,' as we have seen, to which this voice-as-signature appeals through its communication to the senses (and not to the intellect, that unfolkish sphere associated with the non-German), is the property of the German community, the folk-ish group removed from the cold, abstract, and lifeless crafty scheming of those deemed foreign.

But metaphor always has a physical dimension in Wagner, and for him the physiological makeup of the human voice reveals national and racial identity. What distinguishes the German from the non-German voice? What does a foreign vocal instrument sound like? In Wagner's world, the voice of the non-German, both metaphorically and physiologically, is *higher* than that of the German. This notion emerges time and again throughout Wagner's expository production, from his essays of 1840 on the Parisian culture industry to his more celebrated tracts of 1849 to 1851 concerning aesthetic reform and the need for the transformation and purification of German society, and it reappears in his analyses of the legitimate theater penned in the early 1870s following the formation of the Reich.[1] Furthermore, the perception of the voice as an acoustical icon of race and nation appears not only in Wagner's theoretical writings but also decidedly influenced the composition of the vocal music with which he would come to be most closely identified: that of the *Ring*, *Tristan und Isolde*, *Die Meistersinger von Nürnberg*, and *Parsifal*.

Wagner's notion of the non-German voice as higher than that of the German was no private, personal event found only in the idiosyncratic expostulations of his essays and in the unparalleled accomplishments of his musical fantasy, for it reflects, exploits, and perpetuates an iconography of the body that was widespread in European culture of the nineteenth century and that as such appears on both ends of its temporal spectrum, from Rossini's

Mosé in Egitto of 1818 to Richard Strauss's *Salome* of 1905.[2] This feature of Wagner's work — so important to any discussion of a composer primarily associated, after all, with the establishment of a revolutionary, innovative kind of vocal music — is central to an understanding of the role such corporeal images play in Wagner's conception of a new art and of the new society in which he hoped his music of the future would sound.

10. Wagner in Paris, 1840 or 1842. Drawing by Ernest Benedikt Kietz (Nationalarchiv der Richard Wagner–Stiftung/Richard Wagner Gedenkstätte, Bayreuth)

Wagner's search for his own voice began in Paris in the employment of a wealthy German Jew and music publisher, Moritz Adolf Schlesinger, and from this experience in the early 1840s emerged his never-ending association of Jews with the nascent culture industry which he would so vituperatively denounce in 'Das Judentum in der Musik' and other tracts following the 1848 revolution (figure 10).[3] Moritz Adolf Schlesinger was the son of Adolf Martin (actually Abraham Moses) Schlesinger, whose Berlin publishing house ranked as one of the most important of its kind in Prussia.[4] Moritz Adolf enjoyed a similar success in Paris, Europe's operatic center, where he specialized in publications of the very composers Wagner despised: By his retirement in 1846, Schlesinger had produced more than fifty piano-vocal and two dozen full orchestral scores to such works as Meyerbeer's *Robert le diable* and *Les Huguenots*, twelve operas of Halévy, among them *La Juive*, and operas by Adam and Donizetti. He also published complete editions of Beethoven's piano works, string trios, quartets, and quintets and early works of Mendelssohn and Berlioz, including the first edition of *Huit Scènes de Faust* and the full score of *Symphonie fantastique*.[5] Wagner doubtless envied Schlesinger's position in Parisian society, secured in part through the prestigious journal *Gazette musicale de Paris*, which Schlesinger had founded in 1834 and had merged, in the following year, with the successful *Revue musicale de Paris*.[6] The new journal subsidized a series of concerts especially for Schlesinger's favorite composers, many of them Jews, and provided him with a printed forum for their works.[7] Both the concerts and the journal were vehicles Wagner was never able to exploit suc-

cessfully for the furthering of his own fame as a composer, despite his repeated attempts to that end.[8]

In 1840 Schlesinger commissioned from Wagner an article on German music for the *Gazette musicale* that first appeared in two installments, on 12 and 26 July, as 'De la musique allemande' (On German music) and that was later republished in Germany under the title 'Über deutsches Musikwesen.'[9] Just as we have seen how the essay 'Die Kunst und die Revolution' from the immediate postrevolutionary period spelled out issues and associations fundamental to Wagner's later social-aesthetic program, so this early Parisian essay reveals a host of motifs and associated ideas central to his more extensive and mature essays, among them notions represented for him by the human voice. As late as 1871 Wagner deemed the essay important enough to include it in volume 1 of his *Gesammelte Schriften und Dichtungen*, while he omitted there most of the reviews and essays he had written in Paris for the German press: for August Lewald's *Europa: Chronik der gebildeten Welt* in Stuttgart, Schumann's *Neue Zeitschrift für Musik* in Leipzig, and Theodor Winkler's *Dresdner Abendzeitung*. Thus, 'Über deutsches Musikwesen' must have represented even to the older Wagner a valid expression of fundamental constants in his thinking. When Schlesinger commissioned 'De la musique allemande,' Wagner found a vehicle for theoretically justifying his never-ending resentment of the institutional forces governing the arts in the modern world, forces he associated explicitly with Jews, as he would make clear ten years later in 'Das Judentum in der Musik.'[10]

Though Wagner's essay contains many complimentary remarks on the French appreciation of German music and his recognition that the political centralization of France contributes to the strength of French cultural life, and though it closes with the hope that the Germans and French will work together to enhance their differing approaches to art for the betterment of both nations, such passages were most likely intended to forestall consternation over the text's pervasive Francophobic sentiment.[11] The essay unfolds within the very tension between

dependence, envy, and resentment that Wagner experienced in
his work for Schlesinger and opens with the concern that German art is all too easily overpowered by foreign influence:

[One] can say that the French, through their proven willing acknowl-
edgment of foreign productions, have distinguished themselves more
than the Germans, who succumb faster and with less opposition to
every foreign influence than is good for the preservation of a certain
independence. The difference is this: — the German, who does not
possess the ability to initiate a fashion, adopts it without hesitation if it
comes from abroad; in this weakness he forgets himself, and blindly
sacrifices his own judgment to the foreign impression. (DS 5: 152)

The struggle for power that Wagner discerns within the cultural
life of Europe sets up an unequal exchange between diverse
national forces. The despairing martial imagery of overrun borders and impending subordination underscores the plight of the
German artist, for it is he who must strive to preserve the integrity of the besieged homeland. This cognitive model of culture
as a vehicle for national attack and defense will infuse Wagner's
writings to the end of his life and is as readily apparent in the
nationalistic *Deutsche Kunst und deutsche Politik* of 1867 and the
anti-Semitic 'Erkenne dich selbst' of 1881 as it is in this early
xenophobic tract.

To counter this threat, Wagner develops a compensatory argument that robs the competing culture of its validity, though
the assessment of foreign culture as superficial, mercantile, and
lacking in populist support further accentuates the peril facing
Germany. Each national identity is coupled with its representative culture:

The Italian is a singer, the Frenchman a virtuoso, the German a —
musician. The German has a right to be called exclusively 'Musician,'
for of him one may say that he loves Music for its own sake, — not as a
means of charming, of winning money and respect. . . . The German is
capable of writing music merely for himself and his friend, completely
oblivious as to whether it will ever be executed and presented to a
public. . . . Go some winter night and listen to them in their cozy little
room: a father and his three sons sit there at a round table; two play the

violin, a third the viola, the father the cello; what you can hear being performed in the deepest and most heartfelt manner [*so tief und innig*] is a string quartet that that little man composed who is beating time. . . . [The] quartet that he composed is artistic, beautiful, and deeply felt [*kunstvoll, schön und tiefgefühlt*]. (*DS* 5: 153–154)

A number of consistent oppositions emerge here that provide the basis for the development of Wagner's argument. The specific nature of the foreign danger is underscored in polarizations that stress the difference between Latinate and German culture and that anticipate the dialectical arguments of Wagner's post-revolutionary essays: the virtuoso versus the artisan, the implied aristocratic society versus the explicit Biedermeier setting, the public audience versus the private domestic sphere, and, above all, the superficial *Ausland* opposed to the image of Germany's cultural essence as 'deep' — 'tief,' 'innig,' and 'tiefgefühlt.' Such oppositions are grafted onto Wagner's spatial model, discussed in the previous chapter, separating mundane surface from the inner essence of things German. In this way the metaphors of perception (surface versus depth) that we have already examined take on additional, specifically ideological and cultural meaning. It is no coincidence that Wagner's Hans Sachs will later extol his 'liebes Nürnberg' as lying 'in Deutschlands Mitten' (*MN,* 106) or that the Rhinemaidens, as previously stated, will lament at the conclusion to *Das Rheingold*: 'Trusted and true it is only in the depths: False and cowardly is what rejoices above!' (*RN,* 72).

Wagner's image of the human voice, introduced in 'Über deutsches Musikwesen,' should be understood within these ideologically significant, metaphorical oppositions. For Wagner, the voice is both a physiological reality reflecting racial difference and the metaphorical representation of national identity. The notion of deep as better — as more natural, communal, familial, and untouched by the alienation of an inferior and different, 'higher' modern civilization — reemerges in his description of the physiological basis of art south of Germany, specifically of Italian vocal music. In the previous chapter I noted that Wagner adapted the polarity of essential depth versus superfluous and mundane surface appearance, found in the works of his Romantic forebears E. T. A. Hoffmann, Eichendorff, and Novalis, for his visual metaphors of the discerning (Greek and German) eye. Now that metaphorical model is applied not only to the difference between German and non-German culture but to the sonic extremes of deep and high vocal registers as well. Culture as metaphor has for Wagner a realistic, literal component based on the physical properties of those who create, experience, and share it:

> Both nature and the makeup of his homeland set strict boundaries for the German artist. Nature denies him the light and supple development of a head organ, of song [*die leichte und weiche Bildung eines Hauptorganes, des Gesanges*] which we find in the lucky Italian throats; — the political makeup prevents him from [attaining] higher publicity. The opera composer is forced to learn an advantageous singing technique from the Italians, to seek however foreign stages for his works, because he can find none in Germany on which to present himself to a nation. (*DS* 5: 155)

The Italian is a singer and the Frenchman a virtuoso, but only the German, it seems, with his communal life based on a domestic harmony reflected in the physical makeup of his deep vocal registers, is a genuine musician. Ensconced 'deep' within the center of Europe, he must acquire the superficial eccentricities of foreign culture in order to succeed in the 'higher public arena' located in the outer geographical extremities surrounding Germany. High voices are Mediterranean, cultivated, hypercivilized, foreign, and far removed from the lower reaches of the German masses (comprised apparently of bass-baritones), who live in the lower center of the European map.[12] Clearly this metaphorical model scarcely distinguishes between the middle (Nuremberg's position in Germany and Germany's place in the heart of Europe) and the depths (where the essence of the German spirit lies awaiting its recognition, beneath the surface of its appearance, by a like-minded and apparently like-voiced compatriot). Middle and low are equally opposed to the devalued superficiality of the outer and upper registers — of culture and of the voice.[13]

Such physiological metaphors of culture underscore the urgency behind the perception of a purportedly genuine threat to the German nation. To the fantasy of cultural despair that views modern civilization as corrosive and antithetical to a legitimate art and to its reception, the arenas of economic and political power in which inauthentic 'high' art is disseminated are remarkably similar.[14] While the Frenchman is a virtuoso and the Italian a singer, the commodification of higher, literally superior (read: aesthetically and socially inferior) art in France, England, and Italy makes all three countries essentially similar, culturally related, and fundamentally different from Germany. Wagner's ironic description of Italian tenor Giovanni Rubini, for whom Bellini and Donizetti wrote many operatic roles and who enjoyed great success in both Paris and London, makes it clear that the virtuoso is equally at home in the culture industry of all three countries, but not in Wagner's homeland (DS 5: 31–32). Morally, these nations, like their art, resemble one another and are different from Germany as well. The pious religiosity so apparent in the German's attitude to his national art is missing in the sensual, titillating frivolity of Italian and French music and in its reception in the cultural centers of England and France. One has only to recall Wagner's description of modern art as a slave to a 'bigoted English banker' in 'Das Kunstwerk der Zukunft' to appreciate the consistency in his metaphorical reflections on this issue (DS 5: 285). For this reason, when he describes the musical life of Paris, Wagner stresses the notion that the English and the French have mistresses in the French capital who are often found among the artists and dancers of the Opéra, while the Germans do not (DS 5: 50–51). The Germans are morally upstanding, chaste, and presumably baritonal.

Therefore, Wagner suggests, when the German musician elevates his voice, he degenerates morally. He loses his sincerity when he adopts the immoral Italian virtuosity so applauded in

Paris because he has neither the requisite vocal cords nor the vocal technique to effect the elevated pyrotechnics of foreign culture, with its musical virtuosic sensuality:

[The German musician] is pure and innocent, but, for that very reason, noble and sublime. — But set these glorious musicians before a large audience, in a sprawling salon — and they will no longer be the same people. . . . Now they will fearfully attempt to perform for you glittering passages as well; the same voices that sang the lovely German *Lied* so touchingly will quickly study Italian coloratura. But they cannot succeed with these passages and coloratura. . . . These bunglers are the truest artists . . . [and were] ashamed of their own true nature. (*DS* 5: 154–155)

The foreigner can sing such passages and even prefers them, but the genuine German *Musiker* cannot and does not. Culture, then, is understood as related to the physiological characteristics of a people, and as such it is the hallmark of the nation. It is as indelibly inscribed upon the national character as the physiognomy of the national appearance guaranteeing the demarcation of folkish or foreign identity. Wagner implies that you can no more change your innate cultural identity than you can transform your face or the material of your voice, and, for him, the attempt to do so brings with it a loss of traditional values that are associated with a physiologically circumscribed and defined people.[15]

Wagner's remarks concerning the tessitura of vocal music as a criterion of national identity are consistent with his many pronouncements concerning vocal production per se. In 'Das Kunstwerk der Zukunft' he writes that 'language is the condensed element of the voice, the word is the *solidified mass* of the tone' (*DS* 6: 33), and for him, language, as discussed in chapter 1, is one of the elements binding together and defining the community: '*Das Volk*,' he writes in the same essay, 'invented language' (*DS* 6: 20). This is one of the notions that forms a link between the aesthetic tracts, purportedly (according to Wagner's apologists) bereft of racism, and the more explicitly anti-Semitic writings, as comparison of these statements with a passage from 'Das Judentum in der Musik' makes clear: 'A language . . . is not the work of individuals but rather of a historical community: Only he who has unconsciously grown up in this community also takes part in its creations' (GS 13: 13).[16] Language for Wagner is the singular product of a unified people, and for him the Jews, we recall, are cold, loveless, and lacking in familial (read: communal) ties. It is for this reason that Beckmesser so completely misunderstands the text of Walther's dream-poem, a work so representative of the circumscribed bonds of the community to which the hero, Walther, innately belongs and that excludes the cerebral notary. This explicitly anti-Semitic idea had already appeared more covertly in 'Das Kunstwerk der Zukunft,' in which the Jew-as-intellectual is divorced from those that bond together through language: 'Not you intellectuals . . . are inventive, but the *Volk*; because need drives it to invention. . . . It was not you who invented language, but the *Volk*' (DS 6: 20). With language a communal construct perfectly available only to those out of whose bond and common need it arises, it will always be imperfectly accommodated by those who are foreign and, for Wagner, physiologically different.

Because 'language is the condensed element of the voice,' it is not only the semantic but the very sonic component of vocal communication that defines the identity of those who use it. For Wagner, sounds reflect national essence, and therefore the tessitura of speech, like that of song, also provides a sign of national identity. This is true both of the sounds of everyday conversation and of declamation heard in the theater. In his essay 'Über Schauspieler und Sänger' (On actors and singers) of 1872—written one year after he had republished 'Über deutsches Musikwesen'—Wagner argues that the 'higher' culture of French theater, adopted by the German stage and yet antithetical to the German spirit, is based on the different physiology of the French vocal chords. Metaphor ('high' culture) and physical reality (the high voice) combine in one image. The Frenchman on the street speaks in a theatrical, false manner emblematic of his national-cultural essence and inimical to the linguistically and vocally different German: '[This is how] the Frenchman speaks and behaves. . . . But to the German any pathos which somehow comes close to this French [behavior] is completely unnatural; if he feels it is necessary to employ it, he must attempt to imitate it through the ridiculous disguising of his voice and an elevation of all his usual speaking habits [*durch lächerliche Verstellung seiner Stimme und Heraufschraubung seiner Sprachgewohnheiten*]' (*DS* 9: 206). This metaphorical image of foreign culture as higher is meant literally when it is applied to the vocal apparatus producing speech, for these sounds are metabolically antithetical to the German. Wagner goes on here to decry the fact that the sonic dimension of foreign declamatory art has influenced even Germany's greatest poets: ' "Yes," he writes, "even if one has our best poet read his verses to us, he immediately stumbles into the falsetto of his vocal instrument [*verfällt er in eine Falsett seines Sprachorganes*] and uses all those pompous and foolish distortions" ' (*DS* 9: 207). Non-Germans of all kinds sound different from the German, and since art is a reflection of the body and of the social corpus, it sounds wrong if appropriated by a foreigner. If a German tries to sing like an Italian or to speak like a Frenchman, he loses his identity, sounds like a sex-starved eunuch (reminiscent of the castrati so central to the development of foreign opera and anticipating the foreign nature of Wagner's malevolent Klingsor), and makes a fool of himself. Higher speech, then, is unnatural both to the German voice and to the German *Volksgeist* reflected in the voice of the people and in its art.

The social implications of pitch in Wagner's reflections on speech and music in the modern world are not solely related to the nationally identifiable, to the French, the English, and the Italians, for this criterion of inclusion in and exclusion from the German *Volk* plays a prominent role not only in the xenophobic tracts but in the explicitly anti-Semitic writings as well, and, as we have seen, the Jews according to Wagner have infiltrated all nations in the modern world. Long before he wrote 'Über

Schauspieler und Sänger' Wagner had used its image of the
incompatibility of German and non-German theatrical art and
voices when discussing, in 'Das Judentum in der Musik,' musical works composed by Jews: 'Jewish musical works often make
the impression on us as if for example a poem by Goethe were
being read in Jewish jargon' (GS 13: 21). Just as the German
makes a fool of himself when attempting to sing or declaim
a foreign art, and foreign declamatory styles make a travesty
of authentic German poetry, so conversely the Jew seems ridiculous when he attempts to infiltrate the sanctified sphere of
physiologically different German art. We may assume that by
'Jewish jargon' (or, as it was often described in Wagner's time,
Mauscheln, denoting German spoken with a Yiddish accent),[17]
Wagner means here, among other things, the elevated pitch he
associates with foreign declamation. As mentioned in the previous chapter, Wagner claims that the German's antipathy to the
Jew is attributable to the latter's different speech patterns, which
reflect the absence of national-folkish roots, and employs in his
remarks an image of the Jewish voice that conflates with his
metaphor of inferior foreign 'high' culture as superficial and superior German culture as deep:[18] 'It is of central importance . . .
to consider the impression that the Jew makes on us through his
language. . . . The Jew always speaks the language of the nation
as a foreigner. . . . To our ear the hissing, shrill, buzzing, and
gurgling sound of the Jewish manner of speech appears quite
foreign and unpleasant' (GS 13: 12–13). Just as the Jew's *speech*
is perceived as shrill and therefore higher than the German's,
so too is his *singing*, which is also based on his purportedly
natural difference, as another passage from 'Das Judentum in
der Musik' explicitly states: '[The] peculiarities of this Jewish
way of speaking and singing, in all its most shocking abnormality, are to be explained solely on physiological grounds [*rein
physiologisch zu erklären*]' (GS 13: 17–18). Thus the notion of
foreign art, influenced, corrupted, and controlled by the Jews, as
superficial and removed from the authentic depths of German
art is the spatial metaphor that is superimposed on the phys-

iological iconography of polarized and antithetical Jewish and German voices. High art and high voices screech in the elevated regions far above the wondrous art found in the center of the European map and deep within the German soul, commensurate with its deeper vocal instrument.

The sonic image of the Jew's singing as high is a corporeal icon found in both — and thus linking — Wagner's essays and his music dramas. This becomes apparent when one compares Wagner's diverse statements on speech and song with the musical material of his most anti-Semitic works for the stage, *Die Meistersinger von Nürnberg* and *Siegfried.* If we recall that the presence of the Jews in the aesthetic sphere constitutes a danger to the development of German art and to the community it represents, it is only consistent that, for Wagner, the virtuosic music performed in the cultural institutions of France, Italy, and England — all controlled, according to him, by Jews — *had come to resemble the vocal production of the Jews itself,* which Wagner radically separates from the music of the German *Volk.* 'Das Judentum in der Musik' contains a brief, and in this context highly revealing, passage that is important for an analysis of Wagner's musical material: '[The] melismas and rhythms of synagogue chant captivate the musical imagination of the Jew in the same way that the instinctive perception of the melodies and rhythms of our folk song and folk dance [captivate] the actual creative power of the creators of our art song and instrumental music' (GS 13: 20). When Wagner refers to synagogue chant, he assumes that his reader will imagine, like him, a thin, high, and nasal sound, for it was precisely as such that it had existed in the European imagination long before Wagner exploited it in his diverse essays on Jews. The connection between a high voice and a specifically nasal sound as idiosyncratically Jewish is the very connection that, as Sander Gilman has brilliantly shown, Strauss later exploited in his musical allusions in *Salome* to Jewish musician Gustav Mahler.[19] Gilman's comments regarding the cultural background to the anti-Semitic musical codes in

Strauss's early twentieth-century opera bear directly on the tradition within which Wagner's earlier racist conception of vocal music is situated:

There was already a nineteenth-century tradition of representing the Jews' discourse on the operatic stage as different. Stendhal, in his *Life of Rossini*, comments on how an acquaintance of the composer remarked to him, while Rossini was working on *Mosé in Egitto*: 'Since you intend to have a Chorus of Jews, why not give them a nasal intonation, the sort of thing you hear in a synagogue?' . . . Rossini's musical quotation . . . was . . . the use of musical intertextuality to create the illusion of the world of the Jews.[20]

Wagner's reference to synagogue chant in 'Das Judentum in der Musik' drew upon a cultural tradition that viewed the Jewish voice as unusually and idiosyncratically high. That tradition forms the background to the musical characterization of Beckmesser in *Die Meistersinger von Nürnberg*.

The vocal writing of the role of Beckmesser is characterized by an extremely demanding, elevated tessitura. It is significant that the only singer with whom Wagner was dissatisfied at the work's prestigious premiere in Munich in 1868 was the first interpreter of Nuremberg's notary, the Viennese bass Gustav Hölzel, who complained specifically of the role's mercilessly extended notes that rise to extreme heights and stay there, hovering in a part of the voice that would normally be associated, for any extended period of time, with a tenor.[21] Wagner explained to the man: ' "It is a comic character part and can in no way be compared with a bass *buffo* role in the old style: the musically high *tessitura* is the result solely of an impassioned, screeching tone of voice intended to bring out as much as possible." '[22] The composer even explicitly asked the Hamburg bass Rudolf Freny to sing with 'a voice that cracks when [Beckmesser] loses his temper.'[23] In many respects, the role makes the greatest vocal demands of any in the music drama, to which few singers have been equal. It was perhaps because Wagner associated Beckmesser's elevated pitch with the kind of 'Judaized speech' he heard in the legitimate theater, replete with the foreign falsetto sounds of French declamatory styles, that Cosima Wagner, when she staged *Die Meistersinger* in Bayreuth in 1888, assigned the role not to a singer but to an actor, Fritz Friedrichs, whose voice within the opera ensemble must have seemed strange, thin, and, given the extraordinarily high tessitura, undoubtedly nasal and necessarily falsetto-filled as well (see figure 11). It was precisely that sound that provided the signature of Beckmesser's essence to Wagner and to his audience.

In the recent past Paul Lawrence Rose and Barry Millington have drawn attention to the fact that Beckmesser's vocal music is unusually high, but what they have missed, I feel, is the tension in Wagner's musical portrayal between the function of such sounds as metaphor and their place within iconographies associated with Jews in nineteenth-century German culture, for those high sounds are both the musical manifestations of Wagner's notion of Judaized culture as superficial, and hence reprehensible, and themselves part of a tradition of thought that viewed the Jewish body — in this case, his vocal production — as different from that of the non-Jew. When, in act 1 of *Die Meistersinger*, Beckmesser condemns Walther's new music for its lack of coloratura, his criticism is set to a pliant vocal line that lies predominantly above the staff and that, characteristically, rises through florid melismas to a high G♭ (example 1):

Example 1. Beckmesser's praise of coloratura and condemnation of Walther von Stolzing's song in act 1 of *Die Meistersinger*

Beckmesser's music thus demonstrates the very kind of vocal production the influential critic so misses in the aesthetically different song of the future. Melisma and coloratura merge and converge to form similar acoustical signs of non-German influence. Though musicologists distinguish between the melisma

11. Actor Fritz Friedrichs as Sixtus Beckmesser in Cosima Wagner's
production of *Die Meistersinger*, 1888 (Nationalarchiv der Richard
Wagner–Stiftung/Richard Wagner Gedenkstätte, Bayreuth)

('an expressive vocal passage sung to one syllable') and coloratura ('a rapid passage, run, trill, or similar virtuoso-like material, particularly in vocal melodies of eighteenth- and nineteenth-century operatic arias'), these kinds of vocal writing
appear to have had a similar, at times even identical, ideological
significance for Wagner,[24] and they are based on assumptions
concerning the foreign body. Jewish singing, with its melismas
and extended pitch, recalls the coloratura of Italy and France.[25]

These features emerge as acoustical symbols within the music
drama of a figure and a host of associated characteristics re(pre)-
sented as antithetical to Walther and to the German *Volk*. Musical symbolism such as this is, in part, an example of what Peter
Kivy has characterized as 'internal representations' that function 'merely by virtue of a convention internal to the musical
work,' but only in part, for it is important to bear in mind that
this kind of musical representation is based on a racist iconography of the voice that was widespread in Wagner's time.[26] The
composer both calculated his musical effects with it in mind and
in so doing himself contributed to its perpetuation. The internal references within *Die Meistersinger* (coloratura and melisma,
functioning as signs of the foreign) are elements of the work's
musical-semantic vocabulary, but that vocabulary seemed particularly persuasive and credible and hence not the arbitrary
aesthetic decision of a composer within the context of nineteenth-century racist iconographies of the body. Wagner thus
takes the popular image of the Jewish voice and builds his specific signs of Jewish influence on it — melisma (reminiscent for him
of the synagogue) and coloratura (representing the art spheres
of non-German Europe). No wonder Beckmesser's own nocturnal serenade in act 2 is based on a preference for florid, melismatic, high-pitched singing that, characteristically, shows little
feeling for the German language (example 2).[27]

Beckmesser sings the 'melismas . . . of synagogue chant,'
which Wagner describes in 'Das Judentum in der Musik' as 'that
gurgling, yodeling, and blabbering that confounds sense and
mind [*jenes Sinn und Geist verwirrenden Gegurgels, Gejodels und
Geplappers*]' (*GS* 13: 19), and accompanies himself with colora-

Example 2.
Beckmesser's ele-
vated and melismatic
serenade in act 2 of
Die Meistersinger

tura 'ornamentation formulas of sixteenth-century keyboard and lute music.'[28] It is precisely because Beckmesser's singing is so high-pitched that it incites the riot at the conclusion to act 2, for in Wagner's world, the healthy German *Volk* must react violently to the vocal production of those who are racially foreign:[29]

Wer heult denn da? Wer kreischt mit Macht?
Ist das erlaubt so spät zur Nacht? . . .
Man hört nur, wie der Esel schreit! . . .
Heult, kreischt und schreit an andrem Ort! (*MN*, 93)

[Who's howling there? Who's screeching with such gusto? Is that allowed so late at night? . . . All you can hear is a donkey braying! . . . Howl, screech, and scream somewhere else!]

And howling it is, for by rising as high as an a (a′) (in act 3) and often hovering between middle c and f♯ above the staff, the role of the hapless notary lies impossibly high for most basses and even for bass-baritones. Wagner's contemporary audience recognized the notary's high and florid singing to be the composer's ridicule of Jewish art and of the Jewish physiognomy: When the music drama was first performed in Mannheim and Vienna, the Jewish communities of both cities vehemently protested.[30]

But the musical representation of the difference of the Jewish voice is by no means restricted to the vocal writing of *Die Meistersinger*. Wagner also composed instrumental music that provides an acoustical equivalent to the high and pointedly *nasal* sound of his laughable notary, a less-than-subtle allusion to the widespread iconography within his culture of the Jew as typically endowed with an idiosyncratically large nose (exploited, moreover, in many nineteenth-century caricatures of Wagner depicting the composer as himself endowed with a typically 'Jewish' nose; see figures 3 and 4).[31] Egon Voss has written perceptively of Wagner's use of the bassoon (marked 'Fag.1'— or 'first bassoon'—in example 3) in the orchestral passage accompanying Beckmesser's act 3 appearance in Sachs's house the morning after the notary's beating at the hands of the apprentice David (example 3). Voss's remarks are readily apposite to the

Example 3.
Beckmesser's high
and nasal bassoon

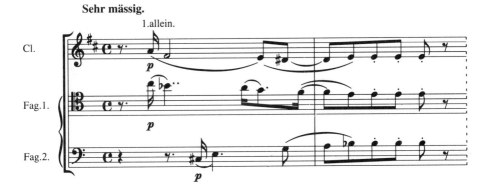

interpretation of Beckmesser's sonic signature as idiosyncratically and characteristically nasal in quality:

A particularly high-lying bassoon is to be found in the third Act of *Die Meistersinger*. At the beginning of the third scene a bassoon sound of this kind seeks to correspond to the maimed Beckmesser. The instrument is to enter on 'c2' and produces primarily tortured sounds because of the register in which the bassoon is used here; but the tones do not only sound tortured because the upper limit of the possible tones of the instrument has been reached but because the constant entrance in the lower register in general does not give the players the opportunity to cultivate and to refine the higher and the highest tones, as readily transpires through the constant practice with the lower tones. Wagner used the fact that the bassoonists do not elegantly and faultlessly succeed with the highest sounds within the marked octaves and that their production is linked to insecurity. In this way, he achieved a sound that is original and very characteristic and that may function as an analogy to Beckmesser's situation, about whom [the stage directions read]: 'Then he limps forward, shudders, and scratches his back.'[32]

Having already established a connection between the notary and high singing, Wagner introduces the figure here to a musical accompaniment that mocks both the injured man himself and the high tessitura that is his acoustical sign. Moreover, the peculiar quality of that sign as a 'nasal' sound, effectively conveyed by Beckmesser's association with the reed instrument, will stay with him throughout the drama. This sonic icon would later be used by Strauss in *Salome* in *his* musical portrayal of Jews; by employing the high, thin, and strained sounds of the oboe in his opera so rife with anti-Semitic under- (and over-) tones, Strauss, writing as the foremost heir (and composer of uppermost airs) of the Wagnerian musical legacy in a culture still imbued with motifs and beliefs central to Wagner's thought, could subtly allude to the notion already discernible in *Die Meistersinger* of 1868 of the Jew as characteristically endowed with a high, thin, and nasal voice, a notion that was pervasive in nineteenth-century European culture and that was based on the perception of the Jew's body as different from the German's.

Wagner's entire metaphorical system, both in his essays and in his works for the stage, is based on the juxtaposition of polarized opposites, and just as the iconography of the Jewish body represents the signs of all that is horrific and threatening to the German, so its opposite, the iconography of the German body, represents the salvation of German art and of the privileged Teutonic community. This is the case with the signs of the body perceived by the eye and with sonic signs as well. German sounds are different from the vocal noise of the foreigner, and their perception serves to reinforce the bonds of the German community based on circumscribed similarity. For Wagner, the authentic reception of German music excludes precisely those elements he despised in the Judaized world, as he implies in 'Über deutsches Musikwesen': 'We . . . may rightfully assume that Music in Germany branches out to the *lowest* and most inconspicuous social strata, yes, perhaps has its roots here. . . . Among these simple, unadorned souls, where the goal is not to entertain a large, *mixed* audience, art divests itself of every coquettish *outward* trapping' (DS 5: 157, my emphasis). The 'low roots' of the German are opposed to the high, 'outward trappings' of non-German art, which — and this is essential — is intended for a *mixed* audience. While the virtuoso performs before a heterogeneous (*gemischtes*) audience in the *Ausland*, German art explicitly requires a uniform reception that does not transpire before a mixed and public crowd but within the national 'family' of like-minded, musical, and physiologically similar individuals whose bodies, as manifest in their voices, are different from those of the non-German (the father and sons playing a deep and deeply felt music in the confines of the metaphorical family-as-community constitute the microcosmic representation of this larger social agenda). As in his remarks on the theater in ancient Greece, the similar here is preferred to the foreign and the uniform to the disparate. The homogeneity of the authentic aesthetic experience thus mirrors the preferred image of the German nation. Mixed means more, and more means different, and different means dangerous and 'higher.'

Because art both reflects its social context and, for Wagner, can offer an anticipatory model for a different, utopian future, his alternative to contemptible cultural practices controlled by Jews not only unfolds before a different kind of audience but also encompasses a different kind of aesthetic material based on a different kind of body. The low-lying German, non-Jewish work will be available not to the virtuosic specialists and to the high-class bankers and frequenters of salons but to all members of an exclusively uniform community, because its aesthetic makeup — unlike the music of the virtuoso — will be suited to the community's Germanic physiology. This idea is discernible in Wagner's description from 1840 of a Protestant congregation participating in its musical traditions. As the German *Volk*, the Lutheran congregation is able to participate because its nonvirtuosic music is written *for the voices of the common people*, who constitute the legitimate *deutsches Musikwesen*:

The glory of German vocal music blossomed in the church; the Opera was left to the Italians. Even Catholic church music is not at home in Germany, but instead exclusively Protestant church music. . . . In the older Protestant churches . . . in place of fancy trappings, the simple chorale sufficed, *sung by the whole congregation* and accompanied on the organ. . . . The Passion music . . . [of Bach] is based on the Savior's sufferings as told by the Evangelists; the text is set to music, word by word; but between the divisions of the tale, verses from the church's hymns, appropriate to the special subject, are woven in, and at the most important passages even the chorale itself, *which truly was sung by the whole assembled congregation*. Thus the performance of such Passion music became a great, religious, solemn occasion in which *artists and congregation* participated equally. . . . Thus church music had *the needs of the Volk* to thank for both its origin and its highest flowering. (DS 5: 161–163, my emphasis)

Everyone in the German congregation can sing the Lutheran chorale. The vox populi thus emerges in the deeper vocal lines of the German liturgy available to all members of the nation. We have only to recall that, for Wagner, the people create language out of 'need' to appreciate the bond here between communal music, language, speech, and race and have only to recall the description of the authentic aesthetic-communal experience in ancient Greece to sense the utopian agenda behind this vision of a German congregation participating in its musical traditions. All forms of vocal expression emerge from a common source and provide authentic vehicles for the confirmation of racial and national identity.[33] (Thus, an implied tension in *Die Meistersinger* concerns two kinds of religious music that for Wagner represent the Jew and the German — the tension between synagogue chant, mentioned in 'Das Judentum in der Musik' and parodied in Beckmesser's nocturnal serenade, and the Lutheran chorale, which Wagner discusses in 'Über deutsches Musikwesen' and which programmatically opens the music drama of the *Volk* [figure 12] and appears in the Festwiese scene in act 3.) The German aesthetic alternative to the sonic sign of the Jew has a social dimension and is based on antithetical images of the German and the Jewish body.

But the dangerous sonic signs of un-German bodies — especially coloratura, which is clearly viewed within the work as music bereft of folkish 'roots' and associated with pedantry and intellectualism — are not solely presented in conjunction with Beckmesser. Because *Die Meistersinger* concerns the *threat* of a nonfolkish, foreign, and illegitimate aesthetics to the development of German art, Wagner makes it clear that the very (to Wagner's mind, reprehensible) music Beckmesser champions has already, by the beginning of the work, begun to infiltrate the acoustical discourse of other members of the Meistersinger guild as well. Beckmesser's coloratura poses a danger to the future of German art, which for Wagner means the future of Germany's cultural essence or identity per se, to 'what is German.' The function of coloratura as a musical representation of pedantry is made manifest when Kothner — a like-minded, conservative supporter of Beckmesser — reads to Walther the rules, engraved (in stone?) in the 'Tabulatur,' governing the makeup of an authentic 'Master-Song.' According to the logic of Wagner's musical iconography, such pedantic intellectualism must be

12. The *Meistersinger* chorale, beginning of act 1, scene 1 in the second complete draft (orchestral sketch), 1862 (Nationalarchiv der Richard Wagner–Stiftung/Richard Wagner Gedenkstätte, Bayreuth)

Example 4.
Kothner reads from
the 'Tabulatur' (A =
psalmodic dis-
course; B = melis-
matic discourse)

couched in the elevated and florid lines of coloratura, that most
non-German of musical discourses. In example 4, the pom-
pously pedantic religious aura surrounding the rules—themselves ossified into a fetish for Beckmesser and for those, such as
Kothner, who sympathize with him—is discernible in the litur-

gical quality of the music at the beginning of each of Kothner's
stanzas (A), and each stanza concludes with the kind of vocal
flourish Beckmesser so admires (B).[34] That it is the coloratura,
and not the pseudo-religious, chantlike incantation at the be-

ginning of Kothner's musical lines, that the work ultimately presents as threatening is demonstrated by the reappearance of these initial lines in Hans Sachs's 'baptism' music in act 3 — in the passage in which the cobbler-artist, beloved by the *Volk* and able to merge aesthetic innovation with German musical tradition, consecrates Walther's oneiric musical fantasy. That art has become a religion is not in itself a concern (as Wagner would later explain in the anti-Semitic essay *Religion und Kunst* [Religion and art] of 1880) so much as the antifolkish pedantic bias that has come to be associated with it and that is reflected in the antipopulist, virtuosic musical lines of Beckmesser's and Kothner's elevated coloratura. Within the spectrum of Wagner's musical vocabulary, Walther's dream-music represents the antithesis of such superficial pedantry. His fantasy is innately folkish, as evidenced not only by the *Volk*'s spontaneous and enthusiastic participation in his prize-song discussed in chapter 1, but by the fact that the music of Walther's dream-song is first heard in the orchestra at the beginning of the drama during the intervals of the chorale intoned by the congregation. Thus, from the outset, Walther's folkish music is opposed to Beckmesser's superficial, technically constructed, and merely virtuosic airs.

When Sachs christens Walther's spontaneous, anti-intellectual, and soon-to-be-populist musical dream that has emerged out of the spirit of the people, Wagner's orchestra sets the ideological stage by accompanying Sachs's statement 'A child was

Example 5. Chorale, act 1, scene 1, and Sachs 'A child was born here ...' with the chorale-melody accompaniment, act 3 of *Die Meistersinger*

born here' with the music of the pseudo-Lutheran chorale heard at the beginning of the drama (example 5). In this scene, the populist chorale, as well as Walther's music, which emerges out of and hence is associated with it, is explicitly opposed to the musical material of Beckmesser's coloratura and hence to the ideas it has come to represent in the drama, especially its deadening influence on the growth of German art. Once the chorale music has been quoted, Sachs intones the opening music

Example 6. Sachs baptizes Walther's song, act 3 of *Die Meistersinger* (A = Kothner's psalmodic discourse; C = chorale melody)

of Kothner's Tabulatur rules but *replaces Kothner's coloratura passages with the music of the opening chorale* (example 6). Wagner's musical material assumes here an 'internally representational' function; it itself conveys through associations constructed within the course of a performance specific ideas that are also expressed verbally throughout the drama. The rules of

the Meistersinger are employed in the celebration of the birth of
Walther's music, underscored by the allusions to Kothner's solemnly cantorial recitation in act 1, but the fact that Walther's
song is folkish, in tune somehow with the people's 'needs' and

essence, is represented by the invocation of the people's chorale at the very moment when, in Kothner's aria, the pedant had employed coloratura. The most unpopular of musical idioms reserved only for specialists is replaced by a vocal music available to the lower voices of the German community, as a comparison of Kothner's virtuosic melismas with the chorale's lower, stolid lines for bass makes clear. Thus, in Sachs's baptismal phrases, Beckmesser's nefarious influence is musically removed and his presence is musically replaced by that of the people, to whom the future of German art, according to the ideology of *Die Meistersinger*, rightfully belongs. Grafted onto the iconography of the human voice, Wagner's musical vocabulary establishes consistent images of fundamentally different and even antithetical kinds of people who, as represented by their vocal signs and their respective kinds of music, constitute members—or outsiders—of a community. By the conclusion to *Die Meistersinger*, Beckmesser's coloratura will have been banished and the people will have been warned by Sachs of the future threat of a corruptingly foreign, *welsch*, non-German presence within Germany's hallowed yet vibrant musical traditions.

Wagner's belief in the different nature of the Jewish voice is discernible in his remarks concerning contemporary European cultural practice and in the music he composed for his parody of the paradigmatic Jew in *Die Meistersinger* and also constitutes the basis for the acoustical idiom of one of the musically most unusual scenes of *Siegfried*, that work so illustrative of racial prejudice. In the encounter between Alberich and Mime in act 2 following Siegfried's fight with the dragon—the first confrontation between the two Nibelungs since the Nibelheim scene of *Das Rheingold*—Wagner portrays in music a parody of characteristics deemed Jewish, of Jewish speech, and above all of the purported physiological difference of the Jewish voice.[35]

While much has been made of the anti-Semitic character of Beckmesser's music, little attention has been devoted to the dialogues between Nibelungs in the *Ring*, which are especially

important for an appreciation of Wagner's conception and portrayal of Jewish speech and of the Jewish voice, because only in
them does his music depict interlocution not between a Teuton
and the foreign Jew but between two members of the Jewish
race. (In addition to the two scenes between Alberich and Mime
in *Das Rheingold* and *Siegfried*, the third dialogue between Nibelungs in the *Ring* occurs in the nocturnal exchange between Alberich and Hagen in act 2, scene 1 of *Götterdämmerung*, which I
will discuss in detail in chapter 5 in terms of its employment of
other corporeal iconographies of difference.)

In the Nibelung dialogues, Wagner highlights what he perceives to be the Jew's attempt to camouflage his speech and
voice when interacting with a non-Jew (as portrayed, for example, in Mime's interaction with Siegfried), because when Alberich and Mime converse, the veil is dropped and they reveal
themselves, through their diction, to be what they 'really' are
(and not, Wagner would have argued, to be representations of
his culturally encoded perception of them). The subject of their
exchange is avarice, that most Jewish of attributes, for the two
figures are obsessed with attaining the Ring and with it limitless
wealth and power. By inventing music of a deprecating and
exaggeratedly grotesque nature, Wagner was able to emphasize
the purported gap between the Jew's 'true' essence and the mask
the foreign being assumes when attempting to intermingle with
(and to the anti-Semitic imagination that means to infiltrate the
community of) the non-Jew.

It is important to bear in mind the shifting nature of the
function of the Alberich-Mime confrontation within the context of the *Ring*'s development. Because Wagner initially conceived of the *Ring* as a single drama — *Siegfrieds Tod* (Siegfried's
death) — and only later added anterior dramas in order to clarify
the actions leading up to the final work, the material he presented in the original version of *Siegfried* was primarily important as *narrative* information.[36] The first drama he added to
Siegfrieds Tod — *Der junge Siegfried* — was primarily intended to
present characters and events on stage that would make the

machinations of the final work more intelligible. It is for this reason that *Götterdämmerung*, *Siegfried*, and *Die Walküre* all contain such extensive narratives recalling the events of *Das Rheingold* (and earlier occurrences as well, as seen in the Norn's exchange in the opening scene of *Götterdämmerung*). Thus, when Wagner first wrote the text to *Der junge Siegfried* in 1851, the narrative material would have been of utmost importance to him in terms of its impartment of information necessary to an understanding of the drama.[37] But when he later came to compose the music for *Siegfried*, having written the texts and composed the music to *Das Rheingold* and *Die Walküre*, this narrative material would have become merely of secondary importance, for it was by then a redundant recapitulation of events already portrayed on stage. Thus, when Wagner set about in the summer of 1857 to compose the scene in *Siegfried* between Alberich and Mime, the *characterization* of the two figures had assumed greater importance than the informational content of their exchange.[38] That characterization is effected through a parody of the perceived idiosyncrasies of Jewish speech and of the Jewish body.

In the narrative of the *Ring* cycle, Alberich and Mime are brothers, but they are not, however, identical. Alberich is the more powerful of the two, the potential ruler who assumes a kind of tragic grandeur in the course of the work, while Mime is more of a *Quetsch* and *Schlemiehl*, a tragic-comic, eternal loser always bewailing his fate and doomed to suffer an ignoble death. When they are contrasted to the young German superhero, Siegfried, their musical characterization is similar, but when they are alone they assume more distinct identities and characterizations. At all times, however, they sound remarkably different from the German superman.

After Siegfried has vanquished Fafner, he enters the dragon's cave, having been guided there by the voice of Nature in the form of the Forest Bird, and when he does so his movement is accompanied by a calm and splendid music in the horns and strings. Once he is lost to sight, however, Wagner's musical material shifts to a hurried, impetuous, and abrupt motive in the woodwinds (marked 'Schnell und drängend'), suggestive of an aggressive and ungainly gait and nervous tension. Mime 'sneaks and creeps' onto the scene ('schleicht heran') and is immediately and violently accosted by his brother (figure 13). In the 'Allegro con impeto' that follows, the vocal lines of the two Nibelungs are characterized by wildly disjunctive, dissonant, and sweeping gestures and staccato attacks in the upper halves of the singers' registers (example 7). Alberich's repeated arpeggios are characterized by a rapid eighth-note movement and numerous accidentals (literally 'foreign' tones in the tonal context), often rising to d′♭, d′, and e′♭, while Mime's outbursts, containing even more rapid, sixteenth-note signs of agitation, hover around e′, f′, and g′♭ and even rise at one point in this opening section to a high and plaintive g′. Wagner claimed that Jewish vocal music, which he associated in 'Das Judentum in der Musik' with Jewish speech, had the effect of a 'prickling restlessness [*prinkelnde Unruhe*]' (GS 13: 21), and, in describing the acoustical idio-

13. Arthur Rackham, 'The dwarfs quarreling over the body of Fafner,' 1911 (From *The Ring of the Niblung*, trans. Margaret Armor, vol.2 [New York: Abaris Books, 1976])

Example 7.
The opening of the exchange between Alberich and Mime in act 2, scene 3 of *Siegfried*

Wo- hin schleichst du ei - lig und schlau, schlim- mer Ge - sell? Ver - fluch- ter

Bru - der, dich braucht' ich hier! Was bringt dich her? Geizt es dich, Schelm, nach mei - nem

Gold? Ver - langst du mein Gut? Fort von der Stel - le! Die Stät - te ist

mein: was stö- berst du hier? Stör' ich dich wohl im stil - len Ge - schäft, wenn du hier

stiehlst? Was ich er- schwang mit schwe - rer Müh', soll mir nicht schwin - den.

syncrasies of such speech, he emphasizes the Jew's 'nervous energy': 'The cold indifference of the idiosyncratic "blabbering" in [Jewish speech] rises for no reason to a stimulation of higher, heart-filled passion [*zur Erregtheit höherer, herzdurchglühter Leidenschaft*]' (*GS* 13: 14). It rises 'for no reason' perceptible to the German other than the innately different, nervous physiology of the Jew. Like Beckmesser's sonic signatures, the musical discourse of the Nibelungs' confrontation — especially in terms of its volatile, 'nervous' character — constitutes an acoustical representation of (this perception of) the Jew's vocal production.[39] The 'hissing and gurgling' of Jewish speech that Wagner emphasizes in 'Das Judentum in der Musik' is discernible in the violent interlocution of the Nibelungs in large part because much of their exchange is set to a staccato and dissonant music in the upper half of their vocal registers.

This becomes particularly pronounced toward the end of their dialogue, just before Siegfried returns from the dragon's lair, when, despite Mime's sycophantic attempts at bargaining and compromise, Alberich tells him that he will never receive an ounce of gold. The tempo accelerates to 'vivace' ('schnell') and both Nibelung voices rise to their maximum heights (marked 'kreischend,' or 'screeching,' for Mime), accompanied by the characteristic musical features of sforzandi, fortissimo, staccato, and grace-note attacks (example 8). Here, Albrich's discourse recalls one of the earliest verbal characterizations of the Nibelung found in the *Ring*, Flosshilde's description of the dwarf's voice as a *Gekrächz* (*RN*, 11), an onomatopoetic expression suggesting a sound somewhat lower than a screech but more abrasive than a squawk and thus, again, similar, though not identical, to Mime's.

Nineteenth-century audiences were sensitive and receptive to the racist implications of Wagner's musical material for the Nibelungs. The representation of purportedly Jewish characteristics in Mime's music was made note of, for example, by none other than Gustav Mahler, a man immensely cognizant of the role anti-Semitism played in nineteenth-century European

Example 8. Mime's hysterical *Mauscheln* in act 2 of *Siegfried*

culture and of the use of music as a cultural code. In a passage from a letter of 1898 to Natalie Bauer-Lechner, Mahler stated what I believe must have been obvious to Wagner's contemporaries: 'No doubt with Mime, Wagner intended to ridicule the Jews (with all their characteristic traits — petty intelligence and greed — the jargon is textually *and musically* so cleverly suggested' (my emphasis).[40] The 'jargon' Mahler has in mind and to which Wagner had referred in 'Das Judentum in der Musik' was defined by the perception of the Jew's voice as different, nasal, nervous, and high, an image of the Jew's body that would later reemerge in *Salome*, with its quintet of Jews set for one bass and *four* tenors. It was no invention of Wagner's but a belief deeply entrenched within his culture that he chose to exploit and to portray on stage in his musical-dramatic caricatures of Jews.

MUSSORGSKY'S NIBELUNGS

The most characteristic feature of the Nibelungs' music is the fundamentally different sonic qualities that segregate their discourse from that of the Teutons. Yet their vocal music is not solely, though most obviously, conceived as a foil to that of the representatives of qualities deemed German — to that of the gods, the first Volsungs, and Siegfried. It is also a music that is based on the juxtaposition of *two* distinct stereotypes of Jews with widespread currency in the nineteenth century: the wealthy and the impoverished Jew.[41] These stereotypes, as we have seen in the previous chapter, are already discernible in 'Das Judentum in der Musik,' in which Wagner devotes a section to the idiosyncrasies of the 'educated Jew' that distinguish the figure from the vast pale of his more 'barbaric' fellow Semites (*GS* 13: 16). *Der gebildete Jude* is more refined, and hence presumably more wealthy, than his more 'Eastern' racial compatriot, but both the upper- and the lower-class Jew — both the figure with pretensions to grandeur and the one more obviously impoverished and despairingly plaintive — are equally removed from the dominant culture that rejects them (and, for Wagner, from an authentic relationship to that culture's art as well). Both types are clichés, each a manifestation of difference set off from Occidental culture, and, despite the fact that their wealth differs, both are defined by unbridled avarice. As caricatures of Jews, Alberich and Mime share similar discursive features, yet, as representatives of the stereotypes of the wealthy and the impoverished Jew, the Nibelungs are given two distinct and characteristically defining sounds that credibly distinguish them to the Western ear. (It was no coincidence that toward the end of his life, in 'Erkenne dich selbst,' Wagner referred to Alberich's ring as a 'Börsenportefeuille,' or 'stock portfolio' [GS 14: 186].[42] Though Alberich is vile, uncouth, and repulsive and hence comparable to the stereotype of the Eastern Jew, he is also clearly — albeit only temporarily — associated with enormous wealth and hence is also a representation of the Western Jew striving for acceptance by a world that will not accept him, as his many resentment-filled comments to Wotan make clear.) Just as the notion of the Jewish voice as higher than that of the non-Jew was part of a cultural vocabulary upon which Wagner drew, so the bifurcation of the Jew into two stereotypes, each with its own distinctive sound, was also not Wagner's invention but was based on anti-Semitic images pervasive in nineteenth-century culture.

Many have been reticent to recognize anti-Semitic stereotypes in the Nibelungs' music because Wagner never labeled them Jews. But comparison of this music with another nineteenth-century composition which does contain such an explicit reference suggests that a little over a hundred years ago, a musical idiom, such as that employed by Wagner, constituted sonic signs that explicitly referred to or at least evoked widely accepted stereotypes. I would argue that the juxtaposition of the music of Alberich and Mime is remarkably reminiscent of the musical portrayal of 'Two Jews, One Rich, One Poor: Samuel Goldenberg and Schmuÿle' in Mussorgsky's *Pictures at an Exhibition* of 1874, composed in commemoration of the painter Victor Hartmann (1834–1873), himself a Jew.[43] The themes of the

Goldenberg   Schmuÿle

Example 9.
Mussorgsky's themes
for Goldenberg and
Schmuÿle

two figures, designated as Jews, are shown in example 9. The similarity between Wagner's and Mussorgsky's musical material casts light on the assumptions and associations that attended Wagner's score in his time. In both Wagner's music drama and Mussorgsky's piece for piano, two contrasting stereotypes of Jews are portrayed in contrasting acoustical idioms that function as musical codes based on the culturally pervasive images of Jews in the nineteenth century. Alberich's and Goldenberg's musical representations are characterized by a sonority of dark, rich colors and agitated, abrupt forte sforzando attacks; to both the nineteenth-century listener, I would argue, and to the ear today, their music evokes self-aggrandizement, authoritarianism, and violence. Their similar musical idioms contrast markedly with the equally similar sonic features assigned to Mime and Schmuÿle. In part, this contrast is effected through the different timbres of the two figures: in Wagner, through the juxtaposition of the bass and the high-tenor voice (despite the fact that Alberich, like Mime, is often singing at the top of his register), and in Mussorgsky through the diverse sonorities of Goldenberg's and Schmuÿle's themes. Mime and Schmuÿle are represented by elevated motives that employ trills and grace notes — in the upper woodwinds and strings for Wagner and in the treble registers of the piano in Mussorgsky — that may be heard to connote wailing and to evoke both sycophantic and hyperactive beings, as the Russian musicologist Mikhail Zetlin's description of Mussorgsky's short piece flatly states: 'Then there is the amusing scene of two Jews arguing, one of them wealthy and pompous and barking away like a bulldog, the other poor and cringing before him in a plaintive treble.'[44] Michael Russ's description of the technical features of Mussorgsky's piece — and of the drama he believes they imply — could,

146 Chapter Two: Voices

with only slight modification, be applied to Wagner's vocal and orchestral music for his Nibelungs:

Goldenberg speaks first in an assertive, blustering way with something of an oriental quality in the rhythmically intricate ornamentation and augmented intervals. He speaks slowly and clearly with a deep powerful voice, in measured lengths, pausing for breath. Then the poor Jew whines almost uncontrollably in a high voice with a triplet tremolo representing his teeth chattering or his body trembling. The B♭♭ minor flourishes at the end of Schmuÿle's idea have a touch of orientalism. In the end, Goldenberg, a nasty, wily and mean character, gives nothing to Schmuÿle, simply sending him off with a flea in his ear.[45]

Both Wagner and Mussorgsky employ acoustical gestures that speak to the prejudicial expectations of their audiences by reminding their listeners of stereotypical images of Jews, images that Hartmann himself must have internalized (and found, moreover, in the various orchestral versions of Mussorgsky's piece as well).[46] While, on the one hand, both Alberich and Mime sing in their upper registers for purportedly metaphorical and physiological reasons and in so doing represent musically one anti-Semitic stereotype (the Jew's nasal and elevated voice), they have, on the other hand, radically distinctive timbres which correspond to the two distinctive clichés of the rich and the poor Jew.

It is precisely through the association of these two stereotypes with their distinctive elocution that a link can be drawn between Wagner and Mussorgsky, for, like the German, the Russian, too, strove to represent the *speech patterns* of his imagined Jewish figures through his music. The musical representation of speech was the key to Mussorgsky's concept of realism, the cornerstone of his aesthetics of composition, which explains his emphasis on vocal music, song, and opera throughout his career. In his discussion of *Pictures at an Exhibition*, Russ underscores this point:

'Truth,' which in Russian means both veracity and justice, is a key concept in realism. In Musorgsky it relates both to truthful translation of Russian speech-tones into music and truth in depicting Russian life. In his songs and operatic projects his principal concern was to depict with accuracy and to draw . . . sound portraits of Russian characters and their speech from many walks of life and in widely different situations. Vocal music is at the heart of realism. . . . In *Pictures* we frequently find him imitating vocal music rather than exploiting the qualities of the piano. . . .

Even without a text, realistic depiction of character types is important in *Pictures* and may be achieved through manner of speech.[47]

If we bear in mind that Wagner drew attention to the Jew's idiosyncratic speech in 'Das Judentum in der Musik' and we hear the discourse assigned to his Nibelungs (restricted to them and idiosyncratic within the musical styles of the *Ring*) as reminiscent of the specific, distinguishing characteristics he identified as typically Jewish, a comparison with Mussorgsky's music — explicitly identified as a representation of Jews — readily emerges. Both composers appear to have striven to represent within their music speech patterns they deemed typical of Jews and relied on similar musical idioms to do so. The similarities in their musical-dramatic portrayals point to widespread and yet consistently standardized images of Jews in the nineteenth century.

*

Just as the sounds of Beckmesser are opposed to the low, communal musical lines of the *Volk* in *Die Meistersinger*, so in the *Ring* the grotesquely elevated sounds of the Nibelungs are set off from the musical interlocution of the Teutonic *Wälsungenpaar*, Siegmund and Sieglinde. The notion of a vocal confirmation of racial and national identity forms the basis of Wagner's musical portrayal of these figures, his metaphor of the German *Volk*, as discussed in the previous chapter, who merge out of 'need' to create the racially pure being Siegfried. Their union is the *Ring*'s microcosmic, symbolic equivalent to the numerically larger unified community of the *Volk* in *Die Meistersinger*. The many visual motifs that underscore their identity as physiologically similar — as 'family' — are accompanied by a host of acous-

tical motifs that have the same metaphorical function. It is of
course their eyes through which the Volsungs initially discern
their shared identity, but Wagner's theoretical reflections on the
Artwork of the Future repeatedly draw attention to the relationship between eye and ear in the makeup of that new, revolutionary work, as the passage from *Oper und Drama* cited at the
opening of this chapter clearly states, and it is therefore only
consistent that by listening to Siegmund's *voice* Sieglinde recognizes herself when she gazes upon her physiologically so similar
twin brother, as she explains to him in their love-duet in act 1:

> was im Busen ich barg,
> was ich bin,
> hell wie der Tag
> taucht' es mir auf,
> wie tönender Schall
> schlug's an mein Ohr,
> als in frostig öder Fremde
> zuerst ich den Freund ersah. . . .
> O still! Laß mich
> der Stimme lauschen:
> mich dünkt, ihren Klang
> hört' ich als Kind —
> Doch nein, ich hörte sie neulich,
> als meiner Stimme Schall
> mir widerhallte der Wald.
> SIEGMUND: O lieblichste Laute,
> denen ich lausche! (RN, 91–93)

[what I harbored in my breast, what I am, rose shining within me like
the day, like a ringing sound it struck my ear when, in the frosty
barren foreign place, I recognized my friend for the first time. . . . Be
still! Let me listen again to that voice: it seems to me I heard its
sound as a child — But no! I heard it not long ago, when the woods
returned the sound of my voice to me.
SIEGMUND: O sweetest sounds to which I listen!]

Their listening serves the same purpose as their vision: They
can scarcely distinguish between their own sounds and those of

their family member, because by listening, they view (hear) the reflection of their own (acoustical) image. Through this process they discern their commonality — their community. This passage is a dramatic parallel to Wagner's statement in 'Das Kunstwerk der Zukunft': 'Only that which loves can make itself understood, and to love means to acknowledge the other person and thus at the same time to recognize one's self' (DS 6: 38). To 'know thyself' is to recognize oneself in the physiological similarity of one's compatriots, not in their visual appearance alone but in their voices as well, and in the voice of the nation's art fashioned through common need. In *Die Walküre*, Wagner's theoretical reflections from *Oper und Drama* concerning the visual and the acoustical components of the Artwork of the Future found their dramatic representation. Recalling his thoughts on the relationship between the different arts in the future, Total Work of Art, eye and ear in act 1 of *Die Walküre* relinquish their 'egotistical' individuation and merge as equal partners in a 'superior communication,' and this process itself provides a metaphor for the process of de-individuation within both the long-lost (Greek) and the future, superior (German) folkish community; sight and sound merge in the Wagnerian artwork, just as the individual Greek or German in Wagner's utopian reflections subsumes his or her identity within the communal body of kindred folk. When writing of the relation between 'eye and ear,' between gesture and 'orchestral language,' Wagner pointedly described the former as 'das schwesterliche Auge [the sibling (or literally "sisterly") eye]' (DS 7: 315), in order to underscore the purportedly natural, familial, and therefore folkish relationship between vision and hearing. In this context the incest of Siegmund and Sieglinde is metaphorically consistent. If the Teutonic family is a metaphor for racial and national community, breeding within domestic boundaries preserves the national essence from the filth of foreign invasion. This is the very idea Wagner later emphasizes in 'Erkenne dich selbst' when he argues that Germany must breed from itself if it is to stave off the threat of Jewish influence. Better to have an inbred national family of musicians (whose superiority is made manifest in the supreme being Siegfried) than to have the high and nervous melismas of a slimy Beckmesser win the German maiden.

At this point it is worth pausing to reflect upon the fact that the essays Wagner wrote prior to his stay in Paris from 1840 to 1842 — before 'Über deutsches Musikwesen' — reveal an altogether different understanding of vocal production. Before working for (and so resenting) Moritz Schlesinger, Wagner appears to have had great *respect* for the art of singing associated with Italy, as his earliest writings from 1834 to his initial work in Paris demonstrate. It was only after the frustrating experiences of the early 1840s that Wagner developed a consistent interpretation of the human voice as an icon of racial identity which he would use metaphorically in his diverse and yet intimately related essays and music dramas. That is, while the cultural vocabulary of early nineteenth-century Europe already contained the acoustical icon of the Jewish voice as providing a high and nasal sound (as reflected in the writings of Stendhal and the music of Rossini), Wagner appears not to have adopted (and adapted) it until his own anti-Semitism had developed into a central component of his understanding of the arts in the modern world.

From the time Wagner wrote his first article, 'Die deutsche Oper' (The German opera), in 1834 to his stay in Paris, his remarks concerning Italian and French opera and the characteristics of superior singing were, in terms of their ideological implications, diametrically opposed to those he would make following his move to the French capital.[48] In his first published tract (which appeared in June 1834 in Heinrich Laube's *Zeitung für die elegante Welt*), Wagner waxed ecstatic about the beauty of Italian vocal production and its superiority over German singing. After deploring the fact that even his beloved Weber did not understand how to write music conducive to the physiological production of song (claiming that he had 'nie den Gesang zu behandeln verstanden') (*DS* 5: 9), Wagner extols the work of the

Italian Bellini and the French opera from Gluck to Grétry and
Auber. Italian opera, he claims, is based on the 'beauty of song
[*Gesangsschönheit*],' which makes its figures 'sensually warm
[*sinnlich-warm*].' He concludes his first, short essay with the
statement that his conception of the ideal opera would be one
that employed the finest features of both the Italians and the
French(!) (*DS* 5: 11–12).

His next essay, 'Pasticcio,' published five months later in November 1834 in the *Neue Zeitschrift für Musik* under the (for our
purposes revealing) nom de plume Canto Spianato ('calm [or]
even song'), expands upon this early denigration of German
singing and its glorification of Italian vocalization. Claiming
that he rejects any instrumentalization of the voice in the manner of Bach's followers (a striking statement, considering the
ideological function of the Bach Passions in his later writings),
Wagner supports instead a German adaptation of the 'good
Italian cantabile style [*den guten italienischen Kontabilitätsstil*]'
based on a natural foundation of breath and articulation (*DS* 5:
18). In this context it is significant that in his later tract 'Bericht
an Seine Majestät den König Ludwig II. von Bayern über eine
in München zu errichtende deutsche Musikschule' (Report to
His Majesty King Ludwig II of Bavaria on a German music
school to be established in Munich) of 1865, Wagner insisted
that a German vocal style should not be based on the 'Modell
des italienischen Gesangs' — he writes instead of a careful, judicious adaptation of the Italian school which emphasizes the
incompatibility of the physiological makeup of the Italian and the
German voice (*GS* 12: 243). Because that German voice, like its
singing, is so intimately, physiologically connected to the German language in his post-1848 writings, Wagner states in his
report to the king that the goal of the future German music
school will be 'to place song in the correct relationship to the
uniqueness of the German language' (*GS* 12: 242). And to the
post-1840 Wagner, only Germans, of course, can speak and sing
like Germans; anyone else attempting to do so sounds like a
foreigner, or even like a parrot. But in 'Pasticcio' of the 1830s,

Wagner is even willing to incorporate into this German adaptation the art of bel canto ornamentation, a statement that would be unthinkable after his interaction with Schlesinger and that *Die Meistersinger* would later portray as nonsensical.

The next essay from this period, 'Der dramatische Gesang' (Dramatic song) of 1837, remains very much in this vein and speaks glowingly of the Italian school's paradigmatic 'highest purity of tone,' 'highest precision and roundedness [*Rundung*],' and the 'highest smoothness of [its] passages' (*DS* 5: 22), the metaphorical quality of which (high = better), of course, Wagner would later reverse. The next tract of 1837, 'Bellini: ein Wort zu seiner Zeit' (Bellini: A word on his time), extols the composer's *Norma* and his talent for writing 'clear, comprehensible melody' (*DS* 5: 26–27). This was also the period in which Wagner wrote works for the stage intentionally (and reverently) modeled on the tradition of Italian and French Grand Opéra: *Die Feen* (The fairies) (called a 'große romantische Oper') from 1833–34; *Das Liebesverbot* (The ban on love) (a 'große komische Oper') in 1835; and *Rienzi* (a 'große tragische Oper'), which he began in 1838, prior to meeting Schlesinger, and completed in Paris in 1840.[49] In 'Eine Mitteilung an meine Freunde' Wagner himself even admitted that the latter was ruled by 'der italienisch-französische Melismus [the Italian-French melismatic discourse] (*DS* 6: 304). In terms of the national provenance of their musical styles, then, *Rienzi* and *Die Meistersinger* would appear diametrically opposed.

It is significant that even in these early, pro-Italian and proFrench essays Wagner writes of the physiological difference between German and non-German voices. Because the foreign cultures are not yet despised as Jew-ridden and inimical to the development of German art, however, he only mentions these physiological differences in passing, stating only that they will make the German adaptation of an Italian vocal school difficult. Even at this early stage he believes in the physiological differences of national vocal production, but he does not yet use them as metaphors of national and racial difference. In 'Pasticcio,' for example, he maintains that the physical, technical, and psychological limitations of the individual (German) singer must be borne in mind when the singer learns the Italian style (*DS* 5: 15), and in 'Der dramatische Gesang' he asks, in speaking of a 'deutschen Belcanto,' 'what can the effect produce if it goes beyond the organic abilities?' (*DS* 5: 23). Clearly here, too, the German is equipped with a different kind of voice—with a lower instrument—but only later will Wagner draw ideological conclusions from this purported physiological difference.

When compared with the essays Wagner penned after his move to Paris and his initial interaction with the 'Judaized' music world, these early tracts offer an ideologically startling contrast to his later understanding of the human voice as an icon of racial and national identity. Having already established in his essays of the 1830s the notion that foreign (Italian and French) voices were higher, and having been raised in a culture replete with corporeal images of Jews denoting their supposed difference and inferiority, Wagner had only to merge his perception of the Jew as influential in the Italian and French music worlds with his belief in the physiological difference of the Jewish and the German voice to discover a powerful icon of race which would speak both metaphorically and realistically to his age. Following his experience with Moritz Schlesinger, the notion of Jewish and Italian voices as diametrically opposed to superior and deeper German sounds would remain a component of Wagner's thought for the rest of his life.

WAGNER'S 'PILGRIMAGE TO BEETHOVEN'

'Über deutsches Musikwesen,' in which the transvaluation of vocal differences first emerges in Wagner's thought, contains more than one alternative to Jewish (and Jew-infested) art and vocal production. Just as the communal chorale in *Die Meistersinger* and the sonic union of the *Wälsungs* in the mythic past of the *Ring* constitute representations of insular moments from Germany's folkish past, so this essay suggests that the chorale no longer corresponds to the needs of the present, and thus, for Wagner, it is not the modern vehicle for the reestablishment of a cultural and national unity threatened by foreign countries and by the racially foreign living within nineteenth-century Germany. Wagner's early essay locates such folkish commonality in another, more contemporary, different, and yet specifically German art that also requires the communal efforts of like-minded, musically inclined members of the nation and that is also intimately associated for him with the physiology of the human voice. The modern vehicle for the aesthetic redemption of the German community is German orchestral music, especially that of Beethoven, which is found throughout the provincial make-up of Wagner's contemporary homeland. Wagner explicitly equates the turn to instrumental music, above all to Beethoven's, with a national message: a rejection of foreign voices and of a foreign vocal technique suited to the expectations of the international music scene:

[The] lack of beautiful vocal training directs the German to instrumental music . . . , where the artist [is] free of every foreign and confining influence. . . . To realize the masterpieces of this genre of art there is no need for precious foreign singers. . . . And is it possible, with the most lavish additions of all the other arts, to erect a more sumptuous and sublime building than a simple orchestra is capable of constructing in the performance of one of Beethoven's symphonies? Most surely not! (DS 5: 158–159)

Beethoven's instrumental music provides for modern Germany the same communal-aesthetic experience once integral to the reception of art in ancient Greece and to the pious *Volk* participating in the liturgical singing of the Bach Passions because, Wagner stated, Germans are innately 'musical' and naturally bond together as a community when they experience the collective performance of an authentically and quintessentially German work of art. Beethoven's symphonies provide a model of hope for modern Germany, and for its future. Little wonder, then, that Wagner repeatedly emphasized the connection be-

tween his own Artworks of the Future and the works of Beethoven; his would constitute the continuation of a, to his mind,
specifically German communal-aesthetic tradition. The icon of
the voice provides a link, then, between Wagner's pronouncements on foreign cultural production and on the superior aesthetics of the most German of his forbears, Beethoven.

Following his employment of the voice as a corporeal sign of
nation and race in 'Über deutsches Musikwesen,' Wagner used it
again in a short story he wrote for Schlesinger entitled 'Eine
Pilgerfahrt zu Beethoven' (A pilgrimage to Beethoven), published shortly after 'Über deutsches Musikwesen' under the title
'Une visite à Beethoven: épisode de la vie d'un musicien alle-
mand' in four issues of the *Gazette musicale* in November and
December of 1840.[50] Indeed, the short story may be read as a
fictional representation of concepts expressed more explicitly in
the earlier essay. In his vindictive autobiography *Mein Leben* of
1870, Wagner characterized Schlesinger as a 'monstrous acquaintance' who had exploited the young composer's destitution
and had forced him to accomplish tasks he detested, such as
providing the publisher with operatic piano-vocal scores, arrangements for trumpet, guitar, and string quartet, potpourris,
and even a pedagogical manual for the *cornet à pistons*,[51] and
these details reappear in trenchant form in his narrative text. In
the autobiographical 'Eine Mitteilung an meine Freunde,' Wagner made it clear that his Beethoven novella, commissioned by
Schlesinger, was an attack on the publisher and everything the
Jew represented:

In order to get me money, the publisher of the *Gazette musicale* assigned
me, along with the arrangements of melodies, the task of writing articles for his journal. Both meant the same to him: but not to me. Just as I
had felt in *the former kind of work* my deepest humiliation, so I seized
upon *the latter*, in order to take revenge for my humiliation. After a few
musical articles of a general nature I wrote a kind of artistic novella, 'A
Pilgrimage to Beethoven.' . . . Here I represented, with invented features and with considerable humor, my own fate, namely in Paris. (DS
6: 234)

Wagner's novella was conceived as an act of revenge. Though the theme of vocal pitch as an icon of racial and national identity is less overt in the 'Pilgerfahrt' than in the previous essay, it can be discerned here as well within a context of competing national characteristics, and the short story, too, is redolent with Francophobic and anti-Semitic sentiment, though Wagner strove to mask them here more than he did in his expository writing. Analysis of this short story establishes once again a connection between Wagner's early Parisian writings on German and non-German culture and his later aesthetic program based on the voice as both racist corporeal icon and metaphor.

When Wagner's protagonist 'R.,' who describes himself as 'a simple German soul' (*DS* 5: 100), meets a group of Bohemian musicians at the outset of his pilgrimage to Vienna, they perform together a septet by Beethoven with the naive spontaneity unique to the German character and antithetical to the superficiality of the international institutions of culture. When they make music, they recall the small domestic ensemble idealized in 'Über deutsches Musikwesen': 'O what delight! Here on a Bohemian country road, under an open sky, Beethoven's Septuor played by dance-musicians with a purity, a precision, and such *depth of feeling* seldom found among the most masterful virtuosi!' (*DS* 5: 90, my emphasis). Immediately following this performance, the nemesis of the story, the villainous Englishman who threatens R.'s pilgrimage at every step of his journey, makes his first appearance and offers the musicians 'a gold coin,' which they refuse. The opposition of superior German musicality and the corrupt mercantilism of the modern, non-German music aficionado is blatantly manifest and will be present with every reappearance of the Englishman throughout the tale. As such, the figure anticipates Wagner's description in 'Die Kunst und die Revolution' of the 'bigoted English banker' as a symbol of the prostitution of art in the modern world (*DS* 5: 285). In the short story, Wagner associates the Englishman with the Jews, the Italians, and the French.[52] Like the internationally foreign and well-to-do Jews, he is wealthy and is himself a composer; at the end of the story, he's off to pay his respects to Italy for the same shallow reason he has visited Beethoven — 'I wish to know Mr. Rossini,' he admits, 'as he is a very famous composer' (*DS* 5: 112) — an example of musical taste that also links him to the Parisians, characterized elsewhere in the story as culture vultures. R., on the other hand, represents the German antithesis to England, Italy, France, and international wealth; he turns 'to the north, uplifted in heart and ennobled' as the 'Pilgerfahrt' closes. For the purposes of his cultural criticism, Wagner could of course have made the foreign nemesis a Frenchman, but he chose to make him English and to associate him with Italy because he was writing for a French audience, who could not know that the three countries were ideologically indistinguishable in Wagner's nationalist and racist cosmology as having all fallen under the horrible influence of the Jews.

For Wagner, the central theme of German musicality threatened by the alienating forces of modern, foreign civilization is played out in Vienna, the goal of R.'s pilgrimage, and it is here that Wagner presents two antithetical images of the human voice, one virtuosic and French and one part of a community and hence *urdeutsch*. In order to underscore the besieged and tenuous position of authentic German art and artistic feeling in nineteenth-century Europe, Wagner portrays Vienna as both German and non-German, as both sharing, through its language, a tie with Germany's folkish cultural traditions and as revealing, through the superficiality of its Parisianlike culture industry, a dystopic vision of a possible future for Germany as well. Wagner's Beethoven — 'a poor German musician' (*DS* 5: 88) — describes the reception of his works in Vienna in terms recalling 'Über deutsches Musikwesen': ' "I do believe . . . that my compositions speak more directly to Northern Germany. The Viennese annoy me often; daily they hear too much bad stuff ever to be disposed to approach in earnest something that is serious" ' (*DS* 5:106). This assessment is initially shared by R., who speaks of the 'somewhat shallow sensuousness of the Viennese' (*DS* 5: 102), but at one point, not coincidentally during a performance of *Fidelio*, the narrator describes the Austrians explicitly as German: 'Wilhelmine Schröder . . . [has] the high distinction of having revealed Beethoven's work to the German public; for truly I saw on that evening even the superficial Viennese seized by the most powerful enthusiasm' (*DS* 5: 102).[53] There is hope for the Viennese after all! They are at least capable of the kind of reception commensurate with German art and might be saved from the influence of foreign culture if they only attended more often to the genius in their midst.

But their taste has come to resemble perilously that of the Parisians. Galops and potpourris, says Beethoven, so beloved by the French, are popular in the Austrian capital (*DS* 5: 111), and in lamenting the trials of an opera composer writing for a Viennese audience with Parisian expectations, Beethoven makes the connection between the two cities explicit: ' "He who has to stitch all kinds of pretty things for ladies with passable voices to get *bravi* and applause should become a Parisian lady's-tailor, but not a dramatic composer" ' (*DS* 5: 107). The notion of the virtuosic voice as an instrument suited to the disjointed and heterogeneous works performed at the Grand Opéra is a notion associated with the French culture industry and, by extension, with its Jewish bankers and publishers. It is a kind of voice that is associated with operatic patchworks intended for a 'barbaric-Judaistic mishmash,' as Wagner would later describe modern civilization in 'Erkenne dich selbst' (*GS* 14: 186). The non-unified, multifarious work reflects its social context, and the high voice is its vocal icon.

The nefarious influence of the culture industry pervades not only German-speaking Austria but (northern) Germany as well, R.'s homeland and the site from which his pilgrimage originates. That the Franco-Jewish commodification of culture has emerged even there is made manifest in R.'s dealings with his German publisher, which recall in vivid detail Wagner's frustrated relationship to Schlesinger. (When the Jew published Wagner's setting of 'Deux Grenadiers' in the *Gazette musicale*, it failed to attract the attention of the influential singers Wagner had longed for and instead only brought Wagner a debt of fifty francs, payable to Schlesinger.)[54]

A few pianoforte-sonatas, which I had composed following the master's model, I carried to the publisher; in a word or two the man made clear to me that I was a fool with my sonatas. He gave me the advice, however, that if I wanted to some day earn a thaler or two with my compositions, I should begin by establishing for myself a little reputation through galops and potpourris. . . . To my misfortune, however, I was not even paid for these earliest sacrifices of my innocence, for my publisher explained that I first must earn myself a little name. I shuddered again and fell into despair. That despair, however, brought forth some capital galops. I actually received money for them. (*DS* 5: 88–89)

The pilgrimage thus constitutes a search for redemption (that Wagnerian idée fixe) for German music from a mercantile approach to art associated with higher and thus superficial (and implicitly Judaized) culture. After meeting Beethoven, R. will never again succumb to the demands of those who exploit culture as a commodity.

This evocation of Schlesinger is more than mere coincidence, because Wagner conceived 'Eine Pilgerfahrt zu Beethoven' as a surreptitious attack specifically on Jewish influence in the modern music world, typified for him by his Jewish employer, and the person of Schlesinger is the clandestine target of Wagner's narrative. While Schlesinger is discernible behind the characterization of R.'s publisher, it was primarily through the Englishman that Wagner ridiculed the entrepreneurial Jew, for the Englishman is nothing less than a portrait of Moritz Schlesinger himself, who had journeyed to Vienna in 1819 on behalf of his father's publishing house in order to secure from the composer the rights to Beethoven's opera 108–112, 132, and 135. It was only after successfully completing his mission that Schlesinger moved to Paris and published there simultaneous first editions of Beethoven's piano sonatas opera 110 and 111 in 1822 and 1823, followed in 1827 by the string quartets opera 130, 132,

133, and 135.[55] Thus, in the very period in which it is set (the early months of 1824, during which Beethoven's Ninth Symphony was completed but not yet performed),[56] the Jewish entrepreneur was involved in the very activities that Wagner's narrative denounces.

But how could the owner of the *Gazette musicale* have so missed the criticism directed at his person, his adopted country, and his race? The answer may lie in the fact that Schlesinger undoubtedly associated Wagner's narrative with another, far more flattering fictional depiction of his journey to Beethoven that he had published in his journal six years earlier and that he himself very likely commissioned. The first two issues of his *Gazette musicale* in 1834 had contained a short story by Jules Janin entitled 'Le Dîner de Beethoven: conte fantastique' that transpires in 1819 and that depicts the visit to Beethoven of a Frenchman who alone, unlike the insensitive Germans, appreciates the musician's genius.[57] Janin's work was obviously a veiled homage to Schlesinger, which the publisher was not averse to distributing in his newly founded journal. Wagner either became acquainted with the piece through Janin himself, whom he mentioned twice in print during his stay in Paris and who, as a colleague of Berlioz and an influential critic with the *Journal des Débats*, was a well-known figure in the Parisian music world, or Schlesinger may have directed his attention to it, implying or stating outright that the text had proven successful with his French readership and could provide a model for Wagner, a young and at that time still inexperienced writer of fiction.[58]

Wagner may have intentionally preserved numerous superficial motivic similarities to Janin's text in order to appeal to his publisher and to his French audience while fashioning a story that clandestinely ridiculed Janin's Francophilic and implicitly pro-Jewish sentiment. Wagner's text, like Janin's, glorifies a visit to Beethoven, but it covertly associates its biographical model, the Jew Schlesinger, with an understanding of art that Wagner despised. Structurally, his most fundamental departure from his model was his bifurcation of Janin's narrating Frenchman into two figures, the Englishman and R., which enabled him to fashion a plot similar to that of the 1834 text while shifting its ideological affiliations.

Janin never identifies the profession of his narrator, but his Beethoven remarks that he is a Frenchman (9), while Wagner introduces R. at the outset as an aspiring musician, that most German of callings. Janin's narrator claims that Beethoven is the *only* true German musician ('le pauvre malheureux Beethoven est encore le seul musicien de l'Allemagne') (10), but such a statement would be unthinkable in the universe of Wagner's story, in which the musical genius is best understood in his fatherland because of the common, shared, and innate musicality of all Germans. Such implications are antithetical to 'Le Dîner de Beethoven: conte fantastique,' at the conclusion of which the narrator exclaims that Beethoven's isolation and neglect make the Frenchman ashamed for Germany and for Europe ('honteux pour l'Allemagne et pour l'Europe de la misère et de l'abandon où je le voyais') (11): Janin implies that only the Frenchman (like Schlesinger?) is capable of appreciating Beethoven's genius, as well as, paradoxically, the English, who have sent the composer a piano as a gift (10, 11). Equally un-Wagnerian is Janin's description of Beethoven's performance on this untuned instrument as the 'plus abominable charivari qu'on pût entendre' (10); Wagner's Beethoven would never make such a fool of himself. Indeed, the most unmusical figure in the 'Pilgerfahrt' is the Englishman, Wagner's surrogate representative of the Judaized culture of France. With Schlesinger's visit to the real Beethoven as a backdrop to the story, the Englishman recalls the publisher racing toward Vienna in a coach with little on his mind but money and prestige, while R. traverses the entire route by foot with the purest of intentions. Wagner thus polarizes Beethoven and the commercialization of art in France, but Schlesinger's journey and Janin's fictional depiction of it had merged the two, and Wagner's only recourse was to invent an artistic allegory that would remove the blemish visited upon the figure he wished to preserve as truly accessible only to the Germans.

And it is only to a German, to R., and not to the Englishman (or Schlesinger) that Wagner's Beethoven reveals the secret of his new aesthetic of the human voice. Beethoven's remarks provide a counter to the Parisian commodification of the virtuosic vocal instrument, and thus the polarization of two kinds of voice in the story accompanies the bifurcation of Janin's narrating Frenchman into the two figures of the Englishman and R.:

'Why should not vocal music, as much as instrumental music, form a grand and serious genre, and its execution meet with as much respect from the thoughtless race of singers as, say, is demanded from an orchestra for a symphony? The human voice . . . is a far more beautiful and nobler organ of tone [*Ton-Organ*] than any instrument in the orchestra. . . . [The] very character that naturally distinguishes the human voice from the character of the instruments would have to be given special prominence, and that would lead to the most varied combinations. . . . May these two elements be brought together, may they be united!' (*DS* 5: 108–109)

If one considers Wagner's writings both immediately prior to his short story and those from the postrevolutionary period, the new vocal production described here by Beethoven comes to imply a vehicle for the emancipation of German music from foreign nations and from the Jews. For this reason Beethoven tells only R. of the Ninth Symphony, the first example of the new German vocal writing that will provide the aesthetic and ideological model for the Artwork of the Future:

'You soon will become acquainted with a new composition of mine, which will remind you of what I have just discussed. It is a symphony with choruses. . . .'

To this day I can scarcely grasp my happiness at thus being helped by Beethoven himself to a full understanding of his titanic Last Symphony, which then at most was finished, but known as yet to no man. (*DS* 5: 109)

Beethoven's vision of a new kind of Artwork of the Future is intended for a different Germany, because an aesthetic that seeks to unite the voice and the orchestra and to treat them as equal partners is based on the notion that these are elements whose unity reflects the unification of the community. While the hierarchical and patchwork proclivities of the foreign Grand Opéra privilege the voice, which it views as a virtuosic instrument, Beethoven sees such an 'organ of tone' as but one component in a group of elements and refuses to characterize it as instrumental. In this respect it is the opposite of the Jewish voice, which can be parodied through the upper registers of a woodwind instrument, the bassoon. The foreign Opéra reflects the disjointed makeup of a heterogeneous society comprised of many nationalities and diverse races, while Beethoven's vision is intended for a homogeneous German audience alone. Because of its nationalist undertones, the Ninth Symphony must remain a secret to the Jew-as-Englishman in the short story, though it will later emerge as the cornerstone of Wagnerian aesthetics. Thus, the multiple negations within Wagner's short story — of Schlesinger, of Janin, of Grand Opéra, of the commodification of culture, and of the French and the English in general — harbor an understanding of the human voice as both cultural metaphor and objective, physiological phenomenon. The rejection of those upper registers brings with it the negation of the cultural practices in which they are heard.

THE INVENTION OF THE *HELDENTENOR*

The theoretical and fictionalized discussions of a national and racist agenda of German music in general, and of vocal music in particular, following Wagner's life in Paris do more than illuminate the ideological implications of his understanding of art in the early 1840s, for they bear direct comparison with the vocal music he composed after he had turned his back on Schlesinger and on the kind of singing associated for Wagner with the Jew.

While his postrevolutionary essays and musical representations of Jews do not constitute isolated events within nineteenth-century culture, as seen through their comparison with the music and letters of Rossini, Mussorgsky, and Mahler, they do, unlike the works of his contemporaries, constitute the flip side of a larger, more extensive, and consistent aesthetic program designed to represent antithetical beings, for Wagner not only composed a kind of vocal music representing the difference of the Jew but also a kind that represented the superiority of the German based on assumptions concerning the privileged difference of the German body. The counterpart to his portrayals of Jews with higher voices is his conceptualization of a new kind of singer never before heard on the operatic stage, the *Heldentenor*, whose new and different sound was the aesthetic product of a xenophobic and anti-Semitic iconography of the human voice.

Wagner's invention of the *Heldentenor* constituted a daring and revolutionary event in the history of operatic composition. The vocal demands of the *Heldentenor* roles in the *Ring, Tristan,* and *Parsifal* require a kind of singer with a vocal apparatus ill-suited to much of the Italian and French operatic repertoire of the mid-nineteenth century and signify a rejection of the sounds he associated with Schlesinger and the Parisian culture industry. The *Heldentenor* often begins his career as a baritone, and the timbre of his mature singing reflects its deeper beginnings. Danish singer Lauritz Melchior, for example, generally considered the greatest interpreter in the twentieth century of Wagnerian heroic tenor parts, sang fifteen bass-baritone and baritone roles before making the transition to the higher vocal category.[59] The kind of singing for which he later became famous was always associated with an unusually dark, deep, and heavy sound. Melchior's biographer Shirlee Emmons describes the Wagnerian tenor thus:

The *Heldentenor Fach* demands a tenor voice of large size, exceptional stamina, and more strength in the lower register than other tenors can summon. This voice often evolves, with maturity, from a high baritone voice. Indeed, it could be characterized as a tenor/baritone. . . . [Melchior's] conviction that a Heldentenor could never be found among lighter-voiced lyric tenors, who lack lower register strength, . . . became well-known. . . . One of Melchior's last accompanists, Leonard Eisner, recalls that 'Melchior believed it was almost mandatory for a real Heldentenor to have been a baritone first. He considered it a logical sequence.'[60]

While the high, lyric, Italianate tenor had to be able to sing an extended tessitura and to execute ringing high c's, the *Heldentenor* requires a powerful *low* c, an octave below middle c (c′) and two octaves below the Italian's celebrated high note, as seen in a passage from Siegmund's monologue in act 1 of *Die Walküre*, the first *Heldentenor* role Wagner composed after writing 'Das Judentum in der Musik' and in the Annunciation of Death scene in act 2 of the same work. Again and again, Siegmund's voice sinks to depths that no composer of Grand Operas would have expected an Italian tenor to reach with confidence. In act 1 Siegmund sings a series of low c's, and in act 2 the tessitura of the role hovers at times between c♯ and f♯ in the bottom fourth of the vocal range (example 10). The *Heldentenor* is only seldom called

Example 10. Siegmund's low Cs at the conclusion of his monologue in act 1 and his deep tessitura in the opening lines of the Annunciation of Death scene in act 2 of Die Walküre

Act I

Siegmund.

da bleicht die Blü - te, das Licht ver - lischt; näch - ti - ges Dun - kel

deckt mir das Au - ge: tief in des Bu - sens Ber - ge glimmt nur noch licht - lo - se Glut.

Act II

Siegmund

Wer bist du, sag, die so schön und ernst mir er - scheint?

Der dir nun folgt, wo - hin führst du den Hel - den?

upon to sing above a high a (a'), a note that Siegmund sings only *once* in the course of *Die Walküre* and that the young Siegfried and Parsifal, too, almost never exceed, but a note that Beckmesser — the *bass-baritone* — sings for *four bars* in act 3 of *Die Meistersinger.* The notary, like most of Wagner's caricatures of Jews, likes to sing high, but Wagner's Germanic heroes generally do not. Interpreters of Siegmund often complain that the role requires power in the lower portion of the voice where it is vocally damaging for a lyric and spinto tenor to sing consistently with great force, and some do not warm up extensively before going on stage because the operatic voice normally rises in the course of a performance.[61] When *Die Walküre* was recorded under Georg Solti in the 1960s, the role was first offered not to a *Heldentenor* but to the celebrated baritone Dietrich Fischer-Dieskau, who declined, before the management engaged James King, a tenor with a powerful middle and lower register who himself, like Melchior, had begun his career as a baritone.[62] In Wagner's time, the *Heldentenor*'s imagined sound was new, darker, and deeper and was associated for him with a purer, more natural Germany unpolluted by 'high' nations and foreign races. This new sound was both metaphor and physiological reality, an ideological-acoustical icon that drew upon a perception in Wagner's culture of the Jew's voice as fundamentally different from that of the German and that expressed metaphorically Wagner's thoughts on the physiologically circumscribed borders of German identity.

Thus the conceptualization of this new vocal category was an aesthetically revolutionary act and also a professional gamble, for by inscribing this vision of a different kind of singer into the scores of his music dramas, Wagner turned his back on the vocal practices found in the operatic institutions of Europe upon which, as a composer, he was dependent. The invention of the *Heldentenor* is therefore a practical example of Wagner's conception of his post-1848 works as revolutionary, paradigmatic models for a different world. The startlingly low, heroic tenor voice is the locus in which the metaphorical dimension of the cor-

14. Gustav Doré, 'Die Heldentenöre' (From Eduard Fuchs and Ernest Kreowski, *Richard Wagner in der Karikatur* [Berlin: B. Behr's Verlag, 1907])

poreal iconographies in Wagner's dramas found its most demanding physical representation. Certainly Wagner was aware of the unusual demands he was making in inventing a new kind of vocal category for the operatic stage, but that is precisely the point; the new work, the Artwork of the Future intended for a different world and for a different audience, rejects the voices associated with those portions of the heterogeneous world Wagner so detested. (Gustav Doré's caricature of this new kind of singer went to the heart of such grandiose pretensions; figure 14.)

The juxtaposition of Mime's higher tessitura and Siegfried's lower vocal music in act 2, scene 3 of *Siegfried* is an example of the ideological implications behind the writing for the high lyric tenor and for the *Heldentenor* voice. Siegfried, let us recall, is the revolutionary, metaphorical representation of a future Germany and of its artwork. Because the Total Work of Art represents the new utopian collective order, it is only fitting that the physiological properties of its paradigmatic emblem — Siegfried — will be different from those Wagner deemed inferior and recognized throughout modern 'Judaized' civilization. The *Heldentenor* voice as the acoustical icon of Siegfried's body is the mirror in which a similarly voiced, physiologically heroic collective would see itself — 'know' itself — reflected. Siegfried's voice, like Walther's in *Die Meistersinger*, is the voice of the *Volk*, whose deeper registers connote for Wagner the German essence. Mime's higher instrument, on the other hand, anticipates the voice of that most anti-Semitic and derisive of musical-dramatic constructions, Sixtus Beckmesser.

Act 2, scene 3 of *Siegfried* is one of Wagner's most remarkable musical-dramatic creations, for here, through a subtle musical and textual device, he creates a bond of identification between the audience and the superhero while portraying the caricature of Jewishness as foreign and dangerous and thereby justifies for his imagined community Mime's murder at the conclusion to the scene. Wagner's Nibelung-Jew is a wily dissembler plotting to poison the son he has fostered in order to attain the Ring, but Siegfried sees (and hears) through Mime's subterfuge; because he has imbibed the magical blood of the dragon, he is able to understand the warblings of the Forest Bird, which warns him of Mime's intentions. Long before Wagner, German folklore harbored the belief that Jews were murderers with a predilection for poison and that they could understand the language of the animals,[63] and these topoi within Germany's cultural traditions may provide an explanation for Siegfried's otherwise startling statement — given the association of birds with Siegfried discussed in chapter 1 — that he had learned from none other than Mime that one could come to understand the language of the birds:

Ein zankender Zwerg
hat mir erzählt,
der Vöglein Stammeln
gut zu verstehn,
dazu könnte man kommen.
Wie das wohl möglich wär'? (*RN*, 203)

[A quarrelsome dwarf told me one could come to understand well the stammering of the birds. How could that be possible?]

But in act 2 of *Siegfried* the hero's superior and natural aural acuity is clearly juxtaposed to Mime's impoverished perception of the natural world, for the dwarf does not hear (or listen to, or understand) the Forest Bird and has no knowledge of Siegfried's insight into his own dissembling performance, an insight vouchsafed the young hero through the voice of Nature itself. The audience never hears the text of Mime's address to Siegfried; instead, like the hero, it hears the words of Mime's innermost thoughts (which Mime himself never puts into words that he himself hears) that reveal his murderous plot. But Wagner's vocal music for Mime acts as an approximation of the text that is never heard, for it sounds sweetly sycophantic, lilting, and unctuous to a Western audience familiar with the musical codes of lullabies and familial love. While Siegfried communes with the Forest Bird, Mime, as a dramatic vehicle for the expression of ideas found in 'Das Judentum in der Musik,' sings like a parrot, mimicking (and miming) the lilting sweetness of the sounds of love, sounds with which he himself has no affinity but which he believes will convince and fool the young German hero. (In this sense Mime's text here anticipates Beckmesser's superficial, parodistic prize-song.) It is Mime's *voice*, then, his *singing*, that gives him away as much as the text of his secret concerns, for only through the tension between the codes of the music and the violence of the verbal statements is Mime revealed as the schemer he is. Throughout the work, Mime attempts to approximate Siegfried's diction and to assume a 'non-Jewish' mode of expression as a means of camouflage, just as Wagner claimed that Jews mimic the culture in which they live in order to hide their 'true' identity. But with the text as a guide, the function of Mime's discourse as camouflage is laid bare, and the audience (Wagner assumes) will identify with the young hero, the target of an unnatural and racially foreign deception. The specific nature of the vocal music that Wagner composed for Mime is a feature of his physiological makeup the dwarf is not able to hide. While

Mime may try to change the tenor of his speech, he cannot but sing as a high tenor, cannot change the nature of his voice, which is physiologically different from that of the Germanic *Heldentenor*. His elevated tessitura, contrasted with the lower vocal writing for Siegfried, gives him away to Wagner's contemporary audience schooled in a culture that understood the Jewish voice to be high, nasal, and different.

This becomes apparent through their contrasting musical idioms when Siegfried asks the dwarf if he is contemplating the hero's injury. While the question is expressed in the middle vocal register, much of Mime's reply lies above middle c (c′) and moves higher and higher in the course of his vain attempts at sycophantic reassurance, with a penultimate phrase of unctuous duplicity on f♯, g′, and high a (a′) (example 11). Similarly, as

Example 11. Diverse tessituras as paradigms of difference in the exchange between Siegfried and Mime, act 2 of *Siegfried*

Mime implores Siegfried to drink the poisoned potion so that
he may win his sword and with it 'helmet and hoard,' the dwarf's
voice rises from c′ to d′, and then to an interpolated e′♮, followed by an f′ and finally a series of cackling, staccato high
g′s, marked 'kichernd,' meaning both 'chuckling' and 'sniggering,' a phrase the German character-tenor Gerhard Stolze often
sang in pure falsetto (example 12). Siegfried's reply is character-

Example 12. Mime's
sniggering high Gs

istically and contrastively set to a lower, deeper, and calmer
vocal line (example 13). This juxtaposition of high, foreign, and

Example 13.
Siegfried's calm
mezza voce

treacherous versus deep, natural, honest, and Teutonic is maintained throughout the scene and provides the basis for Wagner's
musical portrayal of Mime's malicious difference. While Siegfried, warned by and hence on the side of Nature, expresses his
essence in the calm, more powerful, and deeper notes of that
race for which Wagner composed his work (and who he expected would attend its performance and identify with its hero),
the extremely high tessitura of Mime's musical idiom under-

scores his nature as fundamentally different, in terms of his lack of familial bonds, his egotism, and his dishonesty, from that of the superhero and of the audience.

Perhaps the most melodiously beautiful phrase of the entire scene is set to the most reprehensible verbal expression of all, in which Mime explicitly announces his intention to commit murder. Wagner marks the phrase thus: '*Er bemüht sich, den zärtlichsten Ton anzunehmen* [*He makes an effort to assume the tenderest tone*]' (RN, 215). Not coincidentally, this is also the highest phrase of the entire role, rising to a touchingly sweet b'♭, just below that most famous of notes in Italian opera, the high c (c″). In order to underscore the duplicity of the figure singing with the highest of male voices, Wagner slows down his tempo and marks the orchestral accompaniment 'ausdrucksvoll' ('expressive') and 'dolce,' as Mime sings 'I only want to chop the child's head off' (example 14). There is no more succinct example to be

Example 14.
Mime's high B♭: 'I only want to chop the child's head off!'

found in Wagner of an extremely high voice providing an icon of corporeal difference denoting a treachery threatening the German family and hence the German community.

Wagner's paradigm in the *Ring* of the voice as an icon of race may have attended his composition of the vocal writing in *Tristan und Isolde*, often deemed bereft of the ideological baggage so much more obvious in the tetralogy and in *Die Meistersinger von*

Nürnberg.[64] The relationship between ideological meaning and vocal categorization in *Siegfried* may have continued to occupy Wagner when he interrupted the composition of his third *Ring* drama in 1857, at the end of act 2, and turned to the creation of this, his most celebrated (and sensual) paean to love. For while *Tristan* may evince fewer of the more blatant instances of Wagner's racism and nationalism, it is possible that the experience of having just completed the vocal writing for the different tenors in *Siegfried* had an impact on the music he wrote for the tenors in *Tristan*. The vocal and dramatic constellation of Siegfried and Mime could have provided a model for that of Tristan and Melot for the following reasons: Dramatically, Mime and Melot may be compared through their close, life-long proximity to and competition with the central heroes, whom they both plot to destroy in an effort to attain the *Heldentenor*'s possessions — the gold and the golden princess, respectively.[65] Though, unlike Mime, the cameo role of Melot cannot provide the kind of vocal and hence iconographically ideological contrast to the new vocal music written for the central hero, it too suggests a connection between a differently inferior, unheroic kind of voice and such concepts as covetousness, deception, inferior physical prowess, and treachery as found in the *Ring*, and in both works the voice of the hero is fundamentally different from that of the traitor (though it must be added that Melot's vocal material lies much lower than that of Mime). Vocally, Siegfried and Tristan are similar (indeed, most tenors who essay one of the roles, with the notable exception of Jon Vickers, eventually sing the other as well), and both lie significantly lower than most operatic tenor roles and pose unusual, even tremendous demands on the singer's stamina and vocal power.

It could be argued that Wagner would not have written such an unusually high tenor part for his young poet Walther von Stolzing — a role that Melchior, Vickers, and numerous other Wagnerian tenors never sang on stage — if he had been consistently guided by the notion of a high voice as non-Germanic.[66]

Yet the remarks of one Wagnerian scholar, notoriously impatient with investigations concerning Wagner's anti-Semitism, may ironically offer some insight into this apparent inconsistency in the ideology of Wagner's vocal writing for *Die Meistersinger*. Carl Dahlhaus explains Wagner's reasons for composing the kind of music he gave to Walther von Stolzing thus: 'Wagner as a dramatist may have had the idea of furnishing Stolzing, as the representative of musical progress, with the kind of music that was recognized as progressive in the mid-1860s, but as an experienced man of the theatre he knew better: his triumphant heroic tenor [*sic*] needed music that would have an immediate appeal for the audience, who would identify with the crowd on stage.'[67] If Dahlhaus is correct, Wagner may have shied away from giving Stolzing a lower vocal tessitura precisely because such music would have been deemed, ironically, *too* revolutionary, an insight that underscores the iconoclastic nature of Wagner's new vocal category. The vocal writing perceived as less innovative (because it was higher) would have constituted less of a theatrical risk within nineteenth-century European culture than the music of a Siegmund, a Siegfried, or a Tristan, those figures who, unlike Stolzing, so transgress the boundaries of social convention that the consistent programs of their respective dramas demand their death, whereas Stolzing, whose vocal writing is higher and hence more conventional, is integrated into the society of Nuremberg at the conclusion of *Die Meistersinger* — indeed, such integration is clearly one of the key themes of the work. That is, what may appear as an exception in the ideological plan of Wagner's vocal writing may in fact be less than inconsistent: If the tenor is a veritable revolutionary outsider, his voice will be iconoclastically heroic (or low), whereas if his revolution is merged into the social context that he had threatened, his voice will rise accordingly to more conventional heights.

Owing to the extreme demands of his new vocal writing, it is no surprise that Wagner attempted to convince King Ludwig II to finance the establishment of a music school in Munich for the training of German singers, in which a specifically German *Gesangsorgan* would receive a kind of development commensurate with its unique physiological disposition, as he made clear in his 'Bericht an Seine Majestät den König Ludwig II.' Wagner recalled this effort in his impassioned 'Erinnerungen an Ludwig Schnorr von Carolsfeld' (Recollections of Ludwig Schnorr von Carolsfeld), the tenor whom he extolled as the nearly perfect exemplar of the new German vocal art that his works espoused and demanded and who died shortly after performing the title role in the 1865 premiere of *Tristan* in Munich. In his eulogistic recollections, Wagner emphasizes the diametrically opposed singing of emasculated Italy and the new, masculine German Artwork of the Future:

> But the singing voice has hitherto been trained solely after the model of Italian song: there has been no other kind. But Italian song was inspired by the whole spirit of Italian music: and at their best, it was the castrati who suited it to greatest perfection, this spirit being directed only toward sensual well-being without any real anguish of soul, — the youthful male voice, the tenor, being at that time employed not all all, or, as was later the case, in a falsetto castrato manner [*im falsettirenden kastratenartigen Sinne*]. But now the tendency of more modern music, under the inevitably acknowledged leadership of German musical art, has, particularly through Beethoven, elevated itself to heights of true artistic dignity by, for the first time, drawing into the domain of its incomparable expression not only the sensually pleasing but also that which is spiritually vigorous and deeply passionate [*das Geistig-Energische u. Tiefleidenschaftliche*].[68]

It is no coincidence that Wagner's German text stresses the polarity of the *deep* passion of the German and the unnaturally high voice of the Italian, a polarity that he underscores through the explicit and malicious characterization of Italian music as effeminate. Due to political intrigue and Wagner's own intemperate and widely publicized lifestyle, the plan for a German music school was never realized and, with only a few exceptions, the composer remained frustrated for the rest of his life with the quality of singing found on the German stage, even on his own in Bayreuth.[69]

It would be foolish to suggest that Wagner's remarks concerning the human voice constituted a strict program, for, at most, they serve to illuminate repetitive tendencies and implications within his dramas, rather than to reveal a consistent equation of pitch and race. Wagner's conception of the human voice as racial icon undoubtedly influenced his musical portrayals, but it did not provide a *blueprint* for composition. If it had (that is, if Wagner had been consistent), all his heroes would have been basso profundos, and his figures evincing purportedly Semitic features (Alberich, Hagen, Beckmesser, and Klingsor, as well as Mime) would have been cast as high lyric tenors.[70] Nevertheless, insight into the ideological concerns behind Wagner's conceptualization of the *Heldentenor* serve to highlight implications in his musical material that might otherwise go unnoticed. Clearly the demands of operatic traditions (as seen for example in the works of Mozart, Beethoven, and Weber) associating villains with bass-baritones exerted another, vocally different influence on Wagner's compositional strategies. But Wagner's caricatures of Jews do sing a music that sounds different in part because much of its lies at the top of their vocal register, regardless of whether the register in question is that of a bass, a baritone, or a tenor, while his embodiments of superior Germans are inscribed with the physiological metaphors of different bodies, and that means different, lower voices.

THE VOICE OF THE EFFEMINATE JEW

Wagner's comments regarding the 'masculine' nature of Schnorr von Carolsfeld's singing illuminate a sexual dimension that has been latent in the entire discussion of the voice-as-icon thus far: the implicit feminization of the Jew. When Wagner writes about and portrays Jews, he usually means *male* figures who pose a sexual threat. The portrayal of the Jew as idiosyncratically endowed with a high voice, from Wagner's perspective, constituted a slanderous counter to such a danger, a characterization of the Jew as effeminate. This may explain why most of his heroic women are called upon to sing well above high a (a″), while his *Heldentenöre* are not (though it must be added that some of his postrevolutionary soprano roles make unusual demands on the lower vocal registers of the female voice as well, most discernible in Sieglinde's penchant for a tessitura that often falls well below the staff, particularly noticeable in her act 1 monologue 'Der Männer Sippe'). For Wagner, a German woman can sing high with ideological aplomb, but the German man cannot, for to do so is to journey into the metaphorically and physiologically superficial and hence culturally inferior sphere of the foreign. The conflation of the Jew and the feminine may have been widespread in German culture of the mid-nineteenth century; it is explicit in Nietzsche's work of the early 1870s (especially in *The Birth of Tragedy*) and of course became pervasive in Austrian culture by the end of the century.[71] It is already implied in Wagner's earlier writings as well.

One can trace the feminization of Italian song — and of the Jew with whom Wagner came to associate Italian opera — to the composer's early experience of the Italian male soprano Sassaroli, who in Wagner's youth was often a guest in his parents' house and whom Wagner described in *Mein Leben* as 'antipathetic to me' and as terrifying him 'by his very high feminine voice.' Later, whenever he heard Italian spoken or sung, Wagner viewed the language as 'the diabolical work of this spectral instrument.'[72] Such an experience in early youth makes Wagner's enthusiasm for Italian opera in the 1830s all the more remarkable, and the vehemence of his subsequent rejection of the Italian — and Jewish — music world all the more grounded in the depths of Wagner's psyche and expressed in the metaphors available to him through his culture.

Throughout Wagner's theoretical writings and in the metaphorical representations of many of their precepts in his works for the stage, the Jew and the feminine are brought into close proximity. At the end of part 1 of *Oper und Drama*, for example, Wagner characterizes music as a 'feminine,' 'birth-giving,' 're-ceptive' organism (*DS* 7: 112) and poetry as 'masculine,' and these characterizations will be central to the sexual dimension of his metaphorical representation of the Jewish musician: 'the organism of music is able to give birth to the true, living melody if it is inseminated [*befruchtet*] by the thought of the poet. Music is the one who gives birth; the poet is the one who sires [*Die Musik ist die Gebärerin, der Dichter der Erzeuger*]' (*DS* 7: 114). Because of this metaphorical, polarized, gender-specific charac-terization of the two arts, Wagner is able to state that, by itself, each art must be sterile and to suggest that the admixture of the two in his own capacity as both musician and poet under-scores the truly 'productive' and, by implication, sexually active nature of his own artistic creation. Thus, the Artworks of the Fu-ture will be the successful products of a metaphorically hetero-sexual and sexually active, natural-creative (procreative) process. Given his many statements concerning his own status as the inheritor of Beethoven's artistic-'folkish' legacy, it is therefore no surprise that Wagner describes his German forerunner pre-cisely in these sexually redolent metaphorical terms:

With Beethoven . . . we recognize the natural life-drive to give birth to melody out of the inner organism of music. In his most important works he by no means presents the melody as something already com-plete, but rather he allows it, so to speak, to be born before our eyes out of its organs; he initiates us into this act of birth. . . . But the most important thing that the Master finally proclaims to us in his main work is the necessity he feels as a musician to throw himself into the arms of the poet, in order to bring about the act of *procreation* [*den Akt der* Zeugung] of the true, unfailingly real, and redeeming melody. In order to become a *human being* [*Mensch*], Beethoven had to become a *total*, that is, collective, human being subordinate to the conditions of *the masculine and the feminine* [*des Männlichen und Weiblichen*]. (*DS* 7: 109–110)

Beethoven is able to actively produce, because instead of focusing on merely aesthetic form, his artistry successfully merges the feminine and the masculine elements of the future Total Work of Art. And because the authentic artwork is itself a 'reflection' of the collective that beholds it, we may assume that this image of a potent and procreative collective work also says much about the sexual nature of the superior audience it represents — a homogeneous, heterosexually 'productive' audience bereft of Jews. For Wagner, Beethoven's active heterosexual procreative creativity leads to the unification of text and music in both *Fidelio* and the Ninth Symphony, which in its final movement reaches toward Schiller's poetry out of the spirit of music. Both works, of course, are central to the 'Pilgerfahrt' as well; their sexual and vocal implications may be discerned in *Oper und Drama* and in the short story.

Beethoven's conflation of the feminine and the masculine is the sexual parallel to the notion of the authentic aesthetic experience as a 'natural' event in which like kind recognize and find their way to each other, a union that will be productive and will guarantee the future integrity of the nation-as-family. This is precisely the metaphorical function of the union of Siegmund and Sieglinde, who can be said to represent the recognition and the union of the German *Volk* with itself and, at the same time, the union of music (as feminine) and poetry (as masculine). They also metaphorically represent, through the merging of their procreative genders, the component parts of the superior, natural Artwork of the Future, which itself constitutes a mirror of the authentic community.

That community, as we have seen, shuns both difference and particularization, and, given the sexual nature of Wagner's metaphorical discussion of aesthetics, it is no surprise that the Jewish artwork and the Jewish musician are represented in his writings and dramas as sexually different from the authentic German as well. The Jew's body is cursed either with rapacious sensuality or with sterility, and the metaphorical representation of Jewish art brings with it the notion of corporeal difference in general and of sexual inferiority in particular. For Wagner, Meyerbeer, Halévy, and Mendelssohn — the representatives of the successful artistic Jew in the modern age — are a sexual world removed from the procreative, formative power of a Beethoven and the future Master of Bayreuth. They are unable to merge the poetic and the musical, denigrating the former and focusing instead on the latter. Meyerbeer, especially, Wagner maintains, views his librettist Scribe as a subordinate in the process of composing an opera, and thus Meyerbeer's own musical production, according to Wagner, remains impoverished and *sterile* (DS 7: 95–105). These musicians are exclusively concerned with music and not with the generating power of words; theirs is thus a solely 'feminine' artistry.

Consequently, Wagner describes the difference between his own, German works and the foreign operas associated for him with the Jewish music world through socially antithetical images of women: He writes in *Oper und Drama* that the Artwork of the Future can be likened to a relationship between a woman (music) who feels compelled and proud to receive the man she loves (poetry), to the extent that she is willing to be destroyed (and thus Wagner's many heroines called upon to sacrifice themselves take on a metaphorical function within his music dramas). Any woman who does not love 'with the pride of this dedication' does not 'really love,' he claims, and is 'the most unworthy and most repulsive thing [*Erscheinung*] in the world' (DS 7: 115). It is this kind of 'base' woman who represents in Wagner's theoretical reflections the different forms of modern opera, all of which he deems influenced by and closely associated with Jewish musicians and with the financial power of Jews in the music world: The Italian opera is a 'prostitute [*Lustdirne*]' (DS 7: 115); French operatic music is a 'Kokette' (DS 7: 116); and the kind of German operatic music that in truth is a poor relation of Italian and French opera is a 'prude' (DS 7: 116). German men and women meet in a productive union, resulting metaphorically in the superior artwork in Wagner's theories and in the superior, half-godly human being in the *Ring*, but the Jew is innately *female* and hence unable — in his isolation — to 'produce' anything. As late as 1881 Wagner would write in his diary: 'In the mingling of races the blood of nobler males is ruined by the baser female element.'[73] When the discussion is of Jews, the 'female element' (located apparently in both Jewish males and females) constitutes a dangerous and contemptible threat to the German *Volk*. Only when the discussion is of 'noble' blood, as in Wagner's remarks concerning the 'racial' attraction between Siegfried and Brünnhilde cited in the previous chapter, can the feminine have a redemptive function, as it does in virtually all his music dramas and in his discussions of the Artwork of the Future. In this text, Wagner evokes the polarization of the *Volk* as fertile and the Jews as sexually inferior in a passage describing a threat to the future of the German people:

> Thus the *Volk* will bring about redemption by being sufficient unto itself and at the same time by redeeming its own enemies. . . . As long as the conditions [for the domination of the *Volk* by its enemies] exist, as long as they [its enemies] suck their life's blood from the wasted strength of the *Volk*, as long as they — *themselves unable to sire* — devour to no end the fertility of the *Volk* in their egotistical existence — then for just as long all interpreting, creating, changing, improving, and reforming of these conditions will be arbitrary, pointless and fruitless. (*DS* 6: 21, my emphasis)

The vampiric egotism of the foreigner merges with his inability to 'produce,' a notion that both pervades Wagner's metaphors regarding the presence of Jews in the arts and underscores their physical presence as sexually inferior and different.

In 'Das Judentum in der Musik' Wagner makes the connection between race and production explicit: 'historically we must characterize the period of Jewishness in modern music as that of perfected unproductivity' (*GS* 13: 21). In 'Eine Mitteilung an meine Freunde' he took up this theme again and stated explicitly that this modern art is feminine in nature, but now the sexual connotations are, within the moral parameters of his culture, even more pointedly insulting:

That which determines the artist as such are . . . the purely artistic impressions; if his power of reception [*Empfängniskraft*] is completely absorbed by them, so that the life-impressions to be felt later find his ability already exhausted, he will thus develop as an *absolute* artist in the direction which we must solely describe as the feminine, that is, the feminine element of art. In this we find all the artists whose activity nowadays actually constitutes the function of modern art; it is an art world fundamentally separated from life, in which art only plays with itself. (*DS* 6: 217)

Here, the artist of the modern world is not only both feminine and unproductive but is also locked in a l'art-pour-l'art, masturbatory game of self-absorption with no ties to the community and to the 'real' world. (I will discuss the metaphorical and iconographic implications of masturbation for Wagner in greater detail in chapter 5.) Both Mendelssohn's absolute music — his symphonies, for example — as well as the operas of his fellow Jewish colleagues fail to merge the virility of the masculine 'procreative seed of the poetic intent' with the 'wondrously loving woman music' in an act of aesthetic 'birth,' as Wagner characterized his own creative process in *Oper und Drama* (*DS* 7: 231).

Thus the Jew is effeminate, unproductive, masturbatory, and bereft of ties to the life-giving, procreative community. This notion underlies a host of dramatic representations of Jewish stereotypes in Wagner's music dramas, such as Mime, who himself is without offspring, and Beckmesser, who is infertile metaphorically and perhaps even virtually in that, unlike Walther (and Sachs, who has real children), he generates no artistic 'child' and sings accordingly in an impossibly elevated, 'unmasculine' register.[74] Sachs couldn't baptize a song-child of Beckmesser's even if he wanted to, for there is no such child.

Nevertheless, Wagner argues in *Oper und Drama* that Jewish artistry does attempt to overcome these inherent sexual failings. Wagner claims that 'the secret of the sterility of modern music' lies in its desire to have music not only 'give birth, but also to sire [*nicht nur gebären, sondern auch zeugen*],' which he calls 'the height of madness' and associates explicitly with the Jew Meyer-beer (*DS* 7: 114). But, for Wagner, such a desire must fail, be-cause in his world no Jew can truly be productive, can truly change his (all-too-feminine) physiology and surmount the fail-ings that sexuality as a metaphor implies. What constitutes a positive merging of distinct sexual identities in the authentic, German, Wagnerian work of art is denigrated as impossible, inappropriate, and even potentially androgynous when it is lo-cated in the foreign, Jewish work (in a metaphorical hint of this theme, Mime the artist foolishly insists to Siegfried that he is 'both father and mother' to the boy [*RN*, 163]).[75] Sterility, mas-turbation, androgyny, and femininity are all used here meta-phorically, but they all are based on and refer to beliefs concern-ing the purportedly real sexual difference of the Jew's body. All these notions conflate with the image of the non-German voice as high, contemptible, and worthy of laughter.

And it is with laughter that Kundry mocks the castrated Kling-sor in act 2 of *Parsifal*, a work that unabashedly draws upon a host of anti-Semitic images in its scenic representation of a threat to the integrity of a Teutonic and Christian order, the Knights of the Holy Grail. Ever since the publication of Theo-dor W. Adorno's and Robert Gutman's attacks on Wagner, much controversy has surrounded the question of the anti-Semitic nature of *Parsifal* in general and of Klingsor and Kundry in par-ticular.[76] Some scholars have been especially reluctant to ac-knowledge a connection between Wagner's explicit and enthusi-astic employment of Count Arthur Gobineau's racist tracts (in his essay 'Heldentum und Christentum' [Heroism and Chris-tendom] of 1881 — like 'Erkenne dich selbst,' an addendum to *Religion und Kunst* [Religion and art] of 1880) and the text of his final work for the stage.[77] But whether one is willing to accept the notion of diverse kinds of blood alluded to in the work — one racially pure and holy, the other inferior and threatening — as implicitly anti-Semitic or not, no one could deny the remarkable prominence in *Parsifal* of images of castration, associated primarily, though not exclusively, with Klingsor. Such images can be readily compared to the iconographic distinction of the Jew as effeminate in Wagner's writings and other dramas so replete with anti-Semitic imagery.[78]

The 'Jewish' nature of Klingsor can be adduced from a variety of dramatic themes that the sorcerer inherits from Beckmesser and Alberich. Like them, he is fundamentally different from those who constitute the ruling order and, like Beckmesser and Alberich, he seeks the source of power behind a society that refuses to accept him: Beckmesser longs to win the song contest, Alberich the stolen Ring, and Klingsor the Holy Grail. And (most important in the present context), like Alberich and perhaps Beckmesser as well, Klingsor's resentment over his status as a rejected and ridiculed outcast leads to his *sexual* malevolence. Alberich's warning to Wotan in the Nibelheim scene of *Das Rheingold* makes the sexual nature of *his* threat to the ruling order blatantly explicit:

Habt Acht! Habt Acht!
Denn dient ihr Männer
erst meiner Macht,
eure schmucken Frau'n —
die mein Frein verschmäht —
sie zwingt zur Lust sich der Zwerg
lacht ihm Liebe nicht.
Hahahaha!
Habt ihr's gehört?
Hab Acht! (*RN*, 47)

[Beware! Beware! For once you men serve my power, your beautiful women — who scorned my wooing — them the dwarf shall force to pleasure, if love does not smile upon him. Hahahaha! Have you heard? Beware!]

Alberich will indeed penetrate the realm of the sexual Teutonic stronghold when he sires his son, Hagen, through the services of the unfortunate German woman, Grimhild. Beckmesser's sexual threat, of course, is his attempt to win the hand of the perfect German girl, Eva, who finds him repugnant.

But we must bear in mind that the stereotypes of Jewish sexuality constitute extremes: While Alberich represents the lascivious, irrepressibly horny Jew, Mime is his sexual opposite, an effeminate, childless wimp (and thus it is significant that Alberich finds issue while Mime does not). Beckmesser incorporates both stereotypes; he both threatens Eva and is endowed with all the stock clichés of the castrato.[79] As we have seen, one of the key tensions within Wagner's theories and music dramas is that the Jew is both obviously different from the German and at the same time chameleonic, mimicking and thereby infiltrating German society. The anxiety behind this tension is precisely that involved in the polarization of images of the male Jew as both effeminate and at the same time as constituting a malevolent sexual threat, the very tension at the heart of Wagner's differing anti-Semitic caricatures in the *Ring*.

Klingsor, like Beckmesser, is a figure who unites these extremes: He both constitutes a sexual danger and is himself incapable of insemination. He is *truly* a castrato, but he exerts his sexual malevolence through the spell-bound instrument of his anger, the seductress-witch Kundry. By the time Wagner conceived of *Parsifal*, a cultural tradition had long been in place that associated Jews with castration. The sign representing the difference of the Jew's sexual organs, of course, was his circumcision, but in the anti-Semitic imagination that sign evoked castration and was also linked, at least since the Middle Ages, even to the belief that the Jewish male menstruated. In his discussion of the convergence of the motifs of circumcision as a 'wound' and menstruation in Jewish males, Leon Poliakov cites accusations made against the Jews during a case of 'ritual murder' in Tyrnau in 1494: 'the traditions of their ancestors tell them that the blood of a Christian is an excellent means to cure the wound produced by circumcision . . . , suffering from menstruation, both men and women alike, they have noted that the blood of a Christian constitutes an excellent remedy.'[80] This motivic tradition provides a background to the iconic makeup of Klingsor. In act 1 of *Parsifal*, Gurnemanz, more deep-based voice-over narrator than active participant, relates to the young squires and would-be knights of the Grail the terrible story of Klingsor's self-mutilation, the sorcerer's castration:

Ohnmächtig, in sich selbst die Sünde zu ertöten,
an sich legt' er die Frevlerhand. (P, 43)

[Powerless to kill the sin within himself, he lay a sacrilegious hand upon himself.]

It is from this deed that the magician has received his unusual power, with which he threatens the Grail knights:

die Wut nun Klingsorn unterwies,
wie seines schmähl'chen Opfers Tat
ihm gäbe zu bösem Zauber Rat;
den fand er nun. (P, 43)

[anger now taught Klingsor how the offering of his contemptible deed could give him counsel for evil magic; this he then found.]

Klingsor's difference, then, is not only grounded in his irrepressible lascivious nature (the source of his inability to become 'holy,' or 'heilig,' as Gurnemanz mockingly relates) but is also explicitly represented by the physiological sign of his difference — his castration. Such self-mutilation, associated with the Jew since the Middle Ages, in turn is deemed a threat to the order of kindred German spirits, the (medieval) knights of the Grail, whose healthy physiology is altogether different from his.

In *Parsifal*, the motif of castration is not only associated with the evil sorcerer. In all of Wagner's mature music dramas, figures evincing purportedly Jewish features always pose a threat to their Teutonic opposites precisely because their nefarious nature is presented as having crossed communal-racial boundaries. In *Die Meistersinger*, Beckmesser's threat to the development of German art is seen in his influence on Kothner; in the *Ring*, the avarice and licentiousness of Alberich has its lamentable counterpart in Wotan, the founder of the racially superior family, and also leads to the genetic decay of the Teutonic line of the Gibichungs, as seen in his physiologically woeful son, Hagen. In *Parsifal*, too, the traits deemed damnable are not simply portrayed as different and isolated, and hence to be easily banished from the purview of the superior beings, but are closely connected to the insecure future of the superior order as well. Klingsor and the leader of the order of the Grail are remarkably comparable for this very reason; Amfortas suffers precisely from the failings of the outcast magician — indeed, one could argue, on a psychological level, that Amfortas's campaign against the sorcerer constitutes a duel with those parts of himself he so fears and despises (which offers, incidentally, an interesting dramatization of the psychological forces underlying Wagner's own interaction with Jews) — and thus the irony of the king's exalted position, which is painfully expressed in his music, emerges as all the more agonizing. A number of times in the course of Amfortas's two monologues, in acts 1 and 3, each time in the hall of the Grail, music associated with Klingsor accompanies the king when he sings of the flow of his own lascivious blood. This first occurs in the following passage (example 15):

des eig'nen sündigen Blutes Gewell'
in wahnsinniger Flucht
muß mir zurück dann fließen,
in die Welt der Sündensucht
mit wilder Scheu sich ergiessen. (P, 51)

[the waves of my own sinful blood in insane flight must flow back into me, into the world of sinful addiction pour itself with wild trepidation.]

Klingsor's wild chromatic music penetrates Amfortas's modal serenity a second time, in act 3, when he pleads with the knights of the Grail to end his life (example 16):

Taucht eure Schwerte
tief — tief, bis ans Heft! (P, 83)

[Plunge your swords in deep — deep, up to the hilt!]

The ideational implications of the music from act 1 — heard again in act 3 — are not made manifest to the listening viewer

Example 15. The
music of lascivious
blood in Amfortas's
monologue from
act 1 of *Parsifal*

until it reappears in the prelude to act 2, where it is revealed
as the acoustical idiom of the sorcerer (example 17). (Amfortas's first monologue also anticipates yet another passage from
the act 2 prelude in the orchestral accompaniment to his text

'das heisse Sündenblut entquillt,/ewig erneut aus des Sehnens Quelle [the hot blood of sin pours out, eternally renewed from the spring of yearning]' [P, 51]. The musical figure, comprised of two eighth-notes, a dotted eighth, and a sixteenth note, is found here and also reappears in the accompaniment to the passage just cited from act 3; thus, two distinct motives reinforce the connection between the sorcerer and the king, first through adumbration [in act 1] and then through recollection

Example 16. Klingsor's music invades the Hall of the Grail, act 3 of *Parsifal*

Example 17. Music of the sorcerer from the prelude to act 2 of *Parsifal*

[in act 3].) It is the irrepressible yet frustrated nature of Amfortas's sexual longing — represented by his 'hot' blood — that in part links him to the magician, who laments the fact that he continues to be overwhelmed by sexual desire despite his castration, as he makes clear in his short dialogue with Kundry in the opening scene of act 2:

Furchtbare Not!
Ungebändigten Sehnens Pein,
schrecklichster Triebe Höllendrang,
den ich zu Todesschweigen mir zwang —
lacht und höhnt er nun laut
durch dich, des Teufels Braut? (*P*, 57)

[Horrible need! Irrepressible pain of yearning, hellish urge of the most terrible drives, which I forced to deathly silence — does it now laugh and mock through you, the Devil's bride?]

The phrase 'Ungebändigten Sehnens Pein' is introduced by a chromatic, impulsive passage in the strings similar — and related to — that heard in the prelude to act 2 and to that which invades the orchestral accompaniment to Amfortas's two laments (example 18). The musical intertextuality serves to underscore an important point concerning the nature of distinct kinds of blood associated with sanctity versus damnation. It suggests that Klingsor's failings are shared by Amfortas, and these failings are explicitly associated with inferior blood, as the conflation of Klingsor's music and the text of Amfortas's act 1 monologue implies. The lowly, tenacious, lascivious blood of the foreigner — banished to a region on the outskirts (the *Ausland*) of the domain of the Grail — is presented as a foreign agent that enters and attacks the superior realm of the Teutonic and the chaste, deep in the center of the religious and elect.

The similarities of the two figures are also iconographic. The irony of Klingsor's situation is underscored through his control of the 'phallic' spear (Barry Emslie wittily writes that a 'eunuch in possession of a phallic symbol is a laughable contradiction'),[81] which only serves to stress his absence or lack of that which the

Example 18. The musical representation of Klingsor's sinful yearning

audience has been told, long before it ever sees Klingsor, he is missing. But his castration is represented iconographically by an image he shares with his all-too-kindred soul Amfortas as well: namely, the king's gaping wound, 'die Wunde . . . , die nie sich schließen will [the wound . . . that will never close]' (*P*, 42). The polyvalence of this image is powerful indeed, evoking both the male and the female genitalia, both the castration of the testicles and the vagina that, too, 'cannot close' and periodically bleeds, an image that recalls the iconic tradition of male menstruation associated with Jews.[82] (In his cinematic reflection on the music drama, Hans Jürgen Syberberg chose to make the wound visible — and enigmatically depersonalized, as if it were available to all — by having it appear, frothing, bleeding, and explicitly vaginalike, on a dais which is rolled about in the course of the film.)[83] The thematic connections between the king and Klingsor serve to draw attention to their shared image of nearly identical wounds.[84] Amfortas suffers from an opening in the body that, in Wolfram von Eschenbach's *Parzifal*, the literary source for the music drama, is explicitly portrayed as a wound to the loins:

> One day — his nearest and dearest did not approve — the King rode out alone to seek adventure under Love's compulsion and joying in her encouragement. Jousting, he was wounded by a poisoned lance so seriously that he never recovered, . . . through the scrotum. The man who was fighting there and rode that joust was a heathen born of Ethnise, where the Tigris flows out from Paradise. This pagan was convinced that his valor would earn him the Gral.[85]

In the source for *Parsifal*, then, Amfortas's wound is clearly sexual in nature, nearly (or perhaps virtually) equivalent to castration. The 'heathen' from exotic lands in Wolfram's text is not Clinschor, the castrated sorcerer in *Parzifal*,[86] but Wagner combines the two figures (jousting heathen and Clinschor) and has the magician inflict the wound, so similar to his own, upon the king. Klingsor's own, self-induced mutilation is referred to repeatedly in the course of Wagner's drama by Gurnemanz, Kundry, and Klingsor himself. The affinity between the sorcerer and the ailing king, then, was both intentional on Wagner's part and remains, through the musical interconnections and textual references in the work, unmistakable.

Thus, it is only consistent that at the close of the music drama, after the magician has been banished at the conclusion to act 2 by the redeeming power of the 'phallic' spear (triumphantly held aloft by a young *Heldentenor*), the wound of his counterpart Amfortas is also closed by that self-same weapon so suggestive of male images of power and masculinity. And it is therefore equally consistent, indeed all of a piece, that Kundry, the only female role in the work to be heard outside the Magic Garden (with the exception of the disembodied angelic voice at the close of act 1), should also be dispatched. Not only the female but femininity per se is removed, even in the transmogrification of its symbolic manifestations so evocative of castration and menstruation: The castrato is gone, the wound is closed, and the seductive temptress so closely associated with both the eunuch and the wound is gone as well. Like her fellow representative of Jewishness in the work, the all-too-effeminate sorcerer, she is defeated by the return of the 'powerful' spear, taken from the hands of the impure, effeminate, and foreign magician (just as the sword is wrested from Mime in the *Ring*) and returned to its rightful, 'masculine' domain.

A web of iconic traditions within German culture — the male Jew as high-voiced, castrated, effeminate, and menstruating — lends these images, then, a racial dimension in Wagner's music dramas and makes the association of these figures with characteristics deemed Jewish culturally motivated and consistent, both in the imagination of the composer and in the minds of his contemporary audience. The image of the castrated and menstruating Jew merged seamlessly with the perception of the foreigner as sexually inferior, unprocreative, and emasculated — as sexually different from the purportedly virile masculine German as could be. In addition, it lent the metaphorical dimension of Wagner's dramatic representations of Jewish stereotypes a sense of legitimacy and credibility within his culture. Such metaphors are based on the notion of the Jewish body as different, a difference that is always revealed by its corporeal signs. One of the most important of those signs for Wagner as a musician was the elevated voice of the Jew, a sonic icon so redolent of sexual overtones replete with metaphorical implications.

*

To ignore the affinities between Wagner's anti-Semitic diatribes, his aesthetic reformatory writings, and his music dramas is to close our ears to the reprehensible ideology underlying his overwhelmingly seductive music. How easy and tempting it is to forget the message and to revel in the song! But Wagner's contemporaries, schooled in a tradition that perceived Jewish speech as garbled and nasal, may well have heard the anti-

Semitic and sexual undertones — the culturally encoded message of his physiological and metaphorical iconographies — that so often escape our perception today; Mahler and Strauss still heard them at the end of Wagner's century and at the turn of our own, but in our age many refuse to hear such meaning behind Wagner's sonic material. The corporeal images of his works were intended as signposts for the makeup of the ideal audience that would receive the Artworks of the Future, and those signs continued to look and sound familiar, and persuasive, a generation after the composer's death. Today, in that future, we must ask ourselves if we, too, respond to those visual and sonic signs of hatred, or whether the bodily images that Wagner took for granted have taken on different meanings in the more distant, post-Wagnerian age. Does the foreigner still have a high voice within the iconic vocabulary of Western racism? If so, does such a belief inform our response to Wagner's aesthetic constructions, or has that image been lost in the different cultural context of today's Wagnerian reception? What a quandary it would be, when listening to Wagner, to find oneself eavesdropping on his song for Germans, even as one heard the agony behind Beckmesser's shrill and foreign *Coloratur*.

And the scent went straight into them, touched their hearts, and categorically separated friendship from contempt, disgust from desire, and love from hatred. — Patrick Süskind, *Das Parfum: Die Geschichte eines Mörders*

Interaction between the Self and a fellow German deemed similar and between the Self and the Other unfolds in Wagner according to the confirmation of identity afforded by sensual impressions of another's body— by vision and by the sound of the voice. The eye sees and, metaphorically, the ear hears as well, but the I of the subject also receives another sensory indication of corporeal presence in Wagner's world— it smells. Olfactory impressions appear less often in Wagner's writings than do those vouchsafed the eye and the ear, but they serve the same function of establishing and reinforcing national, communal, folkish, and racial boundaries; not surprisingly, Wagner employs aromatic motifs, like those of visual and acoustic stimulation, both as sensual phenomena and as metaphors that evoke a host of ideological issues. In a footnote toward the end of *Oper und Drama*, for example, Wagner uses a metaphor of smell to illustrate his reflections on the etymology of the word *Geist*, which means both 'intellect' and 'spirit,' and thus implicitly associates aroma with idea: 'we may interpret "Geist" very nicely through the similar root "giessen" [to pour]: in a natural sense it is that which *"pours itself out"* from us [*das von uns sich Ausgiessende*], as the aroma is that which the flower spreads out, pours out' (*DS* 7: 318n). By now this image is familiar: Something emanates from the subject and in so doing communicates to the sensory organs of the recipient, who 'knows,' through such corporeal communication, whether to 'recognize' itself in their shared commonality or to define itself through the rejection of that which is different. Like other physiological signs, smell has this specific ideological function in Wagner and thus constitutes an icon of the body as a physiological reality laden with metaphorical implications that is readily comparable to those perceived by the eye and the ear.

Perhaps more than any composer before him, Wagner associated ideas with specific aromas. Raised in an age in which olfactory stimulation came to be categorized and stigmatized according to the dictates and the sensibilities of the developing bourgeoisie (and that therefore carried greater social significance than in the pre-industrial period), Wagner inherited the prejudices and beliefs concerning smell that typified the nineteenth century.[1] Thus, again, he employed an iconography of the body as an expression of his own agenda but in so doing conflated the motivic web of his own theories with the ideological connotations associated with the corporeal icons — in this case, with the perfumes and stench of the body — of his age. Though they occupy a comparatively small space in his theories, smells are everywhere apparent as ideological signs in his music dramas: In his works for the stage, smell, sexual taboo, Judeophobia, and German nationalism form a recurring motivic constellation that exemplifies the cultural material of Wagner's age as the basis for his own social-aesthetic concerns. The associative connection between scent, sex, anti-Semitism, and patriotism pervades his works in much the way such dramatic concerns as redemption and constancy recur with only slight variation throughout his artistic development. The connection illustrates a powerful and culturally encoded psychological mechanism that orders sense perceptions according to ideological and psychological needs: It demonstrates that the sensual perception of the body deemed 'real,' or believed to be grounded in physiological, objectively verifiable reality, is used to pass judgments regarding the perceived object, while that perception is not without values determined by the cultural experience of the community.[2]

Whether experimenting with different taste sensations during the composition of *Tristan und Isolde* or galvanized by an admixture of perfumes while at work on *Parsifal*, Wagner's nose and palate were highly involved in the formulation of ideas at the heart of his music dramas.[3] Robert W. Gutman suggests that Wagner's mania for olfactory stimulation reached its height in old age, during the genesis of *Parsifal*:

> In the late years, with the decay of the senses, his erotic interest in perfumes grew even stronger. He asked Judith [Gautier] to ship limitless amounts of amber, Milk of Iris (he poured half a bottle of it into his daily bath), and Rose de Bengale, and he called for powdered scents to sprinkle over fabrics. . . . His study in Wahnfried was directly over the bath, which he would inundate with rare odors. Seated at his desk and attired in incredible silk and fur outfits douched with sachet, he breathed in the aromatic fumes rising from below. . . . Amid scenes worthy of Huysmans' Des Esseintes, the first act of the 'religious' drama, *Parsifal*, came into being.[4]

But Wagner's fetishistic fascination with odor is far greater than such an anecdotal treatment of his life would suggest, for it functions as an important corporeal subtext in nearly all his major works for the stage: When an odor is introduced into the text of a Wagnerian music drama, it often brings with it a hint of the erotically forbidden, and this moment is of immense ideological importance in the utopian program of Wagner's works. The process of inhaling the aroma of the Other offers a pseudosexual, extrapersonal exchange — if not a foretaste, at least a foresmell of an act that can bring with it associations of defloration. It is a fetishistic, a titillating moment. So it appears, for example, near the conclusion to *Tannhäuser* when Venus arises before the knight in the final act of the drama. She attempts to lure him away from the strictures of his society to an eternal life of debauchery and sexual abandon, and as she approaches, the themes of illicit sex and unusual aromas are briefly intertwined in Tannhäuser's exclamation to his companion Wolfram:

Ha! Fühlest du nicht milde Lüfte? . . .
Und atmest du nicht holde Düfte? (*T*, 66)

[Ha! Do you not feel mild airs? . . . And do you not breathe wondrous fragrances?]

This is the first appearance of the motivic connection in Wagner's works, and it is typical for a number of reasons. In the vocabulary of Wagner's music dramas, *atmen* (to breathe) implies olfaction; it often replaces the less poetic but more straightforward *riechen* to indicate the perception of smell. Similarly, *Duft* (scent) is used in an unusual way. We know that as a librettist Wagner went to great lengths to enhance the language of his texts with antiquated turns of phrase and medieval expressions true to their philological origins. But Wagner most often uses *Duft* in a highly charged and erotic context; any positive connotations it receives in his works depart from the historical usage of the term. When Wagner makes *Duft* a pleasant, enticing aroma, he is projecting into his medieval and Reformation settings a new, more modern understanding of the word; it now evokes solely positive associations, though it originally implied fog, vapor, or a damp wind.[5] Thus the notion of a *Duft* as a seductive fragrance indicating an erotic and threatening dimension must have been more important to Wagner than the fact that it rhymes fortuitously with *Luft* (air), for the consistency of its appearance in a titillating and dangerous setting suggests psychological — as well as metrical — motives for its repeated occurrence.

In the act 3 bridal-chamber scene of *Lohengrin* it again has this function. Here, the foreign knight sings to Elsa of their impending sexual union; flowers and their scents are the metaphors Lohengrin uses to underscore the mystery of his sacred, secret identity, which must be preserved even in the sexual act. In Wagner, when something is sexy it is forbidden and smells wonderful. Lohengrin's and Elsa's fragrant bridal night is not pure bliss, for the motif of smell soon becomes associated with that which is secret, mysterious, and, above all, prohibited:

Atmest du nicht mit mir die süßen Düfte?
O wie so hold berauschen sie den Sinn!
Geheimnisvoll sie nahen durch die Lüfte, —
fraglos geb' ihrem Zauber ich mich hin. — ...
Wir mir die Düfte hold den Sinn berücken,

nahn sie mir gleich aus rätselvoller Nacht:
so mußte deine Reine mich entzücken. (L, 74–75, my emphasis)

[Do you not smell with me the sweet aromas? O how wondrously they bewitch the mind! *Mysteriously* they approach through the air, *unquestioning* I give myself to their magic. — . . . As the aromas bewitch my mind they also approach me out of the mysterious night: in this way your purity had to enrapture me.]

Finally, because breathing implies olfaction in these works, an equation of scents and sex is suggested in Lohengrin's ringing supplication to Elsa during their nocturnal nuptials:

O, gönne mir, daß mit Entzücken
ich deinen Atem sauge ein! (L, 75–76)

[O grant that I may suck in your breath with rapture!]

What is Wagner's consistent motivic vocabulary alluding to? It is nothing less than *incest*, that metaphor of superior, privileged union so replete with ideological, racial, and national significance for Wagner's social-aesthetic theories and for their dramatic representations on stage.[6] This becomes explicit when the sphere of odors and something forbidden in the sexual exchange reappears with even greater clarity in *Die Walküre*, in which the specific nature of the prohibited relationship is revealed as the incestuous act.[7] When Sieglinde sees her brother, Siegmund, for the first time since their childhood, she offers him 'Des seimigen Metes / süßen Trank [a drink of honeyed mead]' (RN, 78), and as their infatuation grows toward recognition and consummation, Siegmund sings his song describing the incestuous union of *Liebe* and *Lenz* — referred to as sister and brother — and highlights his poem with the motif of balmy aromas:

durch Wald und Auen
weht sein Atem, . . .
holde Düfte
haucht er aus:
seinem warmen Blut entblühen

> wonnige Blumen,
> Keim und Sproß
> entspringt seiner Kraft. . . .
> Die bräutliche Schwester
> befreite der Bruder;
> zertrümmert liegt,
> was sie je getrennt;
> jauchzend grüßt sich
> das junge Paar:
> vereint sind Liebe und Lenz! (*RN*, 90–91)

[through wood and meadow his breath blows. . . . sweet aromas he exhales; from his warm blood wondrous flowers arise; bud and bloom spring from his power. . . . The bridal sister is freed by her brother; broken lies what held them apart; shouting with joy the young couple greet each other: united are Love and Spring!]

The incestuous union of *Liebe* and *Lenz*, of course, is a reference to the 'natural' quality of the impending coupling of the Volsung family (Sieglinde pointedly tells Siegmund that he *is* the Spring for which she has yearned [*RN*, 91]), a privileged and positive union that will bring forth the finest of blossoms, Siegfried. No wonder the final line of act 1 is Siegmund's ecstatic reference to their incest as a 'blooming' of 'blood':

> Braut und Schwester
> bist du dem Bruder —
> so blühe denn, Wälsungenblut! (*RN*, 95)

[Bride and sister you are to your brother — so bloom then, Volsung-blood!]

Wagner consistently imbues the Volsungs' union with the sweetest smells of Nature; their incestuous, familial defloration is an act of flowering that makes explicit what had been lurking beneath the surface of Wagner's libretti since *Tannhäuser*: the association in the dramatist's imagination of sensuous aromas and a kind of union rejected by conventional society but vouchsafed those beings who represent the salvation of Germany and of the German race.

Similarly, the thinly veiled Oedipal nature of the relationship between *Tristan und Isolde* (in which the foster son woos his stepmother)[8] also receives an olfactory dimension on a number of occasions in their drama, first in the sexual union of act 2, which begins with the stage direction '*with an increasingly intense embrace, stretching out on a bank of flowers [Blumenbank]*' (TR, 67), and again in Tristan's vision of Isolde in act 3:

Auf wonniger Blumen
lichten Wogen
kommt sie sanft
ans Land gezogen. (TR, 89)

[On the brilliant waves of wondrous flowers she gently comes drawn onto land.]

The same is true of Isolde's orgasmic apotheosis at the conclusion to the drama, after which, especially given its rhythmic and acoustically mimetic evocation of sexual release, we are to assume she is united with her lover. She experiences such union as she is overwhelmed by unparalled aromas:

sind es Wellen
sanfter Lüfte?
Sine es Wogen
wonniger Düfte?
Wie sie schwellen,
mich umrauschen,
soll ich atmen,
soll ich lauschen?
Soll ich schlürfen,
untertauchen?
Süß in Düften
mich verhauchen? (TR, 99)

[Are they waves of gentle airs? Are they waves of wondrous aromas? How they swell, whirl around me, shall I breathe, shall I listen? Shall I drink them, dive beneath? Sweetly in aromas expire?]

Tristan und Isolde, of course, is the most synesthetic of Wagner's works, and the highly charged Oedipal nature of its suggestive psychological content is enhanced by the aesthetic merging of elements in the text. Perhaps the aesthetic goals of synesthesia have as their psychological substratum a desire for the merging of space and the metaphorical crossing of boundaries, a desire momentarily stimulated in the act of perceiving the aroma of the beloved companion. Such merging and crossing is at the center of Wagner's conceptualization of the revolutionary, socially transformative Total Work of Art, the agenda of which is the collapse of both aesthetic and social divisions and categories. That is to say, the psychology of the implications behind olfaction in Wagner may, surprisingly, provide a clue to the urgency discernible behind the many sexualized metaphors with which he discusses his new artwork, an art, moreover, that often depicts sexual transgression and Oedipal desire. In *Tristan und Isolde* the borders are sexual, social, and olfactory; a sexual union is implied in the union of sense perceptions, and the union is, in terms of the society depicted in the drama, a *forbidden* one.

Such a sweet-smelling yet disguised Oedipal relationship gives way in *Siegfried* to an overt association of the most primitive and most forbidden desire — the union of mother and son — with aromatic rapture, and the titular hero, of course, is the revolutionary human being par excellence. Once again, superior smells appear in the company of superior and related beings whose union transgresses the boundaries of a mundane and inferior world. When Siegfried sees Brünnhilde in act 3 of the drama, he believes her to be his mother, and Wagner's associative mechanism brings forth imagery replete with scent sensations by now familiar:

O Mutter! Mutter! . . .
Süß erbebt mir
ihr blühender Mund.
Wie mild erzitternd
mich Zagen er reizt!
Ach! Dieses Atems
wonnig warmes Gedüft! . . .
So saug ich mir Leben

aus süßesten Lippen,
sollt' ich auch sterbend vergehn! (*RN*, 234)

[O Mother! Mother! . . . Sweet her blossoming mouth quivers. How
mildly trembling it entices me, who so hesitates! Ah, the wondrous
warm fragrance of this breath! . . . Thus I shall suck life from the
sweetest of lips, even though I should die!]

After he has wakened her, he asks Brünnhilde 'softly and shyly':

So starb nicht meine Mutter?
Schlief die Minnige nur? (*RN*, 236)

[Then my mother did not die? Did the beloved only sleep?]

In this scene the three motivic criteria of the familial gaze,
voice, and sweet smell are united, and they serve to establish,
through their nature as corporeal icons, Siegfried's and Brünnhilde's status as related, kindred beings. When Siegfried says to
her,

deines Auges Leuchten
seh ich licht;
deines Atems Wehen
fühl ich warm:
deiner Stimme Singen
hör ich süß (*RN*, 237)

[the shining of your eyes I see light; the wafting of your breath I feel
warm: the singing of your voice I hear sweetly]

the signs of familial identity are complete, and nothing stands in
the way of their ensuing consummation.[9] In this context it is
consistent that the Annunciation of Death scene between Siegmund and Brünnhilde is bereft of olfactory motifs; their communication is frustrated, and just as her image grows dark and
cloudy, so the motif of flowers and sweet scents remains linked
solely to the woman with whom Siegmund experiences incest —
Sieglinde. The smell of incest does not waft about Brünnhilde
until she meets Siegfried. After Siegfried has deflowered her,
this constellation of smell and incest will not reappear in the

Ring cycle until Hagen offers the hero a spiced (and, by implication, scented) potion designed to recall this specific, primal, and, within the repressive society of *Götterdämmerung*, highly *forbidden* scene:

Trink erst, Held,
aus meinem Horn:
ich würzte dir holden Trank,
die Erinnerung hell dir zu wecken,
daß Fernes dir nicht entfalle! (*RN*, 318)

[Drink first, hero, from my horn: I spiced a wondrous drink for you, to brightly waken your memory, so that distant things may not elude you!]

As Wagner experimented in his works with variations on the theme of incest — from the mere suggestion of the forbidden in *Tannhäuser* and *Lohengrin* to an overt brother-sister union in *Die Walküre*, a lightly disguised mother-son consummation in *Tristan und Isolde*, and a more overt evocation of such consummation in *Siegfried* — he always associated it with aromatic motifs. In all the above scenes, sexual interdiction automatically arouses an olfactory response in the librettist's imagination. A marriage bereft of forbidden desire, such as that of the bourgeois couple Eva and Walther von Stolzing in *Die Meistersinger*, fails to evoke such imagery (with the exception of Walther's reference to 'Blüt' und Duft [blooms and aroma]' [*MN*, 110] in his prize-song, whose aesthetic makeup is revolutionary but which is accommodated by the society of the *Volk* and the Meistersinger). Only when the identity of the sexual partner carries with it a prohibited dimension hinting at primal desires can the associative mechanism of Wagner's psyche and the natural imagery of his social-aesthetic agenda demand a sweet-smelling yet often engulfing motif. Wondrous smells are for wondrous beings, and for the act that metaphorically preserves their singular, superior nature.

A connection between illicit sex and scent sensations was of course already a cliché by Wagner's time, and its appearance in his works may indicate that it was firmly established within the cultural vocabulary of his age. Yet his music dramas do not simply tie into a cultural-literary tradition that links fragrance to the realm of the mistress, the boudoir, and illicit sex, while assigning a marked absence of odors to the safer world of sex within a socially acceptable, sanctified union, such as marriage. The idiosyncratic aspect of Wagner's recurring use of the connection between aroma and extramarital sex is its ultimate association with forbidden relationships suggesting incest. In Wagner's works, every romantic situation accompanied by enticing fragrances suggests incestuous desire. Wagner thus expands the clichéd opposition of asocial balm versus odorless sex accepted by society to include incestuous relationships versus bourgeois marriage. In this respect, his personal associative patterns linked to the metaphors of his social-aesthetic theories enlarge the motivic tradition.

SMELLS AND WAGNER'S MUSIC

In addition to its consistent repetition in the various similar dramatic situations just cited, the motif of smell also appears in similar musical contexts within the Wagnerian Total Work of Art. That is, the ideological agenda associated with certain dramatic configurations (here, incest and sweet smells) may also be linked to the very musical material of the works for the stage, for just as each appearance of aromatic motifs suggests a forbidden and remarkably superior sexual union connoting incest, and with it all its attendant ideas of racial superiority and community, so they also are accompanied by musical features that evince considerable similarity. While there can be no 'gestural' equivalent in music to olfactory perception, Wagner's works do appear to contain a musical feature — the triplet — that emerges fairly consistently whenever his dramatic situations suggest aromas (as well, perhaps, as the trill, given the sounding of trills in a number of situations suggestive of scent, such as the approach of the siren in *Tannhäuser*, Siegfried's drinking of Hagen's potion, and Isolde's scent-filled death, and in the music associated with Mime's stench and the aromas of Klingsor's Magic Garden, discussed below). This is not to say that the triplet and the trill provide musical *representations* of smells but rather that they are often found in contexts in which a textual reference is made to aromas and hence may constitute a musical device that Wagner associated with the ideas also connected to olfactory perception in his dramas. The triplet serves to provide an acoustical metaphor not for smells per se but for an idea evoked by or linked to an aroma and is found above all whenever Wagner's dramatic situations depict a protagonist experiencing a change of perception associated with olfactory stimulation.

When the penitent Tannhäuser, for example, suddenly perceives in the passage quoted above the approach of Venus near the conclusion to the drama, the rhythmic pulse of the music shifts from the fairly straightforward and predominant 4/4 time (example 19). As the knight feels the 'mild airs' bringing with

Example 19. The conflation of triplets and 'mild airs' in *Tannhäuser*

Ha! Fühl - est du nicht mil - de Lüf - te?

them the 'wondrous fragrances' of sensual delight, the four-square movement of the music, so characteristic of this and of Wagner's other operatic works prior to the *Ring*, is momentarily interrupted or suspended by an interpolated, foreign metrical unit. At the point when the text makes it clear that Tannhäuser inhales the druglike aromas of Venus's sexy perfumes (or her sexual essence?) and thereby experiences a different realm of perception and a different consciousness divorced from the strictures of medieval courtly etiquette, the music briefly evinces metrical slippage — perhaps even intended as a gestural suggestion of a shudder? — clearly indicative of a shift out of the musical-dramatic movement presented prior to Venus's appearance. In a discussion of the Rome Narrative in *Tannhäuser*, Carolyn Abbate felicitously characterizes Wagner's musical material as 'the opera body,' as the acoustical-metaphorical representation of physiological states and of their perception; her observation is readily applicable to a moment such as this, for the metrical slippage evinced here provides a representation of the protagonist's subjective impressions experienced through the sense of olfactory perception.[10] In this, the first example of the motif of scent-and-sex in Wagner's works, his music conflates aromatic rapture with musical rupture.

While such an interpretation by itself might seem to be reading too much into what is admittedly only the most transient of musical phenomena, it is reinforced through the reappearance of the triplet in a host of similar musical-dramatic contexts. In what may otherwise be Wagner's most metrically uniform (and thus metrically most boring) work for the stage, comprised as it is of 4/4 time nearly throughout its entire three acts, the metrical pulse of the music for the bridal chamber scene in *Lohengrin* undergoes a sudden shift when the knight invites Elsa to attend to the 'sweet aromas' of the flower garden (example 20).[11] The

Example 20.
The introduction of triplets and the aromas of the flower garden in *Lohengrin*

repeated triplet patterns in the woodwinds provide what in this opera is an unusual rhythmic contrast to the simple-time note values assigned to the vocal line and to much of the orchestral accompaniment as well. It is with the textual introduction of the motif of scents here that Wagner's musical material displays such sudden metrical shifts. Again, the triplet is not to be understood as an acoustical sign of a scent but provides a musical contrast that accompanies the newly found, suddenly sexy perception through the senses.

And so it goes in Wagner's subsequent phantasmagoric confabulations: Often, when his heroes or heroines achieve a breakthrough out of mundane existence, their new-found experience is accompanied textually by a reference to olfactory stimulation and musically by a shift in rhythmic movement, often of a triplet set either against double time or within a simple-time context. This conflation for Wagner of scent with a flowing triplet meter may account for the shift to 9/8 time (marked '9/8 = 3/4') at the beginning of Siegmund's aria of spring, 'Winterstürme wichen dem Wonnemond,' in which the Volsung sings rapturously of the 'breath,' 'marvelous aromas,' and 'wondrous flowers' of the season of love. Similarly, when Isolde perceives the 'gentle airs' and the 'waves of wondrous aromas' of her Love-Death and asks herself if she should 'sweetly expire' in their fragrances, the musical material of her vocal line suddenly incorporates interpolated triplet figures suggestive of the transformation of her temporal-sensual experience. In all these cases, the idea of rapture and alteration suggested by the text may be associated with the musical material itself, which in these instances may be perceived as a means of conveying the protagonists' experiences of sensuous stimulation and transformed consciousness. It is the imagined nature of this sexy, otherworldly state that gives rise both to the motif of wondrous aroma linked to sensuality and to the musical device of the triplet as a metaphor for a change of perception, a shock out of normalcy, or a sudden physiological and emotional insecurity.

*

Insecurity constitutes the basis for another key dimension in the ideology of aroma in the Wagnerian imagination. The connection between incense and incest, discernible both in explicit form in Wagner's libretti and through evocation in the associations of his music, evokes not only the sweetest rapture of naughty and privileged consummation but also has another, darker dimension related to the ideological content of Wagner's theories and to the biographical trajectory of his hatreds as well, and it smells anything but nice. In the passages cited above, the sense of smell implies a negation of corporeal boundaries. In the act of olfactory perception, limitations of bodily and temporal identity momentarily give way, shifting the subject into a state that suggests suprapersonal communication. The psychological process through which individuation is suspended also explains another tenacious connection in Wagner's associative thinking that is a key to the other, flip side of the positive motifs discussed thus far—a link between smells and Jews. In their chapter on anti-Semitism from *Dialectic of Enlightenment*, Max Horkheimer and Theodor W. Adorno comment on this very process:

Of all the senses, that of smell—which is attracted without objectifying—bears closest witness to the urge to lose oneself in and become the 'other.' As perception and the perceived—both are united—smell is more expressive than the other senses. When we see we remain what we are; but when we smell we are taken over by otherness. Hence the sense of smell is considered a disgrace in civilization, the sign of lower social strata, lesser races and base animals.[12]

Within the discussion of Judeophobia, these remarks serve to explain the mechanism through which one secretly identifies with the despised object—in this case the Jew—and at the same time is compelled to perceive him as a bad smell. We have already examined several features of Wagner's fears concerning his connection to Jews: his suspicion of his possibly Jewish paternal heritage; his fear of being compared professionally with the

Jewish composer Meyerbeer; and the possible horror he may have felt, if Adorno is correct, at recognizing a self-caricature in his original description of the Nibelung dwarf Mime (himself a caricature of a Jew). These anxieties all point to an identification with the image of the Jew at various levels of consciousness within Wagner's psyche. Thus it is not surprising that the same process which calls forth aromatic motifs in conjunction with sexual identification (incest) should also operate when figures associated with Jews appear in the Wagnerian music dramas, for in both cases identification is linked to olfactory perception.

Even if one knew nothing of the long European cultural traditions linking Jews and foul odors, one would expect to find in Wagner's works olfactory equivalents to the other sensory indications of the Jew's body examined thus far—to his different appearance and his elevated voice. Since in Wagner like kind looks and sounds like itself and is endowed with a glorious, superior appearance and a deep, rich, and powerfully ringing heroic voice, one should expect the superior beings to recognize or know—and then to merge with—themselves through the perception of superior fragrances as well, and this is precisely the case in the passages just cited from *Die Walküre*, *Siegfried*, and *Tristan*. Similarly, just as the Self defines itself by perceiving what it is *not* through the physiological signs of the foreigner's appearance and voice, so it is only consistent that that other, foreign body should also be endowed with olfactory signs of its decidedly different, non-German essence.

And different they are. In Wagner's works, stench invariably functions as the olfactory icon of the Jew, and thus it is consistent that the figures analyzed thus far as the bearers of a variety of anti-Semitic icons and attendant associations—Alberich, Mime, and Beckmesser—are all accompanied in their respective music dramas by references to revolting odors. One of the earliest descriptions of Alberich—that small, dark, hairy, money-grubbing outcast—is provided by the Rhinemaiden Wellgunde and underscores the mephitic impression he makes on those around him:

Pfui, du haariger,
höckriger Geck!
Schwarzes, schwieliges
Schwefelgezwerg! (RN, 8–9)

[Pfui! You hairy, humpbacked lout! Black, calloused, sulfurous dwarf!]

Even surrounded by water, Alberich stinks. That this trait is
not unique to the arch Nibelung but belongs to all members
of his 'race' is indicated by the descent to Nibelheim, home
of the dwarves, undertaken through the 'Schwefelkluft [sulfur-
ous chasm]' filled with 'Schwefeldampf [sulfurous fumes]' and
'schwarzem Gewölk [black clouds]' (RN, 37). Of course, sulfur
has traditionally been associated with all kinds of evil figures,
as seen for example in Goethe's *Faust* in the sulfurous residue Mephistopheles leaves behind him after visiting Gretchen's
chamber (a residue that is admittedly only implied but to which
Goethe draws emphatic-mephitic attention).[13] But the reference to sulfur here in *Das Rheingold* is connected to a tradition in
German culture that explicitly links rotten smells to Jews.

When Wagner presented figures constructed out of various
anti-Semitic stereotypes who emit bad smells, he capitalized on
a topos linking Jews and stench that dates back at least as far
as the Middle Ages and that was firmly established in the German cultural consciousness by the nineteenth century. The thir-
teenth-century Austrian poet Seifried Helbling stated flatly that

ez wart sô grôz nie ein stat
sie waer von drîzec juden sat
stankes unde ungloubn.[14]

[There was never a state so large that a mere thirty Jews would not
saturate it with stench and unbelief.]

It is this combination of odor and a lack of piety that characterizes the Jew throughout the Middle Ages.[15] As Sander Gilman
has pointed out, the *foetor judäicus*, or 'odor of the Jews,' was a
motif already popular when the eighteenth-century pamphle-
teer Johann Jacob Schudt attributed it to the Jews' purported

lack of personal hygiene and to their supposedly indiscriminate penchant for garlic.[16] In his anti-Semitic essay 'On Religion' from *Parerga and Paralipomena*, the most important philosopher of the nineteenth century for Wagner, Arthur Schopenhauer, perpetuated the motivic tradition when he wrote explicitly of the 'Jew's pitch [*Judenpech*] and *Foetor Judäicus*.'[17] August von Platen and Wolfgang Menzel later exploited the popular connection between Jew and effluvium in their notorious and vindictive attacks on Heinrich Heine; Menzel's famous comment regarding the German-Jewish poet runs as follows: 'The physiognomy of Young Germany was that of a Jew-boy from Paris, dressed in the newest fashion, but completely pale and enervated by debauchery, with a specific smell of musk and garlic.'[18] Heine himself, in an effort to dissociate himself from the stereotype, described it in his early writings as a feature of Polish (or Eastern) Jews, though later, in *Die Bäder von Lucca*, he penned a caricature of a rotten-smelling, low-class Jew in Hamburg (and in so doing, he was clearly attempting to remove himself from the image of the impoverished Eastern Jew mentioned in the previous chapter).[19] This is not to say that Wagner was indebted to the writings of Platen, Menzel, or Heine on this matter. Rather, the notion of a *foetor judäicus* was so popular in his time that he either consciously exploited the cultural motif or was unconsciously drawn to and assimilated it in his invective portrayals of Jewish stereotypes. Whether he did so intentionally or not is less important than the fact that the motif clearly made sense to him and to his culture and that it lent his metaphorical portrayals of the Jew as the antithesis of the German credibility within his time.

Whenever a pseudo-Semitic figure appears in Wagner's world, he stinks (except in the aromatically unusual *Parsifal*, in which the pseudo-Jew's Otherness is highlighted by a different kind of smell, which I shall discuss below). Thus Mime, like his brother, Alberich, also suffers from a lack of olfactory graces. This is merely suggested in act 1 of *Siegfried* when the dwarf brews a smelly potion from eggs for the hero, who can't stand his cooking and swears: 'Was er kocht, ich kost es ihm nicht! [What he cooks I will not taste!]' (RN, 186). Their relationship is accompanied in the drama by an exchange of unpalatable tastes, a motif implying rotten smells as well that culminates in Siegfried's murder of the dwarf and his outburst:

Schmeck du mein Schwert,
eckliger Schwätzer! (RN, 216)

[Taste my sword, disgusting blabbermouth!]

The motif is taken up again in *Götterdämmerung* when Siegfried relates this event and Hagen comments:

Was nicht er geschmiedet,
schmeckte doch Mime! (RN, 318)

[What he did not forge, Mime nonetheless tasted!]

In Wagner's works, the gustatory always implies olfactory perception. Boundaries of taste and the acceptance or denial of food appear to highlight boundaries of racial purity and thus function much like odors, voices, and visual images in Wagner's sensory cosmology. Siegmund will accept Sieglinde's drink, but there is no indication that he eats with Hunding, though the latter urges him to do so (RN, 81). Mead is passed from Brünnhilde to Wotan, and from his daughter Sieglinde to his son Siegmund, and the Valkyrie promises it to Siegmund as well (RN, 118), but it is never mentioned outside the godly and incestuous family. The nurturing of like kind is a natural event underscored through the taking of food and the perception of smells: In the forest Siegfried observes deer, foxes, and wolves providing their offspring with sustenance (RN, 162). His disgust with Mime's culinary offerings represents his distrust of the dwarf's biological makeup. (It was consistent with the tradition linking Jews to garlic that Arthur Rackham chose to adorn Mime's cave with bulbs of the pungent herb; they hang prominently above the dwarf as he offers the young Siegfried one of his revolting brews [see figure 8].) Wagner presents the exchange as a paradigm of racial difference, for ultimately, acceptance of food from outside the family is equivalent to a danger threatening the Teutonic race. Hagen's potions lead to Siegfried's death, but, as he dies in 'Die Nibelungen Saga (Mythus)' (The Nibelung legend [myth]) — later retitled 'Der Nibelungen-Mythus als Entwurf zu einem Drama' (The Nibelung myth, as sketch for a drama) — the first prose scenario to the *Ring* of 1848, Siegfried has a vision of Brünnhilde bringing him mead: 'Brünhild! [*sic*] Brünhild! You shining Wotan's child! How bright and gleaming I see you approach me! . . . Lead me now, happy man, whom you chose as your mate, to Valhalla, that I in honor of all the heroes may drink Allfather's mead, which you, shining Wish-maid, proffer me! Brünhild! Brünhild! I greet you!'[20] In every case, from the very first conceptualization of the *Ring*, food, like smell, highlights racial identity.

Though it seems that the dwarf has spent sixteen to twenty years of his life preparing meals for the boy, he doesn't appear to be much of a cook, for Siegfried hates Mime's food, and it undoubtedly stinks, since the dwarf himself provides no joy to the discerning nose. An incident during rehearsals to the first complete performance of the *Ring* cycle in 1876 reveals that Wagner thought of Mime as a foul-smelling creature. When Carl Schlosser, the singer portraying the dwarf, failed to hobble about and scratch his back with the requisite verisimilitude in the Nibelheim scene of *Das Rheingold*, Wagner exclaimed to the man: 'You can extend the scratching of your back and heartily scratch your ass! The piccolo flute has such suspicious little trills anyway.'[21] Wagner was joking, of course, but jokes are telling. Unwittingly and yet consistently, Wagner may have been the first composer to invent music for farts.[22] Those 'suspicious little trills' in the uppermost orchestral line serve to highlight a connection between stench and race that is also discernible in both the texts and the music of numerous other Wagnerian dramas — the darker (back)side, as it were, of the trills of rapture associated with Venus's milder airs and with the incestuous rites of spring in *Die Walküre*. Those trills of sulfurous farts are never heard when gods and heroes sing.

In *Die Meistersinger von Nürnberg* Beckmesser, too, could use a good bath. He is associated with pitch and with bad luck in the double entendre of the German word *Pech*, used in the scene in act 2 between Hans Sachs and Eva as the cobbler works on Beckmesser's shoes:

SACHS: Ein Meister, stolz auf Freiers Fuß;
   denkt morgen zu siegen ganz alleinig:
   Herrn Beckmessers Schuh' ich richten muß.
EVA: So nehmt nur tüchtig Pech dazu:
   da kleb' er drin und lass' mir Ruh'! (MN, 75)

[SACHS: A Master proud in courtship's path plans tomorrow to triumph all by himself: Mr. Beckmesser's shoes I must prepare.
EVA: Make sure to take much pitch for that: then he'll stick in them and leave me in peace!]

Die Meistersinger thus adopts the motif of the 'Jew's pitch' that Schopenhauer had exploited in his anti-Semitic essay 'On Religion.' Wagner found — or perhaps only found reinforced — the motif of the Jew exuding the stink of pitch in the works of the writer most influential to his own intellectual development, whose *Parerga and Paralipomena* and *Die Welt als Wille und Vorstellung* (The world as will and representation) he read voraciously in 1854, following his completion of the initial prose drafts of *Die Meistersinger* in 1845 and long before he worked out the final libretto in verse form in 1861–62.[23] (Nietzsche would later observe that 'Wagner's hatred of the Jews is Schopenhauerian.')[24] When Eva exclaims that there is a rotten smell of pitch at the end of the scene with Sachs, she is referring not only to the cobbler, who is working with the stinking substance as he prepares the notary's shoes, but to Beckmesser as well, who she fears will win her hand in marriage:

Gleich, Lene, Gleich! Ich komme schon! Was trüg' ich

hier für Trost davon?
Da riecht's nach Pech, daß Gott erbarm' (MN, 77)

[Yes, Lene! Right away! I'm coming! What kind of help would I get here? Here it stinks of pitch, may God have mercy!]

Because of this connection between miasma and the rival Jew, the idiom of stealing something 'out from under someone's nose' takes on an added dimension. When Eva flirts with Sachs, she suggests that he save her from Beckmesser's airs — both olfactory and musical — in the song contest:

Am End' auch ließ' er sich gar gefallen,
daß unter der Nas' ihm weg vor allen
der Beckmesser morgen mich ersäng'? (MN, 75)

[In the end would he even allow Mr. Beckmesser to sing me out from under his nose in front of everyone tomorrow?]

(The association of stench and Jew in Wagner may be related to the widespread superstition that the large *nose* of the stereotypical Jew is an indication of his sexual difference.[25] The function of pseudo-Jewish figures in his dramatic works, with the exception of Mime, always includes a sexual danger that is based on the perception of the Jew's body as different.)

But not all smells in this most German of music dramas are awful. As in *Die Walküre* and *Siegfried*, both the Jewish threat *and its circumvention* are associated with specific smells in *Die Meistersinger*, and both the foul and the fragrant found here are drawn from long-standing cultural traditions linking aromas with Jews. Beckmesser's danger is signaled by the revolting stench of pitch, but a solution to his wooing of Eva is provided by a heavenly and uniquely German fragrance. Sweet smells in *Die Meistersinger* are *urdeutsch*; they emerge from the tree under which Sachs muses, in the heart (and the central depths) of medieval Germany, on the spontaneous inspiration of Walther's folkish German poetry:

Wie duftet doch der Flieder
so mild, so stark und voll! (*MN*, 72–73)

[How lovely the elder smells, so mild, so strong and robust!]

We learn later in Sachs's expostulatory *Wahnmonolog* that it was
this scent that stirred up the inhabitants of his 'liebes Nürnberg'
to riot ('Der Flieder war's [It was the elder tree]' [*MN*, 107], he
says), a fight that not only interrupts Beckmesser's nocturnal
serenade to Eva but nearly costs him his life. The victim of the
town's animosity and public humiliation, the notary believes the
goal of the riot was his own murder, and that riot was triggered
(not only by the sound of his donkeylike voice, as we have seen,
but also) by a quintessentially German aroma, by a scent naturally directed against the non-German in Wagner's motivically
consistent cosmos:

Wohl grün und blau,
zum Spott der allerliebsten Frau,
zerschlagen und zerprügelt,
daß kein Schneider mich aufbügelt!
Gar auf mein Leben
war's angegeben! (*MN*, 115)

[All black and blue, to the ridicule of the most precious lady, pounded
and beaten, so that no tailor could iron me out! My very life it was that
they were after!]

After he has been soundly battered and ridiculed, the audacity
of the Jew's intrusion into the social-aesthetic and sexual sphere
of purist musical Germany is made manifest. With a magical
aromatic breeze the elder tree has rid Germany of its presump-
tuous foe, and Nuremberg's evil spirit, the devilish Beckmesser,
has been exorcised.[26]

The tree's aroma has its roots in diverse cultural traditions of
Wagner's homeland. Whether the *Flieder* is actually an elder or a
lilac is an open question, one of those potentially intentional
ambiguities so often found in Wagner.[27] Peter Wapnewski

maintains that the time of year in which *Die Meistersinger* takes place necessarily makes it an elder,[28] and the superstitions in German folklore regarding the tree lend credence to this assumption: Hans Bächthold-Stäubli characterizes the elder tree as 'without doubt one of the most folkish (or folkloristic) [*volkstümlichsten*] plants of all.'[29] The attributes assigned to it—and especially to its aroma—in German superstition bear directly on its role in *Die Meistersinger*. It is deemed an ambiguous, powerful plant associated both with evil and with rejuvenative, healing spirits, the very ambiguity (of replenishment and destruction, of good and evil) upon which Sachs reflects in his act 3 *Wahnmonolog* and associated there, too, with spirits (*MN*, 106–107). Wieland Wagner assumed the tree was an elder because of its associations in German culture and accordingly staged act 2 of the drama under enormous, spherical representations of the elder's blossoms, which dominated the scene and replaced the traditional stage picture of *Fachwerkhäuser* and cobbled streets (figure 15).[30] As a plant that, according to Bächthold-Stäubli, 'drives away witches [*hexenabwehrende Pflanze*],' it serves in *Die Meistersinger* to rid Nuremberg of the evil spirit of the notary. Yet its correlate function as a life-affirming, rejuvenative agent is also discernible in the drama: The elder is repeatedly referred to as a *Lebensbaum*—a 'tree of life'—in German folklore, and, as discussed in chapter 1, Walther coins this very term in his metaphorical song of Eva, of life, and of love:

an meiner Seite stand ein Weib,
so schön und hold ich nie gesehn;
gleich einer Braut
umfaßte sie sanft meinen Leib;
mit Augen winkend,
die Hand wies blinkend,
was ich verlangend begehrt,
die Frucht so hold und wert
vom Lebensbaum. (*MN*, 111)

[at my side a woman stood, so beautiful and gracious I had never seen; like a bride she gently embraced my body; beckoning with her eyes, her

15. Act 2 of Wieland Wagner's production of *Die Meistersinger* at Bayreuth, 1956, depicting the elder blossoms on Midsummer's Eve. Photo by Siegfried Lauterwasser (Bayreuther Festspiele)

hand shiningly pointed to what I had so longingly desired, the fruit so gracious and precious of the tree of life.]

The elder is a *Lebensbaum* precisely because it is deemed an *aphrodisiac*, reaching its most intense blossoming, and with it its strongest scents, at the summer solstice. An old proverb from the Thuringian forest runs:

Auf Johannistag blüht der Holler —
da wird die Liebe noch toller.[31]

[On Saint John's Day the elder blooms — then love grows wilder.]

And of course it is precisely on Midsummer's eve that the elder blooms before Sachs's house in act 2 of *Die Meistersinger*, bringing with it an aroma that at once leads to the demise of Beckmesser and that drives the youthful ardor of Walther and Eva to such heights that they would elope, were it not for Sachs's intervention.

But the term *Flieder* can also be rendered into English as 'lilac,' a plant that blooms in the spring, the very season with which Sachs, in the act 2 *Fliedermonolog*, compares the birdsong of Walther's act 1 audition:

Es klang so alt, — und war doch so neu, —
wie Vogelsang im süßen Mai! . . .
Lenzes Gebot,
die süße Not,
die legt' es ihm in die Brust. (*MN*, 73)

[It sounded so old, and yet was so new, — like bird song in sweet May! . . . Spring's command, the sweet need, it placed it in his breast.][32]

This simultaneous polarity and conflation of 'old' and 'new' is one of the central themes of *Die Meistersinger*, and it applies to the implications of different aromas in the drama, lilac blooming in 'sweet May' and the elder in Midsummer. Again, as always in Wagner, the distinction is metaphorical — the bird song of May itself is used metaphorically — and thus abstract and yet placed within a real, physical setting, so that identifying the plant is not simply some positivistic ritual, because that identity leads to diverse and specific implications of a cultural and ideological nature. If it is an elder and not a lilac, its capacity to stimulate young lovers while also protecting the community from evil spirits makes it the producer of an aroma with cultural legitimacy easily adapted to Wagner's own agenda. In act 3 of *Die Meistersinger*, Sachs gleefully ponders the connection between Germany, the *Flieder*'s powerful aroma, and the violent tumult it caused:

Wie friedsam treuer Sitten,
getrost in Tat und Werk,
liegt nicht in Deutschlands Mitten
mein liebes Nürnberg! . . .
und will's der Wahn gesegnen,
nun muß es Prügel regnen,
mit Hieben, Stoß' und Dreschen
den Wutesbrand zu löschen. —

Gott weiß, wie das geschah? . . .
Der Flieder war's: —Johannisnacht! (*MN*, 106–107)

[How peaceful of true customs, trusting in deed and work, lies not in
Germany's middle my dearest Nuremberg! . . . and if chaos will bless it,
blows must come raining down, with punches, slugs, and beatings to
quell the burning rage. —God knows how all that came about? . . . It
was the elder tree: —Midsummer's eve!]

Ultimately Wagner's *Flieder* evokes both the lilac-filled spring
(a season, like in *Die Walküre*, so replete with the aromas of
youthful love) and the midsummer of the elder's blooms, itself
so laden with associations in Germany's cultural heritage. The
'magical' powers of the elder were not Wagner's invention but
were central to the beliefs associated with the tree in the traditions of Germanic folklore. The spirits of the elder (who resemble the magical dwarves found under the tree because they love
its scent)[33] move out of German legends and into the idiosyncratic, personal, anti-Semitic motivic vocabulary of *Die Meistersinger*, providing there a dramatic connection between tradition, magic, a conservative nationalist and folkish agenda, and
a smell that would have appeared familiar and perhaps even
subliminally persuasive to Wagner's contemporary audience
schooled in the same motivic traditions that inform this, one of
the most anti-Semitic dramas ever to have appeared on stage.

The Jew, as a foreign, repulsive, and insidious element threatening the homogeneous sanctity of the German *Volk* and of its art,
is delineated by odors of difference, be they sulfurous, bor-
borygmous, or burned from leather. Could it be that Wagner
surrounded Beckmesser with the smell of pitch and inundated
his own bath with perfume (a practice referred to only later
during work on *Parsifal*) because he wished to distance himself
from confusion with such a figure? The Self needs its Other
in order to recognize the borders that give shape to its own
identity; clearly Wagner's patriotic nationalism is part of a psychological disposition, another expression of which is his anti-

Semitism; each requires the other for its identity, both emerge from a single constellation of needs and fears, and both evoke motifs of smell. These two manifestations of a single senti-ment — nationalism as Judeophobia — appear as poles of a spec-trum filled with aromas that extend from the lowest putrefaction of an inferior race to the magical pollen of a purified Germany. Love and hate are no farther apart in Wagner's mind than their distinguishing and diametrically opposed aromas.

Following Wagner's incorporation of the motif of the *foetor judäicus* in his dramas, the belief in a biological olfactory icon of Jewishness continued to be widely held in the popular culture of Germany. By the end of his lifetime, it even appeared in the pseudo-scientific literature on race. The anti-Semitic biologist Gustav Jaeger, for example, published a treatise in 1880, three years before Wagner's death, entitled *Die Entdeckung der Seele* (The discovery of the soul), which characterized the purported stench of the Jews as a natural sign of their biological differ-ence.[34] In his treatise Jaeger even went so far as to attribute a foul odor to the very *soul* of the Jew. Perhaps the work of Wil-helm Fliess at the end of the nineteenth-century, linking the nose and the genitalia, is related to this motivic tradition, for the argument has been made that Fliess developed his theory through a desire to vindicate his position in society as a Jew.[35] The icon of smell was powerful and tenacious. By the end of Wagner's life, it clearly had adapted to the popularization of the natural sciences, with their emphasis on biological and positiv-istic explanations for natural phenomena. In the twentieth cen-tury it would continue to inform the public perception of the Jew, appearing in such pseudo-scientific proto-Nazi investiga-tions as Hans F. K. Günther's *Rassenkunde des jüdischen Volkes* (Information on the race of the Jewish people), in which Gün-ther claims that the *foetor judäicus* should be studied through chemical analysis.[36] Within Wagner's works, it emerges auto-matically, in a straightforward fashion, and Wagner surely as-sumed that it would be accepted without question because it was such an unquestioned topos in his culture.

While Wagner exploited the scent-filled folkish traditions of Germany with little modification in *Die Meistersinger* through simple references to long-standing motifs, his aromatic adaptation of Teutonic legends and sagas for the *Ring*, *Tristan*, and *Parsifal* was another matter. In these works his ideological concerns demanded a transformation of the literary and legendary sources that provided the basis for his dramatic material. When one compares the sources with the music dramas, it becomes apparent that fetid aromas in the earlier works are suppressed or transplanted in the libretti according to the demands of Wagner's social-racial prejudices and of the motivic associations they evoked within his imagination.

This is only partially the case with respect to the sources of the *Ring*, because in them sweet smells and putrid odors play almost no role at all. In the passages from the *Eddas* and *The Saga of the Volsungs* that provided the models for the union of Siegmund and Sieglinde and of Siegfried and Brünnhilde, aromas can only be occasionally discerned behind references to potions and mead, but flowers, scents, and the like are nowhere to be found.[37] Similarly, the literary predecessors of those who stink in Wagner's *Ring* are remarkably bereft of stench. Thus, Wagner added an olfactory polarity when he adapted his Norse and Germanic sources to the racist and nationalist agenda of his tetralogy, and he did so consistently. When the Volsung heroes are immersed in the smell of spring while Nibelungs fart and stink of sulfur, they do so not in the cultural traditions of northern Europe but only in the music dramas that enact representations of Wagner's thoughts on superior and inferior beings and on a future, homogeneous society rid of those he deemed responsible for the foul demise of his contemporary world.

But in both Gottfried von Strassburg's *Tristan* and Wolfram von Eschenbach's *Parzival* (the primary source material for *Tristan und Isolde* and *Parsifal*)[38] wounds emitting putrid odors play a key role. In *Tristan* attention is drawn to the stench emerging from the hero's wound, suffered in combat with Morold, which is so overpowering as to drive his attendants, well-wishers, and members of the court from his room:

The place where the blow had fallen took on a stench so fearsome that life became a burden to him and his body an offence. . . .

During the whole time that he was playing [the harp] . . . , his vile wound exhaled such an odour that none could remain with him for as much as an hour.

'Tantris,' said the Queen, 'if you should ever happen to reach a point where this stench has left you and people can abide your company, let me commend this girl, Isolde, to your care.'[39]

Similarly, in *Parzival* emphasis is placed on the pollution emerging from Anfortas's (in Wagner, Amfortas's) affliction. Trevrizent explains to the hero that Anfortas is taken to an enchanted lake for its sweet fresh air as a counter to the revolting odor: 'There is a lake called Brumbâne on to which he is taken so that the stench from his gaping wound shall be quelled by the fragrant breezes.'[40] Another passage describes the various means used to counter the foul airs of the wound:

When sharp and bitter anguish inflicted severe discomfort on Anfortas they sweetened the air for him to kill the stench of his wound. On the carpet before him they lay spices and aromatic terebinth, musk, and fragrant herbs. To purify the air there were also theriac and costly ambergris: the odour of these was wholesome. Wherever people trod on the carpet, cardamon, cloves, and nutmeg lay crushed beneath their feet for the sake of the fragrance — as these were pounded by their tread the evil stench was abated.[41]

In both Gottfried's and Wolfram's works, scents offer a revolting and pronouncedly realistic effect, but Wagner erased them in his dramatic adaptations (though it is amusing to note that the 'costly ambergris' that refreshes the air about Anfortas is the very substance Wagner inhaled while composing his music drama based on Wolfram's medieval epic — sent to him by his devoted friend Judith Gautier.[42] When smells enter the texts of the music dramas based on the aroma-filled sagas, they are pleasant and sweet, even enticing, and are limited to characters (such as Isolde) who are unaccompanied by scents in the original sources. Because putrefaction in Wagner is invariably linked to Jews, it has no place among the heroes and Teutonic figures of his artistic imagination, no matter how horrible these figures reek in his sources, and therefore he suppressed it from association with the very protagonists who stink in Germany's literary past.

*

Having discussed the smellier side of Wagner's motivic universe, we can now return to its olfactory opposite, to the realm of those superior and more fragrant beings whose identity is always defined by the horrific bodies their glorious presence rejects and in so doing continually implies. Because they are associated with the kind of sexual union (incest) vouchsafed only the exalted, privileged and heavenly scents bring with them the ideological implications that also attend Wagner's most powerful sexual metaphor. The metaphor of incest, enhanced by aromas, represents Wagner's belief that Germany must isolate itself—*must breed from itself*—if it is to preserve its singular essence and to resist foreign, or *welsch*, corrosion, an idea found throughout his essayistic production and discernible in the metaphors of his dramatic constellations as well. The argument of 'Erkenne dich selbst,' a manifestation of that late phase of Wagner's anti-Semitism grounded in notions of a purportedly biological, verifiable science of race, is based on this premise. Wagner claims that when the German mingles with the 'lesser' peoples of the East (and the East is the purview of the Jew), he degenerates, while the Jew profits from such genetic decay. Following the Thirty Years' War, Wagner explains, 'the great monarchical power relations shifted from genuine [*eigentlichen*] German land to the Slavic East: degenerated [*degenerirte*] Slavs, decaying [*entartende*] Germans form the basis of the history of the eighteenth century, upon which finally in our times the Jew could quite confidently move in from the drained [*ausgesaugten*] Polish and

Hungarian countries' (GS 14: 188–189). This is the very image Wagner had presented in his postrevolutionary essays on the ancient Greek roots of Germany's future cultural and social reform when he described the Oriental and barbaric Jewish hordes penetrating and thereby destroying the communal unity of Greece. When read in conjunction, Wagner's diverse essays suggest that the same fate threatens Germany in the modern age. And what does Wagner hold up as the only possible counter to such a vampiric and dangerously degenerating threat to the future of Germany? 'The unconquerable feeling of relatedness to the *Volk* . . . sympathy . . . for the fate of one's own *family*' (GS 14: 190, my emphasis). The family is the *Volk*, and to breed outside that family is to relinquish the superior material of one's genetic German heritage. Incest, then, with its attendant aromas found only in the company of superior bodies, is the metaphor of Germany's 'real' physiological salvation. The family of the fatherland (and the mother, sister, and brotherland) must breed with (and within) itself to preserve its superior essence. By comparing Wagner's pronouncements in his essays with the music dramas, it becomes clear that aromatic incest, sweet-smelling nationalism, and fetid Jewishness merge in his creative fantasies and in his social theories to form a consistent ideological nexus, for just as the incestuous union produces the superior being who smells wonderful in the works for the stage, so patriotism in both these works and in the essays limits a people's offspring to itself in order to ward off the reeking filth of foreign influence.

While Wagner's use of the motifs of stench and fragrance can be traced to numerous long-standing traditions in his culture, his thoughts on incest mark a break with the assumptions of his time, for they progress in the *opposite* direction of popular contemporary beliefs condemning inbreeding and decay. A widely held belief in the nineteenth century about the Jews equated their supposed degeneration with their suspected inbreeding. The Jews' exclusion of sexual communication outside their population had led, according to the racial attitudes and scientific logic of the time, to the decay of their genetic material. At the end of the century, Freud's French mentor Jean Martin Charcot and such widely read psychiatrists in Germany and the Austro-Hungarian Empire as Theodor Kirchhoff and Richard Krafft-Ebing shared this belief.[43] Wagner's solution to the Jewish threat was diametrically opposed to the pseudo-scientific beliefs of his age and of the time immediately following his death. For him, the physiological incompatibility of the German and the non-German races, ironically, made the Jew a corrosive threat, undiminished — indeed, only exacerbated — by the foreigner's intermarriage, inbreeding, and genetic tenacity, as another passage from 'Erkenne dich selbst' spells out in detail:

> the Jew, on the other hand, is the most amazing example of racial consistency which has hitherto been produced by the history of the world. Without a fatherland, without a mother tongue, he is always led to his inevitably finding himself again, through all peoples, countries, and languages, thanks to the sure instinct of his absolute and ineradicable uniqueness: even mixing with others [*die Vermischung*] doesn't harm him; a male or a female may mix with the races foreign to him [*er vermische sich männlich oder weiblich mit den ihm fremdartigen Rassen*], a Jew always comes out. (*GS* 14: 189)

A passage such as this suggests that the metaphors of interracial union in the *Ring* are grounded in a belief concerning genetic-biological reality; Siegfried emerges from the incest of Siegmund and Sieglinde, while Hagen, a giver of impure potions and described as 'frühalt, fahl und bleich [prematurely old, wan, and pale]' (*RN*, 282), represents the degeneration of a union between the Teutonic Grimhild with Alberich (figure 24). The physiological degeneration of which Hagen speaks — and, as I shall discuss in chapter 5, that his music repeatedly represents — results from the *physically* corrosive effect of a mixture of the Jew's inferior (though tenacious) corporeal features and the blood of a superior, German being. If every union of a Jew and a German results in offspring bearing the corporeal signs of the Jew, the future of Germany is in peril — it will cease to be German, because for Wagner, physiology-as-metaphor is based on the physical reality of the body, and the decay of the German body constitutes that of the German community, of its 'essence.' The terms *degenerirt* and *entartet* connoted in the nineteenth century neurological and biological decay, and Wagner uses them precisely with this meaning in mind. It appears that when the *German*'s body functions as a metaphor, the abstract, theoretical, conceptual dimension of the metaphor may be of greater importance than its physiological sign (as seen in Wagner's use of the image of the eye as the vehicle for the superior community recognizing itself in the work of art), but when the *Jewish* body has a metaphorical function, its physiological dimension comes to the fore, both in Wagner's theoretical writings and in his works for the stage. Though both the (widespread) notion that Jewish inbreeding leads to biological degeneration and the (idiosyncratically Wagnerian) strategy for preserving Germany's racial purity through inbreeding arise from the same racial prejudice, they are obviously opposed in their apparent logic. Thus, Wagner's prejudices forced the associative patterns of his imagination to form motifs at odds with the motivic vocabulary of his age, but he did so consistently and in so doing always underscored the metaphor of incestuous salvation with aromas a world removed from the olfactory signs of those beings the incest would deny. Olfaction for Wagner appears to trigger a process of regression which brings with it such attendant elemental drives as the desire for a return to a mother's embraces and the fear of harm from a Jewish (and hence possibly paternal) foe.[44] The regression suggested by these motivic constellations leads again to the mobilization of atavistic sense perceptions, which in turn tie into primitive desires — in this case, incest — and primitive fears regarding territory or nationalism, both enhanced by the perception of smell in Wagner's emotionally charged imagination.

In his works before *Parsifal*, German racial purity can be preserved only out of the incestuous coupling of the German *Volk* with itself, which, Wagner hopes, will lead to a healthy, pure, and pollen-filled nation rid of the foul presence of a stench-

16. Klingsor's Magic Garden. Oil painting by Max Brückner based on designs by Paul von Joukovsky for the first production of *Parsifal*, 1882 (Nationalarchiv der Richard Wagner–Stiftung/Richard Wagner Gedenk-stätte, Bayreuth)

filled sexual danger. At first glance, *Parsifal* might appear to confound the complex psychological associations connecting Jewishness, aroma, incest, and nationalism in his works, but this is only partially the case. Though the specific constitution of Jewish aromas changes in this final music drama, their function remains the same; they still underscore racial difference. It is not until *Parsifal* that the motif of the Jew as a sexual threat is linked to a *pleasant* odor. Before 1877, pseudo-Semitic figures were simply equated with putrefaction. Now, Klingsor and Kundry, the two representatives of Jewishness in the work, are associated with enticing odors that bring with them a sense of compulsion, entrapment, and sexual urgency. These arise from Klingsor's Zaubergarten, that magic, fantastical place filled with fragrant aromas that paralyze and seductresses who bewitch (figure 16). Klingsor himself is castrated, but his drives cannot be suppressed, and from them his aromatic Magic Garden receives its potency, which poses a threat to the German knights, as Gurnemanz narrates in act 1:

Example 21.
Gurnemanz's evocation of the Magic
Garden in act 1 of
Parsifal

Die Wüste schuf er sich zum Wonnegarten,
d'rin wachsen teuflisch holde Frauen;
dort will des Grales Ritter er erwarten
zu böser Lust und Höllengrauen:
wen er verlockt, hat er erworben;
schon viele hat er uns verdorben. (*P*, 43)

[The desert he created into a wondrous garden, in which grow devilishly sweet women; there he waits for the knights of the Grail for evil lust and the anguish of Hell: whomever he enticed, he has procured; he has already ruined many for us.]

At the appearance of the word 'Wonnegarten,' Wagner employs a variety of musical devices to provide acoustical metaphors for bewitchment (example 21). The flutes play a series of trills, while the clarinets (instruments Wagner had associated with the treacherous difference of Mime in *Siegfried*) emit a syncopated, surging, pulsating motif (later taken up by the strings) that is accompanied, at the words 'holde Frauen; / dort will des Grales Ritter er erwarten,' by a rising and falling movement in the strings — violins and cellos — that may be perceived to constitute a gestural equivalent to a writhing, vinelike embrace evocative of the threatening nature of flowers in the music drama. It is never made clear whether the figures Parsifal beholds in this garden in act 2 are in fact women or flowering plants; the phantasmagoric experience appears to merge vegetation and human being in a musky smell of sexual fascination (figure 17). Parsifal himself asks them:

Wie duftet ihr hold!
Seid ihr denn Blumen? (*P*, 62)

[How wondrously you smell! Are you then flowers?]

to which they reply:

Des Gartens Zier —

17. Costume designs for the Flower Maidens by Paul von Joukovsky for the first production of *Parsifal*, 1882 (Nationalarchiv der Richard Wagner–Stiftung/ Richard Wagner Gedenkstätte, Bayreuth)

— und duftende Geister!
Im Lenz pflückt uns der Meister. (*P*, 62)

[The garden's graceful adornment — and aromatic spirits! In spring the master picks us.]

The *Meister* is Klingsor. Because he wishes to be accepted as a knight of the Holy Grail and thus in effect to eschew his Jewish identity, Wagner's earlier association of family and sweetened stimulation makes the magician adopt the masquerade of the good (familial) smell found in the earlier music dramas — an aroma which before *Parsifal* has solely represented the Teutonic race. That Klingsor's voluptuous flowers smell good is perhaps an olfactory mask, especially if one considers the function of smells in Wagner's earlier works; they are an extension of Klingsor's desire for inclusion among the chosen German knights. Perhaps we are to assume that his *true* aromatic essence is putrid, but whether the magician smells good or bad is less central to his olfactory function than the fact that he — like Kundry — smells *different*. If in the earlier works the Jew stank while Teutonic society smelled sweet, now he adopts a sickly sweet aroma a world removed from the scent of chastity and lofty ideals. Perhaps Wagner's creative imagination and metaphorical system allowed his constructions of anti-Semitic stereotypes to be associated with fragrant aromas in *Parsifal* because here, for the first time in his works, *sexual desire per se* is seen as evil.[45] Pleasant aromas always indicate sexual enticement in his works, but before 1877 such desire is actually presented in a positive light, perhaps as an alternative to the strictures of bourgeois society and as a vehicle for the preservation of the superior German racial family. In the quasi-religious work of the late Wagner, abstention is preferable to wanton sexuality, and each receives a different aroma. (This is ironic, given the fact that the composer was involved in extramarital sexual relations with Judith Gautier — associated for him with perfumes — during work on the very music drama that stigmatizes eroticism and fragrance!)

As the locus of sensuality and temptation, the body emerges in *Parsifal* not as a vehicle through which liberating, natural impulses impel the subject to break out of the unnatural strictures of abstemious and unnatural civilization, as it had functioned in *Tannhäuser*, *Tristan*, and the *Ring*, but as a source of physical impulses depicted solely in a negative light, as the place of drives that lead to the breakdown of a sense of order deemed superior and to the compromise of lofty ideals and superior goals. Perhaps it is for this reason that the most pious and purest figures in Wagner's final music drama are perceived through their voices alone, as *dis*embodied spirits: the nearly dead king Titurel, whom God had chosen as the founder of the order of the Grail, and the (angelic?) voice heard at the conclusion to act 1 that hovers as a reminder and a calling to Gurnemanz to patiently await the coming of the 'pure fool' who will redeem Amfortas's — and Christ's — suffering. Titurel, as his voice informs us during the first temple scene, 'lives on' in the grave through the daily transubstantiation provided by the Grail, painfully presided over by his son, the physically tormented and hence inadequate Amfortas. Time and again, Wagner's text draws attention to the fact that Titurel is holier, purer, loftier, and more pious than other figures, first through Gurnemanz's narrations in act 1 and then through the plaintive antiphonal chant of the Grail knights and the text of Amfortas's prayer to his father in act 3. The absence of Titurel's body is a sign of his sanctity. Never seen, hovering in the grave halfway between the fleshly world of his son and that purer realm of the spirit, Titurel's body assumes metaphorical proportions as the final, solely theoretical link to an earthly realm in which sensual impressions are deemed suspect. After he has died and Amfortas's sinful-sensual wound has been closed, the floating voices of the angels at the conclusion to the work provide an acoustical reminder of that corporeal absence as a sign of virtue, announcing through their invisible sonic impression the beginning of a holier, more abstemious reign to come, a reign devoid of the body. Though Wagner's final dramatic tableau unites the sexual imagery of the spear and the Grail, the implications of his last work deny the physicality of such representations, underscoring instead their abstract, symbolic nature as disembodied conceptualizations. The final scene of the final Wagnerian music drama can be read as a victorious celebration of the demise of the body and, with it, of its threatening sexuality and sensuous odors.

The most threatening body in *Parsifal* belongs to Kundry, Klingsor's supreme flower of seduction. The sorcerer calls her forth with the incantation:

Dein Meister ruft dich Namenlose:
Urteufelin, Höllenrose! (*P*, 55)

[Your master calls you, nameless one: primeval she-devil, Rose of Hell!]

It has often been noted that Kundry is one of the most enigmatic of Wagner's musical-dramatic creations: As a woman who mocked Christ and is punished with the fate of the Wandering Jew (as Wagner himself characterized her), she constitutes his only female anti-Semitic figure, doomed to 'wander' the earth in multifarious guises (dishevelled hag, seductress, and penitent), seeking salvation, which, ultimately, she will find in baptism and death at the conclusion to the drama, recalling Wagner's ambiguous statement in the final passage of 'Das Judentum in der Musik' that the only salvation for the Jews is *der Untergang*.[46] (The question as to whether this term meant 'destruction' or 'assimilation' continues to dominate the debate about Wagner's anti-Semitism today. But many of his defenders forget that in 'Aufklärungen über "Das Judentum in der Musik"' of 1869 Wagner replaced the enigmatic and therefore potentially more humanitarian and inclusive statement at the conclusion to the essay of 1850 with his explicitly stated desire for 'the forcible ejection of the corrupting foreign element' [*GS* 13: 50].)

Because debauchery in *Parsifal* is presented as a source of damnation, it is linked to the Jew through its association with the powers of Klingsor and of the instrument of his will, the wandering Kundry, whose roselike presence threatens to overwhelm the pious German boy Parsifal. For this reason, the perfume of sexual desire is now connected to the Semitic foe as well, replacing or effacing the Jew's effluvia. Because sexuality in *Parsifal* is now debased, the motif of incest, too, undergoes variation and reevaluation. It is no longer a vehicle for circumventing the Jewish sexual influence and for preserving a superior German essence, as it had been in all Wagner's works prior to *Parsifal*, but instead represents the Semitic sexual attack. When Kundry impersonates Parsifal's mother in an attempt to seduce the boy (*P*, 67), incest poses a *threat* to the future of the order of the Grail. Aroma, however, is still linked to eroticism: Kundry can attempt her seduction of Parsifal because she is the *Höllenrose* — her foreign enticing fragrance implying incest has won over the defenses of many a Grail knight — but now in Wagner's cosmology fragrance, sex, and incest represent a danger to the salvation of the German soul, a threat that in *Parsifal* is intimately associated with foreign airs — with the eroticism of the exotic.

At this point it is worth wondering whether Wagner would have had perfumes pumped into the theater at strategic moments in his dramas had the technological means to do so been available to him; one could imagine the Total Work of Art encompassing, and not merely imaginatively evoking, the sensual perception of aromas in such dramatic junctures as the bridal chamber scene in *Lohengrin*, the overwhelming olfactory conclusion to *Tristan*, or the Magic Garden scene of *Parsifal*. In each case, the audience's perception of smell would have been commensurate with Wagner's stated desire that his works communicate through the senses to the 'feeling' instead of the intellect, and thus the often-touted druglike state induced by the more phantasmagoric moments of Wagner's works would have been reinforced by associations linked to olfactory stimulation, as well as to the extraordinarily evocative conflation of music and text in his dramas. And, just to pursue the fantasy to its logical conclusion, one could also imagine a technologically advanced auditorium at Bayreuth equipped for the sensual manipulation of its audience through olfactory as well as visual and acoustical stimuli, exuding at key moments and for short intervals only the stench of garlic or of matter even less seemly and more odoriferous whenever the dramatic situation called for the evocation of anti-Semitic stereotypes. Garlic, sulfur, and flatulence in Nibelheim and in Mime's forest cave, and the stench of pitch and burned leather in the nocturnal scenes of *Die Meistersinger* — truly a 'total' work of art encompassing the spectrum of culturally encoded aromas! Who knows what the sensorial reception in future theaters will entail.

THE ODOR OF THE ORIENT

The exoticism of the Orient brings with it the titillation of aromas that threaten to cast the European (bourgeois) subject outside the pale of respectable accountability, and, accordingly, the Orient's location in the nineteenth-century Western imagination is more closely defined by its ideological function than by its geographical exactitude. The geography of Orientalism, encompassing as it does such spatially diverse yet, in terms of their ideological meaning for the European imagination, remarkably similar locations as North Africa, Turkey, the Near and the Middle East, India, and China, provided Wagner and his European contemporaries with settings for the projection of a host of anxieties concerning difference, be it racial, sexual, national, or religious.[47] While Wagner's works reflect a number of stereotypical features associated with purportedly distinct areas, the ideological implications attending these diverse settings are very much of a piece, for with the assignment of fascinating yet threatening power to the sphere of the largely unknown and hence only imagined realms lying beyond the experience of the Westerner, the desire to control is always present.

That Wagner deems the Jew Oriental, or exotic, is suggested in a passage from 'Die Kunst und die Revolution' cited in chapter 1, in which he juxtaposes the communal spirit of the Greeks (read: Germans) with the egotism of those ancestors of today's 'hero of the stock exchange,' the foreign wheeling and dealing merchants from the outer extremities of the empire — 'the egotistical Orientalized barbarian' (DS 5: 284, 293). The Jew is an Oriental, which in Wagner means simply different because non-European; he is a foreigner from the East bringing with him the exoticism and the threat of a different world and a different body, as Wagner's comments in 'Erkenne dich selbst' regarding the influx of opportunistic and vampiric Jews from the East suggest. Wagner defines and knows himself through the rejection of the image, the sound, and the smell that also define the Other, Eastern being.

Within Wagner's works for the stage, the Oriental always functions as a threat and is often accompanied by exotic odors. But while many figures constructed out of anti-Semitic stereotypes are simply revolting, those evincing Oriental overtones are also often disturbingly enticing; their exoticism makes them scary, but the subject who views their disquieting Otherness does not simply turn away his gaze after recognizing such difference; he surreptitiously keeps one eye (and one nostril) open and continues to slyly perceive the lineaments of that foreign corporeality, inhaling a sexy musk that it would never call European. It is no coincidence that Kundry — the Other as woman, seductress, religious outcast, and Jew — is the figure who has traveled farthest to the East in *Parsifal* in an attempt to garner soothing (and presumably aromatically wondrous) potions for the ailing Amfortas, to a realm that is never seen by the male knights but whose difference is represented in kitchy clichés of a purportedly Oriental nature. It is in her capacity as a messenger from the East that she first enters the drama in act 1 when she rushes in, wild and distraught, witch and Valkyrielike even (she has 'traveled through the air,' so great was her haste), with an unguent she pointedly reveals to be *Arabian* (figure 18):

KUNDRY: (*rushes in hastily, almost falling. Wild garments, tucked high; belt of long snakeskins hanging down; black hair fluttering in loose braids; face a deep brown-red color; stabbing black eyes, at times piercing wildly, more often as if deadly rigid and immovable. She hurries toward Gurnemanz and presses upon him a small crystal phial*)

    Hier! Nimm du! — Balsam . . .

GURNEMANZ: Woher brachtest du dies?

KUNDRY: Von weiter her als du denken kannst.

    Hilft der Balsam nicht,

    Arabia birgt dann nichts mehr zu seinem Heil. —

    Fragt nicht weiter! Ich bin müde. (*p*, 38)

[KUNDRY: Here! Take it! — Balsam . . .

GURNEMANZ: Whence did you bring this?

KUNDRY: From farther than you can imagine. If the balsam does not help, then Arabia holds nothing more for his salvation. — Ask no more! I am weary.]

Gawain, Amfortas's trusted and devoted knight, is the only other figure mentioned who undertakes perilous journeys in order to secure balm for his king, but his potions are not even given a name, are lacking in aromatic distinction, and hence seem pe-

18. Marianne Brandt as Kundry in act 1 of the first pro-
duction of *Parsifal*, 1882. Costume portrait by Hans
Brand (Nationalarchiv der Richard Wagner–Stiftung/
Richard Wagner Gedenkstätte, Bayreuth)

destrian when compared to the exotic perfume offered by Kundry; we may assume that they are garnered from less exotic venues. The brief exchange between Amfortas and the Second Knight on this point suggests the inferiority of this (all-too-European) elixir:

AMFORTAS: Gawan!
ZWEITER RITTER: Herr! Gawan weilte nicht.
   Da seines Heilkrauts Kraft,
   wie schwer er's auch errungen,
   doch deine Hoffnung trog,
   hat er auf neue Sucht sich fortgeschwungen. (P, 39)

[AMFORTAS: Gawain!
SECOND KNIGHT: Sire! Gawain did not tarry; because the power of his healing herb, no matter how laboriously he won it, betrayed your hope, he has sallied forth on a new search.]

The polarity, then, is obvious and is established at the outset of the drama: Kundry as Other — as woman, wanderer, witch, Jewess, and traveler to the East (and hence highly reminiscent of Wagner's Irish princess and daughter of a potion-brewing sorceress, Isolde)[48] — versus Gawain the devout, pious, Western man bearing less potent balsamic remedies. The precise nature of Kundry's magically aromatic potion cannot even be imagined, can only be vaguely evoked by the Western and male mind, but it is more powerful than Gawain's, as one of the squires informs Gurnemanz after Amfortas has bathed in its magic fluids:

GURNEMANZ: Wie geht's dem König?
ZWEITER KNAPPE: Ihn frischt das Bad. (P, 42)

[GURNEMANZ: How is the king?
SECOND SQUIRE: The bath refreshes him.]

Kundry's association with Arabia is essential to the music drama and is reinforced through repeated references. While the apparently extreme manifestations that Kundry assumes in acts 1 and 2 of *Parsifal* draw attention to her chameleonic, quixotic

19. Marianne Brandt as Kundry in act 2 of the first production of *Parsifal*, 1882. Costume portrait by Hans Brand (Nationalarchiv der Richard Wagner–Stiftung/Richard Wagner Gedenkstätte, Bayreuth)

nature, they both serve to underscore her identity as foreign: Her introduction in each (before she has been set on the road toward salvation prior to act 3) emphasizes her status as exotic in general and Arabian in particular. Having journeyed from Arabia as the 'bad witch' before making her entrance in act 1, in act 2 Wagner describes her seductive appearance thus (figure 19): '*A youthful woman of the most intense beauty — Kundry, in a completely transformed shape — on a bed of flowers, in somewhat transparent, fantastical garments — approximately of Arabian style — becomes visible*' (P, 65).[49] Because we learn in this act that Kundry is a wandering — and that means reincarnated — being who moves 'from world to world' (P, 69) as punishment for having mocked Christ, she automatically evokes associations of Buddhism and the Middle East; her soul is born again and again after each individual life manifestation (an intentional reference to Schopenhauer's Buddhist motifs), and the specific nature of her crime calls up a scene in the exotic past and far to the exotic

East of the imagination located in Germany. Therefore it is only fitting that Kundry is the most fragrant of all creatures in *Parsifal's* odoriferous cosmology; it is she who not only smells *like* a rose but, in a metaphorical sense, *is* one, albeit a 'Rose of Hell,' and it is she who brings the exotic 'balsam' unguent from Arabia whose magic flowers we see adorning her upon her appearance in act 2.

Klingsor, too, is a product of the odoriferous Orientalist imagination. Not only his sexual difference as a eunuchlike master of a bewitching harem (whose dark vocal timbre recalls Mozart's eunuch Osmin) but his very appearance marks him as a figure constructed out of stereotypes associated with the East, and his emphatic association with the Magic Garden marks his difference not only as generally evil but as specifically aromatic. Indeed, his iconography points to a specifically Jewish-Eastern heritage, for in the Middle Ages the Jews were closely associated with the necromantic crafts of astrology and alchemy, and they often served as stargazers at the courts of southern Europe following the influx of Moors into Spain.[50] Leon Poliakov writes that in the medieval imagination, the Jews 'are veritable supermen, magicians secretly feared and revered. But at the same time they are weak and sickly, suffering from a thousand malignant afflictions that only Christian blood can cure.'[51] Like the community of the time in general, Luther — no philo-Semite himself — equated alchemists with Jews,[52] and Wagner's scenic introduction of his sorcerer draws directly from, and refers to, this tradition of the Jew as alchemist and magician (figure 20): 'Klingsor's magic castle. In the inner keep of a tower which is open to the sky. Stone steps lead up to the battlements and down into the darkness below the stage, which represents the rampart. Magical and necromantic apparatus' (*P, 55*). One of the sorcerer's first acts is to call forth Kundry with a spell or incantation, as he '*makes gestures of a mysterious nature [ruft, mit geheimnisvollen Gebärden, nach dem Abgrunde*],' and in the Middle Ages Jews were repeatedly charged with invoking demons by magic chants (particularly during the reign of Pope Martin V, in the

20. Karl Hill or Anton Fuchs as Klingsor at Bayreuth, 1882 (Nationalarchiv
der Richard Wagner–Stiftung/Richard Wagner Gedenkstätte, Bayreuth)

early fifteenth century).[53] Stargazer, necromancer, and 'sickly, suffering' outcast longing for the holiest Christian blood ever to have flowed in the medieval imagination, the blood of Christ preserved in the Grail, Klingsor appears as a compilation of exotic notions associated with Jews in the period from which the Parsifal legend developed and incorporates images that still reverberated with anti-Semitic overtones within Wagner's nineteenth-century Germany. Like Kundry, Klingsor poses a powerful and terrifying threat, but he is also fascinating, associated with the exotic attributes of Arabia's aromatic and foreign 'magic.'

Klingsor's music, too, evokes for those conversant with the codes of Western musical traditions the associations triggered by the exoticism of Wagner's visual image, for much of his short scene is grounded in the key of B♭ minor, already discussed in the introduction as a tonal locus arousing notions of darkness and evil in the eighteenth and nineteenth centuries, and it has this function here as well.[54] Not only Johann Friedrich Daniel Schubart but Wagner's revered Beethoven, too, thought of B♭ minor as a 'black' key, and, given its function as an acoustical sign of evil within the musical traditions Wagner inherited (and with which he pointedly associated himself through his glorification of Beethoven as the forerunner of his own works), it is no coincidence that the key emerges in his music dramas in contexts concerning evil and the visual portrayal of darkness. It is fitting that Klingsor—who as the source of sexual malevolence, caster of spells, and terrifying threat to the dominant ruling order of the drama inherits the dramatic function of Alberich— should be assigned music primarily located within the same key with which Alberich and Hagen are associated. But in *Parsifal*, the tradition of the Jew as alchemist and sorcerer is even more prominent than in the *Ring* (Alberich's spells and Hagen's potions notwithstanding), and the key of Klingsor's music (as well as his visual presentation) specifically evokes this very tradition. Carolyn Abbate underscores the representational function of Klingsor's tonality when she describes B♭ minor as 'an iconic key' and explains that for the eighteenth and nineteenth centuries 'associations with magic, the supernatural and the malign were a strong part of its character.'[55] Though she makes no mention of the connection to Jews, we may infer that they are associated with the figure by considering the traditional image of the alchemist in general and the specifically Orientalist construction of Klingsor in Wagner's stage directions. The 'magic, the supernatural and the malign' associated with Klingsor's key conflate with the motivic tradition of the Jew as alchemist, a tradition, moreover, itself associated with the Jewish presence in Arabian lands. In this way textual, visual, and musical icons merge to evoke the Jew in a subtle nexus of cultural references that would have made sense to Wagner's contemporary European audience.

If we think of the caricatures of Jews in the *Ring*, a host of Orientalist characteristics come to mind as well, the mythic, timeless, and geographically ill-defined setting of the tetralogy notwithstanding. Mime is explicitly, and I would argue not coincidentally, connected to the vicinity of the dragon's lair, which lies 'to the East' of the events of *Die Walküre* (RN, 136), and, as previously mentioned, his odor and vampiric schemes associate him with the nineteenth-century stereotype of the Eastern Jew. In her discussion of *Siegfried*, Sandra Corse reminds us that for Hegel—to whom, she argues, Wagner was so indebted for much of the ideational content of his cycle—'the Eastern cultures are based on fear rather than on reason and create a state in which "there is only the status of lord and the status of servant. . . . Thus fear and despotism are the dominants in the East. . . ." Mime attempts to rule by fear.'[56] For the philosophical tradition itself in which Wagner's works are situated, then, the East embodies the locus in which difference from the European community is manifest, the rule of enlightened 'reason' characterizing the Western self-image, while that of 'fear' typified its image of the East. But that fear is itself a projection of the terror that the East represents to the Western mind, as Wagner's description in 'Erkenne dich selbst' of the moving hordes of 'degenerated Slavs' and blood-sucking Jews makes manifest, and the East, the place with which Mime is familiar and to which he leads Siegfried so that the hero may learn fear, is the venue of the Nibelungs.[57]

That East is a dark, dangerous, and smelly place. The Nibelungs are associated with ubiquitous darkness, emerging as they do from a 'home of mist' and themselves evincing the darker complexions of those deemed foreign in the Teutonic imagination. After *Das Rheingold*, Alberich is seen only twice, each time in the dark, before dawn in act 2 scene 1 of both *Siegfried* and *Götterdämmerung*, and Mime, too, is linked to his gloomy forest cave, emerging uncomfortably into the sunlight only to accompany Siegfried to the dragon's lair. But there is yet another culturally far more significant manifestation of the Nibelungs' connection to darkness that is implied throughout the tetralogy but that is directly stated only once and that is rife with the ideology of Orientalism: the perception of the Jew as *black*. To the fantasy of Wagner's age, of course, the appearance of the black constituted a realistic icon of essential difference, despite — or perhaps rather in large part because of — the fact that German culture had had little interaction with blacks by Wagner's lifetime and would not physically experience their presence on a large scale until France occupied Germany with black troops from its North African colonies following World War I.[58] The notion that black represented evil was of course a veritable topos within German culture by the time Wagner penned his works depicting a threat to the essence of the German people by the corrupting influence of modern civilization, a civilization driven by a lust for wealth and by the alienating forces of egotism inimicable to community, forces representing for Wagner evil per se in the modern world. But that culturally pervasive image of evil fit seamlessly into his own ideological agenda: While being black in Wagner is a metaphorical construction borrowed from a communal mythology, it is a metaphor that ties in with the web of corporeal images denoting specific theoretical concerns in his works.

Sander Gilman has shown that in the nineteenth century the notion that Jews were black already had had a long tradition in European culture. It was based on the idea that the Jew's purportedly darker complexion was itself attributable to both his 'origins' in Africa and to the pervasive diseases of the skin associated with Jews at the time.[59] Gilman cites a text by Bavarian writer Johann Pezzl from the 1780s that describes the Jews of Vienna in precisely these terms:

> Their sole and eternal occupation is to counterfeit, salvage, trade in coins, and cheat Christians, Turks, heathens, indeed themselves. . . . This is only the beggarly filth from Canaan which can only be exceeded in filth, uncleanliness, stench, disgust, poverty, dishonesty, pushiness and other things by the trash of the twelve tribes from Galicia. Excluding the Indian fakirs, there is no category of supposed human beings which comes closer to the Orang-Utan than does a Polish Jew. . . . Covered from foot to head in filth, dirt and rags, covered in a type of black sack . . . their necks exposed, the color of a Black . . . the hair turned and knotted as if they all suffered from the 'plica polonica.'[60]

Here the corporeal signs of revolting stench and darker pigmentation are two components that conflate in an image of difference. Having emerged out of Africa, the Jews still evince their affinity with apes, and their skin color — as well as their aroma — also reveals their diseased nature. The notion that their darker pigment was a sign of disease was found both among non-Jews and the Jewish community alike in Wagner's culture, as seen in Joseph Rohrer's comments in 1804 on the 'disgusting skin diseases' of the Jew and in those of Enlightenment physician Elcan Isaac Wolf, who shared the belief that a 'black-yellow' skin color constituted a sign of the Jew's essence.[61] In the middle of the nineteenth century Robert Knox saw the physiognomy of blacks and Jews in virtually identical terms, as his description of the Jew's face makes manifest: 'the contour is convex; the eyes long and fine, the outer angles running towards the temples; the brow and nose apt to form a single convex line; the nose comparatively narrow at the base, the eyes consequently approaching each other; lips very full, mouth projecting, chin small, and the whole physiognomy, when swarthy, as it often is, has an African look.'[62] Such a conflation was part of the Western cultural vocabulary of the nineteenth century. Thus Wolfgang Menzel, in his aforementioned denunciation of Heine, could introduce his attack on the Jewish author by describing Jews as primates, for the connection between primitive, animalistic features — associated for Menzel and his audience with blacks — and the 'non-German' race of the Jews was unquestioned and ubiquitous and therefore constituted at the time a reliable rhetorical device: 'They crawled out of every dark corner, laying bare their teeth in an apelike manner, grinning, and sticking out their tongues [*mit affenartigem Zähneblecken, Grinsen und Zungenherausstrecken*], ridiculing everything that up until then had been holy to the Christian.'[63]

The conflation of the African and the Jew — and for the mid-nineteenth century that meant an emphasis on the purportedly 'apelike' nature they shared — reemerges in Wagner's works as well, where it is situated in a host of corporeal motifs signifying exoticism and difference. The earthen, swarthy nature of diverse pseudo-Semitic figures is only implied in the darkness of Nibelheim, with its attendant mythological attributes of sulfur and fire, but it is stated outright when Wotan, disguised as the Wanderer, describes himself in the first act of *Siegfried* as Alberich's 'lighter' counterpart ('licht Alberich' [*RN*, 172]), refers to the Nibelungs as 'Schwarzalben [black elves]' (*RN*, 171), and directly addresses his Nibelung-nemesis as 'schwarz Alberich' in act 2 of the drama (*RN*, 192). This motif of the polarity between Wotan as the 'light' corollary of the 'black' Alberich was central to Wagner's earliest conception of the drama and was already present in the initial verse version of *Der junge Siegfried* of 1851, in which Wotan (or, as he was then called, 'Wodan') distinguishes between the gods as 'Lichtalben' and the Nibelung dwarves as 'Schwarzalben' in his act 1 narrations to Mime and refers to Alberich as 'schwarzer Albe' before the dragon's lair in act 2.[64] In this context it is worth recalling that one of Wagner's first descriptions of Mime — in the passage from *Der junge Siegfried* he later omitted from the final libretto of the music drama — draws attention to Mime's 'dark ashen color.'[65] Both dwarves, then, were viewed by Wagner as darker than their godly, physiologically superior rival.

Many commentators have drawn attention to Wotan's polarization of himself as 'light' and Alberich as 'dark' in order to underscore the affinity or the parallels it reveals between the two figures, Wagner's two arch rivals and seekers of power in the *Ring*, but no one has sought to read the line as a literal expression, penned in the age of realism, of a racial nature. Writers and composers do not employ imagery for solely private, aesthetically compelling reasons but often find a given motif appropriate or attractive as a response to larger, culturally contextual forces. While it is clear that Wagner found the polarization of 'light elves' and 'black elves' in the sagas from which he drew material for his initial formulation of the drama, such positivistic links only constitute the philological substratum of the cultural implications of such a motif for the nineteenth century, both for the composer and for his audience.[66] To be black in that culture connoted more than simply being evil in a general sense; in the cultural imagination of Wagner's age, the motif of the dark dwarf could have seamlessly evoked both the mythic world of the *Edda*, with its home of mists inhabited by black elves, and the more current catalog of racial stereotypes applied to the image of the foreigner — of the black and the Jew. If we take Wagner at his word, we may interpret this designation of Alberich as *schwarz* as drawing upon a German cultural topos that associates these two groups of racial outcasts, attributing to both such similar and negative stereotypical characteristics as a fetid odor, an enlarged nose, an ungainly deportment, an exotic and foreign appearance, and of course a dark complexion. The attribution of identical features to blacks and Jews was part of the cultural vocabulary upon which Wagner's works drew and due to which, perhaps, they resonated so forcefully in his contemporary audience.

Wotan's characterization of the Nibelungs as 'black elves'

merges with another motif in *Der junge Siegfried*, that of Mime's 'apelike' appearance. Let us recall that in *Deutsche Kunst und deutsche Politik* Wagner likens the aesthetically impoverished mime to an ape (*DS* 8: 290–291), an analogy, as discussed in chapter 1, that attends Mime's function as a metaphor for the inferior artist (a 'mime,' as opposed to the 'idealist' artist Siegfried). But this motif of Mime-as-ape is already apparent in the first prose version of *Der junge Siegfried*, from May 1851, in Alberich's vituperative response to Mime's attempts at reconciliation with his brother: 'Seht doch, will der affe köng [*sic*] sein [What do you know, the ape wants to be king]' he says,[67] and this statement reappears in the verse version of the same work, completed in June 1851, when Alberich exclaims:

dem räudigsten hund
wäre der ring
gerath'ner als dir;
nimmer erringst
du affe den herrscherreif!

[the ring would suit the lousiest dog better than you; never shall you gain you ape the ruling ring!][68]

Both Nibelungs, then, are characterized by the features associated in the nineteenth-century German imagination with blacks, the image of the ape appearing at the time in conjunction with Africans as apposite of their purportedly primitive and decidedly different natural essence. No wonder Wagner described Jewish speech, in 'Das Judentum in der Musik,' as 'aped speech [*nachäffend(e) Sprache*]' (*GS* 13: 17), a formulation with widespread cultural implications. As late as 1881 Wagner would equate Jews with blacks in a despairing passage from 'Erkenne dich selbst': 'What [lies] as a fact [between the area] of everyday communication [*des bürgerlichen Verkehrs*] and that of state politics is the complete right given to the Jews to consider themselves in every respect as Germans — just like the blacks in Mexico were authorized by a law to regard themselves as whites' (*GS* 14: 183). It is altogether consistent at the time that figures evincing numerous anti-Semitic stereotypical features should also be associated with the stereotypical characteristics of blacks, for in the popular imagination the two groups shared defining traits that served to distance them from the German community. But in addition to the icon of darker pigmentation, the marker of a purportedly distinct smell also served to underscore their difference, for, as we have seen, all these figures — whether 'Arabian' or 'African,' enticingly and dangerously exotic or threateningly black — are accompanied by the whiff of difference; be it perfumed or putrid, it is the odor of the exotic Other — the odor of the Orient.

*

We may now return to *Parsifal* to examine that point in the drama in which the exotic aroma of the East and its attendant sexuality are relentlessly banished from the world of the superior German order. In Wagner's final work for the stage, once the world has been rid of the threat of Klingsor's sexual malevolence, *aromas appear sexless* and therefore harmless. In act 3 of the drama, Parsifal contrasts the childlike, prepubescent flowers of Good Friday with those of the Magic Garden:

Wie dünkt mich doch die Aue heut so schön! —
Wohl traf ich Wunderblumen an,
die bis zum Haupte süchtig mich umrankten;
doch sah' ich nie so mild und zart
die Halme, Blüten und Blumen,
noch duftet' all' so kindisch hold. (*P*, 79–80)

[But how beautiful the meadow seems to me today! — It is true that I once encountered wondrous flowers that longingly wrapped around me up to my head; but I never saw such mild and gentle stems, blossoms, and flowers, nor did they smell so childishly lovely.]

Only with the removal of sexuality, of the forbidden, and of the exotic can a *Duft* in Wagner be described as *kindisch*; otherwise it implies prohibited secrets, a desire for forbidden pleasures, or an aroma heralding a repulsive and foreign sexual assault and hence, again, a justification for union with one's own kind.

The motivic tradition of the *foetor judäicus*, as an expression for the Christian world of the difference and the damnation of the Jew, had always contained the logical possibility of the Jew achieving redemption from his stench-filled effluvia. To the medieval mind, this departure from the olfactory icon of Jewishness could only come about through the abandonment of Judaism itself, that is, through the Jew's conversion to Catholicism, which would effectively transform the odoriferous religious foreigner into a sweet-smelling religious compatriot. Only through baptism could the Jew lose his stench, the smell that sets him off from the true believers, and achieve 'the odor of sanctity'; this motif appears time and again in German culture right up to Wagner's day.[69]

In *Parsifal* it is precisely through baptism that the aromas of the devilish flower garden — the olfactory icon of threatening Jewish difference — are replaced by the superior aroma of the prepubescent flowers on Good Friday. With the error of her ways finally made clear to her and the horrors of Klingsor and the Magic Garden a thing of the past, the repentant Kundry kneels before Parsifal in act 3 of Wagner's drama to receive absolution from the knight-as-Redeemer. Maria Magdalene-like, the penitent whore washes his feet with her hair and receives, as his 'first office,' Parsifal's baptismal blessing through the holy water of the spring:[70]

PARSIFAL: Mein erstes Amt verricht' ich so: —
  Die Taufe nimm
  und glaub' an den Erlöser! (*P*, 79)

[My first office I thus perform: — Take baptism, and believe in the Redeemer!]

Wagner thus adapts and transforms the medieval motivic tradition from which he drew so much material in fashioning his final music drama, as seen in the removal of Anfortas's stench mentioned above, but the ideological thrust of disparate smells so central in the Middle Ages to the idea of the Jew finding redemption from his foul religion remains; while to the medieval mind baptism replaced stench with sweetness, Wagner replaces a dangerous and threatening sweetness with 'chaste,' 'childish' aromas, because in *Parsifal* such sweetness is an olfactory icon of the Jew. In each case the odor associated with the Jew constitutes a sign of a threatening difference that is effaced once the Jew has joined the fold of the Christian anointed. It is only by shedding the smell of the Jew through admission into the world of German folkish Christianity that Kundry can fulfill Wagner's ultimate demand at the conclusion to 'Das Judentum in der Musik': 'To become a human being in our community [*gemeinschaftlich mit uns*] means for the Jew first and foremost as much as: ceasing to be a Jew' (*GS* 13: 29). At the conclusion to Wagner's final drama, the olfactory icons of that community appear as Kundry stops her Semitic wandering and believes in the (German) savior.

In this context, the removal of Beckmesser's smelly airs through the victory of Walther's *Preislied* can be seen to emerge out of the same motivic tradition, for the young knight's song, as previously discussed, has been 'baptized' by Sachs and celebrated as such in the ceremony prior to the final scene on the *Festwiese*. Indeed, one could argue that Wagner has Sachs go on at some length about the *Taufe* of the new dream-song-as-child precisely in order to draw attention to its anointed protection and distance from the unholy, inferior, and ugly song of the foreign Beckmesser, which (and who) is so closely associated with the stench of pitch. In some regions of Germany since the Middle Ages, popular folklore equated an unbaptized child with a Jew, claiming that baptismal water 'washed away' the Jewish element, and the first hairs of an unbaptized child were often referred to, therefore, as *Judenhaare*.[71] The musical sphere of Germany, then, is rid of the Jew's olfactory and aesthetic (h)airs and achieves the 'odor of sanctity' in the Nuremberg drama as well. In both *Die Meistersinger* and *Parsifal*, the medieval notion of a baptismal cure of the *foetor judäicus* operates within the complex and yet consistent motivic vocabulary of the works and was both conceived as such by Wagner and may well have been so perceived by his contemporary German audience.

By examining the remarkable consistency in Wagner's associative patterns linking smell and ideology, we are shown a mechanism illustrating the extrapersonal dimension in subjective impressions that was central to Wagner's culture and that is found throughout his theoretical writings and his works for the stage. Perceived as real, objective indications of physiological difference, aromas function in his works and in his world as culturally encoded signs within the racist imagination. Smell is yet one more indication of a culturally constructed message of sex, fear, and hatred contained within the Wagnerian Total Work of Art, whose seductively persuasive power continues to fascinate and to baffle even as it implies a desire for racial destruction.

'Wear comfortable shoes.' — Birgit Nilsson's advice to aspiring
Wagnerian heroines

Having discussed acoustical and olfactory phenomena
in Wagner, let us now turn to additional ocular indications of race in his thinking and in the cultural
traditions from which the corporeal iconographies of his works
were drawn. In Wagner and his world, the visual appearance of
the body is constructed out of a host of specific iconographies
perceptible to the eye. It is not one's physical dimensions in
general that define identity in the Wagnerian cosmos and in his
culture but the detailed makeup of one's body comprised of a
number of specific and presumably irrefutable signs available to
anyone with the eyes to see them.

The foot is one of the features of the body with a long iconographic tradition in European culture that functions much like
the eye, the voice, and aroma within Wagner's model of recognition that is available to the eye's discerning perception. It, too,
provides a sign of racial identity, for in Wagner's works good
figures tread upon good feet and bad beings walk poorly, hobbling about on inferior appendages. As with the other corporeal
icons discussed thus far, the foot both constitutes a metaphor
within Wagner's theoretical reflections on the arts and by the
nineteenth century was replete with associations linked to it in a
number of long-standing (or long-limping) cultural traditions.
Like the voice and smell, the foot provides an image with which
Wagner associates novel aesthetic issues (which for him always
have social implications), but that image was already imbued
with connotations in his culture when he employed it in his
theoretical writings and in the dramatic representations of his
social-aesthetic concerns.

In *Oper und Drama* Wagner maintains that the gestural component of music developed in conjunction with the dance. Musical and physical movement converged, he believed, in the pulsating, natural measurement of rhythm, and this itself—the central metrical fabric holding together the visual and the acoustical delineation of space—is defined for Wagner by the movement of the foot, the corporeal focal point, as it were, in which the progression of the dancer's body and the musical pulse of the conductor's baton meet. The foot is thus the physiological monad that forms a bridge between the 'sister arts' of dance and music and between the long-lost unity of the utopian Greek artwork and that of its refurbished counterpart, the Total Artwork of the Future in a superior and future Germany. It is an image of the body that fuses the function of the eye and that of the ear:

Dance-gesture and orchestra had their most sensual point of contact, that is, the point where both—one in space, the other in time, one to the eye, the other to the ear—necessarily manifested themselves as completely equal and mutual, in *rhythm*, and in this point both must necessarily, following their movement away from it, return again in order therein . . . to remain or to become intelligible. From this point the gesture and the orchestra equally develop their most idiosyncratic linguistic abilities. As the gesture through this ability communicates to the eye what only *it* can express, so the orchestra in its turn communicates to the ear that which corresponds exactly to this expression. . . . The sinking movement of the foot, lowered again after it had been raised, was to the eye exactly the same thing that the accented downward movement of the baton was to the ear; and thus the movement-filled sonic figure [*bewegungsvolle Tonfigur*], performed on instruments that the baton's beating of the measures binds melodically, is also to the sense of sound precisely the same thing as the movement of the foot or other expressive bodily appendages, between its changes corresponding to the baton's downbeat, is to the eye. (*DS* 7: 312)

The dancer's foot, like that of the singing, dramatically moving actor, emerges here as a corporeal signature of the unified Total Work of Art; it is the place of the body where the diverse sensual impressions of the ear and the eye, of music and movement, converge. Because the superior, utopian, folkish total work merges its formerly disparate elements and therein provides a metaphorical mirror for the homogeneous community of those who gaze into and recognize themselves in it, the movement of the foot, as the 'point of origin [*Ausgangspunkt*]' uniting the arts, takes on singular, paradigmatic, and metaphorical importance. As the corporeal basis of the dance, it both itself symbolizes and makes possible the merging, phantasmagoric unity of a work so closely associated in Wagner's mind with the physiological states of superior human beings united in a utopian social order. The movement of the foot is a metaphor for the origins of art as a natural process grounded in the body of those who experience and live it.

But for Wagner, the dance (whose corporeal foundation is the foot) is not only one of the arts, though it be the most basic and generative of the diverse aesthetic forms; it also is itself a metaphor for the unified artwork as well, as Wagner employs it near the beginning of 'Das Kunstwerk der Zukunft':

Dance, Music, and Poetry [*Tanzkunst, Tonkunst* und *Dichtkunst*] are the names of the three unborn sisters, whom we immediately see dancing in a circle [*ihren Reigen schlingen sehen*], wherever the conditions for the appearance of art had come about. By their very nature they cannot be separated without dissolving the dance of art; for in this dance, which itself is the movement of art, they are through the most beautiful affinity and love sensually and spiritually wrapped around one another in such a form and life-giving manner that each one, freed from the dance, without life and movement, can only lead a borrowed life that has only the semblance of art [*künstlich angehaucht*]. (DS 6: 36)

Once the total artwork as the mirror of the community began, like the community it reflected, to disintegrate into its disparate individual component parts, then, the 'sister' arts drifted apart but continued to yearn in the post-Hellenic age for their incestuous reunion, which only the Artwork of the Future will be able to bring about, a reunion that, once again, will emerge out of the dance, itself based on the foot as the appendage allowing the body's movement.

These multiple-metaphorical configurations — the foot as the place where the sonic and the visual meet, as the origin and the link of dance and music, and the dance itself as a metaphor for the Total Work of Art—are central to the imagery of Wagner's postrevolutionary music dramas and to their multilayered implications. For as with the ideology of the eye, of the voice, and of smell, so the foot—and the dance that emerges from it and that itself gives birth to the other arts and represents their union—has an iconic function in Wagner's works for the stage.

But in his dramatic conceptualizations, the foot is an image that merged with a host of motivic traditions central to German culture since the Middle Ages that were still very much a part of the cultural vocabulary of Wagner's contemporary nineteenth-century Germany. Like the voice, the foot has a carefully and consistently constructed metaphorical dimension when it appears on Wagner's stage; it is the symbolical physical locus of the origins of the very works in which it functions, but it also evoked in the nineteenth-century mind specific connotations dependent on the mythical and folkloristic traditions of that culture, many of them imbued with racist meaning.[1]

Both in the classical Greek tradition and in the Norse sources from which Wagner drew material for the *Ring*, the foot has an important and prominent function: It is the site of the body upon which difference, and especially the singularity of the artist, is engraved. In Greek and Norse mythology, *limping* is the sign of the master smith. Both Hephaestus (or Vulcan) in Greek mythology and Völund in the *Völundarkvitha* (The lay of Völund) of *The Poetic Edda* suffer from this defect, which was either imbued them by the primitive imagination as retribution for their unusual abilities as artisans, or, conversely, their skills as artists provided a kind of compensation in the mythological fantasy for their physical impoverishment.[2] Both the Greek and the Norse smith suffer ceaseless torment because they are cursed with a foot that is deformed: Theirs are mutilated or club-feet which mark them as different and outcasts. A highly popular pedagogical text in Germany in Wagner's time, Friedrich Rösselt's *Lehrbuch der griechischen und römischen Mythologie für*

höhere Töchterschulen und die Gebildeten des weiblichen Geschlechts
(Primer of Greek and Roman mythology for institutions of
higher education for girls and for the educated of the female
sex), first published in 1844 and republished in many editions
throughout the rest of the century, contains the following, standard description of the figure of the smith in Greek mythology
(figure 21):

Hephästos was the god of fire, both of the helpful [*wohltuenden*] fire and
the destructive. . . .

The smoke that rises from volcanoes came from his smithy, the
thundering and cacophony in them was the echo of his and the Cy-
clops's heavy beating on the anvil.

Finally, he was also the god of all artistic works with metal. . . . He
also made for himself two slaves out of gold, upon which he supported
himself when he walked; for he was lame. . . .

To be sure, it was inevitable that he always appeared dirty and covered with soot after smithing. . . . He is generally described as a very
ugly god: large, unrefined, broad shouldered, with powerful arms, and
clumsy, so that he often became the target of derision of the other gods.
With his otherwise so strong and large shape, his thin legs stuck out all
the more, and his limping exacerbated his helplessness.[3]

This description of the Greek figure is comparable to that of his
Norse counterpart found in *The Poetic Edda*, in that Völund, the
master smith (described, like Wagner's Alberich, as an *Alben-
herrscher* and, like him, robbed of a golden ring),[4] is lame, though
he suffers this affliction not from birth but at the hands of his
enemies, as the following passage from the *Völundarkvitha*
makes clear in which the queen of his enemies orders his mutilation:

'Let them straightway cut   his sinews of strength
And set him then   in Saevarstath.'

So it was done: the sinews in his knee-joints were cut, and he was set
in an island which was near the mainland, and was called Saevarstath.
There he smithed for the king all kinds of precious things.[5]

Central to the characterization of both figures, then, is the association of limping or lameness with their capacity as master

Hephästos mit den Kyklopen.

Hephästos.

21. Illustrations of the god Hephaestus
(From Friedrich Rösselt, *Lehrbuch der
griechischen und römischen Mythologie für
höhere Töchterschulen und die Gebildeten des
weiblichen Geschlechts*, 5th ed., ed. Friedrich
Kurts [Leipzig: Ernst Fleischer, 1865])

smiths, while their ugly and brutal appearance provides a further motivic feature also associated with their deformity. An audience familiar with the motivic traditions in which he is found would have associated the ugly smith with the physical state that distinguished the figure in the Greek and Norse legends — his lameness.

Wagner's *Ring* draws upon these traditions.[6] Alberich and his fellow Nibelungs are portrayed as a race of dwarves whose handywork is smithing. Before they are enslaved by Alberich and forced to ruin Nature through their incessant delving into rock in search of gold, they fashion jewelry and trinkets for their living, as Mime relates to Wotan and Loge in *Das Rheingold*:

Sorglose Schmiede,
schufen wir sonst wohl
Schmuck unsern Weibern
wonnig Geschmeid,
niedlichen Niblungentand,
wir lachten lustig der Müh. (*RN*, 42)

[Carefree smiths, once we fashioned jewelry for our women, charming Niblungen treasure, we happily laughed at the toil.]

Wagner repeatedly emphasizes the fact that Alberich is a *smith*. It is not solely because he forswears love but also, consistently, because of this identity that he gains access to the secret of shaping the Rhinegold into the form of a ring, and it is due to his affinity with the craft of metallurgy that his new-found wisdom, gained through the theft of the Rhinegold, vouchsafes him insight into the location of veins of golden ore hidden to others, a knowledge of which Mime enviously speaks in Nibelheim:[7]

Durch des Ringes Gold
errät seine Gier,
wo neuer Schimmer
in Schachten sich birgt. (*RN*, 42)

[Through the gold of the ring his greed surmises where a new gleaming is buried in caves.]

Wagner also draws attention to the fact that all the Nibelungs are smiths. Mime, too, is linked to fire, to sulfur, and to dwelling in darkness in the bowels of the earth, and he, of course, is the most gifted smith of the *Ring*; it is not for nothing that Alberich turns to him for the fashioning of the *Tarnhelm*, a magical-aesthetic construct of which Mime is particularly proud and the design of which is based on Alberich's newly gained demonic vision but whose execution is linked to Mime's craft. This identification of Nibelungs as smiths may account for Hagen's knowledge concerning the *Tarnhelm*, as revealed when he explains its mysterious function to Siegfried (RN, 264). It is therefore simply a consistent reinforcement of the association of race and craft when the audience hears the clamor of numerous anvils during the descent to Nibelheim in the orchestral interlude between scenes 2 and 3 of *Das Rheingold* (RN, 37).

Alberich's and Mime's status as smiths is anticipated in a forerunner of the *Ring* cycle, 'Wieland der Schmied, als Drama entworfen' (Wieland the smith, conceived as a drama) of 1850 (itself based on *Völundarkvitha*), in which the eponymous figure is both portrayed as the greatest smith on earth and crippled by the king Neiding (whose name reappears in Siegmund's act 1 narrations in *Die Walküre*), a malevolent monarch who commands his warriors to sever the tendons in Wieland's feet so that the smith will be at his mercy and fashion for him an army's weaponry (DS 6: 178). In despair, Wieland berates himself in a passage replete with images and motifs that would reappear in the *Ring* in conjunction with Alberich: 'Perish then, you lame, limping cripple! You shameful monster! Ridiculed by men, derided by women and children! Perish! You earn only contempt, never revenge, — nor love!' (DS 6: 183). Unlike Alberich, however, Wieland is vouchsafed the opportunity to revenge himself and, in an allegory of artistic flight, he fashions swan wings, Daedaluslike, with which he stirs up the fire in his hearth, ignites the house of his enemies, and flies free of the conflagration. In 'Eine Mitteilung an meine Freunde' Wagner stated explicitly that Wieland learned his craft from *dwarves* (DS 6: 221), thereby underscoring the ideational and iconographic connections underlying the diverse dramatic projects; lameness, smith, and dwarf emerge as three components of a single figure.

When Wagner portrayed the titular villain in his *Ring* cycle as belonging to a race of subterranean master blacksmiths, the associations attending the mythological image would have evoked the malformed outcast in the more cultured members of his audience, and even if the names of Hephaestus and Völund did not come to mind, the association of their craft and their deformity would have been a staple of the cultural vocabulary of the time. Because they are smiths, the Nibelungs must suffer from impoverished perambulation in the minds of those familiar with the mythologies upon which the *Ring* is based.

But this notion of a link between the crafting of metals and deformed feet was not solely a feature of the literary traditions of classical Greek and Norse legends. In Wagner's age it also conflated in the popular imagination of Germany with widespread cultural beliefs, among them the notion that the Jew's body was different. In German folklore since the Middle Ages, stumbling was often associated both with the ability to find hidden treasure (the insight that Mime so envies in his clumsy but prescient bass-brother) *and with Jews*. In his *Handwörterbuch des deutschen Aberglaubens* (Dictionary of German superstition) Hans Bächthold-Stäubli relates a popular German saying that, since the Middle Ages, one shouted when someone stumbled and fell: 'Da liegt ein Spielmann oder ein Musikant, ein Jude, ein Schatz begraben [There a musician or a minstrel, a Jew, a treasure lies buried].' Summing up the motif in popular German culture, Bächthold-Stäubli explains: 'The Jew, whose stumbling is sometimes judged favorably and sometimes unfavorably, stands in the aroma of malevolent magical powers [*steht im Geruch schädlicher zauberischer Kräfte*], and also hoards and finds hidden treasures.'[8] Wagner's works can thus be situated within both the high literary (mythological) and the popular cultural traditions

linking the malformed or inferior foot to a craft associated with
the Jew; indeed, from the Middle Ages on the icon of the impoverished foot emerges in a number of guises as one of the
idiosyncratic signs of the Jew per se. (Interestingly enough, in
Jewish folklore the foot is explicitly associated with the penis, a
conflation of the corporeal iconography of difference and sexuality found in a variety of manifestations within the images of
dominant German culture as well.)[9] In his *Anatomy of Melancholy*, for example, Robert Burton wrote of the Jews' idiosyncratic 'pace' (as well as of their voice and outward appearance)
as a sign of 'their conditions and infirmities,' and Johann Ja-
kob Schudt, the seventeenth-century diagnostician of difference
cited in the previous chapter, drew attention not only to the
Jew's stench (to the *foetor judäicus*) but to the Jews' 'crooked feet'
as a sign of their abnormality.[10] Sander Gilman has pointed out
that in the nineteenth century the notion that the Jew was an
inferior soldier, and hence a bad citizen, was based on this iconographic tradition that located difference in the Jew's foot: In
1804 Joseph Rohrer conducted a study of Jews in the Austrian
monarchy and concluded that the high percentage of Jews re-
leased from military service at the time was attributable to their
'weak feet,' a notion that explains why Theodor Fontane, in his
1870 defense of the Jewish soldiers' conduct in the campaign
against Austria in 1866, singled out the outsider's willingness to
fight despite, he assumed, *the unusually severe pain in his feet.*[11]
Gilman has shown that this image entered the medical discourse
of the late nineteenth century as well, providing the iconographic basis for assumptions concerning the study of flat feet.[12]
When Wagner constructed his representatives of evil out of a
widespread repertoire of anti-Semitic stereotypes, it was only
consistent that he included this sign of the Jew as well. His
caricatures of Jews not only are small and hairy, greedy and
horny, and speak and shriek with nervous energy in a high and
nasal voice, exuding foul odors associated with pitch, flatulence,
and sulfur; they also emphatically *limp.*

THE DEVIL AND THE JEW

It will be obvious that the images I have been discussing concerning the idiosyncratic difference of the Jew are also images associated in Western culture with the Devil. From the sulfur and stench to the irrepressible lechery and the hobbling gait, the catalog of images and attributes linked at least since the Middle Ages to the Jew also relate to Satan and to lesser demons, spirits, and sinister apparitions in both the clerical and the popular motivic traditions of Germany's cultural heritage. The clerical tradition, for example, emphasized the belief widespread since the heyday of the medieval Church that the Jews celebrate the Sabbath together with witches and devils.[13] These traditions form the cultural background to Beckmesser's musical and aromatic 'exorcism' in *Die Meistersinger* and to Klingsor's aforementioned association with cabbalistic crafts, as well as to Kundry's ultimate dissociation from the realm of the Devil and the achievement of 'the odor of sanctity' through baptism in act 3 of *Parsifal*.

The connections between the Devil and the Jew are longstanding in European culture. Leon Poliakov sums up the import of their widespread association thus:

If we examine the legends that circulate about the Jews in legends that cropped up sporadically during the preceding centuries but which now [in the Middle Ages] are accepted throughout Europe, we observe that the Jews are believed to unite in their persons the new attributes of the Devil and those of the witch. The Jews are horned. They are tricked out with a tail and the beard of a goat (that disturbing quadruped which serves as the perfect transmitting agent for all sins); the mephitic odors attributed to them are so violent that they have persisted down through the ages. . . .

In short, combining in their persons the entire gamut of the attributes of evil, the Jews lose their humanity in the eyes of Christians and are relegated to the realm of the occult. Even when they are not assigned strictly diabolical attributes, they are associated with the devils that are often pictured in the background of engravings and paintings representing Jews (thus the devils appear to be of Jewish essence). Elsewhere, Jews are given pigs' ears in place of horns. Popular superstitions abound in the same associations. The Jewish school is a 'black' school; the Jew is the intermediary between the Devil and those who want to sell their souls to him; the cursed pact is sealed with his blood, and if a sick man wants to die, he need only ask a Jew to pray for him. In countless ghost stories, a Jew appears either in human form or as a will-o'-the-wisp. Many of these beliefs and others like them have persisted in the popular imagination down to our own day.[14]

Two of the central icons expressing the affinity between the Devil and the Jew in popular superstition were those of the deformed foot and the limping gait. Thus, when Wagner gave his figures constructed out of numerous iconic anti-Semitic stereotypes the attribute of an inferior foot, he was anchoring the visual imagery of his music dramas to beliefs in both the ecclesiastical and the popular traditions of his culture. The impoverished foot evoked the motivic vocabulary of Greek and Norse mythology, the figures of the dwarf and the ugly smith, the *Bock*, or goat of ill-repute, and the figures of the Jew and the Archfiend. Even in Germanic folklore, the feet of demons, spirits, and dwarves are often of a similarly singular nature, the latter, in particular, often portrayed as malformed or even as resembling the feet of geese or ducks.[15] These images conflate with the popular notion of the Devil as hooved, as walking with a marked and dragging gait characterized by a horse's or goat's foot. In all these diverse yet closely related motivic traditions, moreover, the Devil's foot is explicitly portrayed as black,[16] and we have already examined the darker nature of Alberich's ashen appearance. From a host of traditions, then, Wagner drew an image of horror and of derisive difference linked to the Jew in his construction of the villains within his four-part paradigm of the dangers threatening the future of Germany, a world in peril of being overrun by limping, dark creatures from the East bringing with them overtones of the demonic.

*

The Nibelungs' impoverished appendage automatically emerges, then, through its evocation in the nineteenth-century German viewer's mind via associations with well-known mythological and popular imagery. Because they are dwarves, smiths, and evil, they must have damaged feet. But such feet are also pointedly evoked through the gestural movement of the music that Wagner composed for Alberich as well. Alberich's (but not Mime's) inferior foot is perhaps the only corporeal icon in the Wagnerian work of art solely to be discerned in the music itself. That is, while his status as dwarf and smith may evoke the notion in the cultural imagination, Wagner's text never draws attention to Alberich's foot — but his music does. The motivic material assigned to the strings accompanying the Nibelung's initial appearance, prior to his first lines in *Das Rheingold*, suggests a limping movement (example 22).[17] Alberich's 'limping' motif may be perceived as such within musical conventions that imply a connection between given rhythmic and melodic 'gestures,' as mentioned in the introduction, and the objectified phenomena to which they refer. The graceful movement of the Rhinemaidens evoked by the decreasing sound of the arpeggiated strings and the decrescendo in the falling motives in the woodwinds gives way abruptly with the appearance of Alberich to the darker forte sounds of the basses, cellos, violas, tuba, third bassoon, and clarinets. The conflation of the accented, upward half-step grace-note movement in the cello, followed shortly by a similar figure in the viola, with the forte pizzicato attacks on the unaccented second, third, fifth, and sixth beats in the double basses makes for an irregular, rhythmically lopsided movement, and the juxtaposition of these two sonic-rhythmic configurations will be maintained throughout the scene, giving acoustical representation to the physiological differences between the graceful, fishlike water sprites and the hobbling, toadlike, heavy-footed gnome.

Alberich is clearly one of the clumsiest figures to populate the

Example 22.
Alberich's initial,
limping appearance
in *Das Rheingold*

operatic stage. He has scarcely begun his importunate and unfortunate flirtation with the Rhinemaidens when they cruelly
invite him to negotiate the slippery rocks in order to reach them
in their watery heights — cruelly, because they know he will fail.
His inability to do so underscores both the difference of his
heavier nature and the specific makeup of his body. As he is
dragged down repeatedly to the depths of the Rhine, perhaps by

the weight of his all-too-clublike foot, we are shown the effects of his inferior physical presence. Each time he falls, Wagner's music provides a gestural illustration in the strings that accompanies his downward movement.

Wagner often repeats the limping motif first heard at Alberich's initial appearance or provides a similarly clumsy musical equivalent whenever the dwarf reappears on stage. Such is the case following the orchestral interlude depicting the descent to Nibelheim and preceding the opening of the scene in which Alberich violently accosts his brother, Mime. Prior to their entrance, the orchestration of the Ring motif shifts from the upper to the lower and darker strings, bringing with it the suggestion of weight and of a halting and syncopated movement, and then Alberich drags his brother into view, accompanied by a rolling, clumsy, violent rhythmic pulse in the lower, darker strings (the cellos, with coloristic enhancement by the double basses and the bassoons), similar to the music that was heard as he attempted unsuccessfully to negotiate the slippery rocks in the Rhine (example 23). The ungainly nature of Alberich's perambulatory

Example 23.
Perambulation in
Nibelheim, scene 3
of *Das Rheingold*

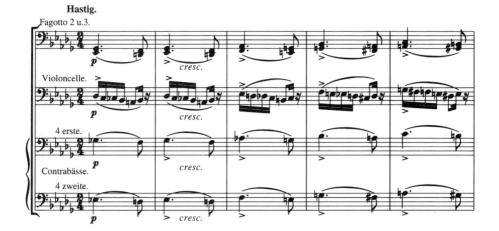

peregrination is implied once again in his entrance at the beginning of his next encounter with Mime, in act 2, scene 3 of *Siegfried*, in which the dwarves argue over the ownership of the Ring (example 24). The syncopated rhythm coupled with the rising movement in the clarinet, bass clarinet, and bassoon provides an acoustical approximation of a hurried and gamboling yet decidedly clumsy gait. In comparing the initial compositional sketches for this scene with the version found in the finished score, Curt von Westernhagen emphasizes the care Wag-

Schnell und drängend. (Dreitaktiger Rhythmos.)

Example 24.
Hobbling dwarves
in *Siegfried*, act 2,
scene 3

ner took in developing a musical portrait of difference, effected in part through its idiosyncratic character within and marked contrast to the surrounding music and through the effect of an iconoclastic rhythmical context intended to denote a picture of disgusting and ungainly movement. In the first sketch to the scene, von Westernhagen explains, 'the semiquaver figure in 2/4 time (in an otherwise 3/4 context) accompanying the slithering motion of the brothers as they rush in to confront each other . . . is completely absent. In its place the sketch has a very hastily scribbled triplet figure. . . . But it is precisely the combination of the three-bar groupings of the vocal parts and the four-bar groupings of the accompaniment [in the finished version of the music drama] that makes the scene so grotesque.'[18] It was in order to paint a persuasive musical picture of two figures characterized by their unnatural, partially comical, and highly caricatured clumsy walk that Wagner invested such effort into the composition and the extensive revision of the scene. Here, the iconoclastic rhythm, which provided a gesturally mimetic device for the depiction of the Nibelungs' carriage, was the key to the musical characterization. (In this context it is worth mentioning that Arnold Schoenberg, in an unpublished essay from 1931, claimed that Wagner's cultural heirs excoriated Brahms's penchant for setting triplets against duple-time figures ['Triolen und Driolen gleichzeitig zu setzen'] as a 'Jewish mania.'[19] Wagner's followers apparently found the musical depiction of the

Nibelungs such an obvious and persuasive portrait of physiological traits deemed Jewish that they subsequently associated its features with Jews whenever they occurred — even in the music of Gentiles.)

Wagner also imbues Mime with impoverished perambulation because he, too, is a Nibelung. Just as their racial nature gives them both inferior eyes, an elevated vocal tessitura, and rotten smells, so they both, as caricatures of Jews, must limp. In his recollections of the rehearsals for the first *Ring* cycle in 1876, Heinrich Porges related that for the Nibelheim scene in *Das Rheingold* Wagner asked his Mime to 'skip around gesticulating,' a request based both on the anti-Semitic stereotype of Jewish conversational mannerisms and on the image of the Jew as a figure with a nervous yet inferior gait.[20] Unlike his brother, Alberich, however, whose clubfootedness is conveyed not through the text but solely through the music and through the associations linked to the figures of the smith and the dwarf, Mime's perambulatory defect is expressed both through his music and through the text of the *Ring*. In the suppressed description of Mime from *Der junge Siegfried* quoted in the introduction, Wagner had drawn attention expressly to the image of the dwarf as 'deformed and hobbling' and to his 'bare feet, with thick coarse soles underneath.'[21] From the outset, then, Mime's characteristic and impoverished gait was one of the central images associated with the figure for Wagner. Siegfried's malicious comments to the dwarf in act 1 of *Siegfried* are based on this initial conception:

Seh ich dich stehn,
gangeln und gehn,
knicken und nicken,
mit den Augen zwicken:
beim Genick möcht' ich
den Nicker packen. (*RN*, 161)

[When I see you standing, loping and going, keeling-over and nodding, with your eyes blinking: by the neck I want to grab the nodder.]

In the measures leading up to this passage Wagner decreases his
orchestration in size and his music in tempo (marked 'poco a
poco rallent.' and then 'Immer noch etwas mehr zurückhalt-
end') and assigns detailed and independent lines for three clarinets, two bassoons, and the violas divided into two sections, instruments closely associated with Mime throughout the drama
(example 25). Their dark sounds produce miniature, staccato
effects as they play the even-note portion of the Nibelung motive, a motive that is often associated with the dwarves' characteristic task of hammering but that now emerges also as part of a
musical portrait of an idiosyncratic gait. It has been argued that
this motive, sketched out in 1851, was the first music Wagner
composed for the *Ring* once he had decided to expand the work
beyond a single drama, and if so it would place both the specific
genesis of the Nibelung's music and the first musical expressions of the cycle as a whole within a year of the publication of
'Das Judentum in der Musik,' a chronological proximity that
makes ideological sense.[22] Perhaps the Nibelung motive lacks
its dotted-rhythm component here because the music not only
represents the dwarf but, more subtly, Siegfried's attempt to
mimic the dwarf's impression on him. The staccato and grace-
note attacks in the three clarinets (similar to those found in the
strings in Alberich's initial appearance in *Das Rheingold*), the
violas (marked 'col legno,' or 'with the wood,' indicating that
the player is to strike the strings not with the hair but with the
wood of the bow, producing a dry, cacophonous, and bizarre
effect perhaps best known in the final movement of Berlioz's
Symphonie fantastique),[23] and in the vocal line convey a sense of
nervousness, clumsiness, and, above all, grossly comic instability. When recalling this scene in act 1 of *Siegfried* in which the
hero derisively imitates the Nibelung, Porges wrote explicitly
of Siegfried's 'mockery of the dwarf's grotesque gait.'[24] Egon
Voss's discussion of the use of the bassoon in the passage beginning 'fur mich drum hüten / wollt' ich den Helm' (RN, 42) that
Mime sings in *Das Rheingold* is immediately apposite to a read-

Example 25.
Siegfried's parody of
Mime's walk, act 1
of *Siegfried*

ing of this music as a sonic representation of the dwarf's unstable movement: 'The third bassoon places a grace note before every tone, which in such a deep register sounds absurd. The trill on "A" also works this way. The other two bassoons are motivically directed as if they "limped" behind the third bassoon. The music portrays the image of the limping dwarf, while he sees himself in possession of the greatest power.'[25] Mime,

then, is as clumsy as his brother, and his bumbling, shuffling, and lopsided gait is evoked through diverse musical means in a variety of dramatic contexts.

Such a musical portrait of Mime's uneven walk reappears in act 2 of *Siegfried* when the hero contrasts the dwarf's pedestrian impression with his own image as surely similar to that of his father, Siegmund: 'small and crooked, hunchbacked and limping, with hanging ears,' a description evoking a deformed, caninelike creature (example 26). Here again Wagner employs the musical devices of act 1 to mimetically evoke Mime's physiological presence generally and his lopsided carriage specifically but also adds devices associated with Alberich as well. The staccato and grace-note attacks, together with the employment of the clarinet and viola, are joined by the use of dotted rhythms and sforzandi by now linked in the listener's mind to Alberich, so that the brief musical portrait underscores the familial-racial affinity of the two Nibelungs and their mutual difference from Siegfried, whose own music is set to a different orchestration, predominantly of strings and French horn (called, significantly enough, the *Waldhorn* in German; Siegfried is, of course, a *Naturmensch*) and containing predominantly even notes and flowing, often boisterous rhythmic movement. Siegfried's music moves evenly, but the Nibelungs' does not. It limps.

At this point it is worth considering another motivic tradition that formed a cultural backdrop to Wagner's portrayal of the Nibelungs, especially of Alberich. The dwarf's apperance is remarkably similar to that of a goat, that animal singled out by Poliakov as the creature so pervasively associated in European cultural history with the Devil. This is precisely how Flosshilde perceives him:

Deinen stechenden Blick,
deinen struppigen Bart,
O säh' ich ihn, faßt' ich ihn stets!
Deines stachligen Haares
strammes Gelock,
umflöss' es Floßhilde ewig! (*RN*, 10)

[Your stabbing glance, your scruffy beard, O if only I saw, if only I held it always! The thick curls of your barbed hair, if only they would flow about Flosshilde forever!]

Alberich's explicitly goatlike appearance (as well as his lascivious nature) draws upon a host of cultural images, most obvious,

Example 26.
Siegfried imagines
what Mime's son
would look like, act
2 of *Siegfried*

perhaps, in addition to his link to the Devil, those of the satyr, the sylvan (or Silenus), and the faun (or Pan) — similar and related figures part goat and part man. The Greek myths in which these figures are found emphasize their carefree nature, but they were reinterpreted and transformed in the medieval imagination into evil and demonic beings, into figures who also came to be associated with such purportedly demonic creatures as monkeys and apes (it is not for nothing that Alberich characterizes his brother as such).[26] Owing to these postmedieval, nefarious associations these figures function as a backdrop to Wagner's characterization of the Nibelungs, whose physiological makeup incorporates the clubfoot and goatlike features of Greek my-

thology but whose emphatically apelike and evil, threatening nature makes them a world removed from their carefree Hellenic forelimpers. Moreover, descriptions of the satyr, Silenus, and Pan from Wagner's time are replete with iconographic features also found in the repertoire of images associated with Jews in the nineteenth-century anti-Semitic imagination and thus would have made the association of Alberich with these figures all the more appropriate in Wagner's mind and in the cultured imagination of his contemporary audience. All three Greek figures, after all, are covered with hair and have searching, active eyes and a hooked nose, all signs that merge with stereotypes of the Jew and with his purportedly salacious nature.[27]

Friedrich Rösselt's *Lehrbuch* once again offers a glimpse into the cultural images to which Wagner's figures referred in his time. The primer clearly demonstrates the similarity of the iconographies shared by the sylvan, the satyr, and Pan and evinces features that, following the Middle Ages, had come to be linked to Jews as well (figure 22):

[The sylvan] is portrayed as an old man with a bald head and fat, rough features, and his face shows an animalistic, goatlike physiognomy. Between his short hairs are usually seen a couple of small horns; the ears rise upward, like goat's ears, in a point; his nose is flat and broad, his beard, like that of he-goats, is pointed. . . . one also sees behind a little tail. . . .

22. Illustration of Silenus, a satyr, and
a faun (from Friedrich Rösselt, *Lehrbuch
der griechischen und römischen Mythologie
für höhere Töchterschulen und die Gebildeten
des weiblichen Geschlechts*, 5th ed., ed. Friedrich Kurts [Leipzig: Ernst Fleischer, 1865])

The satyrs were similar figures. They also had the same human body with animallike facial features, small horns, . . . goat's beard, tail, etc.; but they are younger. . . .

Pan's shape was somewhat similar to that of the satyrs. He too has small horns, pointed ears, a hairy face, a goat's physiognomy, and a tail; but he is distinguished by his crooked nose, since the satyrs and sylvans had one that was squashed flat, and by his goat's feet. When he was born, his wet nurse was so terrified by his ugly appearance that she ran away.[28]

Clearly the ugliness and the unusual feet of the figures recall Hephaestus, while their irrepressible sexual appetites conflate with the popular image of the Devil and the Jew. But it was through their goat's features especially that these figures came to resemble the stereotypical Jew in the German imagination. Joshua Trachtenberg has studied the demonic representation of the Jew in the Middle Ages and makes the following, apposite observation: 'A supposedly characteristic feature of the Jewish physiognomy, which is constantly stressed in the prints and particularly in the folk tales, is the so-called *Ziegenbart* (goat's beard, or goatee). This otherwise obscure detail assumes meaning when we consider it in conjunction with the common representation of the Jew in association with the he-goat. . . . The *Bock* or billy goat, as the Middle Ages knew full well, is the devil's favorite animal, frequently represented as symbolic of satanic lechery.'[29] By imbuing Alberich with the features of a goat, Wagner evoked the sylvan bestiary of classical antiquity, but in doing so he also evoked the Jew, who had come to be viewed in the popular imagination with the same characteristics that accompany these figures (figure 23). Alberich (and Mime) of course cannot simply be *reduced* to an iconographic compendium of the smith's, the Devil's, the satyr's, the sylvan's, and Pan's features, but they can be seen to evoke a host of figures from diverse mythological and popular traditions whose features conflated with diverse anti-Semitic stereotypes in nineteenth-century Europe. One icon shared by all these figures and

23. Karl Hill as Alberich. Photo by Joseph Albert for the 1876 production of *Das Rheingold* at Bayreuth (Nationalarchiv der Richard
Wagner–Stiftung/Richard Wagner Gedenkstätte, Bayreuth)

all these stereotypes is that of the clumsy, animallike, or deformed foot.[30]

The foot also provides an iconic focal point by which the inferior beings of the *Ring* are contrasted with those of more heroic stature. It is worth considering for a moment the sensitive response to Siegfried's final music—his *Trauermarsch*, or funeral march—of the iconoclastic and insightful Wagnerian scholar Dieter Schickling. His description of the mimetic implications of this orchestral passage, one of the most beloved and often-recorded of the entire *Ring* cycle and a staple of the concert hall, is readily apposite to a discussion of the iconography of the limping foot in Wagner:

> The high point in the unleashing of the full orchestra is rhythmically very unusual: Into each rest between the chords of the strong instruments an eighth note on the kettle drum has been inserted; the apparently heroic passage thus acquires a quasi-limping quality that is underscored by the brass instruments, each holding only the last quarter note of the measure—as if someone were dragging a leg behind while slowly walking. . . . That is not being played for a hero but for someone who has been treacherously beaten to death [*für einen tückisch Erschlagenen*].[31]

If one hears the image that Schickling discerns in this passage, the music takes on ideological implications for an understanding of the iconographic function of the foot in Wagner's cosmology of the body. In the present context the key to this reading is its final formulation, because it underscores an interpretation of Siegfried, based upon Wagner's own perception and portrayal of the figure, as a victim of the scheming envy of the Nibelungs, whose antithetical and antipathetic difference to Siegfried is fundamental to the unfolding of *Götterdämmerung*, the original title of which was *Siegfrieds Tod*. It is Alberich's son, Hagen, after all, who at the urging of his dwarvish father, murders the hero. (And Hagen's music shares many of the technical features associated with Alberich, such as sforzandi, dotted rhythms, and syncopations, as I will discuss in chapter 5.) Siegfried is murdered through a stab in the back, an image that would color conservative interpretations of Germany's defeat in 1918 as attributable to a purportedly parasitic Jewish presence driving a deluded government to ruin and defeat.[32] If his musical necrologue gesturally implies that he limps, then, the influence of the Nibelungs in his murder may be heard to be embedded in the musical evocation of an iconography of his body and in the musical commentary on his life and fate, an idea perfectly in keeping with the ideological implications of Wagner's portrayal in the *Ring* of violently incompatible races.

Wagner does not portray the limping quality of the inferior dwarves — or of Siegfried, their superior victim — in motivic isolation but reinforces the image of such lopsided beings by contrasting it with the superior, even, measured, and emphatic perambulatory motion vouchsafed his gods and Volsung supermen. It is only in Siegfried's funeral music that a Volsung can be heard to limp, and then only as a sign of his treacherous and cowardly murder at the hands of a Nibelung; otherwise, the Volsungs' carriage is that of superior beings. It is precisely with an acoustical reference to the image of an aggressive, 'masculine,' running gait that Wagner introduces the first human being of the *Ring* cycle, Siegmund, in the storm music at the opening to act 1 of *Die Walküre*. As a half-god, a symbol of the German *Volk* yearning for the instrument of redemption in his hour of 'need,' and father of the future superhero, Siegmund's tread through the windswept forest is desperate but decidedly heroic (example 27). Even when pursued, unarmed, by Hunding's compatriot warriors and dogs, Siegmund's heroism is apparent in the evenness of his movement, the gestural evocation through the dotted quarter and eighth notes of his halting exhaustion at the close of his second theme notwithstanding. No jittery tumbling and nervous slinking for this superior being.

Though Siegfried's music is decidedly more boisterous than that of his father, it conveys affinity with Siegmund's through its rhythmic evenness and steady progression. Whether fulminating at Mime's ineptitude as a smith in act 1 or prancing about the cave in gleeful anticipation of running off into the world,

Example 27.
Siegmund's running
motives in the pre-
lude to *Die Walküre*

Example 28.
Motives associated
with Siegfried's
surefooted, impetu-
ous nature in act 1
of *Siegfried*

'never to see' the dwarf again, Siegfried's music conveys a lithe, limber, balanced, and 'muscular' quality (which is how Wagner described the movement of his verse in 'Eine Mitteilung an meine Freunde,' as discussed in chapter 1 [*DS* 6: 308–309]) reminiscent of that of his father and altogether different from the rhythms and sounds associated with the Nibelungs (example 28). It was Siegfried, after all, about whom Wagner's initial conception of the *Ring* turned, and his heroic stature and movement provided the antithetical iconographic backdrop to the first music Wagner composed for the work—the nervous, fidgety smithing motive of the hero's limping and inferior foster father.

Just as the eyes of the superior family reflect the similarity of

its members' appearance, so these superior beings all share, then, superior, sure-footed deportment, and because the physical attributes of Wagner's godly breed trickle down from the roving progenitor of Valhalla, it is Wotan himself whom the composer imbues most emphatically with exemplary perambulation. Indeed, from his extramarital rovings referred to by Fricka (*RN,* 20) and his journeys to the depths of Nibelheim and over the rainbow bridge in *Das Rheingold,* to act 3 of *Siegfried,* Wotan is accompanied by the theme of wandering throughout the three *Ring* dramas in which he appears on stage. This is the case even when he is *not* seen by the audience, for example in Sieglinde's act 1 narration in *Die Walküre,* in which she describes to her brother how an old, hale, and venerable man strode into Hunding's hut on her wedding night, for in act 1 of *Siegfried* we recognize the figure Sieglinde had described to be Wotan, dressed in his guise of the Wanderer, when he solemnly appears in the Nibelung's cave.

The musical motive usually labeled 'The Wanderer' is an iconic portrayal of slow and deliberate forward striding, in that its rhythmic progression and the polyphonic movement of its lines are mimetically gestural in character.[33] It is first heard when the figure enters in scene 2, and upon its second sounding Wagner's stage directions read: '*Sehr langsam, immer nur einen Schritt sich nähernd* [*Very slowly, always coming closer only one step at a time*].' The entire first part of the scene between the Wanderer and Mime consists of the optical image of the god moving slowly and deliberately across the stage, a movement that contrasts markedly with the dwarf's shuffling and hurried presence, and their diverse perambulations are underscored by the gestural differences between the Wanderer's motive, which is repeated throughout this opening tableau until he sits at the hearth, and the volatile, agitated music of the Nibelung.

Wagner's reflections on rhythm in 'Das Kunstwerk der Zukunft' provide the theoretical (and characteristically metaphorical) background to the polarity of the rhythmic presence of these two figures and also underscores, again, the close prox-

imity in his thinking between the iconic function of 'gesture'
and musical pulse. The gesture can be seen in the idiosyncratic
singularity of the different tread of the Wanderer and Mime:

> If movement with gesture is itself the heartfelt *tone* of sensation [*gefühl-
> volle Empfindung*], then rhythm is its communicative *language*. The
> faster the change of sensations, the more struck with passion, the more
> unclear is man to himself, and the more unable he therefore is to express
> his sensations in an understandable manner; on the other hand, the
> more peaceful the change, the more vivid is his sensation. Calm is paus-
> ing; a pause in movement, though, is repetition of movement: What is
> repeated can be counted, and the *law* of this counting is *rhythm*. . . .
>
> Only through that which is different from me can I recognize myself;
> that which is different from the movement of the body, however, is that
> which communicates to a different sense than that to which the move-
> ment of the body is revealed, namely the ear. Rhythm, as it emerged
> out of the necessity of the movement of the body striving for communi-
> cation, now communicates as the externally represented, exemplary
> necessity, as law, to the dancer through the sound perceptible to the
> ear, — just as in music the abstract unit of rhythm, the measure, is
> communicated this time to the eye through a recognizable movement.
> (*DS* 6: 42)

'That which is different from me' recalls Wagner's remarks concerning the function of the Jew as the foreign object against
which the German defines himself, while the origin and the
basis for rhythm, it will be recalled, is the foot, the physiological
icon in act 1, scene 2 of *Siegfried* that distinguishes between the
god and the 'race' of dwarves.

The difference between peaceful clarity and 'unclear' restlessness (*deutlich*, or 'clear,' constituting for Wagner the root of
the word *deutsch*) described in this passage is communicated
through the distinctive rhythmic configurations of the two figures of the Wanderer and Mime. The Wanderer is the embodiment of stately calm, and that lofty repose has its pulsing signature, while the Nibelung's music is garbled, 'unclear,' and
altogether *different* from that of the god. The audience's recognition of their racial difference is effected through the percep-

Example 29. The
movement of the
Wanderer, act 1 of
Siegfried

tion of the distinct and idiosyncratically representative sounds
that conflate with their movements. Just as Siegfried, with
whom the audience is supposed to identify, 'knows' the difference that defines the Nibelung as his opposite, so the audience
perceives Mime's rhythmic signature as contrasted to that of the
god. There is no doubt in Wagner's mind that the German
audience will side with Wotan in the ensuing riddle contest, in
part because his sonic signature defines him as different from the
foreign, non-German, limping dwarf. The definition of disparate, antithetical identities is the function of rhythm in Wagner's
theoretical reflections and in the scene between the Wanderer
and Mime.

The Wanderer motive consists of two parts, the first marked
'Mässig und etwas feierlich [Moderate and somewhat solemn]'
spanning four measures, and the second, depending on its dramatic employment, either four or eight. After the motive has
preceded and accompanied Wotan's initial appearance in its
full twelve-measure instantiation, it returns in a shorter, eight-
measure version when the god tells Mime that the world calls
him 'Wanderer' (this time it is shorter because the dwarf abruptly interrupts him) (example 29). The two sections of the motive
are rhythmically similar, defined by common time and a slow,
regular pulse, and both also contain melodic movement that
provides musical representations of the stepwise tread on stage.
The first part consists solely of half notes, and the upper voice
is characterized by a repeated descending gesture that moves
down one whole step (though the interval is written in its different manifestations here as both a whole step and a diminished
third, the ear perceives it as the same melodic distance) and then
rises a half step: from c′ to b′♭ and c′♭ to a in the trumpet (written
in F, a fifth higher than it sounds, in the score), and from b′♭ to
a′♭ and b♭♭ to g′ in the viola. The gestural connotations of
the even symmetry of this first section of the motive are matched
by those of the second. Measures five through eight evince a
rhythmically stable and similar figure in the horns comprised of
an initial half note, followed by a dotted quarter and eighth

notes in the upper voice, while the double basses continue and maintain the even half-note movement, heard in the first four bars, throughout the remainder of the motive. In this second section the first and second horns play the same tone an octave apart, for the length of a measure, in the upper voice through-out, while the contrabasses and second bassoon rise step by step up a fourth, forming a sequential figure every two bars. The inner voices, most notably the cellos, also move in even-measured, step-by-step progressions (marked 'ausdrucksvoll' [expressive]'), and the stability of the horns renders their move-ment all the more pronounced. Through stage directions for the moving actor, the text he sings, and the gesturally evocative and prescriptive music associated with his initial appearance, then, Wagner conveys the stride of the Wanderer as characteristic of the powerful god and in marked contrast to the nervous, jittery, and jerky impressions of his lowly host.

The kind of perambulatory polarity that opposes the Vol-sungs (both fathers and sons) and the Nibelungs is not only a consistent motif found within the *Ring* cycle but a dramatic structure of opposition used consistently by Wagner, with only slight modification, within his other musical-dramatic produc-tions as well. Alberich's and Mime's belabored walk is no result of injury or ill-treatment but appears as a sign of their natural, inborn essence, part and parcel of their stench, slouch, and color. Yet another Wagnerian figure who also constitutes a vehi-cle for the portrayal of anti-Semitic sentiment also acquires the attribute of the clumsy foot in the course of a drama, though in his case as the direct result of attack. Though the source of the specific sign is now different (that is, though it does not appear genetically determined but attributable to injury), the fact that it still appears associated with a parody of a Jew conforms to the ideological program underlying corporeal imagery in Wagner's works. Whether genetically determined or acquired after birth, the ungainly appendage is found solely in association with those figures exhibiting the entire catalog of stock anti-Semitic fea-tures in the Wagnerian imagination.

In *Die Meistersinger von Nürnberg*, the beating that Sixtus Beckmesser suffers at the conclusion to act 2 is so severe that Wagner composed a new, 'limping' motive for the notary for his appearance in act 3, introduced, as discussed in chapter 2, by a high and wailing bassoon (see example 3). Like the Nibelungs' music of impoverished perambulation, Beckmesser's mimetic motive here contains an initial section characterized by a dotted rhythm, followed by one with even notes marked staccato, and, like the musical timbre associated with Mime, Beckmesser's sombre orchestral coloration here relies on the clarinet and bassoons. A few measures later, when this motive is repeated, the musical characterization of the notary employs other devices associated with the poorly perambulatory tenor-Nibelung as well, such as the pizzicato attacks in the violins and syncopations in the woodwind instruments. Wagner's stage directions make Beckmesser's distorted movement — resulting from his brutal beating — something of a caricature:

Walther shakes Sachs's hand; in this manner the latter accompanies him, with a calm, sure step, to the chamber, whose door he opens for him with honor, and then follows him.

Beckmesser comes into view; he appears outside in front of the shop, peers in with the greatest excitement, and, since he finds the workshop empty, hastily enters. . . .

Then he limps forward, shudders, and scratches his back.

He again takes a few steps, but bends at the knee, which he then scratches. . . .

He limps around in an increasingly lively manner and in doing so stares off into space. — As if he were being attacked from all sides, he topples flying in all directions. —

As if in order not to fall down, he holds on to the work table, to which he had tottered, and stares into space. (MN, 113)

(The formulation about 'scratching his back' is a nearly verbatim equivalent to the scatological joke that Wagner later made to Carl Schlosser, his singer of Mime in 1876, as mentioned in chapter 3.) At the conclusion to the scene with Sachs, even after Beckmesser has joyfully received from the cobbler-poet the gift of Walther's song, Wagner repeats his directions to the singing actor portraying Beckmesser's inferior movement and thereby emphasizes the difference between the notary's physiological signs and those of the heroes of the drama, Sachs and Walther, and even of David, another of Beckmesser's sure-footed enemies: '*Beckmesser sways and totters toward the shop door; . . . again runs forward, . . . and then takes off, limping and gesticulating noisily*' (MN, 119). Lest the viewer miss the point that the villainous 'Marker,' so obviously replete with attributes Wagner deemed Jewish, now suffers a limp, the composer had him experience difficulty in negotiating the podium prior to his fruitless attempt in the song contest:

The apprentices lead Beckmesser to a little mound on the lawn in front of the singer's stage, which they have stamped down solid and richly bedecked with flowers; Beckmesser staggers, treads precariously, and sways.
BECKMESSER: Zum Teufel! Wie wackelig! Macht das hübsch fest! (MN, 132)

[BECKMESSER: God damn! How loose! Make that nice and secure!]

Once his performance has started to go sour, the music repeats the tottering motive in the clarinet and bassoon previously associated with his entrance and adds other devices also associated with inferior creatures in Wagner's imagination, such as the trill at one point in the bassoon and throughout in the cello accompaniment to his song, so that we may assume that Beckmesser is on unsure footing, both metaphorically and literally, as he struggles to stand up to his public humiliation. The introduction of the limp motive first heard in Sachs's dwelling makes it clear that the derision visited upon Beckmesser by his fellow members of Nuremberg is focused upon — is intimately associated with — his inferior gait. Once this impression of instability during the song contest has been conveyed musically, the stage directions instruct the singing actor to make it physically as well: '*He again straightens up in order to better stand on his feet. . . . He again totters back and forth; tries to read the page, is not able to; he grows dizzy, in terror he breaks out in sweat*' (MN, 133). (In this respect *Die Meistersinger* is most *literally* a *Satyrspiel*, as Wagner

originally described it; it contains many of the icons of difference also found in the musical-dramatic characterization of Alberich.) It should come as no surprise that German folkore
harbors the belief that if a bride or groom should stumble on
their way to their wedding, bad luck for the marriage will follow.[34] As Wagner's work makes clear, it would be bad luck for
Eva should Beckmesser win her hand, as well as for German art,
and his wobbling is a clear sign of such an ill-suited match.

Just as in the *Ring* cycle every iconic inferiority of the Nibelungs has its superior counterpart in the Volsungs — who are like
fish and not toads; whose eyes are like deer, not 'stabbing,' and
who resemble their natural companions, wolves and bears; who
are beloved by their natural siblings due to their similar and
beautiful faces and figures; whose voices are deep and not falsetto-filled; who smell like the natural aromas of spring rather
than exuding the sulfurous vapors of pitch and flatulence; and
who march with sure-footed determination rather than moving
with clumsy nervousness — so too the iconic difference of Beckmesser's feet is emphasized in *Die Meistersinger* through contrast
with the feet of his foes: the *Volk*, Sachs, Walther, and David.
Immediately prior to Beckmesser's appearance in act 3, after all,
Wagner draws attention to the *'calm and sure step'* with which
Sachs leads Walther out of the shop, and this stage direction has
an iconic function within the web of imagery found throughout
the music drama. After Beckmesser has hobbled out of the cobbler's house and after Sachs has baptized Walther's new song,
the scene shifts to the festival meadows outside Nuremberg,
where the people celebrate amid a parade of guilds, sing their
Lutheranlike chorale 'Wach' auf,' and await the song contest. It
is here that Wagner's polarization of Beckmesser's ludicrous and
pathetic perambulation and the lithe, nimble, and self-assured
athleticism of his enemies is made most manifest. The last image
the audience has had of the notary was of a stumbling, bumbling
old man. And now, on the *Festwiese*, the scene is dominated
initially by the exuberant young, especially by the apprentices,
who dance with the girls of the town. Their extended dance is

one of the most popular orchestral passages of the drama, often performed as a set piece in the concert hall, and is in the nature of a country waltz, or *Ländler*. The purportedly folkish origins of this dance are its raison d'être for inclusion here, as a passage from 'Das Kunstwerk der Zukunft' suggests:

Unique [*Eigentümlich*] is only that which is able to create out of itself: The art of dance was unique through and through, as long as it was able out of its innermost being and needs to create the laws according to which it attained a communicable appearance. Nowadays *only* the *folk-ish*, the *national* dance is unique, for in an incomparable fashion it pronounces out of itself, when it appears, its special being in gesture, rhythm, and measure, whose laws it itself created in the process and that only become recognizable, communicable, when they have truly emerged out of the folkish artwork [*aus dem Volkskunstwerke*]. (DS 6: 48)

The healthy foot, as the basis of and the metaphor for the communal Artwork of the Future, must be associated with the *Volk*, for that work is for (and by) the people, who see themselves reflected in the work they behold. The superior foot and the superior movement it makes possible 'communicate' to the kindred being (and to the kindred, privileged audience) much as the eye, the shape of the body, the voice, and one's smell. One of the images the folkish audience sees is that of the healthy foot as the instrument of the dance, an art that grows out of the folkish spirit and is performed by the *Volk* on stage.

Following as it does the marches and parades of the various guilds (comprised especially of cobblers, tailors, and bakers), the apprentices' charming provincial dance with the girls serves to underscore the folkish character of the entire celebration. Reminiscent of the rustic dance evoked by the music of Beethoven's *Pastoral* Symphony, Wagner's music and the visual image of the dance on stage convey a communal, 'unified' identity manifested in spontaneous and yet collective movement. The one figure who, we can be sure, could not participate in such revelry is the limping notary. Of all the apprentices, it is the folksy David—the boy who single-handedly (albeit with the support of the townspeople) beat Beckmesser within an inch of his life at the end of act 2, as he admits to Sachs ('da hieb ich dem den Buckel voll [then I beat the hell out of him]' [MN, 104]) — who functions most prominently in the dance, tearing himself away only when the Meistersingers appear. The juxtaposition of Beckmesser's two left feet and David's provincial dexterity is thereby musically and visually pronounced and serves to enhance their polarization as combatants in the nocturnal riot of Midsummer Eve. Both images serve to underscore the healthy footing of the community for whom the music drama was composed.

Following the folkish dance, the entrance of the Meistersinger offers yet another manifestation of the superior tread of superior beings; their entrance is accompanied by the motive with which the overture to the drama had opened, a marchlike, stately, somewhat pompous music suggestive of proud and stolid *Staatsbürger*, and one that in this scene is explicitly linked to the visual image of the Meistersinger's self-assured movement across the stage. It is perhaps less than coincidental that the opening bars of this motive, both rhythmically and melodically, bear some resemblance to those of the motive associated with the race of the Volsungs in the *Ring*, a musical affinity, their distinctive harmonic major-and-minor colorations notwithstanding, that may be attributable to the function of both groups, master-singers and super-men, as embodiments of those traits Wagner deemed exemplarily German (example 30). It is this motive of the Volsung race that functions so prominently in the opening pages of Siegfried's funeral march, in which Schickling discerns an acoustical image of the hero's thwarted forward movement, and the similar Meistersinger motive, too, conveys an image of marchlike, albeit more stately progression, underscored by its variant associated with the deferential and immature movements of the youthful apprentices, would-be future Meistersinger. Just as Siegfried's physiognomy is different from that of the evil Nibelungs, so the physiology of the Meistersinger and their apprentices is antithetical to that of their lesser and clumsy adversaries.

Example 30.
Meistersinger and
Volsung motives

Thus, it is not in the music alone but through the conflation of specific scenic enactments (Beckmesser's beating in act 2, his limp in act 3, the apprentices' dance, the entrance of the Meistersinger, and Beckmesser's stumbling on the podium) and the gesturally mimetic music associated with these visual representations that creates a consistent set of images involving the iconography of the inferior foot as a sign of nefarious baseness and inferiority per se. The final image the audience will have of Beckmesser is his resentful, violent, and clumsy perambulation as he exits the scene on the festival meadow following his ridiculous performance and, in Wagner's mind, well-earned excoriation by the *Volk* and by his fellow Meistersinger, all of whom, given Wagner's consistent iconographic vocabulary, walk, march, or dance with greater finesse than the elitist, villainous, and, by his very nature, essentially foreign stereotype of a Jew.

Again and again, Wagner's musical and verbal histrionics incorporate and exploit the icon of the Jew's damaged and different body. Beckmesser's lack of stability is a less explicit reference to the motivic tradition of the lame Jew than that found in the slithering, limping, and clumsy Nibelungs, but it is equally evocative of the image lurking in the back of the cultural imagination in nineteenth-century Germany and was thus appropriate for Wagner's construction of a character so imbued with anti-Semitic stereotypes. It is only fitting that Beckmesser, whose income is gleaned not from the kind of manual labor executed by the other Meistersinger but by cerebral manipulation, whose distance from the *Volk* is underscored throughout, and who lacks any feeling for the German language, should also be identified with this other attribute of the Jew found in the repertoire of anti-Semitic imagery in Wagner's time. Every Jewish stereotype in Wagner's works, as in his culture, is defined by his or her damaged body and is given away by features deemed idiosyncratically different and inferior to those of the German. Among others, impoverished movement stands out because it is so immediately obvious, even from a distance. Though the Jew's voice and stench (or, in the case of *Parsifal*, sexual — and hence different — odor) reveal the Jew in close proximity, the inferior being can even be recognized by the eye of the *Volk* from a vantage point to which no sounds or smells have penetrated.

This icon reappears once again in Wagner's final music drama. In *Parsifal*, once the world has been rid of Klingsor's elevated tessitura and the castrato's damaged body, together with the seductive aromas of his Magic Garden, the instrument of his malevolent difference, Kundry, undergoes a perambulatory transformation linked to her de-Jewification as well. Her transformation had already begun when Parsifal rejected her incestuous advances in act 2, and by the beginning of act 3 she is well on her way to salvation. Having renounced all those nasty Jewish traits such as smelling different, singing wildly disjunctive and dissonant phrases, and attempting to aid Klingsor in the infiltration and destruction of the Teutonic community, Kundry becomes a better, and that means for Wagner more Germanic, figure, worthy of compassion and redemption.

It is therefore perfectly in keeping with Wagner's anti-Semitic corporeal iconography that the dramatist explicitly draws attention in act 3 to the improvement in Kundry's *stride*. While her first appearance in act 1 had been that of a wildly stumbling, nervous, and driven woman (accompanied by an expansive and rapid motive, reminiscent, through its arpeggiation and speed, of coloratura passages from Grand Opéra and assigned to the viola, the instrument so closely associated with that other nefarious stumbler, Mime),[35] her new-found religious and Teutonic demeanor is underscored in act 3 by her noble and sure-footed carriage, as Gurnemanz immediately observes:

Wie anders schreitet sie als sonst!
Wirkte dies der heilige Tag?
O! Tag der Gnade ohnegleichen!
Gewiß zu ihrem Heile
durft' ich der Armen heut'
den Todesschlaf verscheuchen. (P, 74)

[How differently she strides! Did the Holy Day do this? O! Day of mercy without equal! Certainly for her salvation I was allowed to banish the sleep of death from the poor woman.]

In terms of the ideological implications behind her corporeal iconography, the shift from stumbling to noble deportment is identical to that separating Kundry's odoriferous difference and the 'odor of sanctity' that she achieves through baptism and the conversion to Catholicism. She now *must* walk differently, because she is now on the path to salvation — to ceasing to be a Jew. Accordingly, Kundy is finally 'redeemed' at the conclusion to Wagner's last music drama when, having recognized the virtues of abstinence, penance, and religiosity, she dies.[36]

And just as there can be no Nibelung without a superior god or Volsung and no Beckmesser without a superior Walther, Sachs, David, or *Volk*, so the Kundry of act 1, too, requires her superior opposite. That model of Germanic perfection is of course Parsifal himself. He, too, is endowed with a sure foot, surer than Kundry's in act 1 prior to her transformation, for there she vanishes as a penitent hag, crawling into the bushes before Gurnemanz embarks with the eponymous hero on the youth's first journey to the castle of the Grail. In act 3, once she has learned to 'tread differently,' Kundry will join the two

Christian-German men precisely on this path. In act 1 Parsifal remarks that he himself 'scarcely treads,' though he has already moved a 'great distance' (P, 48) on his way to Montsalvat, a journey that in the past Amfortas had also forbidden to Klingsor, who is never granted access to the Grail temple (and of whom, moreover, one could hardly expect pain-free and hence elegant perambulation!). Indeed, immediately following Kundry's disappearance in act 1, the orchestral accompaniment becomes pronouncedly marchlike as Gurnemanz and Parsifal begin their portentous trek to the site of the Grail along a path upon which, as Gurnemanz explains, no one can tread whom it itself has not 'chosen': The notion of elected exclusivity and the icon of superior perambulation are intimately connected. The pure fool has a sure foot that strides easily, and when he holds aloft the holy spear over the newly bleeding Grail at the symbolically androgynous conclusion to the drama (a conclusion that metaphorically merges the sexualized notions of music as the feminine and poetry as the masculine agent and that thereby constitutes a visual representation of the metaphors of the aesthetic theory upon which the Artwork of the Future that has just been enacted is based), the evil of the foreign (both as Jew and as woman-as-temptress) is banished from the world through the demise of Klingsor and the death of Kundry and is subsumed within the holy office of those who firmly stand on the higher moral ground of the sexually and racially pure. The final scenic tableau of Wagner's final work for the stage includes the image of a hero (and a new order) who will tread along the path of the homogeneous and the privileged with the noble gait of the superior being. Germany's racial future, Wagner hoped, was on sure footing, and the image of that stability is grounded in a host of iconic traditions in his culture that identified evil and difference in the bodies of those who could not march with the German.

Just look at these youths — rigid, pale, breathless! These are the Wagnerians. — Nietzsche, *Der Fall Wagner*

Wagner's writings and music dramas repeatedly discuss and portray, through a variety of bodily images and attendant beliefs, the concept of degeneration. From his despairing interpretation in 'Erkenne dich selbst' of Germany's racial future as threatened by a swarm of dark and physiologically inferior Jews from the East, to his numerous dramatic configurations concerning a threat to the preservation of Germany's racial sanctity, Wagner's works time and again return to the image of a pure race threatened by pollution from breeding with a genetically inferior foreigner. That threat is only implicit, to be sure, in the notion of a physically woeful Beckmesser uniting with Eva, the purest of German maidens, because in the course of their music drama such a union never comes to pass; the threat is real but is thwarted before the physiologically antithetical protagonists can consummate a marriage that would spell the end, in Wagner's mind, to the integrity of German society and of its art. Such a threat is equally only implied — but never realized — in the schematic and even symbolic mixture of diverse kinds of blood in *Parsifal*, represented in the antithetical German and foreign fluids of Amfortas's wound and implied in the Eastern sorcerer Klingsor's desire to wrest the holy blood of Christ, contained in the Grail and seen flowing from the spear at the end of the work, from the Teutonic king (as Robert Gutman has shown, comparison of *Parsifal* with Wagner's 1881 essay 'Heldentum und Christentum' [Heroism and Christianity] makes the racist portent of such imagery all the more obvious).[1] In both *Die Meistersinger* and *Parsifal*, the genetic danger to the superior German order never materializes, neither in an inferior child nor in a symbolic, permanent union of Teutonic and inferior blood.

But in *Götterdämmerung*, Wagner's penultimate and far more despairing music drama, such a child is present and functions both as a physical phenomenon and as a metaphor for racial destruction. It is in the four-part drama of the *Ring* cycle that Wagner's portrayal of racial degeneration is most emphatic and most detailed, and it is here that the concept is linked to a figure on stage — to the gloomy and enigmatic Hagen, son of the Nibelung Alberich, murderer of Siegfried and Gunther, and a figure generally regarded as one of the most villainous and terrifying among Wagner's musical-dramatic creations.[2] The threatening image in 'Erkenne dich selbst' of an admixture of antithetical races finds dramatic representation not only in differences between the Volsungs and the Nibelung brothers, Alberich and Mime, but in the younger generation of these races in the *Ring* as well — in the vast genetic-biological gulf separating the body of Siegfried from that of Hagen, whose corporeal makeup receives more attention than even that of his father, Alberich, or of his uncle, the biologically inferior dwarf Mime. It is in the physiological differences between Siegfried and Hagen that Wagner erects his most telling dramatic paradigm of the dangers of interracial procreation.

In the universe of Wagner's *Ring*, Hagen forms the *structural* counterpart not to Siegfried but to Siegmund; they are the sons, and hence the representatives, of the archrivals Alberich and Wotan, and both are sired in the hope that they will regain the Ring. Thus, the fight between the dwarf and the god moves on to their sons. The figures of Siegmund and Hagen are further linked in that they both have mortal Germanic mothers; the unnamed but obviously physiologically superior lover of Wotan (in his guise as 'Wälse'), on the one hand, and Grimhild, the mother of Hagen's half-siblings, Gunther and Gutrune (*RN*, 258), on the other. She either sold her sexual and reproductive services to Alberich in exchange for his gold, as Wotan states in *Die Walküre* (*RN*, 111) (figure 24) or was captured through the

24. Arthur Rackham, 'The wooing
of Grimhilde, the mother of Hagen,'
1911 (From *The Ring of the Niblung*,
trans. Margaret Armour, vol.2 [New
York: Abaris Books, 1976])

dwarf's 'deceit,' as Hagen himself believes (RN, 282). In the 1848 study for the *Ring*, 'Die Nibelungen Saga (Mythus),' Alberich *rapes* Hagen's mother (then called Kriemhild), but when he wrote the final libretto, Wagner exchanged the anti-Semitic stereotype of the lascivious Jew for another, the Jew who exerts power through deceit or money.[3] The structural and functional similarities between the Volsung children of Wotan and the son of Alberich also pertain, moreover, to the psychological damage they experience as offspring of megalomaniacal fathers; both Siegmund's sister, Sieglinde, and Hagen experience recurring nightmares in which their parents play a role, the former appearing near the end of act 2 of *Die Walküre* (RN, 123) and the latter in the opening scene of act 2 of *Götterdämmerung*, startling testimony to the damage inflicted upon these figures by the schemes of their fathers.

But Wagner was not satisfied with merely highlighting the functional parallels between the sons of Wotan and Alberich; his primary interest lay in portraying the physiological differences between the Volsung and the Nibelung that the similarities of their structural positions within the *Ring* would automatically cast into greater relief. It was partly for this reason that the trajectory of the *Ring*'s development is not symmetrical; the introduction of another generation of Volsungs (Siegfried) provides a stark genetic contrast to the inferior physiology of the Nibelung Hagen, for by focusing on the figure who is the product of the incestuous union of superior beings, Wagner underscores the difference between offspring who are racially 'pure' and those who result from the interracial procreation of a German (as represented by Grimhild) and a Jew (represented by Alberich), a theme that often emerges in Wagner's late anti-Semitic tracts as well. Siegfried thus constitutes a metaphor for the salvation of Germany's future, a salvation based upon racial exclusion available to the fatherland if only it were to 'know itself' and to stay within its corporeally recognizable borders, while Hagen's body is a physiological-metaphorical warning to a Germany that refuses to recognize the biological dimension of the purported Jewish threat. Unlike the child of Beckmesser and Eva that is never born and the merging of Klingsor's 'Eastern' blood with that of the Grail that never comes about, Hagen stands before the audience in all his physical horror, a genetic monster constructed out of fears and beliefs in the decay of a superior genetic material that rightfully belongs, in Wagner's thinking, to the race of Germans alone. (In *Die Meistersinger*, the metaphorical equivalent to Siegfried-as-superior child is found in Walther's superior, prize-winning song, whose aesthetic makeup is deemed an organic equivalent of the *Volk* out of whose healthy, racially pure spirit it grows. In speaking of the relationship between the song's verses in act 3 of the drama — the two 'Stollen' constituting the parents of the final 'Abgesang' — Sachs says: 'By looking at the children, you will know whether you've succeeded in finding a genuine couple [ein rechtes Paar . . . das zeigt sich as den Kinden].' Here, too, couched in aesthetic metaphor, the image of the child evokes notions of racial purity versus miscegenation.)

That the physiological connection between Alberich and Hagen, and all it represented for Wagner, was of utmost importance to the composer is demonstrated by the fact that it was a connection he *invented*, for Hagen's status as Alberich's son and Gunther's half-brother is not found in, nor derived from, the *Nibelungenlied*, the source from which Wagner drew so much of his material for *Götterdämmerung*; in the medieval text, Hagen is unrelated to both figures.[4] We have already seen on a number of occasions the ideological implications usually involved when Wagner makes such careful modifications of his sources. Wagner must have invented the relationship because Hagen's evil nature conflated well with his overall scheme of the antipathy of the Volsung and Nibelung races, an antipathy that he imbued, in true nineteenth-century fashion, with a physiological dimension. Yet, as I shall show, Hagen's status as physiologically degenerated is not only a dramatic representation of anti-Semitic stereotypes, for he is constructed out of additional nineteenth-century iconographies of difference and degeneration as well, making him an unusually enigmatic and multifaceted figure within Wagner's works for the stage. Whenever Hagen appears, and whenever he is represented by the idiosyncratic music that illustrates his difference, he evokes the corporeal Other and in so doing represents both Wagner's thoughts on the mixing of races and, as we shall see, additional notions of deviance and decay that were central to the culture in which *Götterdämmerung* was composed and initially received.

Hagen's horrific nature is repeatedly related to the strangeness of his body. Wagner makes the biological distinction between the German superhero Siegfried and his nemesis explicit by having Hagen draw attention, in act 1 of *Götterdämmerung*, to the foreign nature of his blood, that guarantor of racial identity in the nineteenth-century imagination.[5] Hagen's blood is different from both that of Siegfried and his own half-brother, Gunther, whose father, Gibich, was no Nibelung. Hagen emphasizes the genetically determined, iconoclastic nature of his blood when explaining why he has not participated in Siegfried's and Gunther's oath of *Blutbrüderschaft*, or blood brotherhood:

Mein Blut verdürb' euch den Trank!
Nicht fließt mir's echt
und edel wie euch;
störrisch und kalt
stockt's in mir;
nicht will's die Wange mir röten.
Drum bleib' ich fern
vom feurigen Bund. (*RN*, 268–269)

[My blood would spoil your drink! It does now flow true and nobly like yours; stubborn and cold it falters within me; it does not wish to redden my cheek. Thus I keep distant from the fiery covenant.][6]

This motif of Hagen's cold blood was central to the conceptualization of the figure from the beginning of Wagner's work on the *Ring*; the prose draft of *Siegfrieds Tod*, completed before the first verse draft when Wagner still conceived of the *Ring* as a single drama, contains dialogue nearly identical to that found in the final score of *Götterdämmerung*:

Hagen leaned silently on the side: SIEGFRIED *invites him to take part in the vows.*

HAGEN: 'My blood would spoil your drink: it does not flow true and nobly like yours, cold and stubborn is its course and doesn't wish to redden my cheek; therefore leave me out of the fiery covenant.'[7]

From the beginning, then, Hagen was to provide a corporeal contrast to the bodies of the non-Nibelungs (it is not for nothing that Brünnhilde mockingly calls Hagen's attention to the superiority of Siegfried's strength over his [RN, 300–301]).

The idea of physiological difference is not solely portrayed through the dramatic text, however, but through the extraordinarily expressive music Wagner composed for his deviant figure as well. The textual description of Hagen's anemia is reinforced by the halting, sputtering, increasingly slow rhythmic pulse and sparse instrumentation employed in this passage, which is thus singled out through its position following the boisterous duet between Siegfried and Gunther. After their rambunctious music, a change is introduced through Hagen's, which immediately sounds strange (example 31). Here, as elsewhere, Wagner's music provides a metaphorical representation of the difference between the body of the Nibelung and that of the Teuton. Hagen's angular intervals—falling diminished sevenths, at one part a descending chromatic line, and a tritone—conflate with the halting, dotted rhythmic pulse of the Nibelung motive that can be heard to suggest nervousness and that, through its close proximity to Siegfried's and Gunther's music, begs for comparison with their acoustical signs of robust energy.[8] Such devices, together with such other musical signs also found in conjunction with Alberich and Mime as the grace-note attacks, sforzandi, and staccato triplets in the cello accompaniment emerge as part of a musical portrait of Otherness, as part of the aesthetic vocabulary of difference within the overall sonic makeup of the *Ring* per se. While the blood-brotherhood oath concludes

Example 31.
Hagen's description
of his blood, act 1 of
Götterdämmerung

with an orchestral score employing twenty-two instrumental lines for oboes, clarinets, horns, bassoons, trumpets, trombones, tubas, violins, violas, cellos, and double basses, the orchestral accompaniment for Hagen drops to a minimum, employing only horns and cellos, predominantly marked 'piano,' with an occasional coloristic effect in the bassoon and pizzicato attacks in the strings (both so reminiscent of Beckmesser and Mime) or

sustained, quiet sounds in the trombones until, in the final line
of this passage, the Nibelung sings with no orchestral accompaniment at all. Scarcely has Gunther resumed singing, however (with a negative characterization of Hagen as the *unfroh-
en* — the 'unhappy' — man), when the music appears to regain
energy ('Schnell belebend [Quickly enlivened]'; 'Wieder sehr
lebhaft [Again very lively]') with a plethora of strings, brass,

and woodwinds, and Gunther and Siegfried buoyantly rush off to the conquest of Brünnhilde, the object of their impetuous desire.

The musical voice that speaks here is that of 'the opera body'; it is the musical representation of physiological states, audible metaphors of Hagen's blood and of Gunther's and Siegfried's superior physicality.[9] To be sure, many of the musical conventions that are associated with such early nineteenth-century operatic villains as Beethoven's Pizarro and Weber's Kaspar and that are employed in the portrayal of Hagen (such as the diminished-seventh chord, dissonant intervals, and dark timbre of the orchestration and the kind of voice intended for the role) clearly lent the figure credibility to those steeped in the operatic traditions of Germany — to Wagner and to his contemporary audience. But Wagner's construction of evil is unlike that of its villainous predecessors in that it is explicitly based on images of *physiological* difference, and these are reflected, and reinforced, through the music.

While that physiological inferiority makes Hagen readily comparable to other figures in Wagner's works evincing anti-Semitic stereotypical features, there is yet another feature of his characterization that further underscores his difference, both from them and from the Teutons who surround him. It is Hagen's pronounced *sexual isolation* that makes him a unique figure in the *Ring* (with the possible exception, as previously mentioned, of Mime, but Wagner does not draw attention to the dwarf's sexuality). Alberich, Beckmesser, and later Klingsor represent the notion of the Jew as a lascivious, sexual threat, as a bundle of carnal energy that is only partially countered in the anti-Semitic imagination by the portrayal of the Jew as effeminate. Hagen, however, stands out in the Jewish crowd, for he poses virtually no such danger. In a work replete with carnal passion, rape, and tests of sexual prowess, Hagen's lack of a sexual partner is automatically pronounced. He is introduced, after all, in the act of unfolding a plot to procure a wife and husband for his siblings, Gunther and Gutrune, and in so doing tricks Siegfried into forgetting and relinquishing Brünnhilde, the woman with whom the hero has just lost his virginity. Siegfried's sexual drives, it may be recalled, are portrayed as natural and compelling: He learns of love by observing the coupling of wild animals (RN, 162) and then experiences sex with more than one woman in the course of *Götterdämmerung* — with Brünnhilde and Gutrune, and, though he ultimately resists their enticing song, he is nearly seduced in act 3 of the drama by the

Rhinemaidens as well (*RN*, 313). Furthermore, given his position within the dynamics of the plot of the *Ring*, Hagen is also
implicitly contrasted to Siegfried's father, Siegmund, another
figure who experiences love (and perhaps sex) with more than
one woman and whose sexuality Wagner portrays as 'natural'
and healthy.[10]

But while the protagonists around him are primarily concerned with sexual passion, fulfillment, and the vows of wedlock
and constancy, Hagen shows no such interests; his concerns are
with his megalomaniacal drive for power and the physiological
and psychological nature of his difference from others, as he
states in his grim refusal of blood brotherhood. Indeed, the
Nibelung even explicitly *rejects* the kind of sexuality pursued
and enjoyed by Siegfried and Gunther by remarking that he
wishes to remain distant (*fern*) from their 'fiery' vows. Hagen's
distance from fire is his metaphorical distance from the passionate heterosexual activity suggested by the fire that surrounds
Brünnhilde and that Siegfried, in a metaphor of male sexuality,
repeatedly penetrates. (Thus it is worth noting that in both of
Wagner's final two works for the stage a connection emerges
between inferior blood and sexual difference, as a comparison of
Hagen with Klingsor makes clear. As the late Wagner came
increasingly to believe in the biological or hereditary foundation, in the physiological legitimacy of his image of the Jew, the
motif of difference and dangerous blood came increasingly to
the fore in his imagination and merged with the older stereotype of the Jew's sexual difference.)

Within the anti-Semitic iconographic vocabulary of the *Ring*,
then, such sexual isolation gives pause, because it seems to have
no parallel in the cycle. Nevertheless, it is a motif that appears
not only once but that is reinforced through a host of corporeal
icons evoking sexual isolation that operate within the larger
motivic web of the entire tetralogy, especially through the icon
of the *eye*. In the *Ring*, the damaged, sick, or iconoclastically
inferior eye provides a counterpart to the eyes of the gods and of
the German supermen and women and hence, by extension, to

the eyes of the *Volk*, and that damaged bodily icon suggests not only physiological degeneration in general but a decay that is even linked specifically to Hagen's sexual difference. For while the function of the 'good' eye — the eyes of the Volsungs — is a product of Wagner's creative motivic imagination, the notion of the eye as the site of the body in which deviance, decay, and physiological damage could be unmistakenly discerned was by no means his invention but very much a part of the cultural vocabulary of nineteenth-century Germany from which so many of his motifs and images were drawn, and in his world, the eye was an icon not only of racial difference but of a particularly nefarious kind of threatening, sexual deviance linked to physical degeneration as well.

Hagen's iconoclastic physiology and psychology are presented most forcefully in the opening to act 2 of *Götterdämmerung*, which must count as one of Wagner's most unusual dramatic configurations. The scene was of singular importance to the composer, as his recollections of the first complete *Ring* performances in Bayreuth suggest: 'I for my part must admit that I hold the spooky, dreamlike conversation between Alberich and Hagen, at the beginning of the second act of "Twilight of the Gods," to be one of the most accomplished parts of our entire achievement' (*DS* 10: 56–57). In this scene, Alberich appears before Hagen as a nocturnal vision — as ghost, undead, hallucination, somnambulistic apparition, or projection — while his son ruminates '*softly, without moving, so that he appears to remain asleep throughout, although his eyes are fixed and open*' (*RN*, 282). This is the aforementioned 'nightmare' scene in which Hagen is haunted by his oppressive, demanding father; it may be understood as a dramatic representation of the German word for nightmare — *Alptraum* (spelled *Albtraum* in Wagner's time), literally 'elf dream' — and Wotan's apostrophic question to Alberich, 'Rasest du, schamloser Albe? [Are you crazy, shameless elf?]' (*RN*, 56) in *Das Rheingold* and his description of the Nibelungs as 'Schwarzalben' (*RN*, 171) make such an interpretation textually consistent.[11] Hagen, it seems, like Klingsor, may be a raiser of spirits (as well as, like his uncle Mime, a brewer of potions), though Wagner leaves the precise nature of his vision unexplained.

The iconographic significance of Hagen's open, staring, vacuous gaze merges with that of other information provided by the resentful lines he sings to his father. Alberich begins their dialogue with a reference to Hagen's mother, Grimhild, and Hagen's response repeats the motif of anemia found in act 1 while supplementing it with additional, ideologically telling bodily signs that enhance the image of the grim Nibelung staring out into space during his nocturnal visitation:

Gab mir die Mutter Mut,
nicht mag ich ihr doch danken,
daß deiner List sie erlag:
frühalt, fahl und bleich,
haß ich die Frohen,
freue mich nie! (RN, 282)

[Though my mother gave me courage, I cannot thank her for succumbing to your cunning: early-old, wan, and pale, I hate the happy, never rejoice!]

Here, an iconographic portrait of Hagen emerges that reinforces the impression the audience has had of him in act 1 but that, for a nineteenth-century recipient, supplies more specific and detailed images connoting enervation, degeneration, and difference. (Arthur Rackham's 1911 illustration of the scene faithfully incorporates the iconographies reflected in Wagner's libretto [figure 25].) More than any other figure in the *Ring*, Hagen is repeatedly portrayed as both *exhausted* and *pale* — repeatedly, because of his musical metaphors in act 1 and professed feelings of advancing age here, and because of the use of not one but two epithets in this scene denoting a deathly complexion: *fahl*, or wan, and *bleich*.

But are such exhaustion and pale skin stock features of Wagner's image of the Jew? It is true that, upon hearing of the death of Karl Tausig, the composer described his young and devoted

25. Arthur Rackham, 'Swear to
me, Hagen, my son!' 1911 (From
The Ring of the Niblung, trans.
Margaret Armour, vol.2 [New
York: Abaris Books, 1976])

Jewish follower as 'a poor character, *worn out early*, one with no real faith, who . . . was always conscious of an alien element (the Jewish)' and thereby formulated a characterization of the Jew as bereft of energy that conflates with the textual and musical portrayal of Hagen.[12] But the pervasive image of the Jew in Wagner's writings and in his music dramas is rather that of a being imbued with nervous energy and driven by envy and rapacious sexuality. These are the dramatic features of Alberich, Beckmesser, and Klingsor and even of Mime as well, whose sexuality is, in contrast to theirs, a mute point but who always appears as frenetically active.

And yet Wagner repeatedly calls attention to Hagen's exhaustion, both in the text and in the music associated with him. The music of the encounter with Alberich is replete with acoustical evocations of the debilitation already mentioned in act 1 and suggested again by the text here as well. As in the scene depicting Hagen's refusal to participate in the oath of blood brotherhood, the difference between Hagen's music and that of his interlocutor in the opening scene of act 2 is pronounced, even exaggerated. His vocal line and orchestral accompaniment here assume the iconographic function supplied by the textual references to his sallow complexion, depression, isolation, and self-absorption. Hagen's first line, primarily monotone but containing a dissonant, falling tritone and a rising half step, is whispered to a *piano*, tremolo accompaniment in the violins and violas with a pedal point in the cellos, followed by a full measure without any instrumental sound at all (example 32). As in act 1, where Siegfried's and Gunther's energy is suggested by Wagner's tempo indications 'Schnell belebend' and 'Wieder sehr lebhaft,' Alberich's nervous state is stressed through the direction 'wieder lebhaft,' prior to his admonishments, and contrasted by 'wieder langsam' before Hagen resumes singing. It is clear, then, that one of Hagen's characteristic sonic signatures is the comparative lack of energy his music suggests; in the two scenes, following the *Blutbrüderschaft* oath in act 1 and the elven apparition in act 2, few instruments, diminished volume, and

Example 32.
The opening of
Hagen's oneiric dia-
logue with Alberich,
act 2, scene 1 of
Götterdämmerung

longer note values provide an acoustical portrait of a figure whose energy is markedly less than that of those with whom he speaks.

But it is not simply the shifting nature of the musical context — that is, such juxtaposition between him and the blood drinkers Siegfried and Gunther or his own father — that gives expression to Hagen's singularity nor the orchestral setting that illustrates his difference. The vocal music itself that Wagner composed for Hagen is replete with gestures connoting enervation, and it, too, serves to set him off from the frenetic energy of his father. As he expresses his self-loathing, hatred, depression, premature advance in years, and pale appearance, the movement of Hagen's voice provides acoustical signs suggestive of the ideas expressed in his text (example 33). Repeatedly the melodic line begins in the middle of the vocal register and then descends to a dissonant note — a seventh or nearly, but not quite, an octave removed from its point of origin — in the lower regions of the bass instrument. This movement of descent, of sinking or falling, recurs throughout. After commencing on g♭ below c′, the

Gab mir die Mut - ter Muth, nicht mag ___ ich ihr doch

dan - ken, daß dei - ner List sie er - lag: ___ früh - alt ___

fahl und bleich, hass' ich die Fro - hen, freu - e mich nie!

Example 33. The vocal iconography of the onanist, act 2, scene 1 of *Götterdämmerung*

line moves down to ab in the lower register, returns to gb, falls again to ab, and then rises to c'b, its highest point in the scene, only to fall, again, a seventh, and then to return to the middle of the register, ab below c', and then to descend once again, and again, and again, in the following phrases, landing even on the basso profundo note of low F, an octave and a half below c', after it has reached c'b for the second and last time in the scene. Wagner's music evokes here a sense of exhaustion; it is as if the figure repeatedly attempted to express himself but was unable to sustain the intensity of his expression. The voice falls and rests, falls and rests, contains brief outbursts of energy, and then returns to the pattern of descent and extended notes in the lower register as it gives voice to Hagen's characteristics of isolation, envy, and physiological difference. Throughout, the vocal line provides a musical-metaphorical equivalent to the text that both illustrates and gesturally expresses the sentiments the text explicitly states.

But it is not only his exhaustion that sets him off from his father. While Wagner makes Hagen's status as Alberich's issue abundantly clear through repeated references to the figure as the 'Nibelung's son' (*RN*, 111, 270) (and Alberich himself refers to Hagen as 'mein Sohn' no less than six times in the course of his short exchange here [*RN*, 281–284]), he *looks* radically different from his father in one key respect: The stock, stereotypical image of the Jew in the nineteenth-century imagination is that of a dark and dirty being made so either by his genetic affinity with the black or by a life spent in foul conditions (as discussed in chapter 3), but Hagen departs from that image. His complexion is explicitly, even emphatically, described as not only lighter than that of his dark father but of other figures as well, and that lighter complexion, far from constituting a positive link to his Teutonic half-siblings and comrades, appears to connote exhaustion and even bodily damage.

How, then, are we to account for Hagen's singularity within the iconographic vocabulary of the anti-Semitic stereotypes in the *Ring*? What could explain the apparent tension between the fact that, on the one hand, he obviously serves as an example of physiological degeneration resulting from interracial union, while on the other hand so singularly departs from the iconographies of Jewishness so pervasive in Wagner's culture? An answer is to be found in the iconographies of threatening or deviant *sexuality* in Wagner's time, some of which — such as images of effeminacy, castration, and exoticism — have already been discussed. Hagen's isolated, unexplained, or missing sexuality as a component of his difference constitutes a key to understanding the figure's iconographic makeup, for it highlights the fact that he, like other figures in Wagner's music dramas, is constructed out of and refers to a number of iconographies central to nineteenth-century European culture: Hagen is not only formed out of images of the Jew but also from sexual images that depart from the anti-Semitic iconic vocabulary of Wagner's age.

The images of Hagen's unusual sexuality, like all icons denoting the foreign in Wagner, are corporeal images; his musical-dramatic characterization suggests that his psychological (as well as sexual) isolation is grounded in physiological difference. To an audience in Wagner's time, such physiology resonated with sexual overtones. By the middle of the nineteenth century a host of corporeal signs had been established in Western culture that functioned as a catalog of stereotypical symptoms connoting (and revealing) a state of moral and physiological decay resulting from a specific act of sexual deviance, and that nefarious act was *masturbation*. In the portrayal of Hagen, these signs are ever-present.

Granted, masturbation is hardly the first thing that comes to mind when one thinks of Wagner's musical-dramatic paeans to heterosexual passion, or even of *Parsifal*, a work, as we have seen, that damns sexuality of any kind as a threat to the integrity of the Self and the community.[13] But in Wagner, sexuality that falls outside the pale of the mutually engaged, double-gendered, heterosexual corporeal activity (as he metaphorically characterized his own creative process in *Oper und Drama* and with it, by implication, the nature of the community that his works were intended to reflect) is deemed different and brings with it all the ideological baggage of the Outsider found in conjunction with the other notions of difference discussed thus far. We have already seen some of the metaphorical contours of the solo-sexual act in Wagner's theoretical writings, for example in 'Eine Mitteilung an meine Freunde,' where he characterizes the modern art world as 'fundamentally separated from life, in which art only plays with itself' (*DS* 6: 217). But, as is the case with other notions of sexuality in Wagner, masturbation also has an iconic-physiological dimension that serves to lend the ideas behind his metaphor a sense of physicality and corporeal reality — even urgency — that, I believe, granted them a persuasive legitimacy in his time, whether they were consciously perceived or subliminally affected his contemporary audience's reception of his dramatic construction. (I should at least mention in passing that the iconographic nexus of sexuality and disease in *Götterdämmerung* could also have evoked still other associations in Wagner's contemporary audience as well, such as syphilis, the purported signs of which share much with those linked to masturbation. As Linda and Michael Hutcheon have demonstrated, iconographies of syphilis are discernible within the imagery of *Parsifal*, suggesting, again, that notions of physiological and sexual difference are particularly prominent in the late phase of Wagner's life and production. While I will be focusing on the signs associated with masturbation in Wagner's time and in the final drama of the *Ring* cycle, these images were polysemantic and could have evoked numerous notions of sexuality and degeneration, both in his own imagination and in that of his nineteenth-century audience.)[14]

For Wagner, and for his contemporary culture, masturbation was the terrible, reprehensible sexual activity of the Outsider par excellence, for not only was it an act deemed morally indefensible but one that purportedly led to severe physiological damage resulting in the emergence of distinctive corporeal features connoting degeneration that may be discerned in Hagen and that may have lent the final nemesis of the *Ring* cycle a sense of persuasive credibility to Wagner's contemporary audience that we can only dimly imagine today.[15] Masturbation provides a particularly apposite vehicle for demonstrating the culturally circumscribed nature of musical semiology, because a little over a century ago it carried associations that today seem ludicrous but that may have been present during the inception and initial reception of specific moments in Wagner's music drama — and thus with the iconography of masturbation, especially, we can view Wagner himself as a member of his audience, as a reader, like them, of a culturally defined set of images and values.

Clearly we should not think of Hagen as an onanist in any literal sense, engaging in solo-sexual gratification behind the scenes as the drama unfolds. Hagen is no more *literally* a masturbator than Beckmesser, Alberich, or Mime are literally to be understood as Jews (an impossibility, given Beckmesser's social position within sixteenth-century Nuremberg and the timeless, mythic setting of the *Ring*).[16] Rather, like them, Hagen is an aesthetic construct that functions as a screen upon which Wagner and his contemporaries projected and/or in which they recognized diverse signs of difference connoting shared prejudices and fears. The power of the figure lies precisely in the means by which, through him, Wagner evoked various beliefs, concerning both race and sexuality, in the physiological reality of deviance and the borders of a communal identity. To a member of a nineteenth-century audience, Hagen's difference would have been credible precisely because he is constructed out of images that were generally accepted at the time as denoting deviance and decay.

Hagen's makeup is drawn from a long-standing iconographic tradition linking sexuality and degeneration. Some of the very corporeal images discernible in act 2, scene 1 of *Götterdäm-merung* are already used as signs of both disease and masturbation, for example, in a letter of 1800 from Heinrich von Kleist to his fiancée, Wilhelmine von Zenge, that has recently received close scrutiny.[17] The letter makes explicit the diverse signs that would be viewed as symptomatic of the onanist in Wagner's lifetime when Kleist describes an inmate in the Julius-Hospital asylum in Würzberg believed to have suffered a mental and physical breakdown as a result of the 'unnatural sin' of onanism:

An eighteen-year-old youth, who had shortly before been extremely handsome and still bore some signs of this, hung . . . with naked, pale, desiccated limbs; hollow chest, powerless, sunken head, — his dead white face, like that of the tubercular patient, became florid, lifeless, veined. His eyelids fell powerlessly over his dying, fading eyes; a few dry hairs, like those of an old man, covered his prematurely bald head. . . . He could no longer move his tongue to speak, he had hardly the strength even for his piercing breaths. His brain-nerves were not mad but exhausted, completely powerless, no longer able to obey his soul. His entire life was nothing but a single, crippling, eternal swoon.[18]

Here, the masturbator is an adolescent who suffers from neurological damage and internal deterioration that leave their mark on the exterior of the body in the unusual, damaged eyes, pale complexion, and prematurely aged appearance of the subject — the very images conveyed by Wagner's stage directions (the eyes), text (the physiognomy of the prematurely aged youth and the pale complexion), and music (exhaustion) of *Götter-dämmerung*.

The notion that onanism could be discerned through corporeal signs was shared throughout the medical community of

Wagner's time.[19] Features or traits commonly held to be characteristic of the masturbator, already clichés when Kleist wrote his letter and mentioned in the medical literature of the age, included a 'pale sallow face with heavy dark circles around the eyes' and a 'thin and pale and cadaverous [appearance],' the very signs of difference found in Kleist's epistle and in Hagen's description of himself.[20] The damaged eyes, pale skin, premature aging, and inferior physiological constitution are the signs denoting the deviant sexual act in the nineteenth century. At the end of the opening scene to act 2 of *Götterdämmerung*, following Alberich's visual and acoustical disappearance, Wagner's stage directions explicitly state that Hagen continues to gaze '*regungslos und starren Auges* [*motionless and with fixed eyes*]' (RN, 284) at the Rhine: In both Kleist and Wagner, the inferior eye functions as an icon of physiological difference, but this is never the case for the composer with the healthy, gleaming eye. The racial difference separating the Nibelungs and superior beings is the difference of their eyes; Alberich's 'stab' and Mime's 'drip,' while the Volsungs' eyes are doelike or heroic. In *Götterdämmerung*, however, such optical Otherness is not solely racial but is also due to a difference that is sexual in nature.

Kleist and Wagner draw upon a number of common images from the cultural vocabulary of nineteenth-century Germany in responding to, and constructing, representations of deviance. Kleist emphasizes that his subject is a *young* man evincing signs of old age, and this notion is a stereotype of the onanist also found in Wagner. Hagen describes himself precisely in these terms: *frühalt*, or literally 'early-old,' an image of a man robbed of his youth by the deviant nature of his bodily chemistry that has led to his unnaturally premature deterioration or descent into the physiological condition of advanced age. Like the motif of his deviant blood, this notion of Hagen's aged and exhausted appearance was already present in the earliest versions of the scene with Alberich, both in 'Die Nibelungen Saga (Mythus)' of October 1848 and in the prose draft to *Siegfrieds Tod* of May 1851. In the former, Wagner's text states that 'Hagen is pale-colored, earnest and solemn; his features have become prematurely hardened; he appears older than he is'; and in the latter, speaking to his father, Hagen says of his mother and himself: 'Though she gave me strength, yet I must hate her that she succumbed to you: early-old, pale and wan, I hate the world and never wish to rejoice.'[21] From the beginning, then, the image of the 'Nibelung's son' as having never or only briefly experienced youth was central to Wagner's conception of the figure. It is significant that Hagen describes himself as quickly aging, that is, as *prematurely* old, for he and Siegfried are actually the same age: In act 2 of *Die Walküre* Wotan relates to Brünnhilde that Alberich has sired a child, and thus Hagen's conception is roughly contemporaneous with Siegmund's and Sieglinde's one night of passion.[22] Therefore, Hagen should be in the bloom of youth enjoyed by the German superhero, but he is not. Instead, the blood of the adolescent Nibelung moves haltingly and is unnaturally cold, his skin is pallid, and his demeanor is that of an aging, isolated man (and in this respect it is fitting that he is the son of a toadlike and hence presumably cold-blooded creature, as mentioned in chapter 1).

To the nineteenth-century imagination, the admixture of youth, exhaustion, and pallor was a clear indication of solosexual indulgence. Much of the scientific literature of Wagner's time explicitly linked masturbation to childhood and puberty and focused on its danger to the child's body, particularly on the threat it posed to the development into adulthood.[23] This belief was later shared by the young Sigmund Freud, who began his career with an interest in the neurological diseases in children and for this reason worked with Charcot in Paris. In 1893 Freud drafted a paper for Wilhelm Fliess in which he postulated a direct connection between masturbation in adolescence and subsequent neurasthenia, as expressed in such bald, sweeping statements as the following: '*neurasthenia in males* is acquired at puberty and becomes manifest in the patient's twenties. Its source is masturbation, the frequency of which runs completely parallel with the frequency of male neurasthenia.'[24] Hagen's condition is not, then, an isolated case but is based upon and recalls a host of traits, or even symptoms, closely associated in nineteenth-century Western culture with a kind of sexuality deemed nefariously deviant.

The construction of Hagen out of both racial and sexual iconographies made for some inherent logical inconsistencies due to tensions between the iconographies of the Jew and of the onanist upon which Wagner drew in creating his villain. Following a long theatrical tradition in Germany, male Jews were invariably portrayed on the stage of the nineteenth century as old and decrepit.[25] This is precisely the image of both Mime and Beckmesser, described by Siegfried (RN, 200) and Sachs (MN, 56) as old and given, accordingly, the kind of vocal production often found on the operatic stage in the portrayal of old men (early twentieth-century manifestations of which may be heard in the music of Abdisu in Pfitzner's *Palestrina* and of the old king Altoum in Puccini's *Turandot*). In the case of Mime and Beckmesser, the theatrical tradition of the male Jew as old merged easily, then, with Wagner's view of the Jewish voice as inevitably elevated. Because Wagner portrayed Hagen as evincing Semitic stereotypes, he viewed the dramatic figure precisely through the iconography of this theatrical tradition of the male Jew as aged and accordingly portrayed the chronologically young figure as never having enjoyed the carmine blush of adolescence. But since Hagen is the same age as Siegfried, he had to be characterized as *prematurely* decrepit. As an embodiment of stereotypes associated with Jews, Hagen's inferior biological makeup is congenital; he has carried the signs of difference associated with the physical characteristics of Alberich and Mime since his birth. As a sign of a figure bearing specific iconographic indications of masturbation, however (his aged physiology, together with his staring eyes, pale complexion, and exhaustion), his debilitation may be interpreted as the result of nefarious sexual behavior begun after birth, perhaps in adolescence. Thus, there is an inherent logical tension between the interpretation of Hagen's degeneration as related to his Jewish nature and as an indication of masturbation. But such a tension may be accommodated or subsumed within the malleable nature of similar images of difference within a given culture, and Wagner's music drama drew upon and referred to both in its construction of the negativity of its villain.

It was also a commonplace in the nineteenth century that masturbation contributed to a deterioration of the subject's psychological well-being. Given Hagen's statements concerning his resentment and emotional isolation, his premature degeneration could thus have resonated against this belief and would then have seemed part of a consistent syndrome. Already in act 1, at the close of his 'Watch,' Hagen voices his hatred of those who take joy in their youth and camaraderie:

Ihr freien Söhne,
frohe Gesellen,
segelt nur lustig dahin!
Dünkt er euch niedrig,
ihr dient ihm doch,
des Niblungen Sohn. (RN, 270)

[You free sons, happy comrades, just sail merrily away! Though you think him lowly, yet you serve him, the Nibelung's son.]

Dieter Schickling has offered a sensitive and perceptive appraisal of the psychological portrait conveyed by the music of this passage: 'The music reflects the human lack of orientation of the man singing: sired by a father who has taken him from his mother and made him into a criminal. What was done to the child continues to have its effects in the man: he passes on to others the lovelessness he has experienced. Made into a monstrosity, he must also appear to everyone else as a monstrosity. In reality he is an ill man, a human being suffering in despair.'[26] Such a reading is perfectly in keeping with the psychological and sexual portrait of the nemesis in *Götterdämmerung*, whose interaction with his vassals, Gunther, and Siegfried, is usually grim and resentful. It builds upon the isolation and despair associated with the onanist in Wagner's time. Twenty years after the premiere of the *Ring*, a study on the effects of masturbation in children would stress the subject's 'irritability, moroseness and anger,'[27] and in the scene with Alberich, these traits are expressed literally in the same breath in which Hagen describes his lost youth and physiological degeneration.

Even the specific setting of the gloomy opening to act 2 of *Götterdämmerung* may be interpreted through the notions of psychological abnormality associated with onanism in Wagner's time. Several studies of 'masturbatory insanity' contemporaneous with the *Ring* draw attention, for example, to the onanist's propensity for 'hallucinations of hearing.'[28] In his *Physiology and Pathology of Mind* of 1867, for example, English physician Henry Maudsley characterized the onanist's state by 'extreme perversion of feeling and corresponding derangement of thought, in the earlier stages, and later by failure of intelligence, nocturnal hallucinations, and suicidal or homicidal propensities.'[29] With the aid of such a statement, we might view the nighttime scene between Alberich and Hagen as a dramatic portrayal of the idiosyncracies of the onanist's body and deranged mind that would have made sense to the nineteenth-century imagination. Though Hagen never evinces a lack of intelligence, appearing, on the contrary, remarkably adept as a dissembling schemer, such comments as Maudsley's correspond to his representation in Wagner's text and music. It is in the scene with Alberich, after all, that the plan to murder Siegfried is introduced, and when, at the conclusion to act 2, Hagen sings triumphantly of the impending deed, the 'murder' motive harks back to these nocturnal ruminations in which his 'homicidal propensities' first became articulated.[30] In his *Body and Mind* of 1873 Maudsley expanded his findings and described the psychology of the onanist with a host of characteristics readily applicable to Hagen: 'offensively egotistic,' 'full of self-feeling and self-conceit,' 'interested only in hypochondriacally watching his morbid sensations and attending his morbid feelings,' preoccupied with 'extravagant pretensions' and 'great projects engendered by his conceit,' and consumed by 'suspicious self-brooding.'[31] Finally, in 1886, twelve years after Wagner completed the composition of *Götterdämmerung*, an American scientist discussing various conditions associated with a damaged spinal cord (which, as we shall see, was also associated with masturbation) would write of 'melancholia, with delusions of persecution and various hallucinations, depending probably on lesions of the optic, auditory or other sensory nerves.'[32] The 'melancholia,' 'hallucinations,' iconoclastic eyes, and damaged nerves are at the time all intimately related, physiological phenomena and furthermore are all standard features of the onanist; they are all discernible in Hagen's exchange with Alberich.

Understood in this context, Hagen emerges as a representation of a threat to the moral foundation of civilization itself. Discussions of such a danger can be found in works roughly contemporaneous with the genesis of the *Ring*, from Claude-François Lallemand's *Involuntary Seminal Losses* (1842) and Heinrich Kann's *Sexual Pathology* (1844), to Eduard Reich's *History, Natural Laws, Laws of Hygiene in Matrimony* (1864) and his *On Immorality: Hygienic and Political-Moral Studies* (1866).[33] Wagner clearly presents Hagen as such a threat, for if he were to succeed in regaining the Ring (and its retrieval will make it his, as well as Alberich's, as he explicitly states to his father), the world of the *Ring* would fall under the sexual domination of the dwarf and the grim tutelage of his son. Indeed, this is precisely the subject of the Nibelungs' nocturnal ruminations.

Hagen's nature as an outsider is thus constructed out of various images that referred to widespread beliefs in the nineteenth century concerning race and threatening sexual deviance. Precisely for this reason—because of his iconographically ill-defined, pluralistic evocation of diverse notions of the foreign and the terrifying—he would have seemed in Wagner's age all the more multifaceted and powerfully troubling, constituting a veritable conglomeration of icons of horror, and thereby may have been both persuasive and credible to a degree that today can only be dimly imagined.

THE EYES OF THE ONANIST, OR THE

PHILOSOPHER WHO MASTURBATED

Götterdämmerung can thus be read as a work whose iconographic makeup reveals a rejection not only of inferior and foreign races but of a specific kind of sexual activity as well that is deemed antithetical to the German spirit and thus as a work constituting a bridge between the images of effeminate Jewishness in *Die Meistersinger* and *Siegfried* and those of *Parsifal*, with its representation of the non-German as both harboring an inferior kind of nasty-lascivious blood and as castrated. In the older Wagner's imagination, the enemy of the German spirit emerges as both racially foreign and as defined by a number of diverse manifestations of sexual deviance.

At this juncture it is worth considering some of Wagner's extradramatic and nonexpository expressions concerning masturbation, because they demonstrate in an even more explicit manner than the icons of his works for the stage and the metaphors of his essays the nexus of associations linked for him to the solo-sexual act. They can thus provide startling, and by today's standards even embarrassing, evidence of Wagner's growing need to label the foreign and threatening foe as sexually different from the German. It is both consistent and culturally revealing, considering the metaphorical function of the eye in Wagner's theoretical writings and in his works for the stage, that in his personal correspondence toward the end of his life he focused on the image of the damaged eye as a sign of sexual deviance from the German norm: By recognizing that which is foreign in the physiology of the eye, Wagner once again merged the personal, idiosyncratic motivic web of the metaphors he used in his social-aesthetic tracts and music dramas with the standardized images of his age. These linked sexual difference and neurological degeneration to the development of impoverished vision. It bears mentioning, moreover, that Wagner located difference in the iconoclastic eye explicitly in conjunction with those who came to appear threatening or critical of his role as the arbiter of Germany's cultural future; even in his personal life, it seems, the icon of the inferior eye indicated a *threat* to the superior being, and that belief was buttressed by the standard catalog of corporeal images associated with the onanist in the cultural vocabulary of Wagner's time.

A letter from the late phase of his life, written as he was beginning work on *Parsifal* a little over a year following the premiere of *Götterdämmerung*, may be read as a verbal reflection of the iconographies underlying his portrayal of Hagen. In the fall of 1877 Wagner wrote a lengthy communication to Dr. Otto Eiser, Friedrich Nietzsche's physician, friend, and avid Wagnerite, in which the standard nineteenth-century iconography of masturbation is made manifest.[34] When Wagner penned his letter to Eiser, he had not seen Nietzsche since November 1876, when the two had met for the last time in Sorrento.[35] Despite growing estrangement, however, they had continued to correspond, and early in October 1877 Nietzsche had sent the composer a short essay by Eiser on the *Ring* cycle, together with a letter in which he complained of his deteriorating health.[36] It was at Wagner's behest that Hans von Wollzogen contacted Eiser requesting more detailed information about Nietzsche's condition (a request with which the flattered and star-struck physician was only too willing to comply). Though this was not the first time Wagner had expressed his views on masturbation in writing (having denounced his young and devoted follower Karl Ritter as an onanist in a communication to Theodor Uhlig of 31 May 1852), [37] the epistle to Eiser constitutes his lengthiest discussion of the practice. It is significant that this occurred as Wagner's relationship with Nietzsche was coming to a close. The few commentators who have mentioned the letter following its initial publication in 1956 have been concerned primarily with the pomposity, meddling, or malice that it demonstrates on Wagner's part vis-à-vis both Eiser and Nietzsche;[38] but I would argue that of far greater importance is the degree to which it documents both Wagner's acceptance of widespread beliefs in sexual and biological deviance that influenced the iconographic makeup of his music dramas and the manner in which such beliefs influenced his interpretation of a man who was growing increasingly critical of Wagner's self-proclaimed role as the representative of German culture par excellence. The letter is also illuminating in that it openly discusses, and thereby once again demonstrates, the widespread acceptance of an iconography of onanism that could have informed the reception of such images in his works by his contemporary audience.

Cosima Wagner's description of Wagner on the day he penned his letter to Eiser is worth noting, for it suggests that Nietzsche, like Hagen and other figures before him, provided the composer with a vehicle for projecting fears concerning his own physical well-being. With the exhausting premiere of the *Ring* a little more than a year behind him, Wagner had just returned to Bayreuth from a trip to England and was suffering from a variety of physical ailments.[39] Cosima Wagner's diary entry of 23 October records their preoccupation with her husband's bodily functions at the time:

R. again had a wretched night; abdominal troubles — he reads Darwin (*The Descent of Man*), feels cold. I cannot say how sad it makes me to see him, at the start of his great work [*Parsifal*], so hindered by bodily ailments. However, he works in the morning. In the afternoon he writes a long letter to Dr. Eiser in Frankfurt, who wrote a detailed report about our friend Nietzsche's state of health. R. says, 'He (N.) is more likely to listen to the friendly advice of a medical man than to the medical advice of a friend.'[40]

Plagued by his own physical deterioration and embarking on the composition of his final music drama (infused with the purportedly scientific theories of racial difference of Count Gobineau) that would damn sexuality of any kind, Wagner turned to the scornful examination of an increasingly undevoted friend, and especially of his sexuality, in an effort to preserve the integrity of the Self. The associative mechanism of his imagination perceived in the critical Nietzsche the signs of a threat that he had assigned to the nemesis of his last drama — Hagen.

Wagner was concerned with Nietzsche's precarious health characterized by chronic migraines and increasingly impoverished vision (figure 26).[41] In his communication to Hans von Wolzogen, Dr. Eiser had explained that, in his estimation, Nietzsche's severe headaches were due to changes in the fundus oculi, damage to the retina, and chronic inflammation of the eyes but made no mention of any other diagnostic findings. Wagner sent Eiser his own interpretation, buttressed by past 'experiences' he deemed essential to a correct diagnosis of Nietzsche's malady:

Bayreuth, 23 October 1877

My very dear Sir,

. . . In the fateful question that concerns the health of our friend N. I feel an urgent need to inform you, briefly and decisively, of both my opinion and my anxiety — but also of my hope. In my attempts to assess N.'s condition, I have been thinking for some time of identical and very similar experiences which I recall having had with certain young men of great intellectual ability. I saw them being destroyed by similar symptoms, and discovered only too clearly that these symptoms were the result of masturbation. Guided by these experiences, I observed N. more closely and, on the strength of his traits and characteristic habits, this fear of mine became a conviction. I believe it would be wrong of me to express myself more circumstantially on this point, the more so since my only concern is to draw a friendly doctor's attention to the opinion which I have conveyed to you here. It is merely to confirm the great likelihood that I am right that I mention the striking experience I had whereby one of the young friends whom I mentioned, a poet who died in Leipzig many years ago, became totally blind when he was N.'s age, while the other, equally talented, friend, who now ekes out a pitiful existence in Italy, with his nerves completely shattered, began to suffer the most painful eye disease at exactly the same age as N. One thing that struck me as being of great importance was the news that I recently received to the effect that the doctor whom N. had consulted in Naples some time ago advised him first and foremost — to get married. —

I believe I have said enough to enable you to make a serious diagnosis along the lines that I have indicated. It would ill become me to suggest that you should re-examine the symptoms of N.'s illness: it is, after all,

26. Friedrich Nietzsche, 1887 (Courtesy
Archiv für Kunst und Geschichte, Berlin)

clear that the only remedy is to take the greatest possible care of him.
But the need to strengthen and regenerate his nerves and his spinal
cord seems to me far too important for me to conceal from you my very
real wish that something positive be done here. . . . I hope you will
advise him accordingly, and — if necessary — speak to him in all seriousness, without concealing from him the primary cause of his illness. A
friendly *physician* certainly has an authority here which may not be
granted to a physicianly *friend*. . . .

Respectful good wishes from

Your obedient servant
Richard Wagner[42]

Wagner based his comments on a number of shared assumptions of the time concerning a repertoire of physical signs that,
within the European medical community and the general public alike, were deemed such obvious indications of masturbation
that he felt no need to mention them in detail, assuming that the
'traits and characteristic habits' [*Temperamentszüge und charak-
teristische Gewohnheiten*]' that he took to be self-evident indications of the sexual practice were widely accepted as such. This
assumption accounts in part for the circumlocutions and vagaries of the letter ('I believe it would be wrong of me to express
myself more circumstantially on this point'); Wagner relied on
innuendo, based on the cultural vocabulary of his age, to persuade (and, for the record, persuade he did, as Eiser's unctuous
and grateful response clearly indicates).[43] Such indirect, yet persuasive allusions may be compared to the subtle and suggestive evocation of masturbation through the text and the score
of *Götterdämmerung*, an evocation that could only imply, but
not explicitly state the nature of deviance it may have signified
within the iconographic codes of Wagner's culture.

Wagner's concern regarding Nietzsche's nerves and spinal
cord (*Rückenmark*) stems from the belief in a pervasive interior
debilitation suggested by a variety of 'traits and characteristic
habits' that Nietzsche shares with Hagen, such as their 'irritability, moroseness and anger,' and by their status as men suffering
from a pathology associated with adolescence. Wagner stresses

that 'the poet who died in Leipzig' and the 'other, equally talented, friend' were 'young men,' draws therein a comparison with Nietzsche, and in so doing underscores the difference in age between himself and the suffering philosopher (and, perhaps, though probably unconsciously, between himself and Hagen as well). On another occasion Wagner stated that Nietzsche 'should either marry or compose an opera, though doubtless the latter would be such that it would never get produced, and so would not bring him into contact with life.'[44] Wagner's characterization of the modern, Semitic art world, let us recall, evoked the sterility and isolation of onanism; it is for him a world 'fundamentally separated from life, in which art only plays with itself,' and these are the very terms with which he describes the imagined work of his artistically and physiologically inferior and different friend. Wagner clearly implies that his own self-avowed status as the premiere composer of the age fundamentally removed him from the sexual isolation of his wayward philosophizing acquaintance. Young, exhausted, and critical of the German, Nietzsche exhibited the signs of the sexual Other.

But above all it was in the phenomenology of their iconoclastic eyes (comparable to those of Kleist's debilitated asylum inmate) that Wagner recognized deviance from the state of the superior German norm. The individuals Wagner cites as examples of his reliable diagnostic experience were Theodor Apel, the 'poet who died in Leipzig' (and a friend from Wagner's youth with whom he had gone on a riotous holiday to Bohemia in 1834), and Karl Ritter (the 'other, equally talented, friend'), a son of Julie Ritter who herself had generously supported Wagner during his exile in Switzerland, and both, he relates, went blind.[45] Karl Ritter was a young homosexual with whom Wagner had lived in Zurich in the early 1850s, where Ritter functioned as the composer's secretary, factotum, and devotee.[46] By May 1852, however, Ritter had begun to show signs of independence, whereupon Wagner, in the letter cited above to his friend Theodor Uhlig, rejected and calumniated the young man as an onanist, as was later the case with the increasingly distant Nietzsche. But it is only the older Wagner who draws attention to the threatening eye as a sign of sexual deviance, which is why he could reinterpret the fate of his friend Apel to accord with his association of the damaged eye and the onanist: As a close friend, Wagner must have known that Apel's blindness was caused by a fall from a horse at the age of twenty-five, but he either repressed this event or apparently viewed it as less conclusively debilitating than masturbation![47] In Wagner's social-aesthetic theories the eye and vision are metaphors for the mechanisms that determine identity, and their function in this capacity appears to have informed his personal interaction with others as well. The icons of the foreign (critical) foe are discernible by the German, because he can perceive hidden meaning in the depths beneath the surface appearance of the object regarded—in the eyes of the Other. In all these instances, masturbation is intimately linked to its physiological signs, especially to that of the eye, but those signs appear to have emerged in the imagination as increasingly incontrovertible proof of sexual deviance in conjunction with the perception of the acquaintance or friend as increasingly critical of the Self—and to Wagner's mind, criticism was tantamount to attack, as his opening remarks from 'Eine Mitteilung an meine Freunde' suggest, penned some twenty-six years prior to his denunciation of Nietzsche: 'This explanation I intend to direct in this communication to my *friends*, because I can only hope to be understood by them, who feel the inclination and the need to understand me, and only these can be my friends' (*DS* 6: 199). Only those who were 'different' would engage, from the vantage point of skeptical distance, in criticism of the Master, would question the representative of the *Volk*. Leveled from outside the borders of the community, their criticisms would be reduced to the voices of those deemed different, while their eyes grew cold, 'stabbing,' 'dripping,' 'staring . . . without moving,' or altogether blind: Difference had its physiological signs in Wagner's imagination, as in his world.

*

It is worth reflecting on some further implications of Cosima's remarks that cast additional light on the scene between Alberich and Hagen. It is well known that Wagner was an avid reader of the works of Charles Darwin, and a connection may be drawn between his preoccupation with a regression in one's physiological condition owing to sensual stimulation and the very text he was reading before he wrote his letter to Eiser: Darwin's *The Descent of Man* (1871). In this work Darwin discusses 'reversion' as a natural phenomenon 'in which a long-lost structure is called back into existence' and argues that the Greeks 'retrograded' 'from extreme sensuality; for they did not succumb until "they were enervated and corrupt to the very core." '[48] Because the concept of debilitation was central to the recent portrayal of Hagen and to the diagnosis of Nietzsche, it may even account in part for Wagner's fascination with and repeated study of Darwin's theories at the time. Significantly, given the motivic vocabulary of the *Ring*, Darwin also wrote of the homologies man 'presents with the lower animals — the rudiments which he retains — and the reversion to which he is liable";[49] with sexuality and degeneration as shared themes, Darwin's text allows for the reconstruction of a series of associations in Wagner's imagination that would have linked masturbation to physiologically inferior, virtually beastly humans. Such associations would have seamlessly conflated with Wagner's animal imagery linked to different races in his musical-dramatic tetralogy. Seen in this context, Hagen as the bearer of the signs of the Jew and the onanist emerges as a representative of a physiologically primitive stage in human development, as a 'retrograded' being and even as an animal — as the quintessentially inferior outcast per se. No wonder Gunther derides the Nibelung's son as 'der verfluchte Eber [the accursed boar]' (RN, 323) that 'tore apart the noble' Siegfried — the metaphor is not far removed from the notion that Hagen is physiologically somehow closer to animals than to the high, human world of the Gibichungs and, especially, of the Volsungs (despite their animal imagery, for his

animal is the boar, baser than the animal images of the supermen — wolves, foxes, and deer).

Two earlier entries in Cosima's diary concerning, respectively, the primitive nature of Hagen and the scene with Alberich
suggest as much. The first is from 7 February 1870: 'conversation about these characters Gunther and Hagen, the latter re-
pulsively mysterious, impassive, curt. On long-lost naiveté: "All
these heroes appeared to me like a gathering of animals, lions,
tigers, etc.; they also devour one another, but there is no disgusting convention, court etiquette, etc., mixed up in it — everything
is naive." '[50] Wagner uses 'naive' here in the Schillerian sense of
unreflected, spontaneous, and, above all, uncivilized. Yet the
animalistic epithets are not only appropriate for figures deemed
primitive but conflate with the notion of Hagen specifically as a
'retrograded' being and thereby serve to underscore the comparatively baser, more primitive physiological essence of the
outcast. In this context it is worth bearing in mind that at this
time, in the 1870s and 1880s, Wagner often referred to Jews in
the very terms found in Cosima's diary entries. Three years after
the first performance of the *Ring*, for example, Cosima made
note of Wagner's description of Jews as 'calculating beasts of
prey,' the same formulation he later employed in his second-
most notoriously anti-Semitic essay, 'Erkenne dich selbst' of
1881.[51] Wagner's remarks were not meant simply as metaphorical jabs, for a realistic substratum underlies every use of metaphor in his racist vocabulary. Rather, the animalistic epithets
vouchsafed Jews and other 'retrograded' beings, such as masturbators, serve to underscore their comparatively baser, more
primitive physiological essence. Thus, to the anti-Semitic and
sexually conservative imagination, Hagen as a conflation of images of the Jew and the onanist is *truly* an animal. Wagner
himself implied as much on more than one occasion, such as in
another remark recorded by Cosima in a diary entry of 1873,
made during Wagner's work on the orchestration to act 2 of
Götterdämmerung:

Saturday, December 27

—In the morning he plays the scene between Alberich and Hagen and looks forward to the impression it will make when Hill and Scaria sing it. 'It will have the effect of two strange animals conversing together— one understands nothing of it, but it is all interesting.'[52]

The Nibelungs seem to have evoked in the composer's mind atavistic, even primeval, physiologically terrifying connotations, and these may be linked, through Darwin, to regression and to the sphere of the primitive animal. Notions of human inferiority merge with these Nibelung figures as vehicles for the projection of fears regarding racial and sexual difference. For Wagner, to be a masturbator also means to give up 'advanced' human traits (such as, in the case of Nietzsche, walking upright with a straight and healthy back?) and to return to the realm of the beastly from which (non-Semitic) man has advanced. Only non-Jews, non-masturbators (such as Wagner?), and composers of those meta-phorically heterosexual Artworks of the Future, it would seem, can be vouchsafed a haven from the dangers of degeneration and regression, the very haven he hoped Nietzsche, the philosopher-friend so fascinated by the sensuality of the Greeks and in-creasingly so critical of the modern torch-bearer of the Greek heritage, would welcome. As with Wagner's hatred of Jews, his reaction to the image of the masturbator (whether Hagen or Nietzsche) sought to ensure the physiological and moral integ-rity of the communal body to which he belonged and hence of the Self at risk in a world on the verge of self-indulgence, pollu-tion, collapse, and regression.

Yet, as with each of the corporeal icons discussed thus far, it would be wrong to suggest that Hagen's or Nietzsche's idiosyn-cratic natures can be *completely* explained through reference to the associations of masturbation in the nineteenth century, for these figures evoked a variety of concepts through their diverse and enigmatic signs of difference. Again, these iconographies did not provide strict blueprints for consistent composition—

not all heroes sing low Cs, and, as we've seen with Hagen, not all low-voiced figures are good guys—but instead constituted a cultural matrix against which the images in Wagner's texts and music could reverberate with a host of multilayered associations in his culture. Such associations simply reveal the multilayered connotational possibilities of the iconic makeup of Wagner's figures within the nineteenth century. Certainly Hagen is many things and not to be subsumed under or reduced to one rubric: As nemesis and powerful warrior, adept and sly schemer, and murderer of Gunther, he confounds the stereotypical clichés of mental vacuity, empty self-aggrandizement, and meager physical prowess expected of the onanist. Indeed, the ill-defined and often contradictory implications of his portrayal—congenital debilitation as Jew versus acquired degeneration through masturbation; the masturbator as weakling versus Hagen as the powerful leader of his vassals—underscore the complexity and ambiguity of the dramatic figure.

But it is fair to say that Hagen can be seen as an amalgamation of a number of diverse stereotypes of a racial and sexual nature upon which Wagner drew to lend meaning to the nefarious nature of his Nibelung, both for himself and for his contemporary audience. It is simply fitting that this character so essentially unusual—as nemesis, as villain, as a figure who repeatedly draws attention to his own status as Other—received characteristics stereotypically associated with those deemed different in the cultural vocabulary of dominant nineteenth-century German culture. Such connotations appear to have attended the perception by Wagner and his contemporaries of similar stereotypical 'traits' of difference in Nietzsche and others as well. As Nietzsche became increasingly independent of the composer (and critical of his anti-Semitism), his distance from Wagner, and hence his difference, came to be associated in Wagner's mind with signs of masturbation; iconoclastic eyesight, moroseness, irritability, and a sickly demeanor. These are precisely the signs with which Wagner imbued Hagen, his embodiment of untrustworthy and malevolently deviant difference. That is,

Wagner's diagnosis of Nietzsche and his portrayal of Hagan may not *simply* have been acts of malicious calumniation (though they certainly were that, too) but may have been reactions to standard images of difference that made sense within his culture.

Because our valuation of masturbation has changed so much since Wagner's time, we may read the text and the music of Hagen, as well as the contemporary descriptions of Nietzsche, without this component that may have seemed so self-evident to Wagner and to his nineteenth-century opera-going and epistolary audience. But in so doing, we will be ignoring a dimension of the art work (cf. Hagen) and of the human being (cf. Nietzsche) as historical-cultural constructs. Thus, the nineteenth-century perception and subsequent transvaluation of masturbation provide an example of the shifting nature of iconography in general and of musical semiology in particular within different cultural contexts. Such a shift in perception highlights the paradox that Wagner's music dramas, intended as paradigmatic ideological models of Artworks of the Future, were initially anchored in a cultural context from which, once removed, they have lost some of their initial communicative power as documents of hatred. But in the nineteenth century, I would argue, the signs of such hatred were either obvious to the conscious, reflective mind or operated subliminally as persuasive and highly evocative elements in a complex construction of difference. The iconographic codes of Wagner's time regarding sexuality, like those of race, thus reveal his music dramas to be wondrously seductive, startlingly phantasmagoric aesthetic accomplishments that, viewed through the eyes of the future in an act of historical and archaeological-cultural reconstruction, emerge once again as dramatic representations fraught with prejudice, intolerance, and the unbridled malice of those whose superior and penetrating gaze looked down on the purported failings of lesser beings who perennially threatened the racial and sexual norms of the nineteenth-century imagination.

Hans Jürgen Syberberg's cinematic staging of act 1 of *Parsifal* contains an epiphanic moment that metaphorically represents issues addressed in this book. As the various figures of the music drama appear and disappear, they do so against a background of high, mountainous walls of dazzling white and enter and exit the scenes beneath sweeping arches and through cavernous passageways. For a long time it is difficult to determine if this chalky material is a natural outcropping of rock or part of a larger architectural design. It is only as the action progresses from the forest of scene 1 to the hall of the Grail castle, however, that the viewer comes to realize that the arches, hallways, and smoothly white walls are nothing other than the solid material and the diverse apertures of an enormous replica of Wagner's death mask. What had previously been perceived as a natural setting or as portions of a rough-hewn casement are revealed to be representations of insular parts of the clay mold that was pressed upon Wagner's face after he died in the Palazzo Vendramin in Venice on the afternoon of 13 February 1883. Gurnemanz, the squires, Kundry, Parsifal, and the ailing Amfortas had been moving about within the mask, walking or being carried through its eyes, along the sides of its nose and cheeks, within and across its borders. The realization of this remarkable trompe l'oeil is a startling experience.

What is Syberberg saying? Certainly the movement of the camera to a vantage point encompassing and hence revealing the physiognomy of Wagner's death mask, once recognized, evokes a host of associations: the fact that Wagner composed *Parsifal* shortly before his death; that the music drama is preoccupied with the salvation of the soul and hence with the afterlife; and of course the notion that this final work, as Wagner's last musical-dramatic accomplishment replete with its own religious pretensions, constitutes the cornerstone of the cult of the Wagnerites, slaves to the postmortem glorification of the Master and his works.

But Syberberg's visual metaphor implies more. His cinematic enactment also presents the dramatic figures as surrounded by, and trapped within, Wagner's body as the physical locus of his ideas while at the same time implying, through the sterile and lifeless visage, that these ideas have grown anachronistic, have become mere holy relics. The staging of the music drama and of the ideas it represents thus emerges as the staging of the body, so that the former is revealed, literally, to be the embodiment of Wagner's ideological agenda. But if the ideas anchored in the body are recognized as fixed to a historical moment that is past, as Syberberg's literal portrayal of the body as an aging relic suggests, movement away from the historically and culturally determined understanding of that body may also, potentially, provide freedom from the notions whose locus the body had been in Wagner's age: If the body as the site of the Wagnerian agenda is recognized for what it is (for an ideological construct, or a physiological justification for ideas it itself represents in Wagner's culture), then that agenda's pretensions to natural, corporeal legitimacy will have been laid bare and hence undermined. The body will have emerged as the ideological tool that it constitutes in Wagner's writings and in his works for the stage. But this will only be possible to the degree that the post-Wagnerian perspective unfolds in a culture that views the body differently from its nineteenth-century forebears. If that culture continues to define difference through corporeal signs, and if those signs are similar to those at the center of the Wagnerian imagination, his bodily representations of commonality and difference will continue to evoke, perhaps persuasively, his racist agenda.

The tension between these two ideological positions — between entrapment and the recognition of Wagner's anachronism — is the very tension with which we are confronted today when seeking to make moral judgments concerning our own reactions to the Wagnerian Artwork of the Future, for we are that future. Today we must ask ourselves whether Wagner's works still seem powerful, persuasive, or perhaps even credible (and therefore enjoy such popularity) because they reflect assumptions concerning the (corporeal) representational veracity of race and sexuality that continue to inform our own culture as they did Wagner's, or whether the icons of ideology in Western culture have so changed since the nineteenth century that we must speak of a fundamental break between Wagner's intentions, the initial reception of his music dramas, and our own twentieth-century perception of them. It is precisely the degree to which listeners and spectators can determine such cultural distance that will define their own ideological positions vis-à-vis Wagner. For it is not Wagner's music dramas themselves that are so disturbing but the means by which they might once have automatically evoked an agenda of racist and sexual stigmatization without manifestly appearing to do so — through a host of images that defied critical reflection precisely because they seemed, within nineteenth-century European culture, naturally persuasive, credible, and somehow obviously appropriate. The disturbing question is to what extent such images continue to play a role, consciously or not, within the reception of Wagner's works today. Do Wagner's works enjoy such popularity and arouse such fascination in the late twentieth century because audiences still find his images of human nature credible and persuasive?

The difficulty in measuring the distance between our own attraction to Wagner's music dramas and our awareness that they are documents of a different cultural vocabulary with racist and exclusionary implications is one of the reasons they constitute such a controversial force in the late twentieth century. It is, implicitly, the potential connection between the ideology of our world and that of Wagner's culture that lies behind the palpable consternation over the postwar Wagner renaissance discernible in the writings of such scholars as Adorno, Gutman, Zelinsky, Millington, and Rose and that played a role in the recent controversy surrounding Daniel Barenboim's attempts to perform Wagner in Israel.[1] A link between cultural signs and ideological meaning in Wagner is ill defined in part because such meaning in his works has always, at most, been evoked rather than explicitly stated (perhaps because it seemed obvious and persuasive within his time) and because the nexus of associations linking ideas and their representative signs is always in flux. Yet, ironically, it is for this very reason that Wagner's apologists implicitly disavow a connection between his culture and our own, seeing his music dramas as the innocent targets of those who unfairly criticize the Artwork of the Future with the knowledge and hindsight of Auschwitz and the critical skepticism of the post-Holocaust age. I would argue that the former group of critics sees a far too direct connection between the ideology of Wagner's world and the implications of his works' reception today, ignoring the culturally defined shift between sign and significance, while the latter sees too little and seeks refuge behind historical transformation, implying that with the passage of time cultural contexts shift so extensively as to make ex post facto moral judgments in aesthetic matters illegitimate.

But if we can determine that, despite the admittedly remarkable power of the music dramas, the references upon which Wagner relied in the nineteenth century no longer constitute part of our own reception, such an insight may provide a kind of redemption for post-Wagnerian culture from the composer's utopian program. While our world today continues, disturbingly, to share some of the corporeal iconographies found in the Wagnerian work of art (the voice of the effeminate Other, the stench and the color of the despised foreigner, and the enigmatically seductive and yet threatening bodily presence of all that is deemed exotic being the most obvious examples of such bodily signs still found in Western culture today), others (such as the signs of the onanist) are no longer immediately recognized as part of our world. Therefore, our own freedom from Wagner's racist-redemptive notions may lie precisely in the degree to which we can recognize our cultural distance from them — not in an effort to disavow such notions as altogether extrinsic to the

Wagnerian work of art, as his apologists would insist, but first to recognize that they once were central to the Wagnerian agenda and then to question their role in the reception of his works today. If we respond enthusiastically to his music dramas, we should ask ourselves if we are also responding to the corporeal images of racial and sexual exclusion they contain, and, if so, what such a response means about the cultural vocabulary of our own time.

Nevertheless, in seeking to measure such distance we should not be deluded into believing that the ideological impulses behind the iconographies of race, sex, and nation in the Wagnerian Total Work of Art have been overcome. Such impulses have not vanished, and in time and in a cultural setting even more distant from Wagner's age than our own they may be linked to still other corporeal signs that will, once again, make their ideological message appear legitimate and grounded in physiology, made 'real' by the bodily presence that is their nexus in a different, more post-Wagnerian age. They will not be gone but will have simply found new bodies to inhabit. What those bodies will look like, how they will sound, smell, and move, and what sexuality they will be allowed to enjoy are questions that are already implied in the Wagnerian imagination but whose answers will be voiced in a world that is no longer his.

INTRODUCTION: WAGNER AND THE BODY

1. On the question of Wagner's Jewish ancestry, see Deathridge, *The New Grove Wagner*, 1–5; Gutman, *Richard Wagner*, 4–9; Newman, 'The Racial Origin of Wagner,' in *Wagner as Man and Artist*, 387–414. Leon Stein humorously discusses the repercussions this uncertainty has had on the appraisal of Wagner's music: 'There are many . . . who, believing Geyer to have been Wagner's father, and accepting Geyer's Jewish descent as a fact, profess to find definite Jewish qualities in Wagner's music. . . . To these may be added . . . the anti-Wagnerian journalists who found the reasons for Wagner's corrupt music in his Jewish descent.' See Stein, *Racial Thinking*, 228.

2. See Gradenwitz, 'Das Judentum,' 80.

3. See Nietzsche, *Der Fall Wagner*, in *Werke*, 6.3: 35n. On the crest that adorns the first edition of *Mein Leben*, see Deathridge, *The New Grove Wagner*, 2–3. In the 1930s the National Socialists went to great pains to verify Wagner's Aryan pedigree. See, for example, Rauschenberger, 'Richard Wagners Abstammung und Rassenmerkmale'; in 1938 the Geyer thesis was dismissed in Lange, *Richard Wagners Sippe*, 86. A not altogether dissimilar dismissal could still be found in 1985, published under the auspices of the Bayreuth Wagner Foundation: 'Beinahe ein Adler . . .': war Wagner selbst ein Jude?' in Eger, ed., *Wagner und die Juden*, 51.

4. On the significance of this motif for Wagner, see Schickling, *Abschied von Walhall*, 79.

5. Adorno, *In Search of Wagner*, 24. The translation is Ernest Newman's, as are the emphases. See *The Life of Richard Wagner*, 2: 346. The passage Wagner deleted is found in Strobel, ed., *Richard Wagner, Skizzen und Entwürfe*, 99.

6. Adorno puts it succinctly: '[Wagner] pursues his victims down to the level of their biological nature because he saw himself as having only barely escaped being a dwarf.' Adorno, *In Search*, 25.

7. René Girard's remarks concerning the mechanism of the scapegoat are apposite here, in that he stresses the fact that the individual identified as different must in fact *resemble* the group that rejects (and

sacrifices) him, and that the process of identifying the scapegoat must never be recognized for what it is but instead must seem legitimate, grounded in and justified by 'reality.' On the former concept, see *Violence and the Sacred*, 3, 12, 39, 78–79; on the latter, see the same text, 24, 27, 30, 36, 39, 73, 77–85, 87. See also idem, '*To double business bound,*' 187–195.

8. Foucault's remarks on the ideology of the body are found in *Discipline and Punish* (see especially 137ff.); see also his *History of Sexuality*, vol. 1, and *Madness and Civilization*.

9. While this kind of observation has become nearly self-evident to much of the nonmusicological scholarly community today, it has seldom been applied to the investigation of music dramas, a remarkable omission considering the political and social status of such works as highly stylized representations of physicality, power, and community. In this context, see Clement, *Opera, or the Undoing of Woman*, and Robinson, *Opera & Ideas*. As Kittler remarks in a discussion of Wagner, perhaps somewhat too emphatically, 'The facts of physiology . . . are just too stupid or subliminal for most critics.' See his 'Weltatem,' 205.

Two noteworthy exceptions to this tendency to ignore the ideological role of the body in opera are McClary, *Feminine Endings*, and Gilman, 'Strauss, the Pervert, and Avant Garde Opera of the Fin de Siècle,' reprinted in expanded form in Gilman, *Disease and Representation*, 155–181. McClary and Gilman discern corporeal iconographies in the musical vocabularies of specific operatic works within the context of the operas' respective cultures, an approach I find of immense value for an examination of the ideological meaning of such powerful and evocative, multi-aesthetic constructs.

Therefore, I find it disappointing when even one of the most perceptive and persuasive of Wagnerian scholars, Carolyn Abbate in her otherwise superb *Unsung Voices*, analyzes the semiotic nature of Wagner's music *within a cultural vacuum*, without consideration of the cultural context in which the music dramas were constructed and received, as if the codes of which she writes were constitutive in all social contexts and equally ideologically informed in different cultural settings. For her discussions of Wagner's works, see 85–118, 156–249. To a lesser extent this is also the case with the semiotic analyses of Nattiez. See his 'Le Ring comme histoire métaphorique de la musique'; *Music and Discourse*; and *Wagner androgyne*, though Nattiez is far more concerned with Wagner's anti-Semitism than most scholars interested in the semiotic nature of his works, as shown, for example in a passage in this latter text: 87–94. If the music is understood at times to convey connotations of physicality, of bodily presence, its semiotic nature immediately assumes an ideological dimension due to the values associated with the perception of the body in Western culture.

10. On the psychological investment in the exaggeratedly heroic nature of Wagner's heroes, see Rattner, 'Wagner im Lichte der Tiefenpsychologie,' 780.

11. See Gilman, 'Strauss.'

12. Another reason, of course, that such anti-Semitic constructions as Beckmesser and the Nibelung dwarves are never labeled as *Juden* is the fact that the explicit designation of these figures as Jews would have been incompatible with the realistic, historical dimension of Wagner's dramatic configurations; no Jew could have been a prominent notary or town clerk in sixteenth-century Nuremberg, for example, and Jews did not populate the Germanic myths and legends which served as sources for the *Ring*, but neither such a notary nor the mythological constructions need 'be' Jews within their dramatic contexts in order to have evoked the Jew in the nineteenth-century European imagination. It is ironic that it is precisely Wagner's most ardent apologists who fail to appreciate the evocative power of Wagner's multilayered dramatic creations when they argue that the absence of such explicit designations denies the works' anti-Semitic implications: Their reputation for bombast notwithstanding, Wagner's works for the stage are in fact exceptionally subtle and complex constructions based on a host of images and beliefs within German cultural traditions; against the background of the cultural vocabulary of his age, the specter of the Jew — like that of others deemed different and therefore foreign — could have emerged automatically in his time without the aid of a semantically explicit calling card.

13. For an insightful and judicious overview of scholarship on Wagner, see Deathridge, 'A Brief History of Wagner Research.'

14. See Adorno, *In Search*, 23–25; Gutman, *Richard Wagner*. Stein's work from 1950 constitutes an exception to this temporal argument, but he distinguishes between the anti-Semitism in Wagner's life and essays and the ideational implications of the music dramas. See, for example, *The Racial Thinking*, 233.

15. See Mann, 'The Sorrows and Grandeur of Richard Wagner,' 101.

16. See Borchmeyer, *Richard Wagner*, esp. 1–177.

17. Since 1983 Borchmeyer has continued this approach, as his 'Afterword: A Note on Wagner's Anti-Semitism,' in *Richard Wagner*, 404–410, and his review of recent Wagnerian scholarship, 'Wagner-Literatur — eine deutsche Misere,' esp. 36–41, make clear.

18. A very fine exception to this rule is the level-headed work of the prominent Wagnerian scholar John Deathridge.

The apologetic slant of Martin van Amerongen's approach to Wagner is manifested in such statements as the following: 'Like so many of his philosophical ideas, Wagner's hatred of the Jews is for the most part pure theory. When brought face to face with the reality, he was as flexible as anything' (*Wagner*, 58).

Carl Dahlhaus is generally recognized as one of the foremost authorities on Wagner, but he was contemptuous of any attempts to link the composer's anti-Semitism to his music dramas, as seen, for example, in his vituperative dismissal of the work of Hartmut Zelinsky (see note 19).

Martin Gregor-Dellin's major work on Wagner is *Richard Wagner*; Gregor-Dellin's downplaying of Wagner's anti-Semitism is discussed in Zelinsky, 'Rettung ins Ungenaue.'

Burnett James apologetically opines that Wagner's 'anti-Semitic leanings were primarily not social and personal, but artistic' and makes the bizarre claim that the question of Wagner's potentially Jewish background 'is important because Wagner's entire life-work was based upon ideas and theories that ran counter to the basic tenets of Judaism — and that has nothing to do with any form of anti-Semitism.' See his *Wagner and the Romantic Disaster*, 17, 15.

Amazingly, Bryan Magee states that the argument of Wagner's most notoriously and explicitly anti-Semitic tract, 'Das Judentum in der Musik,' 'was almost unbelievably original, and largely correct.' See his *Aspects of Wagner*, 46. Given the fact that this often-cited volume has achieved enormous popularity, such a statement is, to say the least, distressing.

For evidence of L. J. Rather's discomfort with the association of Wagner and anti-Semitism, see his *The Dream of Self-Destruction*, 90, 96; see also his *Reading Wagner*.

Geoffrey Skelton makes almost no mention of anti-Semitism in his discussion of Wagner's relationship with Cosima, a remarkable omission considering the latter's particularly vicious racism, but on occasion he does make such dismissive comments as the following, apparently intended to mitigate the 'Master's' racism through comparison with his contemporaries: 'He was by no means alone in his antipathy towards the Jews.' See *Richard and Cosima Wagner*, 109.

Ronald Taylor's treatment of Wagner's anti-Semitism is, at best, superficial, as seen in his discussion of 'Das Judentum in der Musik' in *Richard Wagner*, 105–107.

Peter Wapnewski has written a number of books on Wagner that seldom mention the composer's racism; the ideological position of his work may be perceived in the vehemence of his attack on Gutman regarding a comparatively marginal philological matter in *Der traurige Gott*, 65–67; see also his *Richard Wagner* and *Tristan der Held Richard Wagners*. I suspect that the vituperative, contemptuous tone of his response to Gutman is at least partly attributable to Gutman's critical approach to Wagner.

Von Westernhagen's relationship to Nazism is discussed in Zelinsky, *Richard Wagner: ein deutsches Thema*, and in Rose, 'The Noble Anti-Semitism of Richard Wagner.'

19. In addition to the works cited in note 18, see Zelinsky, 'Die deutsche Losung Siegfried'; 'Die "Feuerkur" des Richard Wagner oder die "neue Religion" der "Erlösung" durch "Vernichtung"'; 'Der *Plenipotentarius des Untergangs*'; 'Richard Wagners *Kunstwerk der Zukunft* und seine Idee der Vernichtung'; 'Der verschwiegene Gehalt des "Parsifal."' The denunciation of Zelinsky is apparent in Dahlhaus' 'Erlösung dem Erlöser,' and in Kaiser, 'Hat Zelinsky recht gegen Wagners "Parsifal"?'

20. See Nattiez, 'Chéreau's Treachery'; '"Fidelity" to Wagner'; and *Tetralogies*. An example of the conservative rejection of Chéreau's direction can be found in Jordan, 'The *Ring*-Movie and the *Ring*-Text,' 213–218.

21. See Nattiez, '"Fidelity" to Wagner,' 86; *Tetralogies*, 67, 76, 155, 256.

22. Mike Ashman describes the Metropolitan production as 'museum creations' and writes of its 'misplaced conservative intention to rediscover the presumed literalness of Wagner's stage directions in the spirit of *his* times,' a reaction similar to Nattiez's, who writes that 'the result was an aesthetic disaster for the present-day spectator, assuming him or her to be endowed with even a modicum of taste.' See Ashman, 'Producing Wagner,' 44–45; Nattiez, '"Fidelity" to Wagner,' 82.

23. Rose, *Wagner*, 68–72.

24. Millington, 'Nuremberg Trial'; see also Millington's *Wagner*. For a discussion of musical evidence of anti-Semitism in *Parsifal*, see his '*Parsifal*.'

25. Watson, *Richard Wagner*, 318.

26. Stein, *Racial Thinking*, 233.

27. Katz, *The Darker Side*, ix–x.

28. See the remarks by Dahlhaus and Kaiser referred to in note 18.

29. Vaget, 'Wagner, Anti-Semitism, and Mr. Rose,' 233. See also Rasch and Weiner, 'A Response.'

30. Vaget, 'Wagner, Anti-Semitism, and Mr. Rose,' 222.

31. Wagner mentioned this idea in an often-cited letter to Theodor Uhlig of 10 May 1851 describing the (as it turned out, all-too-optimistically short-sighted) plan to expand the *Ring* from a single work to two music dramas, *Siegfrieds Tod* (Siegfried's death) and *Der junge Siegfried* (Young Siegfried): ' "*Der junge Siegfried* would have the tremendous advantage," Wagner claimed, "of conveying the important myths to the audience in the form of a *play*, in the way one conveys a fairy tale to a child. Everything makes a plastic impact, through sharply focused sensual impressions; everything will be understood." ' See Wagner, *Sämtliche Briefe*, 4: 44, cited in Abbate, *Unsung Voices*, 159, from which this translation is taken.

In her discussion of the shift from an emphasis on narrative to scenic enactment in the genesis of the *Ring* texts, Abbate stresses both the physical presence on which she believes Wagner came increasingly to rely as he developed his iconoclastic theories of the Artwork of the Future and the persuasive force vouchsafed by the corporeality of the singer, which she believes Wagner hoped would guarantee the veracity of his ideas: 'The very genesis of the *Ring* attests to a longing for presentation, for the physical force of embodiment in performance, over [narrative] representation and the suspicions attached to the written and silently read word. . . . By stripping away narrators whose reliability will always be uncertain, by eliminating narrations whose significance is not wholly assured, by replacing them with visible incidents, Wagner was attempting to ensure *belief* in his myth. While immediacy, force, and traditional operatic spectacle and action may have been gained, along with them came (he hoped) epistemological certainty' (Abbate, *Unsung Voices*, 160).

32. On this concept, see Franke, 'Musik als Gebärdensprache und das musikalische Gewebe aus "Ahnung und Erinnerung," ' 179–180.

33. Nietzsche, *Der Fall Wagner*, 21–22.

34. For a discussion of the distinction between 'iconic' and 'symbolic' music (the former intended to sound like what it represents), see Kolland, 'Zur Semantik der Leitmotive in Richard Wagners *Ring des Nibelungen*,' 198–199. Peter Kivy's concept of 'internal representations' is similar to Kolland's notion of 'symbolic' music, in that by 'internal representations' Kivy means those that 'are not "inherently" representational, but exist merely by virtue of a convention internal to the musical work.' See Kivy, *Sound and Semblance*, 52. I would argue, however, that both iconic and symbolic representations are ultimately based on the conventions of a culture.

35. See Vetter, 'Wagner in the History of Psychology,' 153.

36. On Wagner's music as a threat to the body in German modernist literature, see my *Undertones of Insurrection*, 13–14, 18–20; see also Koppen, *Dekadenter Wagnerismus*, 278–339.

37. Ehrenfels, 'Wagner und seine neuen Apostaten,' 10.

38. Cited in Ringer, 'Richard Wagner and the Language of Feeling,' 40.

39. On the association of B♭ minor with the Nibelungs, see also Bailey, 'The Structure of the *Ring* and Its Evolution,' 53–54.

40. See Ringer, 'Richard Wagner and the Language of Feeling,' 42.

41. This is the title of Jacob Katz's attempts to relativize, and hence to make light of, Wagner's anti-Semitism (see note 27).

42. The phrase is Andrew Porter's; see his 'Wagner: The Continuing Appeal,' 7.

43. See Hamilton, *Arthur Rackham*, 42.

44. Ibid., 102.

45. Ibid., 99.

46. Lewis, *Surprised by Joy*, 77.

CHAPTER I. THE EYES OF THE *VOLK*

1. In the essays of the immediate postrevolutionary period it is clear that Wagner's desire for the transformation of his society and of the role the arts were to play in it was based on the premise that the theater could function as a vehicle for the transformation of the individual and of the social whole. For a discussion of these issues, albeit without consider-

ation of Wagner's anti-Semitism, see Borchmeyer, *Richard Wagner*, 3–28, 59–74.

Rose points out the difficulty of adequately rendering *Judentum* — the key term in Wagner's anti-Semitic essay — into English: 'Often translated simply as "Judaism," *Judentum* is [often] used polyvalently to denote at least three different ideas, each of which requires separate and specific English terms: "Judaism" for the religion; "Jewry" for the community and nationality; and "Jewishness" for the ethnic traits and mentalities of Jews' (Rose, *Wagner: Race and Revolution*, 3). All three ideas obtain in Wagner's use of the term, but I have opted to employ the latter because of the role the physical presence of the Jew plays in Wagner's thought. Nevertheless, all three, with their diverse implications, are simultaneously involved when Wagner uses the word. An analyst of the recent *Historikerstreit* has attempted to circumvent the polyvalence inherent in the term by insisting on *Judenheit* when 'Jewry' is meant, arguing that the former is more closely equivalent to what Rose would call 'Judaism' and 'Jewishness' (as manifested in the implications of the word *Christentum*); see Geiss, *Die Habermas-Kontroverse*, 70.

2. See Hegel, *The Phenomenology of Mind*, 225–233. Corse has devoted nearly an entire and often highly perceptive book to an examination of this cognitive model of mutual self-recognition within Wagner's thought, but she focuses her investigation almost exclusively on Wagner's indebtedness to Hegel and Feuerbach. While the connections she has discerned are undeniably valid, the place of this metaphorical device within Wagner's racism, his utopian agenda, and the ideological plan behind the scenic representations of his music dramas remains unexplored. See Corse, *Wagner and the New Consciousness*, 24–28; on Hegel and Feuerbach, see esp. 142.

3. For an insightful examination of this model in Hoffmann, see Wellbery, 'E. T. A. Hoffmann and Romantic Hermeneutics.'

4. See my 'Richard Wagner's Use of E. T. A. Hoffmann's "The Mines of Falun." '

5. Novalis, *Monolog*, 102.

6. Ibid., 134.

7. *Deutsche Gedichte*, 369.

8. For an interesting account of the technical arguments in this text, see Gerlach, 'Musik und Sprache in Wagners Schrift *Oper und Drama*,' 9–39.

9. On the notion of a lost unity in ancient Greece, see Nattiez, *Wagner androgyne*, 33–40. Wagner's glorified image of classical Greece as implicitly Aryan was typical of the romantic image of antiquity, as discussed (without reference to Wagner) in Bernal, *Black Athena*, vol. 1: *The Fabrication of Ancient Greece, 1785–1985.*

10. On the pervasiveness of this notion from the Middle Ages to the nineteenth century, see Carlebach, *Karl Marx and the Radical Critique of Judaism*; Lowenthal, *The Jews of Germany*, 53–69, 224–225; Poliakov, *A History of Anti-Semitism*, 3: 166, 179, 190, 422–423; Strauss, 'Juden und Judenfeindschaft in der frühen Neuzeit,' 66–87, here 77–82; Weinberg, *Because They Were Jews*, 85; Wistrich, *Antisemitism*, 26–39.

In Wagner's anti-Semitic cosmology, the male Jew occupies a far greater presence and constitutes a far greater threat than the Jewess, and accordingly there is only one female representation of notions deemed characteristically Jewish in his music dramas. Therefore, when I refer to 'the Jew,' unless otherwise noted I will mean Wagner's image of the *male* Jew.

11. See Nattiez, *Wagner androgyne*, 43–45.

12. On Wagner and Meyerbeer, see Thomson, 'Giacomo Meyerbeer.' At the end of his life Wagner was still at it, with a vengeance. In a letter to King Ludwig II of Bavaria of 22 November 1881 he wrote: 'I consider the Jewish race the born enemy of pure humanity and all that is noble in man: there is no doubt but that we Germans especially will be destroyed by them' (Wagner, *Selected Letters of Richard Wagner*, 918 [#489]).

13. The literature on this text is extensive. For a sample, see Stein, *The Racial Thinking of Richard Wagner*, 105–112; Gilman, *Jewish Self-Hatred*, 209–211; Katz, *The Darker Side of Genius*, 20–21, 31–77; Rose, *Wagner*, 77–88, 114–118; and my 'Parody and Repression,' 140–141.

14. See Wagner, *Sämtliche Briefe*, 3: 406–409 (#106), here 408. Wagner often adopted the affectation of writing nouns in lowercase.

15. This passage is discussed in Rose, *Wagner: Race and Revolution*, 103–104.

16. See *Richard Wagner an August Röckel*, 39; in English in Newman, *The Life of Richard Wagner*, 2: 349.

17. Weininger, *Geschlecht und Charakter*, 404.

18. Ernst Bloch is one of the few critics to have devoted serious attention to Beckmesser's prize-song, but he ignores its implied sce-

nario of public torture and execution, discussing instead the text's affinity with such later authors and literary movements as Morgenstern and Dada. See his 'Über Beckmesser's Preislied-Text.'

19. This passage is discussed in Rose, *Wagner: Race and Revolution*, 55–56.

20. Jahn's work is discussed in George Mosse, *Germans and Jews*, 11–13.

21. *Heldenlieder der Edda*, 21; *The Poetic Edda*, 261.

22. Initially, Wagner intended to have Wotan enter the hut after Siegmund's arrival and to have him offer Hunding the sword (called at this stage 'Balmung') as a gift for his hospitality. This plan is apparent both in the prose sketch to *Die Walküre* of May 1852 and in a book of notes from that year, in which Wagner expanded some of the ideas of the sketch. See Strobel, ed., *Richard Wagner, Skizzen und Entwürfe*, 212; see this page also for the plan to have Wotan function as a witness to the incest; for Wotan's appearance in the prose sketch, see 235.

23. Ibid., 251.

24. See Finney, 'Self-Reflexive Siblings.'

25. See Abbate, *Unsung Voices*, 229. For her entire discussion of the scene, see 225–229.

26. Can it have been a coincidence that these two works, the most blatantly anti-Semitic of Wagner's music dramas, were, with the exception of the apprentice-piece *Das Liebesverbot* of 1835, the only works initially characterized by the composer as 'comedies'? See Deathridge, *The New Grove Wagner*, 166. Wagner termed *Die Meistersinger* a 'comic' opera in the prose draft of 1845 and a 'grand comic' opera in the 1861 version (but the adjective was deleted for the 1868 premiere). See Deathridge, Geck, and Voss, *Verzeichnis der musikalischen Werke Richard Wagners und ihrer Quellen*, 483. Originally Wagner conceived of *Der junge Siegfried* as a comic opera intended as a contrast to *Siegfrieds Tod*. See Corse, *Wagner and the New Consciousness*, 132.

27. On this scene, see Newman, *Wagner as Man and Artist*, 340; Wapnewski, *Der traurige Gott*, 164–166.

28. Newman, *The Life of Richard Wagner*, 2: 346.

29. See Deathridge, *The New Grove Wagner*, 52–53.

30. At least one critic has pointed out the association of 'actor' evoked by the name of the dwarf for a German audience: see Gradenwitz, 'Das Judentum,' 79.

31. See Borchmeyer, *Richard Wagner*, 261.

32. Robert Donington draws attention to the similarities of these motives and points out that the music of the sunlight shining on the gold in the first scene of *Das Rheingold* bears similarly striking resemblance to that of Siegfried's forest murmurs. Apparently Wagner provided a number of musical parallels between the 'naive,' unsullied, natural state of the opening of the *Ring* and his characterization of Siegfried as a 'natural' being. See Donington, *Wagner's 'Ring' and Its Symbols*, 176–177, 272–273. Egon Voss discusses the musical portrayal of Siegfried-as-Nature-incarnate, especially with reference to Wagner's use of the French Horn, in his *Studien zur Instrumentalmusik Richard Wagners*, 176–178.

33. Hans Bächthold-Stäubli points out that in Germanic folklore the toad was associated with Jews: 'The Jew hates . . . the Christian god. On his altar sits a toad.' See *Handwörterbuch des deutschen Aberglaubens*, 'Jude, Jüdin,' 4: 808–833, this quote 817; on the role of the toad in the history of Germanic folklore, see 'Kröte,' 5: 608–635.

34. See Magee, *Richard Wagner and the Nibelungs*; Byock, 'Introduction' to *The Saga of the Volsungs*, 1–29, here 3, 27.

35. *The Saga of the Volsungs*, 58.

36. A later passage in the tale makes it clear that it also provided the basis for Fafner's murder of Fasolt (though it is his father, Hreidmar, not his brother, whom Fafnir kills in the saga), his transformation into a dragon, and Mime's labor as a smith. See *The Saga of the Volsungs*, 58–59.

37. The earliest formulation of this scene, in *Der junge Siegfried*, is nearly identical to that found in *Siegfried*, which suggests that from the earliest inception of the *Ring* this motif of recognition and familial familiarity was central to Wagner. See Cohen, 'The Texts of Wagner's "Der junge Siegfried" and "Siegfried," ' 19.

38. See Strobel, ed., *Richard Wagner, Skizzen und Entwürfe*, 99.

39. John Deathridge has wittily argued that the motive is suggestive of the movement of a serpent and that, because it appears shortly before the consummation of Brünnhilde and Siegfried, it constitutes a 'dubious joke' on Wagner's part. From a review of new recordings of *Siegfried* and *Götterdämmerung* broadcast on radio by the BBC on 17 October 1992.

40. Cosima Wagner, *Diaries*, 2: 932.

CHAPTER 2. VOICES: COLORATURA VERSUS *TIEF UND INNIG*

1. On the applicability of the 'culture industry' thesis to the Paris of this period, see Bürger, 'Literarischer Markt und autonomer Kunstbegriff.' I am indebted to Peter Uwe Hohendahl for this reference.

2. See Gilman, 'Opera, Homosexuality, and Models of Disease,' in *Disease and Representation*, 155–181; for *Salome*, passim, and for reference to Rossini's work, 170.

3. Moritz Adolf (also referred to as Maurice Adolphe) Schlesinger's true name was Mora Abraham Schlesinger; see 'Schlesinger,' in *Riemann Musik Lexikon*, 580. On Wagner's experience in Paris at this time, see Devraigne, 'Hungerjahre in Paris,' 93–96; on Wagner's disavowed indebtedness to the Parisian Opera, see Borchmeyer, *Die Götter tanzen Cancan*, 45–143.

4. The firm of Adolf Martin Schlesinger owned the rights to Weber's music and printed the works of Spontini, Mendelssohn, Loewe, Beethoven, Bach, Berlioz, Cornelius, Liszt, and Chopin. By 1836, four years before Wagner began working for his expatriated son, Adolf Martin's firm had published over two thousand titles. See Elvers, 'Schlesinger,' 660.

5. MacNutt, 'Schlesinger, Maurice,' 660–661.

6. F. J. Fétis had founded the journal in 1827; the joint publication began in November 1835 with vol. 2, no. 44 and was thereafter referred to both as *Gazette musicale de Paris* and *Revue et gazette musicale de Paris*; it ceased publication in 1880. See ibid., 661; Hatin, *Bibliograpic historique et critique de la presse périodique française*, 591; Guichard, *La Musique et les lettres au temps du romantisme*, 172–178. I would like to thank Seymour S. Weiner for sharing with me his invaluable bibliographic expertise in clarifying the publication history of this journal.

7. On this journal and its concerts, see Douchin, *La Vie érotique de Flaubert*, 25; Bart, *Flaubert*, 26–28, 81–82, 108, 116, 185. Mention is made in these works of the *Gazette musicale* because Flaubert was infatuated for a time with Schlesinger's wife.

8. In his autobiography Wagner admitted that the performance of his *Columbus* overture in the concert series 'bored everybody'; see *My Life*, 185–186.

9. Wagner's first published essay was 'Die deutsche Oper,' which appeared on 10 June 1834 in the *Zeitung für die elegante Welt*, but 'De la musique allemande' was the first essay in which the ideological plan of

his future theories emerged in clear form. On 'Die deutsche Oper,' see Deathridge, *The New Grove Wagner*, 13; Rose, *Wagner*, 24. Due to his poor command of French, Wagner had to write his texts in German and pay half his honorarium to a translator, who fashioned a French rendition for publication in the *Gazette*. See Wagner, *My Life*, 186; Jacobs and Skelton, *Wagner Writes from Paris . . .* , 12–13; Gutman, *Richard Wagner*, 75. Of the nine texts Wagner wrote between July 1840 and October 1841 ('Über deutsches Musikwesen' [On German music], '*Stabat Mater* de Pergolèse par Lvoff' [Pergolesi's *Stabat Mater*], 'Der Virtuos und der Künstler' [The virtuoso and the artist], 'Eine Pilgerfahrt zu Beethoven' [A pilgrimage to Beethoven], 'Über die Ouvertüre' [On the overture], 'Ein Ende in Paris' [An end in Paris], 'Der Künstler und die Öffentlichkeit' [The artist and publicity], 'Ein glücklicher Abend' [A happy evening], and '*Der Freischütz*: an das Pariser Publikum' [*Der Freischütz*: To the Paris public]), eight were published in the *Gazette musicale*, and another ('*La reine de Chypre* d'Halévy') was to follow there in the spring of 1842. See Jacobs and Skelton, *Wagner Writes from Paris . . .* , 196–197.

10. Scholarship often mentions the early Parisian texts solely for the comparative clarity of their style and therefore their resemblance to works of E. T. A. Hoffmann and Heine; they have received surprisingly little attention as the first evidence of Wagner's aesthetic-social program. See, for example, Mayer, *Richard Wagner in Selbstzeugnissen und Bilddokumenten*, 12; Borchmeyer, *Richard Wagner*, 1, 104–105; Gregor-Dellin, *Richard Wagner*, 101–102; Rather, *Reading Wagner*, 35; Deathridge and Dahlhaus, *The New Grove Wagner*, 24, 69. Like many before him, Bryan Magee assumes that 'Das Judentum in der Musik' was written because of Wagner's antipathy to Meyerbeer and Halévy but does not mention Schlesinger in this context. See his *Aspects of Wagner*, 50–51.

11. After the close of 'Ein glücklicher Abend' (A happy evening) the narrating editor's remarks begin thus: 'The following articles I publish from among my dead friend's papers. To me this first one ['Über deutsches Musikwesen'] *seems to have been intended to win friends among the French for his Parisian undertaking*, whereas its successors unmistakably betray the deterrent impressions already made on him by Parisian life' (*DS* 5: 151–152, my emphasis).

12. On the continuing presence of this metaphor in Western culture

today, and on the notion that it is grounded in physiology, see Johnson, *The Body in the Mind*, xii–xv; Lakoff and Johnson, *Metaphors We Live By*, 14–30.

13. Ironically, Wagner's vituperative and despairing regaling against the unnaturally elevated pathos of French opera can be situated within a tradition of French criticism itself, for none other than Jean-Jacques Rousseau, in his *Lettre sur la musique française*, decried 'the shrill and noisy intonations' of the recitative of the French opera of his day — though not, however, of its more melodious music — and thereby articulated a characteristic of French opera — its elevated tessitura — which indeed was objectively verifiable and not merely Wagner's invention but upon which Wagner projected judgments and values altogether different from those found in Rousseau's remarks. See Aprahamian, 'Debussy's "Pelléas et Mélisande,"' 10; see also Gülke, *Rousseau und die Musik*, 145–159.

14. On the history of this tradition in nineteenth- and twentieth-century Germany, see Stern, *The Politics of Cultural Despair.*

15. The distorted view critics have held of Wagner's Parisian writings from the early 1840s exemplifies the tendency of much Wagnerian scholarship to make light of or to ignore altogether the reprehensible ideology behind his social-aesthetic writings from this period. The following, amazingly one-sided assessment stems from Jacobs and Skelton: '[Wagner] writes . . . with an open mind. . . . How very human he is . . . and yet how impressive and endearing: an impassioned idealist, a penetrating thinker, a shrewd observer, warm-hearted, courageous and brimming over with high spirits, poetry and humour' (Jacobs and Skelton, *Wagner Writes from Paris . . .* , 14); Ernest Newman was equally generous when he described 'Über deutsches Musikwesen' as 'very touching in its wistful little vision of tiny, cozy German towns' (Newman, *Wagner as Man and Artist*, 193).

16. See Stein, 'Volk, Kultur, Language, and Music,' in *The Racial Thinking of Richard Wagner*, 3–42, esp. 24.

17. Sander Gilman has written extensively on *Mauscheln*; see his *Inscribing the Other*, 177–178, 253–254; *The Jew's Body*, 16, 21, 27, 88, 134–135, 206; *Jewish Self-Hatred*, 139–141, 145, 155, 219, 255, 260–266, 276.

18. On the tradition characterizing Jewish voices as higher than others, see Gilman, *Inscribing the Other*, 197–200.

19. For this discussion of Mahler, see Gilman, *Disease and Representation*, 179–181.

20. Ibid., 170.

21. On Wagner's dissatisfaction with Hölzel, see Bauer, 'Die Auffüh-rungsgeschichte in Grundzügen,' 651.

22. See 'Drei unbekannte Schreiben Richard Wagners an Gustav Hölzel, mitgeteilt von Marie Huch in Hannover,' trans. in Wagner, *Selected Letters of Richard Wagner*, 222; Millington cites this letter in his 'Nuremberg Trial,' 257.

23. See Wagner, *Selected Letters of Richard Wagner*, 814–815; Mill-ington mentions this letter as well in his 'Nuremberg Trial,' 257.

24. See Apel, 'Melisma,' 516; 'Coloratura,' 184.

25. For a discussion of Beckmesser's act 2 aria as a parody of syna-gogue chant, see Millington, 'Nuremberg Trial,' 252–254.

26. Kivy, *Sound and Semblance*, 52.

27. Ernst Bloch made note of Beckmesser's 'ridiculous coloratura on insignificant syllables,' but he dismissed it as merely ('bloße') 'Musik-Travestie' and thereby missed the larger iconographic context in which this music functions. See his 'Über Beckmessers Preislied-Text,' 259.

28. Apel, 'Coloratura,' 184. Dahlhaus writes of Beckmesser's 'me-chanical coloratura, modal melodies and perfunctory accompani-ments'; see *The New Grove Wagner*, 160. Rose writes that Beckmesser's serenade is 'a parody of Jewish cantorial style, with long melodic wail-ing syllables sung in a near falsetto tessitura'; see Rose, *Wagner: Race and Revolution*, 112. Egon Voss has discussed the parodistic nature of Beckmesser's coloratura in 'Wagners *Meistersinger* als Oper des deut-schen Bürgertums,' 27.

29. On the mutual antipathy between Beckmesser and the *Volk*, see Rappl, 'Beckmesser als psychologische Schlüsselfigur.'

30. See Fischer-Dieskau, *Wagner and Nietzsche*, 44. For a sampling of Jewish critiques of *Die Meistersinger* from the perspective of a National Socialist, see Stock, 'Jüdische Kritikaster über Richard Wagners "Mei-stersinger,"' 202–206. On Mannheim, see Cosima Wagner, *Diaries*, 1: 120 (entry for 4 July 1869). My thanks to Hans Rudolf Vaget for bring-ing the uprisings in Mannheim to my attention.

31. On the iconography of the Jewish nose, see Gilman, *The Jew's Body*, 169–193.

32. Voss, *Studien zur Instrumentalmusik Richard Wagners*, 173–174, my translation.

33. Adolf Martin Schlesinger published the first edition of Bach's St. Matthew Passion, a fact Wagner undoubtedly knew and the irony of which, given his desire to monopolize Bach as uniquely German, he no doubt resented. See Elvers, 'Schlesinger,' 660.

34. Joachim Herz is one of the few commentators to have noticed that Kothner's music is 'decorated with solemn coloratura [*geschmückt mit feierlicher Koloratur*]'; see his 'Der doch versöhnte Beckmesser,' 214.

35. For Adorno's remarks concerning the connection between 'Das Judentum in der Musik,' with its emphasis on the speech patterns of Jews, and the musical discourse of Mime and Alberich, see his *In Search of Wagner*, 24.

36. For a particularly insightful discussion of the genesis of the *Ring*, see Abbate, *Unsung Voices*, 157–161; see also Deathridge, *The New Grove Wagner*, 32–36.

37. On the genesis of the text of *Siegfried*, see Coren, 'The Texts of Wagner's "Der junge Siegfried" and "Siegfried."'

38. For the dates of the composition of the music to *Siegfried*, see Deathridge, *The New Grove Wagner*, 170.

39. This notion of Jewish speech and Jewish music as 'nervous' is pervasive, and in this context it is worth mentioning that it is always interesting, and I would argue revealing, to observe how Wagner's more apologetic critics occasionally adopt the composer's discourse. One such example is Joachim Kaiser's description of Hagen's 'Watch' — from *Götterdämmerung* — as one of the composer's '*nervös*-gespannter Nachtstücke' (my emphasis). See 'Die Bayreuther Revolution in Permanenz,' 192.

40. De la Grange, *Mahler*, 1: 482; this statement is referred to in Rose, *Wagner: Race and Revolution*, 71; Cooke, *I Saw the World End*, 264; and Kennedy, *Mahler*, 82.

41. Adorno refers to the stereotypical characteristic features that distinguish Mime and Alberich in *In Search of Wagner*, 23.

42. See also Borchmeyer, *Die Götter tanzen Cancan*, 165.

43. See Abraham, 'The Artist of *Pictures from an Exhibition*,' 229–236. For reproductions of two watercolor paintings of Jews by Hartmann which may be similar to the pencil drawings Mussorgsky owned, see Frankenstein, 'Victor Hartmann and Modeste Musorgsky,' photos

between 282–285. Frankenstin believes that these pencil drawings were the inspiration for Mussorgsky's music and that Hartmann fashioned another, single drawing of two Jews, entitled 'Samuel Goldenburg [*sic*] und Schmuÿle,' which Mussorgsky's earlier biographers mistook as the source of the music in *Pictures at an Exhibition* (see 285). These photos are also found in Russ, *Musorgsky*, figs. 2, 3.

44. See Zetlin, *The Five*, 252. See also Schwarz, 'Musorgsky's Interest in Judaica,' 93.

45. Russ, *Musorgsky*, 44.

46. For reasons unknown to me, Theo Hirsbrunner claims that Ravel omitted this scene from his 1922 orchestration of Mussorgsky's music for piano, while Russ's book on *Pictures at an Exhibition* contains a description of Ravel's setting. See Hirsbrunner, *Maurice Ravel*, 311; Russ, *Musorgsky*, 80.

47. Russ, *Musorgsky*, 10.

48. On Wagner's essayistic production in the 1830s and its ideologically idiosyncratic position within his entire career, see Kühnel, 'Wagners Schriften,' 471–476.

49. See Deathridge, *The New Grove Wagner*, 166.

50. The story appeared in the *Gazette musicale* on 19, 22, and 29 November and 3 December 1840; the original German text was published on 30–31 July and 2–10 August 1841 in the *Dresdner Abendzeitung*; Wagner writes in *My Life* that 'the 1841 volume of this publication, then published by Arnold in Dresden but long since defunct, contains the only printed version of this manuscript' (198). See also letter of 1 June 1841 to Theodor Winkler in *Sämtliche Briefe*, 1: 493–495. For its republication in vol. 1 of his *Gesammelte Schriften und Dichtungen* the text had to be retranslated from the French. See Borchmeyer, 'Nachwort zu Band V' (*DS* 10: 297).

51. See Wagner, *Sämtliche Briefe*, 478–480 (letter to Schlesinger of 27 April 1841); Wagner, *My Life*, 174; see also 'Eine Mitteilung an meine Freunde' (*DS* 6: 233–234). On Wagner's work as an arranger for Schlesinger, see Deathridge, *The New Grove Wagner*, 19–20.

52. On the equation of Jews and the English in the German imagination of the nineteenth century, see Gilman, *Disease and Representation*, 160; see also Tuchman, *Bible and Sword*, 212.

53. A formative experience for Wagner's initial understanding of the human voice was a performance of Bellini's *I Capuleti e i Montecchi* that he attended in March 1834 in Leipzig, in which he first heard Wilhel-

mine Schröder-Devrient. Later, in *My Life*, Wagner would backdate the experience of his initial encounter with the singer to 1829, maintaining that he first heard her in *Fidelio*, but, as Deathridge insightfully points out, Wagner changed the time, the work, and the composer of the event 'in order to make his supposed inheritance of Beethoven's legacy, and with it his destiny as the creator of a specifically German music drama, seem inevitable from the outset.' Inevitable it was not, for Wagner was initially thrilled both by Schröder-Devrient in an Italian opera and by the works of Bellini themselves, replete with elevated bel canto vocal lines, as his essays from 1834 to 1837 demonstrate. See Deathridge, *The New Grove Wagner*, 7, for his proof of Wagner's falsification of the date, composer, and work involved.

54. Wagner, *My Life*, 192–193.

55. Elvers, 'Schlesinger,' 660; MacNutt, 'Schlesinger, Maurice,' 660–661.

56. See Grout and Palisca, *A History of Western Music*, 547; Solomon, *Beethoven*, 278.

57. References to Janin's work will be given parenthetically. On this text, see Hofer, 'Expérience musicale et empire romanesque,' 306. Wagner's work actually refers to, or at least joins, a minor French literary tradition of texts treating the motif of Beethoven which had appeared in Schlesinger's journal. Honoré de Balzac's 'Gambara' had appeared in the *Gazette musicale* between 23 July and 20 August 1837, only three years after the publication of Janin's work and three prior to the appearance there of Wagner's story. On this text, see Guichard, *La Musique*, 180–186. (For Wagner's own comments on Balzac's *La Comédie humaine* in *Deutsche Kunst und deutsche Politik*, see DS 8: 315–316). Thus, beginning with its first issue, Schlesinger's journal published a text every three years that alluded to his own visit to Beethoven.

58. Wagner mentioned Janin twice after his 'Pilgerfahrt' had appeared, the first time in a 'Bericht für die Dresdner Abendzeitung' of 23 February 1841 and again in an article on a Parisian performance of *Der Freischütz* published in the *Gazette musicale* on 23 and 30 May of the same year (DS 5: 71); see Jacobs and Skelton, *Wagner Writes from Paris...*, 152. It has often been argued that Wagner based his fictitious account of an aspiring musician's visit to Beethoven on Johann Friedrich Reichardt's *Vertraute Briefe, geschrieben auf einer Reise nach Wien und den österreichischen Staaten zu Ende des Jahres 1808 und zu Anfang 1809*, but the year of the 'Pilgerfahrt' (1824) is much closer to Janin's

1819 than to the year of Reichardt's text. On Wagner's indebtedness to Reichardt, see Borchmeyer, 'Nachwort zu Band V' (DS 10: 298). It was Wagner who informed Cosima, and Cosima who noted in her diary, that the 'Pilgerfahrt' was based on the German text and, given its ideological implications, it is hardly likely that either would have readily emphasized its relation to a French source.

59. See Emmons, *Tristanissimo*, 411.

60. Ibid., 7, 14; in the foreword to the book (x), Wagnerian soprano Birgit Nilsson describes Melchior's voice as having 'a darkness that there should be in a Wagnerian tenor.'

61. Already in 1888 Nietzsche had written, in *The Case of Wagner*, that 'one only sings Wagner with a ruined voice!' See *Werke*, 6: 32.

62. See Culshaw, *Ring Resounding*, 218.

63. See Bächtold-Stäubli, *Handwörterbuch des deutschen Aberglaubens*, 'Jude, Jüdin,' 4: 808–833, here 826, 812.

64. Rose has analyzed the ideological implications of *Tristan* through a discussion of Wagner's 'Jesus von Nazareth' of 1849, which the composer never set to music but which Rose views as a precursor to the later music drama. See Rose, *Wagner: Race and Revolution*, 54–56, 97–98.

65. Rose writes of Melot's implied affinity with anti-Semitic stereotypes in Wagner. See ibid., 98.

66. Melchior never sang Walther on stage, but he did make several recordings of excerpts from the role. See Emmons, *Tristanissimo*, 411–451. One could argue that Walther's vocal music requires a sound reminiscent of Lohengrin and Erik, a lighter, higher, brighter sound not heard in the heroic tenor roles of the *Ring, Tristan und Isolde*, or *Parsifal*. Some singers believe that Wagner wrote his *Heldentenor* roles with two kinds of tenor in mind, one reminiscent of the dramatic Italian tenor, the other demanding a different, more baritonal kind of voice.

67. Dahlhaus, *The New Grove Wagner*, 160–161.

68. See Wagner, *The Diary of Richard Wagner, 1865–1882*, 141–142; I have modified this translation. For the original German, see Wagner, *Das braune Buch*, 168–169.

69. For a detailed examination of Wagner's attempts to establish an educational program for the training of German singers, see Fischer, 'Sprachgesang oder Belcanto?'

70. On Alberich, Beckmesser, and Mime as caricatures of Jews, see

Adorno, *In Search of Wagner*, 20–26; on Klingsor as a Jew, see Gutman, *Richard Wagner*, 428–430.

71. On the conflation of the Jew and the feminine at the turn of the century, see Mosse, *Nationalism and Sexuality*, 143–146.

72. Wagner, *My Life*, 28.

73. Wagner, *The Diary of Richard Wagner*, 202 (entry of 23 October 1881).

74. Walther Jens perceptively describes Beckmesser as 'impotent' in his 'Ehrenrettung eines Kritikers,' 249.

75. On this concept in Wagner, see Nattiez, *Wagner androgyne*, 59–65.

76. On Klingsor's and Kundry's status as Jews, see Gutman, *Richard Wagner*, 428–430; Zelinsky, 'Der verschwiegene Gehalt des "Parsifal,"' 247.

77. Four scholars who have recognized the connection between these late essays and *Parsifal* are Gutman, *Richard Wagner*, chap. 15; Poliakov, *The History of Anti-Semitism*, 3: 429–457; Millington, *Wagner*, 102–109; and Rose, *Wagner: Race and Revolution*, 144–169. Their positions are opposed to those of Dahlhaus, as seen in his remarks in *Parsifal: Texte, Materialien, Kommentare*, 269, and Borchmeyer, 'The Question of Anti-Semitism,' 182–184.

78. Wagner himself preferred to view Klingsor as sharing an affinity with the failings of the Jesuits, as suggested in an entry of 2 March 1878 from Cosima's diary: 'Comparison between Alberich and Klingsor; R. tells me that he once felt every sympathy for Alberich, who represents the ugly person's longing for beauty. In Alberich the naivete of the non-Christian world, in Klingsor the peculiar quality which Christianity brought into the world; just like the Jesuits, he does not believe in goodness' (Cosima Wagner, *Diaries*, 2: 33). It goes without saying, however, that the figure could evoke and even intentionally refer to a host of traits deemed representative of a number of groups perceived as different and threatening within nineteenth-century German culture, in this case Jesuits and Jews alike. Wagner himself may have associated Klingsor first and foremost with the Catholic Church, against which he had fulminated in 'Die Kunst und die Revolution' of 1849 and which would continue to be the object of his scorn until his death. Nevertheless, as analysis of Wagner's early sociocritical tracts shows, it is important to bear in mind that Catholicism and the Jews occupy a similar position in his thought, both forming an antagonistic, corrosive force

in his model of the ancient world that ultimately led to the demise of Greek culture, and the Jews occupy such a position in the corollary of classical antiquity in modern Europe — in a Germany threatened by the Jew as Other. On Klingsor as Jesuit and as Jew, see Rose, *Wagner: Race and Revolution*, 163.

79. Walter Jens has described Beckmesser's voice as a 'Kastraten-stimme'; see Jens, 'Ehrenrettung eine Kritikers,' 249.

80. Poliakov refers to Anton Bonfin, *Rerum Hungaricum Decades*, Dec. 5, Book 4. See *A History of Anti-Semitism*, 1: 143n. See also Trachtenberg, *The Devil and the Jews*, 48. This belief was widespread in the Middle Ages and is to be found in much literature of postmedieval Germany as well.

81. Emslie, 'Woman as Image and Narrative in Wagner's *Parsifal*,' 117.

82. On the vagina as a wound and as evidence of castration, see Freud, 'Femininity' and 'Female Sexuality,' in *The Standard Edition of the Complete Psychological Works of Sigmund Freud*, vol. 21.

83. Jeremy Tambling writes of the cinematic depiction of the wound: 'in the film, Amfortas carries his wound round with him on a cushion, as if to make the Nazi-type point that a decadent Europe has made a fetish out of its being feminised, and that its religion is a displacement of its sexual fear. . . . The wound is like a bleeding vagina: it thus belongs, in Oedipal terms, to the male's fear of that as the memory of castration. Here it seems that Syberberg is only working on motifs that are in the subconscious of the operatic text' (Tambling, *Opera, Ideology and Film*, 204).

84. Robert Donington writes of the image that 'it is apparently all one wound in principle' (*Opera & Its Symbols*, 134).

85. Eschenbach, *Parsifal*, 244.

86. Ibid., 440.

CHAPTER 3. SMELLS: THE TEUTONIC
DUFT AND THE *FOETOR JUDÄICUS*

1. On the social and ideological function of smell at the end of the eighteenth century in Europe, see Corbin, *The Foul and the Fragrant*.

2. For this reason I disagree with Carl Dahlhaus, who writes the following (referring to Wagner's notorious penchant for silks and perfumes and to Schiller's own avowed stimulation of his creative powers through pungent stench): 'What an artist needs to stimulate his crea-

tive powers, whether it be brocade or the smell of rotten apples, is his business and his alone' (*The New Grove Wagner*, 89). Such extolment of the private sphere misses the implications of Wagner's purportedly personal or idiosyncratic reactions to sensual stimuli as representative of widespread ideological phenomena in his culture.

3. On the role of taste sensations during the composition of *Tristan und Isolde*, see my 'Zwieback and Madeleine.'

4. Gutman, *Richard Wagner*, 396. In Wagner's correspondence with Judith Gautier he repeatedly discusses perfumes; see *Die Briefe Richard Wagners an Judith Gautier*, 146–147, 151–153, 155, 159, 167, 171, 175, 178, 181, 183, 189–192. The scene Gutman refers to is described in a letter written sometime between 17 and 21 December 1877: 'You frighten me with all your "extracts." They could make me do foolish things: in general I prefer powders, since they cling more gently to fabrics, etc. But, once again, be prodigal, above all in the quantity of oils to put in the bath, such as the "ambergris" etc. I have my bathtub below my "studio," and I like it when the aromas ascend' (Wagner, *Selected Letters of Richard Wagner*, 879 [#460]; I have modified this translation). For the original German, see *Die Briefe Richard Wagners an Judith Gautier*, 171. It is interesting to note that in 1937 the 'racial psychologist' Walther Rauschenberger strove to explain Wagner's predilection for strong perfumes as 'non-Nordic,' 'Dinaric' psychological features that were, racially speaking, fundamentally different from such purportedly Nordic characteristics as Wagner's boldness, tenacity, and creativity. Rauschenberger thus attempted to deny the biographically documented connection between creativity and scents. See Rauschenberger, 'Richard Wagners Abstammung und Rassenmerkmale,' 161–171.

5. See Grimm and Grimm, *Deutsches Wörterbuch*, "Duft, " 2:1500–1502; Paul, *Deutsches Wörterbuch*, "Duft," 2:133. Wagner uses *Duft* as a synonym for fog in the extensive stage directions to the first scene of *Tannhäuser* (*T*, 35–37) but never when his characters sing of sexual and sensuous rapture. Interestingly, in his essay on the music drama, Baudelaire failed to recognize this link between sense and sex and instead associated aromas with the realm of the gods from which Venus has been expelled. See the passage quoted in Borchmeyer, *Die Götter tanzen Cancan*, 98.

6. On the Oedipal nature of Lohengrin's relationship with Elsa, see Rank, *Die Lohengrinsage*, 135–151.

7. See Rank, *Das Inzest-Motiv in Dichtung und Sage*, 587–595; Rath-

er, *The Dream of Self-Destruction*, 45–63; Finney, 'Self-Reflexive Siblings.'

8. On the Oedipal nature of their relationship, see 'Tristans Grabstein,' in Wieland Wagner, ed., *Hundert Jahre Tristan*, 201.

9. On this scene, see Kittler, 'Weltatem,' 204–205.

10. See Abbate, *Unsung Voices*, 112, 138.

11. The original draft of the work was in 4/4 time throughout. I am indebted to John Deathridge, who is currently preparing a critical edition of *Lohengrin*, for this information.

12. Horkheimer and Adorno, *Dialectic of Enlightenment*, 188.

13. The evocative, well-known lines run thus: 'Es ist doch so schwül, so dumpfig hie, / und ist doch eben so warm nicht drauß' (Goethe, *Werke*, 3: 88).

14. Quoted in Güdemann, *Geschichte des Erziehungswesens und der Cultur der abendländischen Juden während des Mittelalters und der neueren Zeit*, 1: 145.

15. See also Trachtenberg, *The Devil and the Jews*, 48.

16. Schudt, *Von der Franckfurter Juden Vergangenheit* (*Sitten und Bräuchen*); Gilman, *Jewish Self-Hatred*, 174–175.

17. See Schopenhauer, 'On Religion,' in *Parerga and Paralipomena*, 2: 370. This work is discussed very perceptively in Rose, *Wagner*, 94–95.

18. See Menzel, 'Die tiefste Korruption der deutschen Dichtung,' 337–338; on Platen, see Schloesser, *August Graf von Platen*, 2: 137.

19. See Gilman, *Jewish Self-Hatred*, 174–180; see also Poliakov, *A History of Anti-Semitism*, 1: 142.

20. Strobel, ed., *Richard Wagner, Skizzen und Entwürfe*, 32.

21. After an incident recorded by Heinrich Porges and quoted in Gregor-Dellin, *Richard Wagner*, 426. I have modified this translation.

22. With his joke in mind it is somewhat amusing to read musicologist Egon Voss's characterization of the dramatic use to which the composer employed the piccolo flute — the instrument implied as the voice of flatulence: 'Wagner often uses the sharp and harsh sound of the small flute to make visible the whistling of wind and storm.' How right Voss may have been. . . . See Voss, *Studien zur Instrumentalmusik Richard Wagners*, 125. Voss also writes of Wagner's use of this instrument for the purpose of caricature, as in the musical accompaniment to Loge's ironic praise of Alberich, beginning 'den Mächtigsten muß ich dich rühmen' (*RN*, 48). See ibid., 126.

23. See Deathridge, *The New Grove Wagner*, 172.

24. Nietzsche, *Die fröhliche Wissenschaft* (The gay science), chap. 99 in *Werke*, 5: 132.

25. See Bächthold-Stäubli, *Handwörterbuch des deutschen Aberglaubens*, 'Nase,' 6: 970.

26. M. Owen Lee points out that 'the [positive main] characters [in *Die Meistersinger*] are even named for scriptural sinners who need redeeming . . . Eva must be saved from Beckmesser—a devil indeed: Walther and David say as much, Sachs finishes his shoes with pitch, not wax, and Beckmesser himself exclaims "zum Teufel" at every crisis. . . . [Beckmesser is] exorcised (that is what happens at baptisms)' (Lee, 'Wahnfried,' 66, 68).

27. I would like to thank John Deathridge for drawing my attention to this ambiguity.

28. In the German version of his discussion of the music drama Wapnewski writes: 'Fliederduft (das meint Holunder, wie die Jahreszeit des Johannistags deutlich macht . . .),' but in the English version he merely states that the term *Flieder*, though it can be translated as both 'lilac' and 'elder,' 'clearly means elder' and omits his temporal explanation. See 'Die Oper Richard Wagners als Dichtung,' 323; 'The Operas as Literary Works,' 77.

29. See Bächthold-Stäubli, 'Holunder,' 4: 262.

30. On the political implications of this production, see Hohendahl, 'Reworking History: Wagner's German Myth of Nuremberg,' 41.

31. Bächthold-Stäubli, 'Holunder,' 266.

32. If Wagner had wished to invent direct musical representations of smells themselves, rather than acoustical and rhythmic evocations of ideas associated with them, the *Fliedermonolog* would have been the place to do so, but here, at most, one can only discern a potential representation of the movement of breezes in the tremolos of the string section, a movement of air which brings with it the aroma of the elder tree. Voss writes, 'Naturally neither the horns nor the string instruments with their tremolos on the bridge are supposed to represent the elder and its aroma' (Voss, *Studien*, 179).

33. Bächthold-Stäubli, 'Holunder,' 263.

34. Jaeger, *Die Entdeckung der Seele*, 106–109; cited in Gilman, *Jewish Self-Hatred*, 300.

35. See Kris, 'Wilhelm Fliess' wissenschaftliche Interessen,' 8–11; Masson, ed., *The Complete Letters of Sigmund Freud to Wilhelm Fliess, 1887–1904*, 1–14, and *The Assault on Truth*, 55–78, 94–103.

36. Günther, *Rassenkunde des jüdischen Volkes*, 260–268; cited in Poliakov, *The History of Anti-Semitism*, 1: 142.

37. I would like to thank my colleague Kari Ellen Gade, a specialist in Old Norse literature, for pointing this out to me.

38. See Gutman, *Richard Wagner*, 163–164, 185; Wapnewski, *Der traurige Gott*, 38–83, 205–246.

39. Strassburg, *Tristan*, 138, 145. I would like to thank Sidney M. Johnson for drawing my attention to these passages.

40. Eschenbach, *Parzival*, 249.

41. Ibid., 392.

42. See note 4.

43. See Gilman, *Difference and Pathology*, 53–56.

44. On the connection between regression and the perception of smell, see Horkheimer and Adorno (who refer to Freud), *Dialectic of Enlightenment*, 232–233.

45. On the component of Wagner's personal feelings of guilt as manifested in *Parsifal*, see Voss, 'Wagners "Parsifal"—das Spiel von der Macht der Schuldgefühle,' 18.

46. On Kundry as the Wandering Jew, see *The Diary of Richard Wagner*, 54; see also Millington, *Wagner*, 47; Zelinsky, 'Die "Feuerkur" des Richard Wagner oder die "neue Religion" der "Erlösung" durch "Vernichtung"'; Rose, *Wagner: Race and Revolution*, 37.

47. The classical study on the subject is Said, *Orientalism*. For a fine examination of one European representation of the East in nineteenth-century music, with numerous references to the growing scholarship in this area, see Locke, 'Constructing the Oriental "Other."'

48. Though the specific connotations of the geographical polarity in *Tristan* is diametrically opposed to that of *Parsifal* (the West being the domain of the exotic in the earlier drama), the two works are remarkably similar in terms of their association of woman-as-exotic and aromas. A number of passages in *Tristan* refer to the potions of Isolde's mother, and of the princess herself, in terms that anticipate the text associated with Kundry. Isolde's outburst in act 1, scene 1 runs thus:

O zahme Kunst
der Zauberin,
die nur Balsamtränke noch braut! (*TR*, 32)

[O tame art of the sorceress, who now only brews balsamic potions!]

This motif reappears in her narrative to Brangäne in act 1, scene 3:

Isoldes Kunst
ward ihm bekannt;
mit Heilsalben
und Balsamsaft
der Wunde, die ihn plagte,
getreulich pflag sie da. (*TR*, 39)

[Isolde's art became known to him; with healing salves and balsamic juice she dutifully tended his wound that plagued him.]

And finally, Brangäne's catalog of the Irish queen's unguents in act 1, scene 4 repeats the connection between exotic woman and exotic elixirs:

So reihte sie die Mutter,
die mächt'gen Zaubertränke.
Für Weh und Wunden
Balsam hier;
für böse Gifte
Gegengift. (*TR*, 44)

[Thus the mother arranged them, the powerful magic potions. For woe and wounds, balsam here; for evil poisons, antidote.]

49. Barry Emslie dismisses this portrayal of Kundry as 'slightly silly and scarcely original: the woman as representative of the harem, full of Eastern sexual promise.' But the fact that it is *not* original underscores precisely its importance as a cultural construct composed of motifs with wide currency in the nineteenth century. See Emslie, 'Woman as Image and Narrative in Wagner's *Parsifal*,' 118.

50. See the chapter on 'The Jew as Sorcerer' in Trachtenberg, *The Devil and the Jews*, 57–155, here 72–73.

51. Poliakov, *The History of Anti-Semitism*, 1: 142.

52. Trachtenberg, *The Devil and the Jews*, 72–73.

53. Ibid., 72.

54. Kundry's and Klingsor's music contains standard European acoustical representation of the East, as seen in the motives usually described as 'Klingsor,' 'Klingsor's magic,' and 'Kundry's flight.' A host of additional examples of the musical portrayal of Orientalism from this period come to mind, such as Verdi's *Aida* of 1871, the exoticism of

the music Bizet composed for his gypsy seductress in *Carmen* of 1875, and the 'moorish' ballet in Verdi's *Otello* of 1887, as well as the pseudo-gypsy music in Franz Schmidt's *Notre Dame* and the japaniserie of Puccini's *Madama Butterfly*, both of 1904 (comparable ideologically to the chinoiserie of *Turandot* of 1926). On Bizet's Orientalism, see Mc-Clary, 'Images of Race, Class and Gender' and ' "Exoticism" in *Carmen*,' in *Georges Bizet: Carmen*, 29–43, 51–58.

55. See Abbate, 'Parsifal: Words and Music,' 51.

56. Corse, *Wagner and the New Consciousness*, 139.

57. In this respect the images of Wagner's conservative imagination anticipate those of his cultural heirs, the proto-fascist *Freikorps* of the Weimar years, as brilliantly discussed (without reference to Wagner) in Theweleit, *Male Fantasies*.

58. On Germany's interaction with blacks, see Gilman, *On Blackness without Blacks*; on the cultural repercussions of the French occupation of Germany following World War I, see my *Undertones of Insurrection*, 123–136.

59. See Gilman, *The Jew's Body*, 99–100, 171–176.

60. Pezzl, *Skizze von Wien*, 107–108; cited in Gilman, *The Jew's Body*, 172.

61. See Rohrer, *Versuch über die jüdischen Bewohner der österreichischen Monarchie*, 26; Wolf, *Von den Krankheiten der Juden*, 12; cited in Gilman, *The Jew's Body*, 173.

62. See Knox, *The Races of Men*, 133; cited in Gilman, *The Jew's Body*, 174.

63. Menzel, 'Die tiefste Korruption,' 335.

64. See Strobel, ed., *Richard Wagner, Skizzen und Entwürfe*, 139–140. See also Coren, 'The Texts of Wagner's "Der junge Siegfried" and "Siegfried," ' 26–27.

65. See Strobel, ed., *Richard Wagner, Skizzen und Entwürfe*, 99; Newman, *The Life of Richard Wagner*, 2: 346.

66. On the saga-sources for the motif of 'light-elves' and 'black-elves,' see Magee, *Richard Wagner and the Nibelungs*, 136–137.

67. Strobel, ed., *Richard Wagner, Skizzen und Entwürfe*, 84.

68. Ibid., 158. In the final version set to music Wagner changed *affe* to *Rüpel*, or 'boor' (RN, 209).

69. See Trachtenberg, *The Devil and the Jews*, 48; and Poliakov, *The History of Anti-Semitism*, 1: 143n, who traces the motif of the 'odor of sanctity' and its connection to the Jews. It is still discernible in a collec-

tion of *Märchen* by Richard von Volkmann-Leander that was extremely popular in Wagner's time. First published in 1871, the story 'Wie der Teufel ins Weihwasser fiel' (How the Devil fell into the holy water) concerns the loss of the Devil's stench after his accidental baptism; the motif of the story bears comparison with the tradition of the *foetor judäicus* and the potential for a loss of the Jewish odor through baptism because of the association of the Jew and the Devil, who shared iconographies of difference and attending heretical implications throughout the Middle Ages. In this popular text of the late nineteenth century, the Evil One attains the 'odor of sanctity' through baptismal waters, much as his relative the Jew had been able to in the German imagination since the age of Wolfram von Eschenbach. See Volkmann-Leander, *Träumereien an französischen Kaminen*, 21–22.

70. On Kundry as a Mary Magdalene figure, see Emslie, 'Woman as Image,' 123–124.

71. Bächthold-Stäubli, 'Jude, Jüdin,' 4: 808–833, here 823.

CHAPTER 4. FEET: CLUBFOOT, HEROIC FOOT

1. For an analysis of the notion, widespread in the nineteenth century and the fin de siècle, that the Jewish foot was unusually enlarged, see Gilman, *The Jew's Body*, 38–59.

2. See Stoneman, 'Hephaestus,' in *Greek Mythology*, 84–85. In writing of the motif of lameness in the mythological imagination, J. E. Cirlot asks, 'May it not be that certain talents are given to men to compensate for some physical defect?' (see Cirlot, *A Dictionary of Symbols*, 111).

3. Rösselt, *Lehrbuch der griechischen und römischen Mythologie für höhere Töchterschulen und die Gebildeten des weiblichen Geschlechts*, 97–99.

4. *Heldenlieder der Edda*, 21.

5. *The Poetic Edda*, 261.

6. See Donington, *Wagner's 'Ring' and Its Symbols*, 47.

7. For this motif Wagner also drew upon a prose adaptation of a short story by E. T. A. Hoffmann that he had written on commission in 1841 shortly before turning to the subterranean imagery of *Tannhäuser.* See my 'Wagner's Use of E. T. A. Hoffmann's "The Mines of Falun." '

8. Bächthold-Stäubli, *Handwörterbuch des deutschen Aberglaubens*, 'Stolpern,' 8: 493, 494.

9. See Levy, 'Die Schuhsymbolik im jüdischen Ritus.'

10. For references to much of the material for my discussion here I

am indebted to Gilman, *The Jew's Body*, 39–42. On Burton and Schudt, see 39.

11. See Rohrer, *Versuch über die jüdischen Bewohner der österreichischen Monarchie*, 25–26; Fontane, *Der deutsche Krieg von 1866*, 1: 413.

12. See Gilman, *The Jew's Body*, 40; Gilman refers to an illustration of a flat foot used in an article by Gustav Muskat on the diseases of the feet, found in Max Joseph, *Handbuch der Kosmetik* (Leipzig: Veit & Comp., 1912); the illustration is reproduced in *The Jew's Body*, 41. For an earlier medical discussion of the clubfoot from the end of Wagner's century, see Thorndike, 'The Treatment of Club-Foot.'

13. See Poliakov, *A History of Anti-Semitism*, 1: 142–144; see also Trachtenberg, *The Devil and the Jews*, 44.

14. Poliakov, *The History of Anti-Semitism*, 1: 142, 144.

15. See Bächthold-Stäubli, 'Fuß,' 3: 225; see also 'Hinken,' 4: 58–61.

16. See Bächthold-Stäubli, 'Fuß,' 3: 226.

17. Sandra Corse describes Wagner's music for Alberich's initial appearance in scene 1 of *Das Rheingold* thus: 'a limping rhythm played by the orchestra. . . . Alberich's entrance provides . . . a musical difference' (Corse, *Wagner and the New Consciousness*, 77).

18. Westernhagen, *The Forging of the 'Ring,'* 156–157.

19. Cited in Gradenwitz, 'Das Judentum,' 89.

20. Porges, *Wagner Rehearsing the 'Ring,'* 30.

21. Strobel, ed., *Richard Wagner, Skizzen und Entwürfe*, 99; Newman, *The Life of Richard Wagner*, 2: 346.

22. On the dating of the initial composition of the Nibelung motive, see Bailey, 'The Structure of the *Ring* and Its Evolution,' 53–54. The earliest music for the *Ring* was to the Norn's scene in *Siegfrieds Tod*. See Deathridge, *The New Grove Wagner*, 171.

23. Egon Voss discusses the use of the 'col legno' effect in the violas in the passage 'Vom Spieße bring' ich den Braten: / versuchtest du gern den Sud? / Für dich sott ich ihn gar' (*RN*, 159) in act 1 of *Siegfried*. See his *Studien zur Instrumentalmusik Richard Wagners*, 97.

24. Porges, *Wagner Rehearsing the 'Ring,'* 82.

25. Voss, *Studien*, 173.

26. See Grootkerk, 'The Satyr,' 211–213.

27. See Borges and Guerrero, *The Book of Imaginary Beings*, 198.

28. Rösselt, *Lehrbuch*, 136–137.

29. Trachtenberg, *The Devil and the Jews*, 46–47.

30. In his *Tannhäuser* essay, Baudelaire describes Venus as 'the Queen

384 Notes to Chapter 4

of all she-devils, of the female faun- and satyr-people who, since the death of great Pan, have been banned to the subterranean realm to live there with the indestructible and irresistible Venus.' Quoted in Borchmeyer, *Die Götter tanzen Cancan*, 99–100. Thus, already in a prerevolutionary drama, the realm of the faun, satyr, and Pan figures represent through their association with Venus a threat to a Wagnerian hero.

31. Schickling, 'Wagner beim Wort genommen,' 795–796; William Kindermann writes of 'the total absence of . . . accents of tragedy' in the Funeral March. See his 'Dramatic Recapitulation in Wagner's *Götter-dämmerung*,' 108. In this context, see also Wintle, 'The Numinous in *Götterdämmerung*.' On the question of the heroic character of Siegfried's music and of the figure himself, see Mayer, *Richard Wagner in Selbstzeugnissen und Bilddokumenten*, 236–241.

32. See Hanisch, 'The Political Influence and Appropriation of Wagner,' 196–197.

33. The label of 'Der Wanderer' was first applied to this leitmotif by Hans von Wolzogen and can still be found in many popular guides to the *Ring* today. See Wolzogen, *Führer durch die Musik zu Richard Wagner's Festspiel* Der Ring des Nibelungen, 57–58; see also Wagner, *Der Ring des Nibelungen: Vollständiger Text mit Notentafeln der Leitmotive*, 182. Hubert Kolland analyzes this motif extensively in his 'Zur Semantik der Leitmotive in Richard Wagners *Ring des Nibelungen*,' 199–201.

34. Bächthold-Stäubli, 'Stolpern,' 8: 493.

35. Voss explains that the viola is often used in connection with Kundry in act 1 of *Parsifal* and with Loge throughout the *Ring*, two figures who share much with other anti-Semitic representations. See Voss, *Studien*, 96–97. Loge's status as a figure constructed out of anti-Semitic stereotypes is less unequivocal than that of the Nibelungs, though he shares some of them: like one of Alberich's models, Hephaestus, he is crafty, associated with fire, smoke, and the underworld, and calls Alberich 'cousin' (though that could be an unctuous and yet condescending apostrophe); moreover, he is the maliciously untrustworthy (financial!) adviser to a court, to Wotan and the gods, who rely on him while suspicious of his every word, the very image of the court Jew so central to European anti-Semitism. On Loge as an anti-Semitic figure, comparable to Wagner's image of Heinrich Heine, see Rose, *Wagner*, 206, n49.

36. On Kundry as the Wandering Jew, see Richard Wagner, *The Diary of Richard Wagner*, 54; Millington, *Wagner*, 47; Zelinsky, 'Die

"Feuerkur" des Richard Wagner oder die "neue Religion" der "Erlö-sung" durch "Vernichtung"'; Rose, *Wagner*, 37, 163–164, 172. On her death and its connection to Wagner's remarks concerning the annihi-lation, negation, or eradication of Judaism in 'Das Judentum in der Musik,' see Zelinsky, 'Der verschwiegene Gehalt des "Parsifal"'; Mill-ington, '*Parsifal*.'

CHAPTER 5. ICONS OF DEGENERATION

1. See Gutman, *Richard Wagner*, 420–431.

2. John Culshaw's description of Gottlob Frick's interpretation of the role as 'the embodiment of evil' is a case in point. See his *Ring Resounding*, 193.

3. See Strobel, ed., *Richard Wagner, Skizzen und Entwürfe*, 28.

4. See Mertens, 'Wagner's Middle Ages,' 249.

5. For references to the extensive literature on nineteenth-century racial theories, see Gilman and Chamberlain, eds., *Degeneration*; see also Mosse, *The Crisis of German Ideology*, 88–102, and *The Culture of Western Europe*, 85–94.

6. On this scene, see Schickling, *Abschied von Walhall*, 86; Zelinsky, 'Die deutsche Losung Siegfried,' 205.

7. Strobel, ed., *Richard Wagner, Skizzen und Entwürfe*, 41.

8. On the relationship between the perception of rhythm and the physical state of the *listener*, with an explicit reference to the listener's blood, see Williams, *The Long Revolution*, 66, cited in McClary, *Femi-nine Endings*, 23.

9. See Abbate, *Unsung Voices*, 112, 138.

10. Originally, in the prose text 'Die Nibelungen Saga (Mythus)' of October 1848, Wagner made it clear that Siegmund (then called 'Sige-mund') was married before being reunited with his sister, Sieglinde ('Sigelind'); see Strobel, ed., *Richard Wagner, Skizzen und Entwürfe*, 27. At this stage in the *Ring* project, this earlier marriage produces no children. When Wagner wrote the verse draft of *Der junge Siegfried* in 1851, he preserved this motif and had Brünnhilde relate to Siegfried that his father, Siegmund, had been married prior to meeting Sieg-linde; in this version both Siegmund and Sieglinde have become par-ents before the beginning of *Die Walküre*, albeit of children inferior to Siegfried ('yet only timid sons / they sired; / for more heroic buds / the fulsome line of the Volsungs / yearned'; see ibid., 186). In the final version of the drama, however, it is unclear what Siegmund's sexual

experiences have been with the women he describes in his act 1 narrations (*RN*, 83–84). Wotan attests to the natural character of Siegmund's love for Sieglinde thus:

Was so Schlimmes
schuf das Paar,
das liebend einte der Lenz?
Der Minne Zauber
entzückte sie:
wer büßt mir der Minne Macht? (*RN*, 98)

[What was the terrible thing the couple created that the Spring lovingly united? The magic of love charmed them: who pays penance to me for the power of love?]

11. In act 2, scene 1 of *Götterdämmerung* Hagen refers to Alberich as 'Albe' (*RN*, 282) and himself is referred to as 'Albensohn' by Gunther (*RN*, 323). It may be illuminating to recall the contexts in which the term *Alp* occurs in Wagner's writings, for in one of the earliest revolutionary tracts, 'Wie verhalten sich republikanische Bestrebungen dem Königtum gegenüber?' (How do republican movements act toward the monarchy?) of 1848, Wagner claimed that 'the complete emancipation of mankind' would come about in a society based on the 'activity of the limbs' rather than on money and claimed 'like a bad nocturnal elf/ dream [*wie ein böser nächtlicher Alp*] this demonic concept of money will vanish from us' (*DS* 5: 214). Here, in the year in which the first plan for the *Ring* emerged, the damnation of modern civilization was linked to money, described in the vocabulary of the Nibelungs. Hagen's 'bad dream' may be the metaphorical representation for Wagner of the nightmare of Jewishness in nineteenth-century Germany.

12. See Cosima Wagner, *Diaries*, 1: 391 (entry for 18 July 1871).

13. One of the few commentators to mention the importance of masturbation in Wagner's thinking is Dieter Schickling, but his treatment of the issue is cursory and eschews discussion of its role in the semiology of Wagner's music, and, though he discerns suggestions of masturbation in textual passages associated with Beckmesser and Klingsor, he does not mention Hagen. See Schickling, *Abschied von Walhall*, 73–76. Lindsay A. Graham has written an entertaining article that includes some remarks on Wagner's 'guilt over masturbatory fantasies.' See Graham, 'Wagner and *Lohengrin*.'

14. I would like to thank Linda and Michael Hutcheon for allowing me to read in manuscript their chapter on *Parsifal* from their forthcoming book on opera and disease (Lincoln: University of Nebraska Press), a pioneering work on the cultural iconographies in opera.

15. For overviews of the nineteenth-century literature on masturbation as deviant and dangerous, see Hare, 'Masturbatory Insanity'; Engelhardt, 'The Disease of Masturbation.'

16. See Borchmeyer, 'The Question of Anti-Semitism,' 183.

17. The letter is analyzed in detail in Gilman, *Disease and Representation*, 67–73.

18. Kleist, *Sämtliche Werke und Briefe*, 2: 559–562; trans. and cited in Gilman, *Disease and Representation*, 68.

19. In Samuel La'mert's *Self-Preservation*, an illustration depicting a severe case of corona veneris shows the purported effects of onanism on the masturbator's skin. Cited in Gilman, *Inscribing the Other*, plate 13. Belief in the external signs of onanism is also documented in Deslandes, *A Treatise on the Diseases produced by Onanism, Masturbation, Self-Pollution, and other Excesses.* On the continent (in France, Germany, and Austria), discussions of onanism appear to have been somewhat less vituperative than their more strident, moralizing, and condemning counterparts in England and America, but they all contained similar, shared assumptions concerning the debilitating effects, and the external signs thereof, associated with the sexual practice. These distinctions are discussed in Hare, 'Masturbatory Insanity,' 4–9. Additional nineteenth-century German texts concerning onanism can be found in Hohmann, ed., *Schon auf den ersten Blick*, 36–44. In a little-known lecture presented before a private club in Paris in 1879, Mark Twain lampooned the widespread notion that masturbation could be detected through the damage it inflicted upon the body and the psyche: 'The sign[s] of excessive indulgence in this destructive past-time are easily detectable. They are these: A disposition to eat, to drink, to smoke, to meet together convivially, to laugh, to joke, and tell indelicate stories — and, mainly a yearning to paint pictures' (Twain, 'Some Thoughts on the Science of Onanism' [originally published under the title '1601']).

20. The former passage is from Howe, *Excessive Venery, Masturbation and Continence*, 73; the latter is found in F. A. Burdem, 'Self-Pollution in Children,' 339, cited in Engelhardt, 'The Disease of Masturbation,' 237, 27n.

21. Strobel, ed., *Richard Wagner, Skizzen und Entwürfe*, 28, 44.

22. Inexplicably, Robert Bailey argues that a 'lapse of a generation . . . occurs between [*Siegfried*] and *Götterdämmerung.*' See his 'The Structure of the *Ring* and Its Evolution,' 49.

23. See Gilman in Gilman and Chamberlin, eds., *Degenerations*, 73; see also Russell, 'Cases illustrating the influence of exhaustion of the spinal cord in inducing paraplegia,' 456.

24. The paper was dated 8 February 1893; see Freud, *The Standard Edition of the Complete Psychological Works of Sigmund Freud*, 1: 180.

25. See Mosse, *Nationalism and Sexuality*, 135; Gilman, *Difference and Pathology*, 151.

26. Schickling, *Abschied von Walhall*, 86.

27. See Burdem, 'Self Pollution in Children,' 341.

28. See Wilhelm Griesinger, *Mental Pathology and Therapeutics*, cited in Hare, 'Masturbatory Insanity,' 6.

29. Henry Maudsley, *The Physiology and Pathology of Mind*, cited in ibid., 7.

30. See Newman, *The Wagner Operas*, 611; Rappl, *Wagner-Opernführer*, 115.

31. Henry Maudsley, *Body and Mind*, 86–87, cited in Gilman, *Disease and Representation*, 78.

32. See Stedman, 'Some of the Mental Aspects of Nervous Disease,' 422.

33. See Lallemand, *Des pertes séminales involontaires*, 3: 479; Kann, *Psychopathia sexualis*; Reich, *Geschichte, Natur- und Gesundheitslehre des ehelichen Lebens* and *Über Unsittlichkeit*. Kann's and Reich's works are discussed by Gilman in Gilman and Chamberlin, eds., *Degenerations*, 73, 76–77.

34. The letter was first published in an appendix to Westernhagen, *Richard Wagner*, 527–529; it was republished in Wagner, *Briefe*, 597–598 (#193). References to the original German will be to this edition. Long before 1956, Wagner's biographer Carl Friedrich Glasenapp appears to have been familiar with the letter's contents, but he may have suppressed its publication for reasons of propriety. He mentions a 'detailed, sympathetic communication of which we cannot say with exactitude whether or not it has been preserved.' See Glasenapp, *Das Leben Richard Wagners in sechs Büchern dargestellt*, 5: 404. Thus, prior to its publication, many scholars knew of its existence and knew that it had troubled Nietzsche profoundly, but they could only surmise as to what its contents might have been. An example of this scholarly conundrum

can be found in Griesser's *Nietzsche und Wagner*, in which Griesser said that he assumed the letter contained references to Nietzsche's purported infatuation with Cosima Wagner (!) (292–293).

35. On this final meeting, see Newman, *The Life of Richard Wagner*, 4: 543–544; Mayer, *Richard Wagner in Selbstzeugnissen und Bilddokumenten*, 156; Gregor-Dellin, *Richard Wagner*, 440; Gutman, *Richard Wagner*, 359–360.

36. Eiser's text was not published until 1978; see Eiser, 'Richard Wagners "Der Ring des Nibelungen." '

37. See Wagner, *Sämtliche Briefe*, 4: 383–384.

38. On Wagner's correspondence with Eiser, see Gutman, *Richard Wagner*, 360; Fischer-Dieskau, *Wagner and Nietzsche*, 159; Schickling, *Abschied von Walhall*, 74; Gregor-Dellin, *Richard Wagner*, 451–456; Vogel, *Nietzsche und Wagner*, 294–298.

39. See Mayer, *Richard Wagner*, 168. Wagner had conducted several concerts with Hans Richter in London's Albert Hall in an attempt to keep the Bayreuth festival solvent. See Fischer-Dieskau, *Wagner and Nietzsche*, 159.

40. Cosima Wagner, *Diaries*, 1: 989.

41. The literature on Nietzsche's physiological illness is extensive. For overviews, see Janz, *Friedrich Nietzsche*; Volz, *Nietzsche im Labyrinth seiner Krankheit*. On Eiser's remarks concerning Nietzsche's 'mental derangement,' see Newman, *The Life of Richard Wagner*, 4: 590.

42. See Wagner, *Selected Letters of Richard Wagner*, 873–874. Given the widespread assumption that the body would be irreparably damaged by the debilitating effects of premature and solitary sexual indulgence, many physicians in the nineteenth century came to believe that any heterosexual sex would be preferable to onanism, a notion that can be traced at least to the beginning of the eighteenth century. For example, in his influential *Tentamen de Morbis ex Manustrupatione* of 1758, Simon-André Tisson wrote: 'We have seen that masturbation is more pernicious than excessive intercourse with females.' See Tisson, *Onanism*, 45: anonymous trans. of *Tentamen de Morbis ex Manustrupatione*. Tisson incorporated many ideas found in the anonymous English publication *Onania, or the Heinous Sin of Self-Pollution, and all its Frightful Consequences, in both Sexes, etc*, cited in Hare, 'Masturbatory Insanity,' 2. On occasion, nineteenth-century physicians went so far as to advise (male) masturbators to engage in intercourse with prostitutes or a mistress. See, for example, Mayes, 'Spermatorrhoea, Treated by the lately

invented Rings,' 352; Parvin, 'The Hygiene of the Sexual Functions,' 606. Such a practice forms the background to Wagner's remarks concerning the advice of Nietzsche's Italian physician that Nietzsche marry.

43. See Eiser's letter to Wagner of 26 October 1877 in Wagner, *Briefe*, 529–530.

44. See Cosima Wagner, *Diaries*, 1: 749 (entry of 4 April 1874).

45. On the identity of Apel as the deceased poet, see Wagner, *Briefe*, 657; on Wagner's holiday with him, see Phillip Hodson, *Who's Who in Wagner's Life & Work*, 5; on Ritter as the unnamed friend, see Wagner, *Selected Letters*, 873n; Wagner, *Briefe*, 657.

46. On Wagner's relationship to Karl Ritter, see Schickling, *Abschied von Walhall*, 73; Gregor-Dellin, *Richard Wagner*, 252.

47. On Apel's injury, see Bauer, *Richard-Wagner-Lexikon*, 53.

48. Darwin, *Selected Writings*, 160; this text is persuasively discussed in Dijkstra, *Idols of Perversity*, 211–212.

49. Darwin, *Selected Writings*, 696.

50. Cosima Wagner, *Diaries*, 1: 187.

51. Both of these statements are cited in Rose, *Wagner*, 152–153.

52. Cosima Wagner, *Diaries*, 1: 715. The references are to Karl Hill and Emil Scaria, who were scheduled to sing the roles of Alberich and Hagen, respectively. Before the premiere, Scaria was replaced by Gustav Siehr, who learned his role in two weeks. See Wagner, 'Ein Rückblick auf die Bühnenfestspiele des Jahres 1876' (*DS* 10: 57).

AFTERWORD: WAGNER'S EMBODIMENT

1. On Barenboim's failed campaign, see Bar-Am, 'Wagner still "verboten" '; Bernheimer, 'Wagner vs. Wagnerism in Israel'; Goddard, 'Israel and Germany and Richard Wagner'; Haberman, 'Israel Philharmonic Puts Off Wagner Concert'; Hecht, 'The Wagner "Rehearsal" '; Oestreich, 'Wagner, Nazis and the Israeli Soul'; Rhein, 'Barenboim Takes Step in Returning Wagner to Israel'; Rothstein, 'What Is the Politics of "Tristan"?'; Shattner, 'Israel Philharmonic Cancels Wagner Recital amid Protests'; Taruskin, 'Only Time Will Cover the Taint'; 'Wagner Concert Postponed after Furor'; Walsh, 'The Case of Wagner—Again'; Ward, 'Listeners Look Beyond the Music for Meanings'; Zadrozny, 'Israel Orchestra Bans Classical Music Antisemitism.'

The controversy over Barenboim's attempt to perform Wagner in Israel evinces the very ideological positions regarding the question of the ideational implications of music discussed in the introduction. While those who seek to distinguish between Wagner the man and his music also disregard the cultural context in which the music is performed as essential to such a discussion, others, most notably Rothstein and Taruskin, are far more perceptive. The former approach is typified by such remarks as the following: 'Is there anything antisemitic in [*sic*] Wagner's music? Of course not. One simply cannot write antisemitic music' (Bar-Am); 'The case asks us to distinguish between the man and his music' (Goddard); 'The overwhelming consensus continues to be that whatever Wagner's music is, it isn't anti-Semitic. . . . So far, however, no one has found the means to equate Wagner's music itself, rather than early 20th-century trappings surrounding it, with anti-Semitism' (Ward). Rather than viewing the music as an aesthetic construct that exists in a historical-cultural vacuum and that is violated by a post-Holocaust reading, Rothstein and Taruskin make the following, apposite observations: 'Music can indeed have political meanings. Music is never purely abstract. . . . But its meanings are not literal' (Rothstein); 'It does no good to argue that the music itself is inherently nonpolitical and nonracist. The music does not now exist, nor has it ever existed, in a social vacuum. Its meanings are not self-contained. They are inscribed not only by its creator but by its users, Nazi and Jew alike' (Taruskin).

Works by Richard Wagner

AUTOBIOGRAPHICAL WRITINGS AND DIARIES

Das braune Buch: Tagebuchaufzeichnungen 1865 bis 1882. Zurich: Atlantis, 1975.

The Diary of Richard Wagner, 1865–1882: The Brown Book. Annotated by Joachim Bergfeld. Trans. George Bird. London: Gollancz, 1980.

Mein Leben. Ed. Martin Gregor-Dellin. Munich: List, 1963.

My Life. Trans. Andrew Gray. Ed. Mary Whittall. Cambridge: Cambridge University Press, 1983.

(= Hans von Wolzogen.) 'The Work and Mission of My Life.' *North American Review* 223–224 (August–September 1879): 107–124, 238–258.

LETTERS

Briefe. Ed. and introduction by Hanjo Kesting. Munich: Piper, 1983.

Briefe an Hans Richter. Ed. Ludwig Karpath. Berlin: Zsolnay, 1924.

Briefe an Hans von Bülow. Jena: Diederich, 1916.

Briefe Richard Wagners an eine Putzmacherin. Ed. Daniel Spitzer. Vienna: Carl Konegen, 1906.

Die Briefe Richard Wagners an Judith Gautier. Ed. Willi Schuh. Zurich: Rotapfel, 1936.

Briefe Richard Wagners an Otto Wesendonck. Berlin: Duncker, 1905.

'Drei unbekannte Schreiben Richard Wagners an Gustav Hölzel, mitgeteilt von Marie Huch in Hannover.' *Die Musik* 12 (1912–13): 171–172.

Family Letters of Richard Wagner. Trans. William Ashton Ellis. London: Macmillan, 1911.

Richard Wagner an August Röckel. 2d ed. Leipzig: Breitkopf & Härtel, 1912.

Richard Wagner an Mathilde Wesendonck: Tagebuchblätter und Briefe, 1853–1871. Ed. Wolfgang Golther. Berlin: Duncker, 1904.

Richard Wagner an seine Künstler. Ed. Erich Kloss. Berlin: Schuster & Loeffler, 1908.

Richard Wagner an Theodor Apel. Leipzig: Breitkopf & Härtel, 1910.

Sämtliche Briefe. Ed. Gertrud Strobel and Werner Wolf. Leipzig: Deutscher Verlag für Musik, 1979–.

Selected Letters of Richard Wagner. Trans. and ed. Stewart Spencer and Barry Millington. London: Dent, 1987.

and Franz Liszt. *Briefwechsel zwischen Wagner und Liszt.* 2 vols. Leipzig: Breitkopf & Härtel, 1900.

and King Ludwig II. *König Ludwig II und Richard Wagner: Briefwechsel.* Ed. Otto Strobel. 5 vols. Karlsruhe: Braun, 1936–1939.

WORKS

Dichtungen und Schriften. Ed. Dieter Borchmeyer. 10 vols. Frankfurt am Main: Insel, 1983.

Gesammelte Schriften. Ed. Julius Kapp. 14 vols. Leipzig: Hesse & Becker, 1911.

Richard Wagner's Prose Works. Trans. William Ashton Ellis. London: Kegan Paul, Trench, Trübner & Co., 1892–1899. Repr. 8 vols. New York: Broude Brothers, 1966.

Der Ring des Nibelungen: vollständiger Text mit Notentafeln der Leitmotive. Ed. Julius Burghold. Munich: Wilhelm Goldmann, 1981.

Sämtliche Werke. Ed. Carl Dahlhaus. Mainz: Schott, 1970–.

Other Sources

Abbate, Carolyn. 'Erik's Dream and Tannhäuser's Journey.' In *Reading Opera.* Ed. Arthur Groos and Roger Parker. Princeton: Princeton University Press, 1988. 129–167.

———. 'Opera as Symphony, a Wagnerian Myth.' In *Analyzing Opera: Verdi and Wagner.* Ed. Carolyn Abbate and Roger Parker. Berkeley: University of California Press, 1989. 92–124.

———. 'Parsifal: Words and Music.' In *Parsifal.* Ed. Nicholas John. English National Opera Guide Series 34. New York: Riverrun Press, 1986. 43–58.

———. *Unsung Voices: Opera and Musical Narrative in the Nineteenth Century.* Princeton: Princeton University Press, 1991.

Abbate, Carolyn, and Roger Parker, eds. *Analyzing Opera: Verdi and Wagner.* Berkeley: University of California Press, 1989.

Abraham, Gerald. 'The Artist of Pictures from an Exhibition.' In *Musorgsky: In Memoriam 1881–1981.* Ed. Malcolm H. Brown. Russian

Music Studies 3. Ann Arbor: University of Michigan Research Press, 1982. 229–236.

Ackermann, Peter. *Richard Wagners 'Ring des Nibelungen' und die Dialektik der Aufklärung.* Tutzing: Hans Schneider, 1981.

Adorno, Theodor W. *In Search of Wagner.* Trans. Rodney Livingston. London: New Left Books, 1981.

———. 'Wagner, Nietzsche, and Hitler.' *Kenyon Review* 9 (1947): 155–162.

Adorno, Theodor W., and Max Horkheimer. *Dialectic of Enlightenment.* Trans. John Cumming. New York: Seabury Press, 1972.

Amerongen, Martin van. *Wagner: A Case History.* Trans. Stewart Spencer and Dominic Cakebread. London: Dent, 1983.

Anonymous. *Onania, or the Heinous Sin of Self-Pollution, and all its Frightful Consequences, in both Sexes, etc.* London: n.p., ca. 1726.

Apel, Willi. *Harvard Dictionary of Music.* 2d ed. Cambridge: Harvard University Press, 1977.

Appia, Adolphe. *Staging Wagnerian Drama.* Trans. and introduction by Peter Loeffler. Basel: Birkhäuser Verlag, 1982.

Aprahamian, Felix. 'Debussy's "Pelléas et Mélisande."' Brochure to Claude Debussy, *Pelléas et Mélisande.* EMI Records Ltd. CDS7 49350-2. 7–11.

Ashman, Mike. 'Producing Wagner.' In *Wagner in Performance.* Ed. Barry Millington and Stewart Spencer. New Haven: Yale University Press, 1992. 29–47.

Bächthold-Stäubli, Hans. *Handwörterbuch des deutschen Aberglaubens.* 9 vols. Berlin: de Gruyter, 1927–1941.

Bailey, Robert. 'The Structure of the *Ring* and Its Evolution.' *19th-Century Music* 1 (July 1977): 48–61.

Balzac, Honoré de. 'Gambara.' In *Le Chef-d'oeuvre inconnu: Gambara, Massimilla Doni.* Introduction and annotation by Marc Eigeldinger and Max Milner. Paris: Flammarion, 1981. 73–138.

Bar-Am, Benjamin. 'Wagner still "verboten."' *Jerusalem Post,* 19 December 1991, section 'Opinion.'

Bart, Benjamin F. *Flaubert.* Syracuse: Syracuse University Press, 1967.

Barth, H., D. Mack, and E. Voss, eds. *Wagner: A Documentary Study.* London: Thames & Hudson, 1975.

Bauer, Hans-Joachim. *Richard-Wagner-Lexikon.* Bergisch Gladbach: Gustav Lübbe, 1988.

Bauer, Oswald G. 'Die Aufführungsgeschichte in Grundzügen.' In

Richard-Wagner-Handbuch. Ed. Ulrich Müller and Peter Wapnewski. Stuttgart: Alfred Körner, 1986. 647–674.

——. *Richard Wagner: die Bühnenwerke von der Uraufführung bis heute*. Foreword by Wolfgang Wagner. Frankfurt am Main: Propyläen, 1982.

Beckett, Lucy. *Richard Wagner: Parsifal*. Cambridge: Cambridge University Press, 1981.

Bein, Alex. *Die Judenfrage: Biographie eines Weltproblems*. Stuttgart: Deutsche Verlags-Anstalt, 1980.

Berl, Heinrich. *Das Judentum in der Musik*. Berlin: Deutsche Verlagsanstalt, 1926.

Bermbach, Udo. 'Die Destruktion der Institutionen: zum politischen Gehalt des "Ring."' In *In den Trümmern der eignen Welt: Richard Wagners 'Der Ring des Nibelungen.'* Ed. Udo Bermbach. Berlin: Reimer, 1989. 111–144.

——, ed. *In den Trümmern der eignen Welt: Richard Wagners 'Der Ring des Nibelungen.'* Berlin: Reimer, 1989.

Bernal, Martin. *Black Athena: The Afroasiatic Roots of Classical Civilization*. London: Vintage, 1991–.

Bernheimer, Martin. 'Wagner vs. Wagnerism in Israel.' *Los Angeles Times*, section 'Calendar,' part F, p.1, col.5.

Bloch, Ernst. 'Über Beckmessers Preislied-Text.' In Richard Wagner, *Die Meistersinger von Nürnberg: Texte, Materialien, Kommentare*. Ed. Attila Csampai and Dietmar Holland. Reinbek bei Hamburg: Rowohlt, 1981. 243–248.

Bokina, John. 'Wagner and Marxist Aesthetics.' In *Wagner in Retrospect*. Ed. Leroy Shaw, Nancy R. Cirillo, and Marion S. Miller. Amsterdam: Rodopi, 1987. 138–151.

Borchmeyer, Dieter. *Die Götter tanzen Cancan: Richard Wagners Liebesrevolten*. Heidelberg: Manutius-Verlag, 1992.

——. '"Parsifal": Erlösung und Wiederbringung der Dinge.' In *Liebe und Erlösung: über Richard Wagner*. Ed. Wolfgang Böhme. Karlsruhe: Gebr. Tron KG, 1983. 49–67.

——. 'The Question of Anti-Semitism.' Trans. Stewart Spencer. In *Wagner Handbook*. Ed. Ulrich Müller, Peter Wapnewski, and John Deathridge. Cambridge: Harvard University Press, 1992. 166–185.

——. *Richard Wagner: Theory and Theatre*. Trans. Stewart Spencer. Oxford: Clarendon Press, 1991.

——. 'Wagner-Literatur—eine deutsche Misere. Neue Ansichten

zum "Fall Wagner."' Internationales Archiv für Sozialgeschichte der deutschen Literatur. 3. Sonderheft. Forschungsreferate 2. Folge. Tübingen: Niemeyer, 1992. 1–62.

Borges, Jorge Luis, and Margarita Guerrero. *The Book of Imaginary Beings.* Trans. Norman Thomas di Giovanni. New York: Discus-Avon, 1970.

Botstein, Leon. 'Wagner and Our Century.' *19th-Century Music* 11 (1987–88): 92–104.

Branscombe, Peter. 'The Dramatic Texts.' Trans. Stewart Spencer. In *Wagner Handbook.* Ed. Ulrich Müller, Peter Wapnewski, and John Deathridge. Cambridge: Harvard University Press, 1992. 269–286.

Brod, Leo. 'Richard Wagners jüdische Propagandisten.' In *Wagners Werk und Wirkung: Festspielnachrichten Beiträge 1957 bis 1982.* Ed. Lorenz Ellwanger. Bayreuth: Lorenz Ellwanger, 1982. 25–29.

Brody, Elaine. 'The Jewish Wagnerites.' *Midstream* (February, 1986): 46–50.

Bronsen, David, ed. *Jews and Germans from 1860 to 1933: The Problematic Symbiosis.* Heidelberg: Siegen, 1979.

Brown, Malcolm H., ed. *Musorgsky: In Memoriam 1881–1981.* Russian Music Studies 3. Ann Arbor: University of Michigan Research Press, 1982.

Burbridge, Peter, and Richard Sutton, ed. *The Wagner Companion.* London: Faber, 1979.

Bürger, Peter. 'Literarischer Markt und autonomer Kunstbegriff: zur Dichotomisierung der Literatur im 19. Jahrhundert.' *Zur Dichotomisierung von hoher und niederer Literatur.* Ed. Christa Büger, Peter Bürger, and Jochen Schulte-Sasse. Frankfurt am Main, 1982. 241–265.

Burke, Kenneth. 'The Thinking of the Body. Comments on the Imagery of Catharsis in Literature.' *Psychoanalytic Review* 50 (Fall 1963): 25–68.

Burton, Robert. *The Anatomy of Melancholy.* Ed. Holbrook Jackson. New York: Vintage, 1977.

Busi, Fred. 'Wagner and the Jews.' *Midstream* (February 1986): 37–42.

Byock, Jesse L. Introduction. *The Saga of the Volsungs: The Norse Epic of Sigurd the Dragon Slayer.* Trans. Jesse L. Byock. Berkeley: University of California Press, 1990. 1–29.

Carlebach, Julius. *Karl Marx and the Radical Critique of Judaism.* London: Routledge & Kegan Paul, 1978.

Chamberlain, Houston Stewart. *The Wagnerian Drama: An Attempt to Inspire a Better Appreciation of Wagner as a Dramatic Poet.* London: John Lane the Bodley Head, 1923.

Cicora, Mary A. *Parsifal-Reception in the Bayreuther Blätter.* New York: Peter Lang, 1987.

Cirlot, J. E. *A Dictionary of Symbols.* 2d ed. Trans. Jack Sage. London: Routledge & Kegan Paul, 1971.

Clement, Catherine. *Opera, or the Undoing of Woman.* Trans. Betsy Wing. Foreword by Susan McClary. Minneapolis: University of Minnesota Press, 1988.

Cooke, Deryck. *I Saw the World End: A Study of Wagner's 'Ring.'* London: Oxford University Press, 1979.

Corbin, Alain. *The Foul and the Fragrant: Odor and the French Social Imagination.* Cambridge: Harvard University Press, 1986.

Coren, Daniel. 'The Texts of Wagner's "Der junge Siegfried" and "Siegfried."' *19th-Century Music* 6 (1982–83): 17–30.

Corse, Sandra. *Wagner and the New Consciousness: Language and Love in the* Ring. London: Associated University Presses, 1990.

Csampai, Attali, and Dietmar Holland, eds. *Lohengrin: Texte, Materialien, Kommentare.* Reinbek bei Hamburg: Rowohlt, 1989.

——. *Die Meistersinger von Nürnberg: Texte, Materialien, Kommentare.* Reinbek bei Hamburg: Rowohlt, 1981.

——. *Parsifal: Texte, Materialien, Kommentare.* Reinbek bei Hamburg: Rowohlt, 1984.

——. *Tannhäuser: Texte, Materialien, Kommentare.* Reinbek bei Hamburg: Rowohlt, 1986.

——. *Tristan und Isolde: Texte, Materialien, Kommentare.* Reinbek bei Hamburg: Rowohlt, 1983.

Culshaw, John. *Ring Resounding.* New York: Viking Press, 1967.

Dahlhaus, Carl, ed. *Das Drama Richard Wagners als musikalisches Kunstwerk.* Studien zur Musikgeschichte des 19. Jahrhunderts 23. Regensburg: Gustav Bosse, 1971.

——. 'Erlösung dem Erlöser.' In *Parsifal: Texte, Materialien, Kommentare.* Ed. Attila Csampai and Dietmar Holland. Reinbek bei Hamburg: Rowohlt, 1981. 262–269.

——. *The New Grove Wagner.* London: Macmillan, 1990. 68–164.

——. *Realism in Nineteenth-Century Music.* Trans. Mary Whittall. Cambridge: Cambridge University Press, 1985.

———. *Richard Wagner's Music Dramas.* Trans. Mary Whittall. Cambridge: Cambridge University Press, 1979.

———. 'Soziologische Dechiffrierung von Musik: zu Theodor W. Adornos Wagnerkritik.' *International Review of Music Aesthetics and Sociology* 1 (1970): 137–147.

———. 'Das unterbrochene Hauptwerk: zu Wagners Siegfried.' In *Das Drama Richard Wagners als musikalisches Kunstwerk.* Ed. Carl Dahlhaus. Studien zur Musikgeschichte des 19. Jahrhunderts 23. Regensburg: Gustav Bosse, 1971. 235–238.

———. *Vom Musikdrama zur Literaturoper: Aufsätze zur neueren Operngeschichte.* Munich: Katzbichler, 1983.

———, ed. *Richard Wagner: Werk und Wirkung.* Studien zur Musikgeschichte des 19. Jahrhunderts 26. Regensburg: Gustav Bosse, 1971.

Darcy, Warren. 'The Pessimism of the *Ring.*' *Opera Quarterly* 4 (Summer 1986): 24–48.

Darwin, Charles. *Selected Writings.* Ed. Philip Appleman. New York: W. W. Norton, 1970.

Deathridge, John. 'A Brief History of Wagner Research.' In *Wagner Handbook.* Ed. Ulrich Müller, Peter Wapnewski, and John Deathridge. Cambridge: Harvard University Press, 1992. 202–223.

———. 'Götterdämmerung: Finishing the End.' Brochure to Richard Wagner, *Götterdämmerung.* Deutsche Grammophon. 429 385-2GH4. 66–72.

———. *The New Grove Wagner.* London: Macmillan, 1990. 1–66, 165–193.

———. 'The Nomenclature of Wagner's Sketches.' *Proceedings of the Royal Musical Association* 101 (1974–75): 75–83.

———. Review of recent recordings of the *Ring* broadcast on radio by the BBC on 10 and 17 October 1992.

———. 'Through the Looking Glass: Some Remarks on the First Complete Draft of "Lohengrin."' In *Analyzing Opera: Verdi and Wagner.* Ed. Carolyn Abbate and Roger Parker. Berkeley: University of California Press, 1989. 56–91.

———. 'Wagner and the Post-Modern.' *Cambridge Opera Journal* 4, no. 2 (July 1992): 143–161.

———. 'Wagner's Sketches for the "Ring": Some Recent Studies.' *Musical Times* 118 (May 1977): 383–389.

Deathridge, John, Martin Geck, and Egon Voss, eds. *Verzeichnis der musikalischen Werke Richard Wagners und ihrer Quellen.* Mainz: Schott, 1984.

Deslandes, Leopold. *A Treatise on the Diseases produced by Onanism, Masturbation, Self-Pollution, and other Excesses.* 3d ed. Boston: Otis Broaders & Co., 1841.

Deutsche Gedichte: von den Anfängen bis zur Gegenwart. Ed. Theodor Echtermeyer and Benno von Wiese. Düsseldorf: August Bagel, 1980.

Devraigne, Pierre. 'Hungerjahre in Paris.' In *Wagners Werk und Wirkung: Festspielnachrichten Beiträge 1957 bis 1982.* Ed. Lorenz Ellwanger. Bayreuth: Lorenz Ellwanger, 1982. 93–96.

DiGaetani, John Louis, ed. *Penetrating Wagner's "Ring": An Anthology.* Rutherford, N.J.: Fairleigh Dickinson University Press, 1978.

Dijkstra, Bram. *Idols of Perversity: Fantasies of Feminine Evil in Fin-de-Siècle Culture.* New York: Oxford University Press, 1986.

Dippel, Paul Gerhardt. *Richard Wagner und Italien.* Emsdetten: Lechte, 1966.

Donington, Robert. *Opera & Its Symbols: The Unity of Words, Music, & Staging.* New Haven: Yale University Press, 1990.

——. *Wagner's "Ring" and Its Symbols.* New York: St. Martin's Press, 1963.

Douchin, Jacques-Louis. *La Vie érotique de Flaubert.* Paris: J. J. Pauvert, 1984.

Douglas, Mary. *Natural Symbols.* New York: Pantheon Books, 1970.

Eger, Manfred, ed. *Wagner und die Juden: Fakten und Hintergründe: eine Dokumentation zur Ausstellung im Richard-Wagner-Museum Bayreuth.* Bayreuth: Druckhaus Bayreuth, 1985.

Ehrenfels, Christian von. 'Wagner und seine neuen Apostaten.' *Der Auftakt: moderne Musikblätter* 11 (1931): 5–12.

Eisen, A. M. 'Nietzsche and the Jews Reconsidered.' *Jewish Social Studies* 48 (1986): 1–14.

Eiser, Otto. 'Richard Wagners "Der Ring des Nibelungen": ein exegetischer Versuch.' *Bayreuther Blätter* 1 (1978): 309–317, 352–366.

Elvers, Rudolf. 'Schlesinger.' In *The New Grove Dictionary of Music and Musicians.* Ed. Stanley Sadie. London, 1980. 16: 660.

Emmons, Shirlee. *Tristanissimo: The Authorized Biography of Heroic Tenor Lauritz Melchior.* New York: Schirmer Books, 1990.

Emslie, Barry. 'Woman as Image and Narrative in Wagner's *Parsifal*: A Case Study.' *Cambridge Opera Journal* 3, no. 2 (July 1991): 109–124.

Engelhardt, H. Tristram Jr. 'The Disease of Masturbation: Values and the Concept of Disease.' *Bulletin of History of Medicine* 48 (1974): 234–248.

Eschenbach, Wolfram von. *Parzifal.* Trans. and introduction by A. T. Hatto. London: Penguin, 1980.

Ewans, Michael. *Wagner and Aeschylus: The Ring and the Oresteia.* London: Faber, 1982.

Fehl, Philipp P. 'Wagner's Antisemitism and the Dignity of Art.' In *Wagner in Retrospect.* Ed. Leroy Shaw, Nancy R. Cirillo, and Marion S. Miller. Amsterdam: Rodopi, 1987. 197–201.

Field, Geoffrey G. *Evangelist of Race: The Germanic Vision of Houston Stewart Chamberlain.* New York: Columbia University Press, 1981.

Finney, Gail. 'Self-Reflexive Siblings: Incest as Narcissism in Tieck, Wagner, and Thomas Mann.' *German Quarterly* 56, no. 2 (March 1983): 243–256.

Fischer, Jens Malte. 'Sprachgesang oder Belcanto? Wagners Sänger und die Bayreuther Schule.' In *Richard Wagner 1883–1983: die Rezeption im 19. und 20. Jahrhundert.* Ed. Gerhard Croll, Franz Hundsnurscher, Ulrich Müller, and Cornelius Sommer. Stuttgarter Arbeiten zur Germanistik 129. Stuttgart: Akademischer Verlag H.-D. Heinz, 1984. 475–490.

Fischer, Klaus-Uwe. 'Von Wagner zu Hitler: Annahme oder Ablehnung einer These von Ludwig Marcuse.' In *Richard Wagner: wie antisemitisch darf ein Künstler sein?* Musikkonzepte 5. Munich: Text & Kritik, 1978. 34–40.

Fischer-Dieskau, Dietrich. *Wagner and Nietzsche.* Trans. Joachim Neugroschel. New York: Seabury Press, 1976.

Fontane, Theodor. *Der deutsche Krieg von 1866,* vol. 1: *Der Feldzug in Böhmen und Mähren.* Berlin: Verlag der königlichen geheimen Ober-Hofbuchdruckerei, 1870.

Foucault, Michel. *Discipline and Punish.* New York: Pantheon, 1977.
———. *The History of Sexuality.* Vol. 1. Trans. Robert Hurley. New York: Random House, 1978.
———. *Madness and Civilization: A History of Insanity in the Age of Reason.* Trans. Richard Howard. New York: Random House, 1965.
———. *The Order of Things: An Archaeology of the Human Sciences.* New York: Random House, 1970.

Franke, Rainer. *Richard Wagners Zürcher Kunstschriften: politische und ästhetische Entwürfe auf seinem Weg zum 'Ring des Nibelungen.'* Hamburger Beiträge zur Musikwissenschaft 26. Hamburg: Karl Dieter Wagner, 1983.

Frankenstein, Alfred. 'Victor Hartmann and Modeste Musorgsky.' *Musical Quarterly* 25 (1939): 268–291.

Freud, Sigmund. *The Standard Edition of the Complete Psychological Works of Sigmund Freud.* London: Hogarth Press, 1971.

Fuchs, Eduard, and Ernest Kreowski. *Richard Wagner in der Karikatur.* Berlin: B. Behr's Verlag, 1907.

Fuchs, Hanns. *Richard Wagner und die Homosexualität: unter besonderer Berücksichtigung der sexuellen Anomalien seiner Gestalten.* Studien zur Geschichte des menschlichen Geschlechtslebens 7. Berlin: H. Barsdorf, 1903.

Furness, Raymond. *Wagner and Literature.* Manchester: Manchester University Press, 1982.

Gallagher, Catherine, and Thomas Lacquer, eds. *The Making of the Modern Body: Sexuality & Society in the 19th Century.* Berkeley: University of California Press, 1987.

Gay, Peter. *Freud, Jews, and Other Germans: Masters and Victims in Modernist Culture.* New York: Oxford University Press, 1978.

Geck, Martin. *Die Bildnisse Richard Wagners.* Studien zur Kunst des 19. Jahrhunderts 9. Munich: Prestel Verlag, 1970.

Geiss, Imanuel. *Die Habermas-Kontroverse: ein deutscher Streit.* Berlin: Siedler Verlag, 1988.

Gerlach, Reinhard. 'Musik und Sprache in Wagners Schrift *Oper und Drama*: Intention und musikalisches Denken.' In *Richard Wagner: Werk und Wirkung.* Ed. Carl Dahlhaus. Studien zur Musikgeschichte des 19. Jahrhunderts 26. Regensburg: Gustav Bosse, 1971. 9–39.

Gilman, Sander L. *Difference and Pathology: Stereotypes of Sexuality, Race, and Madness.* Ithaca: Cornell University Press, 1985.

——. *Disease and Representation: Images of Illness from Madness to AIDS.* Ithaca: Cornell University Press, 1988.

——. *Inscribing the Other.* Lincoln: University of Nebraska Press, 1991.

——. *Jewish Self-Hatred: Anti-Semitism and the Hidden Language of the Jews.* Baltimore: Johns Hopkins University Press, 1986.

——. *The Jew's Body.* New York: Routledge, 1991.

——. *On Blackness without Blacks: Essays on the Image of the Black in Germany.* Boston: G. K. Hall, 1982.

——. 'Strauss, the Pervert, and Avant Garde Opera of the Fin de Siècle.' *New German Critique* 43 (Winter 1988): 35–68.

——. 'The Struggle of Psychiatry with Psychoanalysis: Who Won?' *Critical Inquiry* 13, no. 2 (Winter 1987): 293–313.

Gilman, Sander L., and J. Edward Chamberlin, eds. *Degeneration: The Dark Side of Progress.* New York: Columbia University Press, 1985.

Girard, René. *'To double business bound': Essays on Literature, Mimesis, and Anthropology.* Baltimore: Johns Hopkins University Press, 1988.

——. *Violence and the Sacred.* Trans. Patrick Gregory. Baltimore: Johns Hopkins University Press, 1979.

Glasenapp, Carl Friedrich. *Das Leben Richard Wagners in sechs Büchern dargestellt.* 6 vols. 5th ed. Leipzig: Breitkopf & Härtel, 1905–1912.

Glass, Frank W. *The Fertilizing Seed: Wagner's Concept of the Poetic Intent.* Ann Arbor: University of Michigan Research Press, 1983.

Goddard, Peter. 'Israel and Germany and Richard Wagner.' *Toronto Star*, 16 March 1992, section 'Entertainment,' B4.

Goethe, Johann Wolfgang von. *Goethes Werke.* Ed. Erich Trunz. 14 vols. Hamburg: Christian Wegner, 1949–1960.

Golomb, J. 'Nietzsche on Jews and Judaism.' *Archiv für Geschichte der Philosophie* 67 (1985): 139–161.

Gradenwitz, Peter. 'Das Judentum: Richard und Cosima Wagners Trauma.' In *Richard Wagner 1883–1983: die Rezeption im 19. und 20. Jahrhundert.* Ed. Gerhard Croll, Franz Hundsnurscher, Ulrich Müller, and Cornelius Sommer. Stuttgarter Arbeiten zur Germanistik 129. Stuttgart: Akademischer Verlag H.-D. Heinz, 1984. 77–91.

Graham, Lindsay A. 'Wagner and *Lohengrin*: A Psychoanalytic Study.' *Psychiatric Journal of the University of Ottawa* 3, no. 1 (March 1978): 39–49.

de la Grange, Henri-Louis. *Mahler.* New York: Doubleday, 1973.

Greenblatt, Robert. 'Richard Wagner (1813–1883): The Voluptuary Genius.' *British Journal of Sexual Medicine* 10, no. 93 (March 1983): 17–18.

Gregor-Dellin, Martin. *Richard Wagner: eine Biographie in Bildern.* Munich: Piper, 1982.

——. *Richard Wagner: His Life, His Work, His Century.* Trans. J. Maxwell Brownjohn. New York: Harcourt, Brace, Jovanovich, 1983.

Griesinger, Wilhelm. *Mental Pathology and Therapeutics.* Intro. Erwin H. Ackerknecht. London: n.p., 1867; repr. New York: Hafner, 1965.

Griesser, Luitpold. *Nietzsche und Wagner: neue Beiträge zur Geschichte und Psychologie ihrer Freundschaft*. Vienna: G. Freytag, 1923.

Grimm, Jacob, and Wilhelm Grimm. 'Duft.' In *Deutsches Wörterbuch*. Leipzig: S. Hirzel, 1860. 2: 1500–1502.

Grimm, Reinhold, and Jost Hermand, eds. *Re-reading Wagner*. Madison: University of Wisconsin Press, 1993.

Groddeck, Georg. 'Der Ring.' *Die Arche* 3, no. 11 (November 1927): 11–31.

Groos, Arthur. 'Appropriation in Wagner's *Tristan* Libretto.' In *Reading Opera*. Princeton: Princeton University Press, 1988. 12–33.

Groos, Arthur, and Roger Parker, eds. *Reading Opera*. Princeton: Princeton University Press, 1988.

Grootkerk, Paul. 'The Satyr.' In *Mythical and Fabulous Creatures: A Source Book and Research Guide*. Ed. Malcolm South. New York: Greenwood Press, 1987. 207–223.

Grossmann-Vendrey, Susanna. *Bayreuth in der deutschen Presse: Beiträge zur Rezeptionsgeschichte Richard Wagners und seiner Festspiele*. 3 vols. Regensburg: Gustav Bosse, 1977–1983.

Grout, Donald Jay, and Claude V. Palisca. *A History of Western Music*. 3d ed. London: J. M. Dent & Sons, 1983.

Güdemann, Moritz. *Geschichte des Erziehungswesens und der Cultur der abendländischen Juden während des Mittelalters und der neueren Zeit*. 3 vols. Vienna: Alfred Hölder, 1880–1888.

Guichard, Léon. *La Musique et les lettres au temps du romantisme*. Paris: Presses Universitaires de France, 1955.

Gülke, Peter. *Rousseau und die Musik, oder, Von der Zuständigkeit des Dilettanten*. Wilhelmshaven: Heinrichshofen, 1984.

Günther, Hans F. K. *Rassenkunde des jüdischen Volkes*. Munich: J. F. Lehmann, 1930.

Gutman, Robert W. *Richard Wagner: The Man, His Mind, and His Music*. 2d ed. New York: Harcourt, Brace, Jovanovich, 1990.

Haberman, Clyde. 'Israel Philharmonic Puts Off Wagner Concert.' *New York Times*, 23 December 1991, section C, p. 11, col. 1.

Hall, Calvin S. 'Wagnerian Dreams: One Hundred Years after Richard Wagner's Death, a Study of the Composer's Dreams Offers Clues to His Odious Behavior.' *Psychology Today* 17 (January 1983): 34–39.

Hamilton, James. *Arthur Rackham: A Life with Illustration*. London: Pavilion, 1990.

Hanisch, Ernst. 'The Political Influence and Appropriation of Wagner.' Trans. Paul Knight. In *Wagner Handbook*. Ed. Ulrich Müller,
Peter Wapnewski, and John Deathridge. Cambridge: Harvard University Press, 1992. 186–201.

Hare, E. H. 'Masturbatory Insanity: The History of an Idea.' *Journal of
Mental Science* 108, no. 452 (1962): 2–25.

Hart Nibbrig, Christiaan L. *Die Auferstehung des Körpers im Text*. Frankfurt am Main: Edition Suhrkamp, 1985.

Hartmann, Otto Julius. *Die Esoterik im Werk Richard Wagners*. Freiberg
i. Br.: Verlag Die Kommenden, 1960.

Hatin, Louis Eugène. *Bibliographie historique et critique de la presse périodique française*. Paris: Didot, 1866.

Hecht, Reuben. 'The Wagner "Rehearsal." ' *Jerusalem Post*, 13 January
1992, section 'Opinion.'

Hegel, G. W. F. *The Phenomenology of Mind*. Trans. J. B. Baillie. 2d ed.
London: George Allen and Unwin, 1931.

Heldenlieder der Edda: Auswahl. Trans., introduction, and annotation by
Felix Genzmer. Stuttgart: Phillip Reclam Jr., 1961.

Hermand, Jost. 'Gralsmotive um die Jahrhundertwende.' *Deutsche Vier-
teljahrsschrift für Literaturwissenschaft und Geistesgeschichte* 36 (1962):
521–543.

——. 'Wagner's Last Supper: The Vegetarian Gospel of His Parsifal.'
In *Re-reading Wagner*. Ed. Reinhold Grimm and Jost Hermand.
Madison: University of Wisconsin Press, 1993. 103–118.

Herz, Joachim. 'Der doch versöhnte Beckmesser: noch eine Wagner-
Polemik (1961).' In Richard Wagner, *Die Meistersinger von Nürnberg:
Texte, Materialien, Kommentare*. Ed. Attila Csampai and Dietmar
Holland. Reinbek bei Hamburg: Rowohlt, 1981. 213–215.

Hirsbrunner, Theo. *Maurice Ravel: sein Leben, sein Werk*. Laaber: Laaber Verlag, 1989.

Hodson, Phillip. *Who's Who in Wagner's Life & Work*. London: Wei-
denfeld & Nicolson, 1984.

Hofer, Hermann. 'Expérience musicale et empire romanesque: Hoff-
mann musicien chez Jules Janin, Champfleury et Alexandre Dumas.'
In *E. T. A. Hoffmann et la musique*. Ed. Alain Montandon. Bern: Peter
Lang, 1987. 303–314.

Hohendahl, Peter Uwe. 'Reworking History: Wagner's German Myth
of Nuremberg.' In *Re-reading Wagner*. Ed. Reinhold Grimm and Jost
Hermand. Madison: University of Wisconsin Press, 1993. 39–60.

Hohmann, Joachim S., ed. *Schon auf den ersten Blick: Lesebuch zur Geschichte unserer Feindbilder.* Darmstadt: Luchterhand, 1981.

Hollinrake, Roger. *Nietzsche, Wagner and the Philosophy of Pessimism.* London: Allen and Unwin, 1982.

Horawitz, Adalbert. *Richard Wagner und die nationale Idee.* 2d ed. Vienna: J. Gutmann, 1874.

Howe, Joseph S. *Excessive Venery, Masturbation and Continence.* New York: Bermingham, 1884.

Huber, Martin. *Text und Musik: Musikalische Zeichen im narrativen und ideologischen Funktionszusammenhang ausgewählter Erzähltexte des 20. Jahrhunderts.* Frankfurt am Main: Peter Lang, 1992.

Ingenschay-Goch, Dagmar. *Richard Wagners neu erfundener Mythos: zur Rezeption und Reproduktion des germanischen Mythos in seinen Operntexten.* Bonn: Bouvier, 1982.

Jacobs, Robert L. 'A Freudian View of *The Ring.' Music Review* 26 (1965): 201–219.

Jacobs, Robert L., and Geoffrey Skelton, trans. and eds. *Wagner Writes from Paris . . .* London: Allen & Unwin, 1973.

Jaeger, Gustav. *Die Entdeckung der Seele.* Leipzig: Ernst Fünther, 1880.

James, Burnett. *Wagner and the Romantic Disaster.* New York: Hippocrene Books, 1983.

Janin, Jules. 'Le Dîner de Beethoven: Conte fantastique.' *Gazette musicale de Paris* n.s. 1 (5 January 1834): 1–3; *Gazette musicale de Paris* n.s. 2 (12 January 1834): 9–11.

Janz, Curt Paul. *Friedrich Nietzsche: Biographie.* 3 vols. Munich: Hanser, 1978.

Jens, Walter. 'Ehrenrettung eines Kritikers: Sixtus Beckmesser.' In Richard Wagner, *Die Meistersinger von Nürnberg: Texte, Materialien, Kommentare.* Ed. Attila Csampai and Dietmar Holland. Reinbek bei Hamburg: Rowohlt, 1981. 249–257.

Johnson, Mark. *The Body in the Mind: The Bodily Basis of Meaning, Imagination, and Reason.* Chicago: University of Chicago Press, 1987.

Jordan, Gerda. 'The *Ring*-Movie and the *Ring*-Text.' In *Wagner in Retrospect: A Centennial Reappraisal.* Ed. Leroy R. Shaw et al. Amsterdam: Rodopoi, 1987. 213–218.

Josserand, Frank B. *Richard Wagner: Patriot and Politician.* Washington, D.C.: University Press of America, 1981.

Kahler, Erich. 'Ursprung und Wandlung des Judenhasses.' In Kahler, *Die Verantwortung des Geistes.* Frankfurt am Main: 1952. 53–91.

Kaiser, Joachim. 'Die Bayreuther Revolution in Permanenz.' In Richard Wagner, *Die Meistersinger von Nürnberg: Texte, Materialien, Kommentare.* Ed. Attila Csampai and Dietmar Holland. Reinbek bei Hamburg: Rowohlt, 1981. 191–193.

——. 'Hat Zelinsky recht gegen Wagners "Parsifal"?' In *Parsifal: Texte, Materialien, Kommentare.* Ed. Attila Csampai and Dietmar Holland. Reinbek bei Hamburg: Rowohlt, 1984. 257–259.

Kalfus, Melvin. 'Richard Wagner as Cult Hero: The Tannhäuser Who Would Be Siegfried.' *Journal of Psychohistory* 11 (Winter 1984): 315–382.

Kann, Heinrich. *Psychopathia sexualis.* Leipzig: Leopold Voss, 1844.

Karbaum, Michael. *Studien zur Geschichte der Bayreuther Festspiele (1876–1976).* Regensburg: Gustav Bosse, 1976.

Katz, Jacob. *The Darker Side of Genius: Richard Wagner's Anti-Semitism.* Hanover, N.H.: University Press of New England, 1986.

——. *From Prejudice to Destruction: Anti-Semitism 1700–1933.* Cambridge: Harvard University Press, 1980.

Kelly, Alfred. *The Descent of Darwin: The Popularization of Darwinism in Germany 1860–1914.* Chapel Hill: University of North Carolina Press, 1981.

Kennedy, Michael. *Mahler.* 2d ed. London: Dent, 1990.

Kerman, Joseph. *Opera as Drama.* 2d ed. London: Faber, 1989.

——. 'Wagner and Wagnerism.' *New York Review of Books*, 22 December 1983, 27–37.

Kesting, Hanjo. *Das schlechte Gewissen an der Musik: Aufsätze zu Richard Wagner.* Stuttgart: Klett-Cotta, 1991.

Kindermann, William. 'Dramatic Recapitulation in Wagner's *Götterdämmerung.' 19th-Century Music* 4 (Fall 1980): 101–112.

Kisch, Guido. *The Jews in Medieval Germany: A Study of Their Legal and Social Status.* Chicago: University of Chicago Press, 1949.

Kittler, Friedrich. 'Weltatem: On Wagner's Media Technology.' In *Wagner in Retrospect.* Ed. Leroy Shaw, Nancy R. Cirillo, and Marion S. Miller. Amsterdam: Rodopi, 1987. 203–212.

Kivy, Peter. *Sound and Semblance: Reflections on Musical Representation.* Princeton: Princeton University Press, 1984.

Kleist, Heinrich von. *Sämtliche Werke und Briefe.* Ed. Helmut Sembdner. 2 vols. Munich: Carl Hanser, 1961.

Knox, Robert. *The Races of Men: A Fragment.* Philadelphia: Lea and Blanchard, 1850.

Kolland, Hubert. 'Zur Semantik der Leitmotive in Richard Wagners *Ring des Nibelungen.*' *International Review of the Aesthetics and Sociology of Music* 4 (1973): 197–211.

Koppen, Erwin. *Dekadenter Wagnerismus: Studien zur europäischen Literatur des Fin de Siècle.* Berlin: de Gruyter, 1974.

Kris, Ernst. 'Wilhelm Fliess' wissenschaftliche Interessen.' In *Siegmund Freud, aus den Anfängen der Psychoanalyse: Briefe an Wilhelm Fliess. Abhandlungen und Notizen aus den Jahren 1887–1902.* London: Imago, 1950. 8–11.

Kropfinger, Klaus. *Wagner and Beethoven: Richard Wagner's Reception of Beethoven.* Trans. Peter Palmer. Cambridge: Cambridge University Press, 1991.

Kühnel, Jürgen. 'The Prose Writings.' Trans. Simon Nye. In *Wagner Handbook.* Ed. Ulrich Müller, Peter Wapnewski, and John Deathridge. Cambridge: Harvard University Press, 1992. 565–651.

Kulka, O. D. 'Richard Wagner und die Anfänge des modernen Antisemitismus.' *Bulletin des Leo Baeck Instituts* 4 (1961): 281–300.

Kusche, Ludwig. *Wagner und die Putzmacherin, oder Die Macht der Verleumdung.* Wilhelmshaven: Heinrichshofen, 1967.

Lakoff, George, and Mark Johnson. *Metaphors We Live By.* Chicago: University of Chicago Press, 1980.

Lallemand, Claude-François. *Des pertes séminales involontaires.* 3 vols. Paris: Bechet Jeune, 1838–1842.

La'mert, Samuel. *Self-Preservation: A Medical Treatise on Nervous and Physical Debility, Spermatorrhoea, Impotence, and Sterility.* London: n.p. [ca. 1860].

Lange, Walter. *Richard Wagners Sippe: vom Urahn zum Enkel.* Leipzig: Max Beck Verlag, 1938.

Large, D. C., and William Weber, eds. *Wagnerism in European Culture and Politics.* Ithaca: Cornell University Press, 1984.

Lee, M. Owen. 'Wahnfried: Some Metaphors in *Die Meistersinger.*' In *Wagner in Retrospect: A Centennial Reappraisal.* Ed. Leroy R. Shaw et al. Amsterdam: Rodopoi, 1987. 63–69.

Lee, Vernon. *Music and Its Lovers: An Empirical Study of Emotion and Imaginative Responses to Music.* London: George Allen & Unwin, 1932.

Leppert, Richard. *The Sight of Sound: Music, Representation, and the History of the Body.* Berkeley: University of California Press, 1993.

Levy, Ludwig. 'Die Schuhsymbolik im jüdischen Ritus.' *Monatschrift für Geschichte und Wissenschaft des Judentums* 62 (1918): 178–185.

Lewis, C. S. *Surprised by Joy.* London: Geoffrey Bles, 1955.

Locke, Ralph P. 'Constructing the Oriental "Other": Saint-Saëns's *Samson et Dalila.*' *Cambridge Opera Journal* 3, no. 3 (November 1991): 261–302.

Lorenz, Emil Franz. 'Die Geschichte des Bergmanns von Falun, vornehmlich bei E. T. A. Hoffmann, Richard Wagner, und Hugo von Hofmannsthal.' *Imago* 3 (1914): 250–301.

Lowenthal, Marvin. *The Jews of Germany: A Story of Sixteen Centuries.* New York: Russell & Russell, 1970.

Mack, Dietrich, ed. *Richard Wagner: das Betroffensein der Nachwelt.* Darmstadt: Wissenschaftliche Buchgesellschaft, 1984.

——, ed. *Theaterarbeit an Wagners Ring.* Munich: Piper, 1978.

MacNutt, Richard. 'Schlesinger, Maurice.' In *The New Grove Dictionary of Music and Musicians.* Ed. Stanley Sadie. London, 1980. 16: 660–661.

Magee, Bryan. *Aspects of Wagner.* New York: Stein and Day, 1969.

Magee, Elizabeth. *Richard Wagner and the Nibelungs.* Oxford: Clarendon Press, 1990.

Manilla, Morton. 'Wagner in the History of Anti-Semitism.' *Midstream* (February 1986): 43–46.

Mann, Thomas. *Pro and Contra Wagner.* Trans. Allan Blunden. Introduction by Erich Heller. London: Faber, 1985.

Marcuse, Ludwig. *Das denkwürdige Leben des Richard Wagner.* Zurich: Diogenes, 1973.

Masson, Jeffrey Moussaieff. *The Assault on Truth: Freud's Suppression of the Seduction Theory.* New York: Farrar, Straus and Giroux, 1985.

——, ed. *The Complete Letters of Sigmund Freud to Wilhelm Fliess, 1887–1904.* Cambridge: Harvard University Press, 1985.

Maudsley, Henry. *Body and Mind.* London: Macmillan, 1873.

——. *The Physiology and Pathology of Mind.* London: Macmillan, 1867.

Mayer, Hans. *Richard Wagner in Bayreuth 1876–1976.* Stuttgart: Belser, 1976.

——. *Richard Wagner in Selbstzeugnissen und Bilddokumenten.* Reinbek bei Hamburg: Rowohlt, 1974.

——. *Richard Wagner: Mitwelt und Nachwelt.* Stuttgart: Belser Verlag, 1978.

Mayes, J. A. 'Spermatorrhoea, Treated by the lately invented Rings.' *Charleston Medical Journal & Revue* 9 (1854): 351–353.

McClary, Susan. *Feminine Endings: Music, Gender, and Sexuality*. Minneapolis: University of Minnesota Press, 1991.

———. *Georges Bizet: Carmen*. Cambridge: Cambridge University Press, 1992.

McCreless, Patrick. *Wagner's Siegfried: Its Drama, History, and Music*. Ann Arbor: UMI Research Press, 1982.

McDonald, William E. 'Words, Music, and Dramatic Development in *Die Meistersinger*.' *19th-Century Music* 1 (1978): 146–160.

McGrath, William J. *Dionysian Art and Populist Politics in Austria*. New Haven: Yale University Press, 1974.

Menzel, Wolfgang. 'Die tiefste Korruption der deutschen Dichtung.' In *Das Junge Deutschland: Texte und Dokumente*. Ed. Jost Hermand. Stuttgart: Philipp Reclam Jun., 1976. 335–341.

Mertens, Volker. 'Wagner's Middle Ages.' In *Wagner Handbook*. Ed. Ulrich Müller, Peter Wapnewski, and John Deathridge. Cambridge: Harvard University Press, 1992. 236–268.

Millington, Barry. 'Nuremberg Trial: Is There Anti-Semitism in *Die Meistersinger*?' *Cambridge Opera Journal* 3, no. 3: 247–260.

———. '*Parsifal*: A Wound Reopened.' *Wagner* 8 (1987): 114–120.

———. *Wagner*. London: Dent, 1986.

Mosse, George L. *The Crisis of German Ideology: Intellectual Origins of the Third Reich*. New York: Grosset and Dunlap, 1964.

———. *The Culture of Western Europe: The Nineteenth and Twentieth Centuries*. 3d ed. London: Westview Press, 1988.

———. *Germans and Jews: The Right, the Left, and the Search for a 'Third Force' in Pre-Nazi Germany*. New York: Howard Fertig, 1970.

———. *Nationalism and Sexuality: Middle-Class Morality and Sexual Norms in Modern Europe*. Madison: University of Wisconsin Press, 1985.

zur Mühlen, Patrik von. *Rassenideologien: Geschichte und Hintergründe*. Berlin: Dietz Verlag, 1977.

Müller, Ulrich. 'Wagner and Antiquity.' In *Wagner Handbook*. Ed. Ulrich Müller, Peter Wapnewski, and John Deathridge. Cambridge: Harvard University Press, 1992. 227–235.

Nattiez, Jean-Jacques. 'Chéreau's Treachery.' *October* 14 (Fall 1980): 71–100.

——. ' "Fidelity" to Wagner: Reflections on the Centenary *Ring*.' In
Wagner in Performance. Ed. Barry Millington and Stewart Spencer.
New Haven: Yale University Press, 1992. 75–98.

——. *Music and Discourse: Toward a Semiology of Music*. Trans. Carolyn
Abbate. Princeton: Princeton University Press, 1990.

——. 'Le Ring comme histoire métaphorique de la musique.' In *Wagner in Retrospect: A Centennial Reappraisal*. Ed. Leroy R. Shaw et al.
Amsterdam: Rodopoi, 1987. 44–49.

——. *Tetralogies — Wagner, Boulez, Chéreau: essai sur l'infidelité*. Paris:
Christian Bourgois, 1983.

——. *Wagner androgyne: essai sur l'interprétation*. Paris: C. Bourgois,
1990.

Newcomb, Anthony. 'The Birth of Music out of the Spirit of Drama.'
19th-Century Music 5 (1981–82): 38–66.

Newman, Ernest. *The Life of Richard Wagner*. 4 vols. Cambridge: Cambridge University Press, 1933.

——. *Wagner as Man and Artist*. London: Victor Gollancz, 1963.

——. *The Wagner Operas*. New York: Alfred A. Knopf, 1972.

Nietzsche, Friedrich. *The Complete Works of Friedrich Nietzsche*. New
York: Russell and Russell, 1964.

——. *Untimely Meditations*. Trans. R. J. Hollingdale. Cambridge:
Cambridge University Press, 1989.

——. *Werke: Kritische Gesamtausgabe*. Ed. Giorgio Colli and Mazzino
Montinari. Berlin: de Gruyter, 1967–.

Nietzsche, Friedrich, and Richard Wagner. *The Nietzsche-Wagner Cor-
respondence*. Ed. Elizabeth Förster-Nietzsche. Trans. Caroline V.
Kerr. Introduction by H. L. Mencken. London: Duckworth and
Co., 1922.

Novalis (= Friedrich von Hardenberg). *Monolog, Die Lehrlinge zu Sais,
Die Christenheit oder Europa, Hymnen an die Nacht, Geistliche Lieder,
Heinrich von Ofterdingen*. Ed. Curt Grützmacher and Sybille Claus.
Reinbek bei Hamburg: Rowohlt, 1963.

Oestreich, James R. 'Wagner, Nazis and the Israeli Soul.' *New York
Times*, 12 January 1992, section 2, p.1, col.2.

Panizza, Oskar. 'Bayreuth und die Homosexualität: eine Erwägung.'
Die Gesellschaft: Monatsschrift für Literatur, Kunst und Socialpolitik 11
(1895): 88–92.

Parvin, Theophilus. 'The Hygiene of the Sexual Functions.' *New Or-
leans Medical & Surgical Journal* 11 (1884): 598–612.

Paul, Hermann. 'Duft.' In *Deutsches Wörterbuch*. Halle: Niemeyer, 1956. 2: 133.

The Poetic Edda. Trans., introduction, and annotation by Henry Adams Bellow. London: Oxford University Press, 1926.

Poliakov, Leon. *The Aryan Myth: A History of Racist and Nationalist Ideas in Europe*. London: Sussex University Press, 1971.

———. *The History of Anti-Semitism*. Trans. Richard Howard, Natalie Gerardi, Miriam Kochan, and George Klin. 4 vols. Vols. 1–3: London: Routledge & Kegan Paul, 1974–1975. Vol. 4: Oxford: Oxford University Press, 1985.

Porges, Heinrich. *Wagner Rehearsing the 'Ring': An Eye-Witness Account of the Stage Rehearsals for the First Bayreuth Festival*. Trans. Robert L. Jacobs. Cambridge: Cambridge University Press, 1983.

Porter, Andrew. 'Wagner: The Continuing Appeal.' In *Wagner in Retrospect: A Centennial Reappraisal*. Ed. Leroy R. Shaw et al. Amsterdam: Rodopoi, 1987. 7–18.

Radkau, Joachim. 'Richard Wagners Erlösung vom Faschismus durch die Emigranten.' In *Exilforschung: ein internationales Jahrbuch*. Vol. 3. Munich. Text & Kritik, 1985. 71–105.

Rank, Otto. *Das Inzest-Motiv in Dichtung und Sage: Grundzüge einer Psychologie des dichterischen Schaffens*. Leipzig: Franz Deuticke, 1926.

———. *Die Lohengrinsage: ein Beitrag zu ihrer Motivgestaltung und Deutung*. Leipzig: Franz Deuticke, 1911.

Rappl, Erich. 'Beckmesser als psychologische Schlüsselfigur.' In *Wagners Werk und Wirkung: Festspielnachrichten Beiträge 1957 bis 1982*. Ed. Lorenz Ellwanger. Bayreuth: Lorenz Ellwanger, 1982. 199–203.

———. *Wagner-Opernführer*. Regensburg: Gustav Bosse, 1967.

Rasch, William, and Marc A. Weiner. 'A Response to Hans Rudolf Vaget's "Wagner, Anti-Semitism, and Mr. Rose."' *German Quarterly* (Summer 1994): 400–408.

Rather, L. J. *The Dream of Self-Destruction: Wagner's 'Ring' and the Modern World*. Baton Rouge: Louisiana State University Press, 1979.

———. *Reading Wagner: A Study in the History of Ideas*. Baton Rouge: Louisiana State University Press, 1990.

Rattner, Josef. 'Wagner im Lichte der Tiefenpsychologie.' In *Richard-Wagner-Handbuch*. Ed. Ulrich Müller and Peter Wapnewski. Stuttgart: Alfred Körner, 1986. 777–791.

Rauschenberger, Walther. 'Richard Wagners Abstammung und Rassenmerkmale.' *Die Sonne: Monatsschrift für Rasse, Glauben, und Volk-stum im Sinne nordischer Weltanschauung und Lebensgestaltung* 14 (1937): 161–171.

Reich, Eduard. *Geschichte, Natur- und Gesundheitslehre des ehelichen Lebens.* Cassel: C. J. Krieger, 1864.

———. *Über Unsittlichkeit: hygienische und politisch-moralische Studien.* Neuwied: J. H. Heuser, 1866.

Reichardt, Johann Friedrich. *Vertraute Briefe, geschrieben auf einer Reise nach Wien und den österreichischen Staaten zu Ende des Jahres 1808 und zu Anfang 1809.* Introduction and annotation by Gustav Gugitz. 2 vols. Munich: Georg Müller, 1915.

Renk, Herta A. 'Ammerkungen zur Beziehung zwischen Musiktheater und Semiotik.' In *Theaterarbeit an Wagners Ring.* Ed. Dietrich Mack. Munich: Piper, 1978. 275–288.

von Rhein, John. 'Barenboim Takes Step in Returning Wagner to Israel.' *Chicago Tribune*, 23 January 1992, section 'Tempo,' p. 3.

Ringer, Alexander. 'Wagner and the Language of Feeling.' In *Wagner in Retrospect: A Centennial Reappraisal.* Ed. Leroy Shaw, Nancy R. Cirillo, and Marion S. Miller. Amsterdam: Rodopi, 1987. 37–44.

Robinson, Paul. *Opera & Ideas: From Mozart to Strauss.* New York: Harper & Row, 1985.

Rohrer, Joseph. *Versuch über die jüdischen Bewohner der österreichischen Monarchie.* Vienna: n.p., 1804.

Rothstein, Edward. 'What Is the Politics of "Tristan"?' *New York Times*, 12 January 1992, section 2, p. 25, col. 5.

Rose, Paul Lawrence. 'The Noble Anti-Semitism of Richard Wagner.' *Historical Journal* 15 (1982): 751–763.

———. *Revolutionary Antisemitism in Germany from Kant to Wagner.* Princeton: Princeton University Press, 1990.

———. *Wagner: Race and Revolution.* London: Faber and Faber, 1992.

Rösselt, Friedrich. *Lehrbuch der griechischen und römischen Mythologie für höhere Töchterschulen und die gebildeten des weiblichen Geschlechts.* 5th ed. Ed. Friedrich Kurts. Leipzig: Ernst Fleischer, 1865.

Rürup, Reinhard. *Emanzipation und Antisemitismus: Studien zur 'Judenfrage' der bürgerlichen Gesellschaft.* Göttingen: Vandenhoeck & Ruprecht, 1975.

Russ, Michael. *Musorgsky: Pictures at an Exhibition.* Cambridge: Cambridge University Press, 1992.

Russell, James. 'Cases illustrating the influence of exhaustion of the spinal cord in inducing paraplegia.' *[London] Medical Times & Gazette* 2 (1863): 455–459.

Sabor, Rudolph. *The Real Wagner.* London: Andre Deutsch, 1987.

The Saga of the Volsungs: The Norse Epic of Sigurd the Dragon Slayer. Trans. and introduction by Jesse L. Byock. Berkeley: University of California Press, 1990.

Said, Edward. *Orientalism.* New York: Pantheon, 1978.

——. *The World, the Text, and the Critic.* London: Vintage, 1991.

Schickling, Dieter. *Abschied von Walhall: Richard Wagners erotische Gesellschaft.* Stuttgart: Deutsche Verlags-Anstalt, 1983.

——. 'Richard Wagners Männer und Frauen: Zur emanzipatorischen Psychologie des "Ring." ' In *In den Trümmern der eignen Welt: Richard Wagners 'Der Ring des Nibelungen.'* Ed. Udo Bermbach. Berlin: Reimer, 1989. 163–180.

——. 'Wagner beim Wort genommen: zur Psychologie seiner Opern.' In *Richard-Wagner-Handbuch.* Ed. Ulrich Müller and Peter Wapnewski. Stuttgart: Alfred Kröner, 1986. 792–802.

'Schlesinger.' *Riemann Musik Lexikon: Ergänzungsband Personenteil L–Z.* Ed. Carl Dahlhaus. Mainz, 1975. 580.

Schloesser, Rudolf. *August Graf von Platen: ein Bild seines geistigen Entwicklungsganges und seines dichterischen Schaffens.* 2 vols. Munich: R. Piper & Co., 1913.

Schudt, Johann Jacob. *Von der Franckfurter Juden Vergangenheit (Sitten und Bräuchen): aus Johann Jacob Schudts 'Jüdische Merkwürdigkeiten.'* Ed. Efraim Frisch. Berlin: Schocken, 1934.

Schüler, Winfried. *Der Bayreuther Kreis von seiner Entstehung bis zum Ausgang der wilhelminischen Ära: Wagnerkult und Kulturreform im Geiste völkischer Weltanschauung.* Münster: Verlag Aschendorff, 1971.

Schwarz, Boris. 'Musorgsky's Interest in Judaica.' In *Musorgsky: In Memoriam 1881–1981.* Ed. Malcolm H. Brown. Russian Music Studies 3. Ann Arbor: University of Michigan Research Press, 1982. 85–94.

See, Klaus von. *Deutsche Germanen-Ideologie: Vom Humanismus bis zur Gegenwart.* Frankfurt am Main: Athenäum, 1970.

Seelig, Lutz Eberhardt. *Wagners Sehnsucht nach Kongenialität: Sentas Emanzipation im Fliegenden Holländer.* Cologne: Hermann Böhlaus, 1984.

Seelig, Wolfgang. *Ambivalenz und Erlösung: Parsifal: menschliches Verständnis und dramatische Naturdarstellung.* Bonn: Bouvier, 1983.

Sehulster, Jerome R. 'The Role of Altered States of Consciousness in the Life, Theater, and Theories of Richard Wagner.' *Journal of Altered States of Consciousness* 5 (1979–80): 235–258.

Shattner, Marius. 'Israel Philharmonic Cancels Wagner Recital amid Protests.' *Agence France Presse*, 20 December 1991, section 'News.'

Shaw, George Bernard. *The Perfect Wagnerite: A Commentary on the Niblung's Ring.* 4th ed. London: Constable & Co. 1923; repr. New York: Dover, 1967.

Shaw, Leroy, Nancy R. Cirillo, and Marion S. Miller, eds. *Wagner in Retrospect: A Centennary Reappraisal.* Amsterdam: Rodopi, 1987.

Shawe-Taylor, Desmond. 'Wagner and His Singers.' In *Wagner in Performance.* Ed. Barry Millington and Stewart Spencer. New Haven: Yale University Press, 1992. 15–28.

Silbermann, Alphons. *Der ungeliebte Jude: zur Soziologie des Antisemitismus.* Frankfurt am Main: Edition Interfrom, 1981.

Skelton, Geoffrey. *Richard and Cosima Wagner: Biography of a Marriage.* London: Victor Gollancz, 1982.

Solomon, Maynard. *Beethoven.* New York: Schirmer, 1977.

Sommer, Antonius. *Die Komplikationen des musikalischen Rhythmus in den Bühnenwerken Richard Wagners.* Schriften zur Musik 10. Giebig am Chiemsee: Musikverlag Emil Katzbichler, 1971.

Sontag, Susan. 'Wagner's Fluids.' *London Review of Books*, 10 December 1987, 8–9.

Stedman, Henry R. 'Some of the Mental Aspects of Nervous Disease.' *Medical Communications of the Massachusetts Medical Society* 13 (1886): 415–430.

Stein, Jack M. *Richard Wagner and the Synthesis of the Arts.* Detroit: Wayne State University Press, 1960.

Stein, Leon. *The Racial Thinking of Richard Wagner.* New York: Philosophical Library, 1950.

Stekel, Wilhelm. 'Nietzsche und Wagner: eine sexualpsychologische Studie zur Psychogenese des Freundschaftsgefühls und des Freundschaftsverrats.' *Zeitschrift für Sexualwissenschaft und Sexualpolitik* 4 (1917): 22–28, 58–65.

Stendhal. *The Life of Rossini.* Trans. Richard N. Coe. Seattle: University of Washington Press, 1972.

Stern, Fritz. *The Politics of Cultural Despair.* Berkeley: University of California Press, 1974.

Sternfeld, Richard. *Richard Wagner und der heilige deutsche Krieg.* Oldenberg: Gerhard Stalling, 1916.

Stock, Richard Wilhelm. 'Jüdische Kritikaster über Richard Wagners "Meistersinger." ' In Richard Wagner, *Die Meistersinger von Nürnberg: Texte, Materialien, Kommentare.* Reinbek bei Hamburg: Rowohlt, 1981. 202–206.

Stoneman, Richard. *Greek Mythology: An Encyclopedia of Myth and Legend.* London: Acquarian Press, 1991.

Strassburg, Gottfried von. *Tristan: With the 'Tristan' of Thomas.* Trans. and introduction by A. T. Hatto. London: Penguin, 1967.

Strauss, Herbert A. 'Juden und Judenfeindschaft in der frühen Neuzeit.' In *Antisemitismus: von der Judenfeindschaft zum Holocaust.* Ed. Herbert A. Strauss and Norbert Kampe. Frankfurt am Main: Campus Verlag, 1988. 66–87.

Strobel, Otto, ed. *Richard Wagner, Skizzen und Entwürfe zur Ring-Dichtung, mit der Dichtung 'Der junge Siegfried.'* Munich: F. Bruckmann, 1930.

Subotnik, Rose Rosengard. *Developing Variations: Style and Ideology in Western Music.* Minneapolis: University of Minnesota Press, 1991.

Syberberg, Hans Jürgen. *Parsifal: ein Filmessay.* Munich: Heyne, 1982.

Tambling, Jeremy. *Opera, Ideology and Film.* Manchester: Manchester University Press, 1987.

Tarasti, Eero. *Myth and Music: A Semiotic Approach to the Aesthetics of Myth in Music, Especially that of Wagner, Sibelius and Stravinsky.* Helsinki: Suomen Musiikkitieteellinen Seura, 1978.

Taruskin, Richard. 'Only Time Will Cover the Taint.' *New York Times,* 26 January 1992, section 2, p. 25, col. 5.

——. Review of Carolyn Abbate, *Unsung Voices: Opera and Musical Narrative in the Nineteenth Century. Cambridge Opera Journal* 4, no. 2 (July 1992): 187–197.

Taylor, Ronald. *Richard Wagner: His Life, Art and Thought.* London: Paul Elek, 1979.

Theweleit, Klaus. *Male Fantasies.* 2 vols. Minneapolis: University of Minnesota Press, 1989.

Thomson, J. L. 'Giacomo Meyerbeer: The Jew and His Relationship with Richard Wagner.' *Musica Judaica* 1 (1975–76): 54–86.

Thorndike, Augustus. 'The Treatment of Club-Foot.' *Medical Communications of the Massachusetts Medical Society* 17 (1898): 287–294.

Tisson, Simon-André. *Onanism.* New York: Collins & Hannay, 1832.

———. *Tentamen de Morbis ex Manustrupatione*. Lausanne: M. M. Bousquet, 1758.

Trachtenberg, Joshua. *The Devil and the Jews: The Medieval Conception of the Jew and Its Relation to Modern Antisemitism*. New Haven: Yale University Press, 1943.

Tuchman, Barbara. *Bible and Sword: England and Palestine from the Bronze Age to Balfour*. New York: Ballantine Books, 1984.

Twain, Mark. 'Some Thoughts on the Science of Onanism.' Charlottesville, Va.: n.p., 1964.

Twitchell, James B. *Forbidden Partners: The Incest Taboo in Modern Culture*. New York: Columbia University Press, 1987.

Vaget, Hans Rudolf. 'Wagner, Anti-Semitism, and Mr. Rose: *Merkwürd'ger Fall!*' Review of Paul Lawrence Rose, *Wagner: Race and Revolution*. *German Quarterly* 66, no. 2 (Spring 1993): Forum Section, 222–236.

Vetter, Isolde. 'Wagner in the History of Psychology.' Trans. Stewart Spencer. In *Wagner Handbook*. Ed. Ulrich Müller, Peter Wapnewski, and John Deathridge. Cambridge: Harvard University Press, 1992. 118–155.

Vogel, Martin. *Nietzsche und Wagner: ein deutsches Lesebuch*. Bonn: Verlag für systematische Musikwissenschaft, 1984.

Vogt, Matthias Theodor. 'Taking the Waters at Bayreuth.' In *Wagner in Performance*. Ed. Barry Millington and Stewart Spencer. New Haven: Yale University Press, 1992. 130–152.

Volkmann-Leander, Richard von. *Träumereien an französischen Kaminen*. 31st ed. Leipzig: Breitkopf & Härtel, 1905.

Volz, Pia Daniela. *Nietzsche im Labyrinth seiner Krankheit: eine medizinisch-biographische Untersuchung*. Würzburg: Königshausen & Neumann, 1990.

Voss, Egon. *Studien zur Instrumentalmusik Richard Wagners*. Studien zur Musikgeschichte des 19. Jahrhunderts 24. Regensburg: Gustav Bosse, 1970.

———. 'Wagners *Meistersinger* als Oper des deutschen Bürgertums.' In *Die Meistersinger von Nürnberg*. Ed. Attila Csampai and Dietmar Holland. Reinbek bei Hamburg: Rowohlt, 1981. 9–31.

———. 'Wagners "Parsifal" — das Spiel von der Macht der Schuldgefühle.' In *Parsifal: Texte, Materialien, Kommentare*. Ed. Attila Csampai and Dietmar Holland. Reinbek bei Hamburg: Rowohlt, 1984. 9–18.

'Wagner Concert Postponed after Furor.' *Facts on File World News Digest*, 31 December 1991, 1005 G3.

Wagner, Cosima. *Die Briefe Cosima Wagners an Friedrich Nietzsche*. Ed. Erhart Thierbach. 2 vols. Weimar: Nietzsche-Archiv, 1940.

——. *Diaries*. Ed. and annotation by Martin Gregor-Dellin and Dietrich Mack. Trans. and introduction by Geoffrey Skelton. 2 vols. New Haven: Harcourt Brace Jovanovich, 1978–1980.

——. *Die Tagebücher*. Ed. Martin Gregor-Dellin and Dieter Mack. 2 vols. Munich: Piper, 1976–1977.

Wagner, Siegfried. *Erinnerungen*. Stuttgart: Engelhorn, 1923.

Wagner, Wieland, ed. *Hundert Jahre Tristan*. Emsdetten: Lechte, 1965.

Walsh, Michael. 'The Case of Wagner — Again.' *Time*, 13 January 1992, 57.

Wapnewski, Peter. 'The Operas as Literary Works.' Trans. Peter Palmer. In *Wagner Handbook*. Ed. Ulrich Müller, Peter Wapnewski, and John Deathridge. Cambridge: Harvard University Press, 1992. 3–95.

——. 'Die Oper Richard Wagners als Dichtung.' In *Richard-Wagner-Handbuch*. Ed. Ulrich Müller and Peter Wapnewski. Stuttgart: Alfred Körner, 1986. 223–352.

——. *Richard Wagner: die Szene und ihr Meister*. Munich: Beck, 1978.

——. *Der traurige Gott: Richard Wagner in seinen Helden*. Munich: C. H. Beck, 1978.

——. *Tristan der Held Richard Wagners*. Berlin: Severin & Siedler, 1981.

Ward, Charles. 'Listeners Look Beyond the Music for Meanings.' *Houston Chronicle*, 26 January 1992, section 'Zest,' 10.

Weinberg, Meyer. *Because They Were Jews: A History of Antisemitism*. Contributions to the Study of World History 4. New York: Greenwood Press, 1986.

Weiner, Marc A. 'Gerhart Hauptmann's *Die versunkene Glocke* and the Cultural Vocabulary of Pre-Fascist Germany.' *German Studies Review* 11, no. 3 (October 1988): 447–461.

——. 'Parody and Repression: Schnitzler's Response to Wagnerism.' *Modern Austrian Literature* 19, nos. 3–4 (1986): 129–148.

——. 'Richard Wagner's Use of E. T. A. Hoffmann's "The Mines of Falun."' *19th-Century Music* (1982): 201–214.

——. *Undertones of Insurrection: Music, Politics, and the Social Sphere in the Modern German Narrative*. Lincoln: University of Nebraska Press, 1993.

———. 'Wagner and the Vocal Iconography of Race and Nation.' In *Rereading Wagner*. Ed. Reinhold Grimm and Jost Hermand. Madison: University of Wisconsin Press, 1992. 78–102.

———. 'Wagner's Nose and the Ideology of Perception.' *Monatshefte* 81, no. 1 (Spring 1989): 62–78.

———. 'Zwieback and Madeleine: Creative Recall in Wagner and Proust.' *Modern Language Notes* (German) 95 (Spring 1980): 679–684.

Weinfeld, H. 'Wagner und Meyerbeer.' In *Richard Wagner zwischen Beethoven und Schönberg*. Musik-Konzepte 59. Munich: Text & Kritik, 1988. 31–72.

Weingart, Peter, Jürgen Kroll, and Kurt Bayertz. *Rasse, Blut, und Gene: Geschichte der Eugenik und Rassenhygiene in Deutschland*. Frankfurt am Main: Suhrkamp, 1988.

Weininger, Otto. *Geschlecht und Charakter: eine prinzipielle Untersuchung*. 25th ed. Vienna: Wilhelm Braumüller, 1923.

Wellbery, David E. 'E. T. A. Hoffmann and Romantic Hermeneutics: An Interpretation of Hoffmann's "Don Juan."' *Studies in Romanticism* 19, no. 4 (1980): 455–473.

Wessling, Bernd. W., ed. *Bayreuth im dritten Reich: Richard Wagners politische Erben*. Weinheim: Beltz, 1983.

———. *Meyerbeer: Wagners Beute — Heines Geisel*. Düsseldorf: Droste, 1984.

Westernhagen, Curt von. *The Forging of the 'Ring': Richard Wagner's Composition Sketches for 'Der Ring des Nibelungen.'* Trans. Arnold and Mary Whitall. Cambridge: Cambridge University Press, 1976.

———. *Richard Wagner: sein Werk, seine Wesen, sein Welt*. Zürich: Atlantis, 1956.

———. *Richard Wagners Dresdener Bibliothek, 1842–1849: neue Dokumente zur Geschichte seines Schaffens*. Wiesbaden: F. A. Brockhaus, 1966.

———. *Wagner: A Biography*. Trans. Mary Whittall. Cambridge: Cambridge University Press, 1986.

Williams, Raymond. *The Long Revolution*. London: Cox & Wyman, 1961.

Wintle, Christopher. 'The Numinous in *Götterdämmerung*.' In *Reading*

Opera. Ed. Arthur Groos and Roger Parker. Princeton: Princeton University Press, 1988. 200–234.

Wistrich, Robert S. *Antisemitism: The Longest Hatred*. London: Methuen, 1991.

Wolf, Elcan Isaac. *Von den Krankheiten der Juden*. Mannheim: C. F. Schwan, 1777.

von Wolzogen, Hans. *Führer durch die Musik zu Richard Wagner's Festspiel* Der Ring des Nibelungen: *ein thematischer Leitfaden*. Leipzig: Feodor Reinboth, 1896.

Woolf, Virginia. 'Impressions at Bayreuth.' *Times* (London), 21 August 1909; repr. *Opera News* 41, no. 2 (August 1976): 22–23.

Zadrozny, Ilse. 'Israel Orchestra Bans Classical Music Antisemitism.' *Gazette* (Montreal), 25 January 1992, section 'Entertainment,' F4.

Zelinsky, Hartmut. 'Die deutsche Losung Siegfried: oder die "innere Notwendigkeit" des Juden-Fluches im Werk Richard Wagners.' In *In den Trümmern der eignen Welt: Richard Wagners 'Der Ring des Nibelungen.'* Ed. Udo Bermbach. Berlin: Reimer, 1989. 201–250.

———. 'Die "Feuerkur" des Richard Wagner oder die "neue Religion" der "Erlösung" durch "Vernichtung."' In *Richard Wagner: wie antisemitisch darf ein Künstler sein?* Ed. Heinz-Klaus Metzger and Rainer Riehn. Musikkonzepte 5. Munich: Text & Kritik, 1978. 79–112.

———. 'Der *Plenipotentarius des Untergangs.*' *Neohelicon* 9 (1982): 145–176.

———. 'Rettung ins Ungenaue: zu M. Gregor-Dellins Wagner-Biographie.' In *Richard Wagner: Parsifal*. Ed. Heinz-Klaus Metzger and Rainer Riehn. Musikkonzepte 25. Munich: Text & Kritik, 1982. 74–115.

———. *Richard Wagner: ein deutsches Thema: eine Dokumentation zur Wirkungsgeschichte Richard Wagners 1876–1976*. Frankfurt am Main: Zweitausendeins, 1976.

———. 'Richard Wagners *Kunstwerk der Zukunft* und seine Idee der Vernichtung.' In *Geschichtsprophetien im 19. und 20. Jahrhundert*. Ed. Joachim H. Knoll and J. H. Schoeps. Stuttgart: Burg Verlag, 1984. 84–106.

———. 'Richard Wagners letzte Karte.' In *Parsifal: Texte, Materialien, Kommentare*. Ed. Attila Csampai and Dietmar Holland. Reinbek bei Hamburg: Rowohlt, 1984. 252–256.

———. 'Der verschwiegene Gehalt des "Parsifal."' In *Parsifal: Texte,*

Materialien, Kommentare. Ed. Attila Csampai and Dietmar Holland. Reinbek bei Hamburg: Rowohlt, 1984. 244–251.

Zetlin, Mikhail. *The Five: The Evolution of the Russian School of Music.* Trans. and ed. George Panin. New York: International Universities Press, 1959.

In the *Texts and Contexts* series